PEASANTS AGAINST GLOBALIZATION

- collective action, even in rural areas

- comparative advantage + insad production

- legacy of previous organization → integration into global economy, not destabilizing (throughout)

- conflict btwn. demands of peasants & market competition

- structural adjustment & globalization

- victory of sorts: p. 148

- p.154 declared innocent: democracy at work

- p. 160 transnational organizing

- p. 164-5 peasants appropriate the language of the free market

PEASANTS AGAINST GLOBALIZATION

Rural Social Movements in Costa Rica

MARC EDELMAN

STANFORD UNIVERSITY PRESS

Stanford, California

Stanford University Press
Stanford, California
© 1999 by the Board of Trustees of the
Leland Stanford Junior University

Printed in the United States of America
CIP data appear at the end of the book

To the memory of my grandmother,
Frances Israel Hochberg —
teacher, activist, beloved friend

The case in which . . . it is proper to restore the free importation of foreign goods, after it has been for some time interrupted, is, when particular manufactures, by means of high duties or prohibitions upon all foreign goods which can come into competition with them, have been so far extended as to employ a great multitude of hands. Humanity may in this case require that the freedom of trade should be restored only by slow gradations. . . . Were those high duties and prohibitions taken away all at once, cheaper foreign goods . . . might be poured so fast into the home market, as to deprive all at once many thousands of our people of their ordinary employment and means of subsistence. The disorder which this would occasion might no doubt be very considerable.

ADAM SMITH,
An Inquiry into the Nature and Causes of the Wealth of Nations
(1976 [1776]), 1:491

ACKNOWLEDGMENTS

The invisible hand—Adam Smith's potent metaphor for how individual self-interest promotes the common good—was an object of study in two senses when I began this book. Most immediately, I had witnessed and was interested in the devastating effects of free-market policies—and grassroots responses to them—in rural Costa Rica in the late 1980s and 1990s. More broadly, I considered the transition from statist to free-market economies, and its consequences for social well-being, to be one of the central issues of our time.

In reflecting now on what has gone into the writing—the people to thank, the institutions which aided me—I am struck by how market logic affected so many of them, and only sometimes in ways that contributed to the common good. Both the experience of researching this book and life in the late twentieth century lead me to agree with Oscar Wilde's remark that "the market knows the price of everything and the value of nothing." But the rapaciousness of the era is such that even astute "anti-market" commentary isn't immune from appropriation. Hillary Rodham Clinton employed Wilde's caustic comment in a 1993 speech on the "Politics of Meaning." Around the same time, Volvo featured it in advertisements for one of their luxury models, a car said to amply reward "those who recognize the difference between civility and ostentation." Similarly, neoclassical economists have seized upon even Adam Smith's "invisible hand" imagery, subtly converting it— as Heinz Lubasz (1992) has shown—from an "invisible hand" of "nature" or "Providence" to an "invisible hand" of the "market." As the book's epigraph indicates, Smith was hardly as unambivalent an advocate for laissez-faire extremism as his contemporary epigones would have it.

Some of the ideas and portions of the text appeared earlier (and in much different form) in the *American Ethnologist, Peasant Studies*, and *NACLA Report on the Americas*. Rodolfo Monge Oviedo, coauthor of the 1993 *NACLA Report* article that prefigured parts of the argument in Chapter 1, has generously let me integrate some of our collaborative work into the present text. The publishers of all three journals kindly granted permission to incorporate this and other copyrighted material into the book. Ricardo Solano, director of the Centro Nacional de Acción Pastoral, Rubén Vega, director of the Documentation Department of *La Nación,* and the Costa Rican National Archives provided permission to reproduce several of the photographs that are published here. Numerous colleagues and friends provided detailed comments on pieces of the manuscript in one or another of its former incarnations. My profound appreciation goes to Peggy Barlett, Michael Blim, Philippe Bourgois, John Burdick, Margaret Everett, Mario Fernández Arias, Lesley Gill, Charles R. Hale, Jack Hammond, Angelique Haugerud, Judith Adler Hellman, Douglas Kincaid, María Lagos, Susan Lees, Fabrice Edouard Lehoucq, Deidre McFadyen, Lynn Morgan, Martin Murphy, June Nash, Ciska Raventós, Isabel Román, Fred Rosen, Jeffrey Rubin, Jorge Rovira Mas, Lynn Stephen, Carlos Vilas, Robert G. Williams, and Ann Zulawski. For providing documentary materials, places to stay, meals, loans of vehicles and computer equipment, and much stimulating discussion, I am grateful to Heidi Arce, Carlos Camacho Nassar, Gerardo Campos Alpízar, Yves Fournier, Marcelo Gaete, Jayne Hutchcroft, Enrique March, Iván Molina, Abelardo Morales, and Eduardo ("El Nica") Morales Parrales, as well as to many of the protagonists mentioned in the book. Patricia Mathews Salazar helped to transcribe taped interviews and offered spirited observations on what she heard. Ramiro Campos, undergraduate extraordinaire and erstwhile *subcomandante* of the Hunter College Student Government, served as an able research assistant during the final stages of the project; I hope that at least some of the less-than-electrifying tasks I assigned him paid off in a better understanding of recent developments in his ancestral home. Martha Soler, the best mother-in-law anyone could wish for, kindly polished my Spanish prose in a large number of research-related documents. Many thanks also to Muriel Bell and Nathan MacBrien of Stanford University Press and to copy editor Ruth Steinberg for seeing this project through to completion.

My heartfelt appreciation goes to several institutions which provided generous support during various stages of this project. Fieldwork funds came from the American Council of Learned Societies, the Wenner-Gren Foundation for Anthropological Research (grant 5180), and several small grants from Yale University. A Yale Senior Faculty Fellowship in 1993–94 permitted me to write much of the manuscript. I can now confess that I wrote the final lines at the School of Social Science of the Institute for Advanced Study in Princeton during the first weeks of a year-long fellowship, when I was supposed to be working on a different, though related, book. I can only hope that this transgression—for me, a kind of intellectual clearing of the decks—will be forgiven, or at least overlooked.

Following the first of these two luxurious writing leaves, I moved from Yale to the City University of New York, just as proponents of the magic of the marketplace and tax cuts for the rich began their most recent, mean-spirited assault on public higher education. As targets of the invisible hand, colleagues and students at Hunter College and the CUNY Ph.D. Program in Anthropology have more in common with rural Central Americans than either group would necessarily think. Both groups have prompted me to reflect on the commonalities of these two worlds, rather than simply succumbing to the traditional anthropological preoccupation with difference and otherness.

In Costa Rica in the 1980s and early 1990s, the Centro de Estudios para la Acción Social (CEPAS) produced much of the best scholarly work on economic trends, agrarian issues, and popular movements. Three CEPAS sociologists—Sandra Cartín, Isabel Román, and Rolando Rivera—were kind enough to organize a seminar in 1990 to discuss an early version of Chapter 4; as I have described it in the Introduction, this event was not only a useful, if trying, intellectual interchange for me, but it had complex and unexpected repercussions on the peasant movement I was studying. CEPAS had to shut its doors in the mid-1990s, a victim of funding cutbacks rooted ultimately in the very neoliberal economic upheaval it had so assiduously documented and analyzed. Its demise is a major loss for Costa Ricans seeking to understand their own society, as for those of us from abroad who long relied on its staff and databases for research support.

One of the arguments of this book is that even when popular organizations "fail" or fade away, their members' "social energy" (as Albert Hirschman called it, ironically invoking Adam Smith) manifests itself in new forms in future efforts for change. This has certainly been true for most of the people involved with CEPAS. Sadly, though, Rolando Rivera will not have this chance. A talented and committed social scientist, and loyal friend, his promising career and life were cut short in 1995 at the untimely age of 32, when an inept and fatigued Aviateca pilot crashed a Costa Rica–bound jetliner into El Salvador's Chichontepec volcano. Post-crash investigations revealed that pilots had recently begun flying extra-long shifts, following a company downsizing campaign.

Débora Munczek, my *compañera*, is not an anthropologist, but I've learned more about how to listen from her than I ever could from any course or book on ethnographic field methods. Accompanying her during her research with victims of human rights abuses in Honduras has been an inspiration for me. I am grateful beyond measure for her constant warmth, love, and support. My older son Daniel does not remember my regret that we had to celebrate his first birthday several days late because I was in the middle of a critical period of fieldwork in rural Santa Cruz and Nicoya. He does recall several longer and more recent absences, and I can only thank him once again for being so resilient, so confident in himself and in me, and so forgiving, both of my travels and of my so often preempting his computer-game time in order to write—with what he thinks of as the dullest software ever invented. The arrival of my younger son, Benjamin, coincided almost to the day with the e-mail message from Stanford accepting this book for publication. That I was able to complete the final revisions was due only to the priceless support of my extended family—parents, in-laws, *tíos políticos*, and various fictive kin—who provided some respite from the wonderful but exhausting work of parenting a newborn.

Finally, this research project, more than any other in which I have been involved, has brought home to me a lesson that is perhaps obvious, though too often forgotten when one is immersed in that rarified "life of the mind" of North American academia: our finest teachers are often those we meet outside of the lecture hall and seminar room. I dedicate this book to the memory of one such extraordinary teacher, my grandmother, Frances Israel Hochberg (b. 1895 Poland, d. 1976 New York). Like many immigrant women of her generation, she happened to be a teacher by profession (as well as a formidable grammarian of English, her second language). But—certainly at least as important—she was also a union organizer and a lifelong civil rights and peace activist. Like many of the peasant activists I came to know in Costa Rica, she loved justice and talking about politics.

M. E.

CONTENTS

Eight pages of photos follow p. 90

TABLES AND ILLUSTRATIONS

ABBREVIATIONS

The following abbreviations are used throughout the text, notes, and references:

AID	U.S. Agency for International Development
ALCORSA	Algodones de Costa Rica, S.A. (Cottons of Costa Rica)
ALUNASA	Aluminios Nacionales, S.A.(National Aluminum Company)
APRA	Alianza Popular Revolucionaria Americana (American Popular Revolutionary Alliance)
ASBANA	Asociación Bananera Nacional (National Banana Producers Association)
ASPPAS	Asociación de Pequeños Productores del Pacífico Seco (Association of Small Producers of the Dry Pacific Region)
BAC	Banco Anglo-Costarricense (Anglo-Costa Rican Bank)
BCAC	Banco Crédito Agrícola de Cartago (Agricultural Credit Bank of Cartago)
BCR	Banco de Costa Rica (Bank of Costa Rica)
BCIE	Banco Centroamericano de Integración Económica (Central American Economic Integration Bank)
BCCR	Banco Central de Costa Rica (Central Bank of Costa Rica)
BDPC	Banco Popular y de Desarrollo Comunal (Peoples Savings and Community Development Bank)
BNCR	Banco Nacional de Costa Rica (National Bank of Costa Rica)
CACs	Centros Agrícolas Cantonales (Cantonal Agricultural Centers)
CACM	Central American Common Market

CADESCA	Comité de Acción de Apoyo al Desarrollo Económico y Social de Centroamérica (Committee for Action and Support of the Economic and Social Development of Central America)
CAN	Consejo Nacional Sectorial de Desarrollo Agropecuario y de Recursos Naturales Renovables [formerly Consejo Agropecuario Nacional] (National Council on Agricultural Sector Development and Natural Resources)
CAT	Certificado de Abono Tributario (Tax Payment Certificate)
CATIE	Centro Agronómico Tropical de Investigación y Enseñanza (Center for Tropical Agronomic Research and Training)
CATSA	Central Azucarera del Tempisque, S.A. (Tempisque Sugar Mill)
CBI	Caribbean Basin Initiative
CCA	Coordinadora Campesina del Atlántico (Peasant Coordinating Committee of the Atlantic)
CCSS	Caja Costarricense de Seguro Social (Costa Rican Social Security Fund)
CECADE	Centro de Capacitación para el Desarrollo (Center for Development Training)
CEMPASA	Cementos del Pacifico, S.A. (Pacific Cement Company)
CEMVASA	Cementos del Valle, S.A. (Del Valle Cement Company)
CENADA	Centro Nacional de Abastecimiento (National Supply Center)
CENAP	Centro Nacional de Acción Pastoral (National Center for Pastoral Action)
CENPRO	Centro de Promoción de Exportaciones e Inversiones (Center for Promotion of Exports and Investments)
CEPAS	Centro de Estudios Para la Acción Social (Center for Studies of Social Action)
CEPC	Consorcio de Exportación de Productos Costarricenses, S.A. (Costa Rican Export Products Consortium)
CIGRAS	Centro de Investigación de Granos y Semillas (Center for Research on Grains and Seeds)
CINDE	Coalición de Iniciativas para el Desarrollo (Coalition for Development Initiatives)

CITA	Centro de Investigación y Tecnología de Alimentos (Center for Research and Food Technology)
CNAA	Cámara Nacional de Agricultura y Agroindustria (National Agriculture and Agroindustry Chamber)
CNFI	Compañía Nacional de Fuerza y Luz (National Power and Light Company)
CNP	Consejo Nacional de Producción (National Production Council)
CODESA	Corporación Costarricense de Desarrollo, S.A. (Costa Rican Development Corporation)
CONAI	Comisión Nacional de Asuntos Indígenas (National Commission on Indigenous Affairs)
CONAPE	Consejo Nacional de Préstamos para Educación (National Educational Loan Council)
CONARIEGO	Comisión Nacional de Riego (National Irrigation Commission)
CONCACOOP	Consejo Nacional Cooperativo (National Cooperative Council)
CONICIT	Consejo Nacional de Ciencia y Tecnología (National Science and Technology Council)
COOPEAGRI	Cooperativa Agrícola Industrial y de Servicios Múltiples El General (Agricultural, Industrial and Multiple Services Cooperative of El General)
COPAN	Comité Patriótico Nacional (National Patriotic Committee)
CORYC	Consejo Rural y Campesino (Rural and Peasant Council)
CSUCA	Confederación Superior Universitaria Centroamericana (Central American University Confederation)
DAISA	Desarrollo Agroindustrial, S.A. (Agroindustrial Development Company)
DCC	Distribuidora Costarricense de Cemento, S.A. (Costa Rican Cement Distribution Company)
DINADECO	Dirección Nacional de Desarrollo de la Comunidad (National Community Development Directorate)
DNC	Dirección Nacional de Comunicaciones (National Communications Directorate)

EARTH	Escuela de la Agricultura de la Región Trópical Húmeda (Agricultual School for the Region of the Humid Tropics)
ECAG	Escuela Centroamericana de Ganadería (Central American Livestock School)
ECLA	United Nations Economic Commission for Latin America
ECR	Editorial Costa Rica (Costa Rica Publishers)
EFF	Extended Fund Facility
ESPH	Empresa de Servicios Públicos de Heredia (Public Service Enterprise of Heredia)
ESF	Economic Support Funds [from USAID]
ETA	Escuela Técnica Agropecuaria de Santa Clara (Agricultural Technical School of Santa Clara)
FECOPA	Federación de Cooperativas Agrícolas (Federation of Agricultural Cooperatives)
FECOSA	Ferrocarriles de Costa Rica, S.A. (Railroads of Costa Rica)
FEDEAGRO	Federación Nacional de Cooperativas Agropecuarios (National Federation of Agricultural Cooperatives)
FENAC	Federación Nacional Campesina (National Peasant Federation)
FERTICA	Fertilizantes de Centroamérica (Fertilizers of Central America)
FESIAN	Federación Sindical Agraria Nacional (National Agrarian Union Federation)
FINTRA	Fiduciaria de Inversiones Transitorias (Transitory Investments Trust)
FNCA	Fondo Nacional de Contingencias Agrícolas(National Agricultural Contingencies Fund)
FNL	Fábrica Nacional de Licores (National Liquor Factory)
FODEA	Ley de Fomento a la Producción Agropecuaria (Law for Fomenting Agricultural Production)
FODEIN	Fondo de Desarrollo Industrial (Industrial Development Fund)
FOPEX	Fondo de Promoción de las Exportaciones (Export Promotion Fund)
GATT	General Agreement on Tarriffs and Trade

ICAA	Instituto Costarricense de Acueductos y Alcantarillados (Costa Rican Water and Sewer Institute)
ICE	Instituto Costarricense de Electricidad (Costa Rican Electrical Institute)
ICODE	Iniciativas de Comunicación para el Desarrollo (Communication Initiatives for Development)
ICPP	Instituto Costarricense de Puertos del Pacífico (Costa Rican Pacific Ports Institute)
ICT	Instituto Costarricense de Turismo (Costa Rican Tourism Institute)
IDA	Instituto de Desarrollo Agrario (Agrarian Development Institute)
IDB	Inter-American Development Bank
IDC	Instituto de Defensa del Café (Coffee Defense Institute)
IFAM	Instituto de Fomento y Asesoría Municipal (Institute for Development and Municipal Advisement)
IICA	Instituto Interamericano de Cooperación para la Agricultura (Inter-American Institute for Agricultural Cooperation)
IMAS	Instituto Mixto de Ayuda Social (Mixed Social Aid Institute)
IMF	International Monetary Fund
INA	Instituto Nacional de Aprendizaje (National Training Institute)
INFOCOOP	Instituto de Fomento Cooperativo (Cooperative Development Institute)
INS	Instituto Nacional de Seguros (National Insurance Institute)
INVU	Instituto Nacional de Vivienda y Urbanismo (National Housing and Planning Institute)
ITCO	Instituto de Tierras y Colonización (Land and Colonization Institute)
ITCR	Instituto Tecnológico de Costa Rica (Technological Institute of Costa Rica)
JAAE	Junta Administrativa de Acueductos de Escazú (Escazú Water Board)
JAPDEVA	Junta de Administratión Portuaria y Desarrollo Eco-

	nómico de la Vertiente Atlántica (Atlantic Zone Port and Economic Development Board)
JASEC	Junta Administrativa de Servicios Eléctricos de Cartago (Cartago Electrical Services Board)
JDT	Junta de Defensa del Tabaco (Tobacco Defense Board)
JPC	Junta de Protección a la Agricultura de la Caña (Cane Agriculture Protection Board)
JUNAFORCA	Junta Nacional de Forestación Campesina (National Peasant Forestry Board)
LAICA	Liga Agrícola e Industrial de la Caña de Azúcar (Agricultural and Industrial Sugar Cane League)
MAG	Ministerio de Agricultura y Ganadería (Ministry of Agriculture and Livestock)
MAI	Ministerio de Agricultura e Industria (Ministry of Livestock and Industry)
MEIC	Ministerio de Economía, Industria y Comercio (Ministry of Economy, Industry and Commerce)
MEP	Ministerio de Educación Pública (Ministry of Public Education)
MIDEPLAN	Ministerio de Planificación Nacional y Política Económica (Ministry of National Planning and Economic Policy)
MNC	Mesa Nacional Campesina (National Peasant Roundtable)
MOPT	Ministerio de Obras Públicas y Transportes (Ministry of Public Works and Transport)
MRP	Movimiento Revolucionario del Pueblo (Revolutionary People's Movement)
NGOs	Nongovernmental Organizations
NSMs	New social movements
NTAX	Nontraditional Agricultural Exports
OFICAFE	Oficina del Café (Coffee Office)
OFIPLAN	Oficina de Planificación Nacional y Política Económica (Office for National Planning and Economic Policy)
OIJ	Organismo de Investigación Judicial (Judicial Police)
ONS	Oficina Nacional de Semillas (National Seeds Office)
OPSA	Oficina de Planificación del Sector Agropecuario (Office for Agricultural Sector Planning)

PAE	Programa de Ajuste Estructural (Structural Adjustment Program [see SAL])
PANI	Patronato Nacional de la Infancia (National Child Welfare Board)
PL-480	U.S. Public Law 480 (Agricultural Trade Development and Assistance Act [also known as "Food for Peace"])
PLN	Partido de Liberación Nacional (National Liberation Party)
PPC	Partido del Pueblo Costarricense (Costa Rican Peoples Party)
PRN	Partido Republicano Nacional (National Republican Party)
PUSC	Partido Unidad Social Cristiana (Social Christian Unity Party)
PVP	Partido Vanguardia Popular (Popular Vanguard Party)
RACSA	Radiográfica Costarricense, S.A. (Costa Rican Long Distance Communications Company)
RECOPE	Refinería Costarricense de Petróleo (Costa Rican Petroleum Refinery)
SAL	Structural Adjustment Loan
SBN	Sistema Bancario Nacional (National Banking System)
SENARA	Servicio Nacional de Aguas Subterráneas, Riego y Avenamiento (National Subsurface Water, Irrigation and Drainage Service)
SENAS	Servicio Nacional de Aguas Subterráneas (National Subsurface Water Service)
SEPSA	Secretaría Ejecutiva de Planificación Sectorial Agropecuaria y de Recursos Naturales Renovables (Executive Secretariat of Agricultural Sector and Renewable Natural Resources Planning)
SITRACAÑA	Sindicato de Trabajadores de la Caña (Sugarcane Workers Union)
SNE	Servicio Nacional de Electricidad (National Electricity Service)
TFB	Tempisque Ferry Boat, S.A.
TRANSMESA	Transportes Metropolitanos, S.A. (Metropolitan Transport Company)

UCADEGUA	Unión de Campesinos de Guatuso (Peasant Union of Guatuso)
UCR	Universidad de Costa Rica (University of Costa Rica)
UCTAN	Unión Campesina de Trabajadores del Atlántico Norte (Peasant Union of Workers of the North Atlantic)
UNA	Universidad Nacional Autónoma (National Autonomous University)
UNAC	Unión Nacional Campesina (National Peasant Union)
UNACOOP	Unión Nacional de Cooperativas (National Union of Cooperatives)
UNDP	United Nations Development Program
UNED	Universidad Estatal a Distancia (State Distance Learning University)
UNSA	Unión Nacional del Sector Agropecuario (National Union of the Agricultural Sector)
UPAGRA	Unión de Pequeños Agricultores de la Región Atlántica (Atlantic Region Small Agriculturalists Union)
UPANACIONAL	Unión Nacional de Pequeños y Medianos Productores Agropecuarios (National Union of Small and Medium Agricultural Producers)
UPAP	Unión de Productores Agropecuarios de Puriscal (Union of Agricultural Producers of Puriscal)
UPIAV	Unión de Productores Agropecuarios Independientes de Pérez Zeledón (Union of Independent Agricultural Producers of Pérez Zeledón)
USAID	U.S. Agency for International Development
WTO	World Trade Organization

PEASANTS AGAINST GLOBALIZATION

Debt Crisis, Social Crisis, Paradigm Crisis

From one day almost to the next—"*de la noche a la mañana,*" as people say in Spanish—it seemed that the world was coming apart at the seams. All of a sudden, once comfortable and self-satisfied Costa Ricans beheld rapidly growing numbers of disheveled children singing for coins on buses, more and more beggars and rag collectors going door to door, and homeless families huddled under bridges. In the capital, surly men in mirrored sunglasses and embroidered *guayabera* shirts clogged downtown sidewalks, compulsively tapping numbers into their pocket calculators and calling out ever higher prices for the wads of dollars clutched in their fists. In the little stores that had long been centers of village and neighborhood gossip and social life, grocers doubled and quadrupled prices and then still went bankrupt when it turned out that they hadn't sufficiently estimated real replacement costs for their stock. The middle class panicked; the poor tried anything simply to survive.

This was the beginning of the "lost decade" of the 1980s, Latin America's worst economic crisis since the Great Depression. Throughout the continent, the social advances and economic growth of the preceding thirty years stalled

1

or reversed in a deadly combination of spiraling indebtedness, stagflation, trade and budget deficits, and plummeting living standards. Many specialists date the onset of the crisis to Friday, August 13, 1982, when Mexico provoked worldwide consternation by announcing that it could not pay foreign banks the interest due on its $80 billion debt. Fully a year before the famous "Mexico weekend," however, Costa Rica declared a moratorium on its foreign debt payments. This action by a small Central American country, with a population of less than three million and a total debt of less than $4 billion, attracted little attention in newsrooms, academia, or international financial circles.[1]

Costa Rica's unenviable distinction as the first Latin American country to default on its foreign obligations might have been nothing more than a footnote to the larger story of the 1980s debt crisis.[2] Small countries, after all, do not have the international clout of their larger neighbors, and nonpayment of a mere $4 billion was hardly likely to cause more than a minor ripple in the world financial system. The importance of the Costa Rican case derives not from its scale, but from what the country was before—and what it became after—the economic cataclysm of 1981–82. At the end of the 1970s, when the first serious signs of crisis loomed, Costa Rica was a model social democratic welfare state, with significant public-sector involvement in the economy and a vast array of government social programs. Toward the end of the 1980s, in contrast, neoliberal opponents of "statist" economics began to paint Costa Rica—one of the first countries in the region to initiate a World Bank–sponsored structural adjustment program—as a free-market success story and a beacon for the rest of the hemisphere, along with much larger Chile and Mexico.[3]

By 1980, after more than three decades of reformist policies, Costa Rica boasted health and social welfare indicators that approached those of developed countries. The average life expectancy at birth of 73.5 years and the infant mortality rate of 19.1 per thousand were unmatched by any other country in Latin America except Cuba. The adult literacy rate of 93.1 percent was surpassed only by Cuba and the more developed countries of the southern cone of South America—Argentina, Chile, and Uruguay (MIDEPLAN 1990, 22, 31; IDB 1985; ECLA 1984).[4] Costa Rica also enjoyed a sterling reputation as a stable democracy, no small advantage at a time when Washington was about to launch a sustained campaign against "totalitarian" Sandinista Nicaragua just to the north.

But just two years later, by 1982, Costa Rica was widely regarded as an economic basket case. Not only had it defaulted on its loans, inflation had soared to near 100 percent, unemployment had more than doubled since 1979, and real wages had plummeted, impoverishing much of the population and threatening stability. Alarmed political analysts cautioned that Costa Rica might follow the route of Uruguay, another democratic social welfare state, where a stable constitutional system dating from the turn of the century had been replaced with a brutal military dictatorship in 1973 (Vega 1982).

By the early 1990s it had become commonplace for the business media to assert that the Latin American debt crisis was "over" (see *Journal of Commerce*, 20 July 1992, 2), and some economists even claimed that "a decade of hope" had begun (IDB 1991, 2). In Costa Rica, President Rafael Angel Calderón Fournier was trumpeting the "stability" of Costa Rica's "transformed" economy and boasting that "the World Bank, the Inter-American Development Bank and the International Monetary Fund . . . describe us as a human and economic miracle" (*New York Times*, 5 Oct. 1992, A12). Foreign Minister Bernd Niehaus claimed in 1990 that Costa Rica was becoming a "locomotive pulling the other economies of Central America toward . . . development" (*Tico Times*, 25 May 1990, 1). Echoing Oscar Arias, Costa Rica's president from 1986 to 1990, and Eduardo Lizano, Central Bank director from 1984 to 1990, Niehaus maintained that this small Central American republic could soon be the first developed country in Latin America (Alvarez 1988, 9; Lizano 1988a, 36; 1988b, 48).[5] But the 1995 Mexican peso crisis dampened the hyperbolic bravado of the business press, even as academic experts and policymakers throughout the region began to speak of a "third wave" of economic restructuring (Phillips 1997). Even earlier, however, many Costa Ricans harbored doubts about their country's supposed "miracle." The shift from a statist to a market-oriented economic system mirrored broader processes taking place throughout the world, and, as elsewhere, in Costa Rica the transformation inevitably produced "winners" and "losers" (Frieden 1989).

This book is about the effects of sudden economic change on people in the countryside, particularly those peasant smallholders who produce maize, rice, and other basic grains. It examines their struggles for survival, their efforts to understand the often distant and unseen forces threatening their livelihood, and the ways they acted politically to confront and then adapt to the free-market juggernaut. The book is also an examination of the possible roles of the state in the economy and social welfare. In an era in which states are decidedly unpopular, it is essential to point out that, at least in Costa Rica, the state contributed enormously to economic and social progress, and that legacy (despite the claims of the champions of the free market) goes a long way toward explaining the "success" of today's neoliberalism (see Chapter 1). In its broadest sense, the account that follows is about the theory and practice of development (and of social movements and anthropology) in the contemporary rural Third World.

The story I relate is not, however, a heroic tale of "resistance to capitalism" or one of those "grand" or "meta"-narratives that seek to legitimize "political or historical teleologies" involving the "great 'actors' and 'subjects' of history—the nation-state, the proletariat, the party, the West," or, in this case, "the peasantry" (see Jameson 1984, xii). Rather, the lessons of this study are a good deal more ambiguous, stemming not only from the complexity of the processes and people central to the research, and from their uncertain future, but from my dissatisfaction with a number of the analytical frameworks that social scientists have recently employed to examine economic change and collective action in the rural Third World. In particular, much of the current anthropological writing on knowledge and power takes a peculiarly devitalized approach to the latter category; it often views power primarily as a product of abstract discursive processes and gives only scanty attention to real human beings or to the material historical processes that both produce and reflect discourses and in which concrete political conflicts are embedded. Moreover, as I will discuss in more detail below, those scholars of development and social movements who stress "discourse" and "identity politics" at the expense of political economy often tend to give insufficient attention to the ways in which the concepts central to their analyses have been constructed over long periods of time, or to the sometimes remote but nonetheless powerful cultural histories of those groups that are today moved to collective action (see C. R. Hale 1997).

The absence here also of what some might perceive as modernist certainties derives, too, from ambivalences and shifts inherent in the issues this work raises about *campesino* movements. Almost everywhere, peasant organizations tend to rise and fall or change political direction with startling rapidity, as other scholars have amply demonstrated (see Zamosc 1986). In the late twentieth century, however, these oscillations take on an added dimension. Agriculturalists' associations and other grassroots groups sometimes evolve into "imagined organizations," which exist primarily in the minds of their leaderships and foreign donors. It would be easy, of course, to dismiss such "paper" groups as a perverse manifestation of opportunism, of the NGO boom of the 1980s and 1990s, and of neoliberal development policies gone awry. But as I suggest in Chapter 5 and in the Conclusion, the same individuals who head phantom unions and aggrandized "coalitions" are sometimes those with the deepest and most selfless commitments to fundamental change and the greatest capacities for envisioning creative solutions to profound development dilemmas. And "imagined organizations" (along with "imaginary leaders") can themselves undergo metamorphoses that lead to their reemergence and reinsertion in a vital and genuine political practice. Ambiguity and ambivalence thus reflect very real complexity, but they should not be considered synonymous with radical skepticism (cf. Comaroff and Comaroff 1991, 13).

"The fashion process," as Stanley Aronowitz remarks, "operates as much among intellectuals as it does in the dress industry" (1988, xviii). My rejection of "meta-narratives" does not, I hope, imply uncritical acceptance of the relativist and agnostic vogue characteristic of postmodernism and related "isms" (poststructuralism, deconstruction, etc.). This book aims instead to reassert both the importance of studying the complex interplay between culture, power, and material realities and the possibility of a responsible account, of "an anthropology-with-one's-feet-on-the-ground" or "a 'good enough' anthropology," in Nancy Scheper-Hughes's (1992, 4) memorable phrasing. It does not claim to have resolved the methodological and epistemological conundrums posed by today's trendy "isms." Rather, it departs from the premise—ultimately as much a product of the author's political outlook and values as is the case with any academic postmodernist—that these concerns, while deserving of attention, need to be held in abeyance, or at least denied center stage, if we are to advance knowledge of other, more pressing issues. Understanding the human tragedy of the contemporary Third World, to mention just one, is better served by a social scientific practice that attempts, however imperfectly and incompletely, to document and to come to grips with the forces creating, resisting, and reconceptualizing change. The book is also an argument for the continuing importance of political economy in such accounts. This requires an examination not just of the ephemeral, plural, and hybrid realities (or representations thereof) cherished by postmodernists, but of the countervailing, culturally and politically *homogenizing* tendencies inherent in contemporary capitalism. These processes, as David Harvey remarked even before the absolute ascendence of neoliberalism as *the* single, unchallenged economic model on the world scene, "are becoming ever more universalizing in their depth, intensity, reach and power over daily life" (1989, 117).

Thus, when I use the term "political economy," I am not referring to the newly popular notion that categories such as "development" and "under-development" are mere "fictitious construct[s]" or "narratives . . . woven of fact and fiction" (Escobar 1995, 19; 1988, 429; 1984, 389). I suggest instead that such representations, however ideologically laden they may be, are worth examining in all their messy, particular concreteness. They are not simply "discourses" that "reorganize" Third World societies in ways that key postmodernist critics of "development" prefer to leave largely unexamined and that serve, in a manner reminiscent of the homeostatic processes beloved by colonial-era functionalist anthropologists, primarily to reproduce the "discourses" themselves (rather than, say, specific economic sectors, interest groups, social classes, or families).

Like a number of commentators (Sangren 1988, 405), I find myself "simultaneously intrigued and appalled" by much postmodernist writing.[6] Despite, or perhaps because of this ambivalence, I recognize that in the context of the present inquiry three linked areas of thought—all in danger of being monopolized by purveyors of postmodern angst—deserve at least a brief discussion (which obviously cannot be anything but partial, in both senses of the term). These are: (1) the anthropology of "development" discourse; (2) "new social movements theory," one of the main paradigms for studying collective action; and (3) the problems and possibilities of "situated" or "engaged" research.

The connections between these three areas stem not only from the affirmations of some advocates of postmodernist approaches that new social movements in the Third World constitute a potentially emancipatory answer to a "development encounter" replete with unequal power relations. Rather, as I will describe shortly, the necessity of positioning the author in the research process and in written accounts of the research may, in the case of studies of social movements, in particular, derive from the "relations of fieldwork" themselves rather than from a preexisting abstract commitment to reflexivity or a predisposition toward narcissism (or "I-saying"). Moreover, a brief analysis of some postmodernist claims in the areas of development, social movements, and "positionality" suggests that discussion around all three themes has been insufficiently historicized (despite critic Fredric Jameson's widely cited injunction to the postmodernists, "Always historicize!" [quoted in B. Palmer 1990, 43]). This lack of attention to political-economic processes and intellectual antecedents makes it easier to accord "discourse" analytical priority and to attribute to it a kind of autonomous power over and above other kinds of power relations. It also leads to dubious assertions of intellectual originality and to obscuring, albeit largely unintentionally, incorporations of earlier scholars' insights (see Nash 1997, 21–22).

Underdevelopment in Quotation Marks?

Since the mid-1980s, a growing coterie of scholars has attempted to apply one or another variant of Foucauldian discourse analysis to the study of Third World development (see Apfell, Marglin, and Marglin 1990; DuBois 1991; Esteva 1988; Ferguson 1990; García Canclini 1993; Mitchell 1991; Prakash 1990; I. Sachs 1976; W. Sachs 1992).[7] Echoing a favorite maxim of postmodernist critics of ethnographic writing (Clifford 1983,6; 1988,80), several even assert that "underdevelopment" is a "fictitious construct" (Escobar 1988, 429; 1984, 389; see also DuBois 1991, 25; Esteva 1988, 667).[8] In so doing, they seek both to shock readers and to call attention to the historically conditioned nature of some unquestioned and perhaps cherished assumptions. Insofar as this kind of iconoclasm achieves these objectives it may represent a salutary antidote to much overly complacent mainstream thought and practice. But to the extent that such pronouncements divert attention from the profound inequalities that separate what are conventionally known as First World and Third World societies (or regions and classes within each) they cannot help but be deeply troubling.[9]

The claim that "underdevelopment" and—by extension, one assumes—"development" are "fictions" is intended to emphasize that a particular set of "discourses" and associated "strategies" propagated by powerful international agencies (such as the World Bank) and their local allies contribute to altering not only social and economic relations in the targeted countries but also "cultural meanings and practices" (Escobar 1988, 438). This is hardly controversial (though it does tend to make something of a mockery of the semantic conventions and shared subjectivity necessary for scholarly or other interchange [see Rosenthal 1992]).[10] "Discourses" do categorize people, and sometimes the labels are denatured caricatures of what those people are or believe themselves to be. It does not follow, however, that researchers must eschew all sociological categories simply because some social scientists or social engineers employ pejorative terms or labels that implicitly blame the labeled rather than the labelers. Indeed, it is curious that the same scholars (Escobar 1988, 435–36; 1991, 667–68) who are highly critical of designations such as "small farmers," "beneficiaries," and "pregnant and lactating women," use other such highly problematical categories—"peasant," for example—without the least acknowledgment of the hand-wringing and debate that they have caused among pre-postmodernist scholars (Leeds 1977; Shanin 1982). It is surprising too that, in discussing the power of labeling discourses, they downplay or ignore altogether another, contradictory tendency that is also a key postmodernist concern—the capacity of subalterns to appropriate labels (and more complex discourses) and infuse them with new and often positive meanings (but see Escobar 1995, 48–52). In an example close to the case at hand, I discuss in Chapter 4 how in Costa Rica the term "small farmer" (*pequeño agricultor*) changed from a relatively bland category favored by government officials and agricultural-sector lobbyists to a highly charged, politicized badge of pride. Some agriculturalists, in the heat of struggle, not only adopted it as a new form of self-definition, but employed it—at times ironically and at other times unconsciously—as a virtual synonym for outlaw status.

Nor is it always true that in the "development encounter"—successor, of course, to the ignoble "colonial encounter" (Asad 1973)—"states, dominant institutions, and mainstream ways are strengthened and the domain of their action is inexorably expanded" (Escobar 1991, 667; cf. 1984, 388). This assertion—central to James Ferguson's study of the World Bank in Lesotho (1990, 253; cf. DuBois 1991, 11 and Mitchell 1991, 30)—completely misses the point about the main theory and practice of contemporary neoliberal development policy (as well as denying to subordinate groups, through its emphasis on the inexorableness of the "development" process, any possibility of political efficacy).[11] The basic premises of neoliberalism—the reigning "development" model today—include the need to *drastically reduce* the reach of the state and, more broadly, that of the public sector. Somehow, postmodernist students of "development" have missed—have, in fact, inverted—this fundamental postulate of neoliberalism.

The deficiencies of the postmodernist anthropology of development are most obvious in its silences (or its "not-saids," to borrow an apt expression from Foucault [1972, 25]). Flesh-and-blood human beings—the victims of development gone awry—might be, one supposes, the obvious subjects of an engaged and outraged anthropological investigation (as, for example, in Scheper-Hughes's 1992 tour-de-force, *Death Without Weeping*). But they are conspicuously absent in most of the writings of postmodernist critics of "development," such as those of Escobar and DuBois, which are generally pitched at such a high level of abstraction as to preclude analysis (or, at times, even mention) of historical examples or illustrative cases. Similarly missing is any serious attention to (or frequently any reference to) the relative differences in levels of living or the highly skewed distributions of wealth and income that distinguish Third World from First World societies. It is not necessary to favor the conventional indicators employed by the major aid and lending institutions (per capita GDP, etc.) or even to adopt the increasingly problematical "Third" and "First World" categories at all to recognize that hundreds of millions of people are not meeting their basic needs for food, clothing, and shelter (or that alternative measures of this fundamental problem exist—such as the effort to adjust per capita GDP figures to reflect purchasing power in different countries [Summers and Heston 1988]; the Overseas Development Council's physical quality of life index [Morris 1979]; the United Nations Development Program's human development index [UNDP 1995]; or Amartya Sen's [1987] appealing notion that a measure of living standards should include a level of happiness, satisfaction of desires [i.e., "utility"], and choice). Recognition of this vast human tragedy need not imply uncritical acceptance of the accuracy or validity of much of the quantitative data that become "naturalized" and serve to justify the existence of the entire "development industry." But what is striking about the postmodernist critics of "development" is how frequently they exclude from view *both* the affected people *and* the relevant macroeconomic and social indicators. They thus end up trivializing the day-to-day experience and aspirations of those who suffer by either ignoring their grinding poverty, by carping about the bureaucrats and social scientists who attempt to measure it, or by locating it and all efforts to reverse it at the level of an elite discourse. Despite these scholars' frequent exaltation of "civil society" as a panacea for the ills wrought by "development," a discourse-centered approach to power can lead to blanket cynicism about even innovative efforts for change. Marc DuBois, for example, a self-described follower of Foucault, charges that

> those small development organizations that operate on a grass-roots level, those often considered to be the most effective and certainly the most sensitive to local populations, appear to be potentially the most dangerous if a Foucauldian sense of power is used to examine development anew. (1991, 19)

Discourse certainly figures in the reproduction of the wretched poverty afflicting so much of the world's population. But so do other phenomena, such as forms of accumulation and distribution and the other, nondiscursive, largely material aspects of the physical and social reproduction of the classes, sectors, corporations, and family groups that make up any contemporary economy, but that pass largely unexamined in the postmodernist critiques of "development." Apart from frequent condemnation of the theoretical main-stream's association of "development" with industrialization, and of the in-stitutionalization and expansion of the "development industry" itself, the postmodernist critics rarely mention any specific economic sector or even social reproduction in general except as a problem of competing discourses.

The rhetorical undermining of semantic conventions that pervades the postmodernist anthropology of "development" also gives rise to dubious syllogistic reasoning about the aspirations of the world's poor. Escobar (1991, 670), for example, questions Thayer Scudder's (1988, 366) assertion that "the large majority of the world's population want development for them-selves and their families." "How can Scudder demonstrate this point?" Es-cobar asks. "It is not difficult to show . . . that there is widespread resistance to development projects in many parts of the Third World."

But do Scudder and Escobar intend the same thing when they say "devel-opment"? Certainly not. Scudder clearly means something like "improved well-being" or "rising living standards." For Escobar, on the other hand, "development" signifies a destructive discourse and its associated institu-tional manifestations. Having assigned this negative meaning to the term, he rightly questions whether people want it. But it hardly follows that "the large majority of the world's population" does not desire improved well-being. Indeed, poor people's opposition to development projects is usually rooted in their perception, too frequently well founded, that such schemes threaten their living standards (whether economically or culturally defined). Escobar would likely agree. But is this evidence of opposition to develop-ment, as he claims? Only in a world in which idiosyncratic understandings of everyday words and rhetorical sleight-of-hand substitute for empirical in-vestigation and reasoned argument.[12] In the Costa Rican context examined in this book, to provide just one counterexample, militant peasant groups, following the common Latin American practice of appending aspirations or martyrs' names to the titles of popular organizations, proudly added the words "Justice and Development" to the name of the national-level coalition they founded in 1989 (Consejo Nacional de Pequeños y Medianos Produc-tores Justicia y Desarrollo 1991). "Development," like "small agricultural-ist," could be appropriated and infused with new meanings.

The postmodernist critique of "development" constitutes a useful correc-tive to mainstream theory in several respects. James Ferguson (1990), for ex-ample, brilliantly deconstructs the image of Lesotho presented in reports of the World Bank and other lending and aid agencies and shows how self-defeating, counterproductive "development" projects flow from an erroneous, ahistorical vision of this small, south African country as a nation of subsistence peasants (rather than of migrant laborers). Similarly, Tim Mitchell (1991) analyzes how development agency studies of Egypt employ a common leitmotif, the image of a dense, rapidly growing population crammed into the narrow Nile Valley, in order to elide questions of resource and income distribution. But it says a lot about the usefulness of the paradigm in question that in Ferguson's and Mitchell's work the Foucauldian framework is quite understated. Indeed, similar critiques of neo-Malthusianism's refusal to acknowledge inequality and of the ahistorical social science that saw "natural economy" and "isolation" at every turn but ignored conspicuous evidence of capitalist exploitation had attracted wide attention in anthropology at least since the early 1970s (Hewitt 1984; Mamdani 1973; Vincent 1990), well before Foucault became part of the disciplinary canon.

A common thread in the postmodernist anthropology of development literature is the insistence that "development" arose full-blown in the post–World War II era as an ideology and practice with few significant historical or intellectual antecedents (e.g., Escobar 1988; 1995, chap. 1; Kearney 1996, 34; Sachs 1976). The most engaging and specific articulation of this position is from Mexican scholar-activist Gustavo Esteva:

> Until well into the nineteenth century, the word *development* [*desarrollo*] in
> Spanish was employed to describe the operation of unrolling a parchment: it sig
> nified to return an object to its original form. During the last century [the term]
> migrated through at least three scientific disciplines, where it was employed as a
> metaphor for opening new fields of knowledge. It remained for a long time con
> fined to technical usage. In economics, neither Marx nor Schumpeter succeeded
> in gaining it general acceptance, except for very specific uses. But in 1949 some
> thing very strange occurred with *development*. Never before had a word achieved
> universal acceptance the very day of its political coining. On January 10, 1949,
> when Truman employed it in a speech, it immediately acquired a specific, distin
> guished meaning as Point Four of the Truman Doctrine. In a few days, two bil
> lion people became underdeveloped.[13] (Esteva 1988, 665, italics in original)

Esteva goes on to note—correctly—that "today development is an amoeba word, without precise meaning, but full of connotations" (665). Unfortunately, however, this semiotic sensitivity is not accompanied by a similar appreciation of the concept's complicated trajectory.[14] "Development" and "underdevelopment" were not, as the postmodernists claim, simply invented in a post–World War II effort to "remake" the Third World. These "constructs" have instead varied and complex roots in at least three historical-ideological watersheds: nineteenth-century Liberalism (and evolutionism), turn-of-the-century U.S. neocolonialism, and the debates between Latin American Marxists and populists that date to the 1920s.[15]

It is beyond the scope of this Introduction to elaborate the argument in much detail. A bare outline should suffice, however, to make the point, at least as regards Latin America. Most Latin American countries attained independence burdened with weak notions of nationhood, property controlled by religious and community corporations, and economies which, despite a century of Bourbon reforms, were still shaped largely by metropolitan-oriented trade in a few primary products. Liberalism took root in post-independence Latin America as a *modernizing, developmentalist* ideology and practice aimed at overcoming this colonial heritage (C. A. Hale 1989; Katz 1991; Love 1988). Whether articulated as a struggle for "civilization" against "barbarism" (as in Argentina) or in more explicitly racist and Social Darwinist terms (as in Mesoamerica and the Andes), Liberal ideology contained definite notions of development (or "modernity") and underdevelopment (or "backwardness"). While the periodization and the specific practice of Liberalism varied in different settings, the Liberals' adoption of free-market, secular policies usually involved, among other things, increased foreign indebtedness to finance construction of transport infrastructure, especially railways; the creation in government executive branches of "Development Ministries" (Ministerios de Fomento);[16] the privatization of church, community, and state lands; and major giveaways to foreign capital which, it was hoped, would facilitate the transition to "modernity." In Costa Rica, during the Liberals' late-nineteenth-century apogee, virtually the entire "national project," as articulated by intellectuals and politicians, "was precisely to come to be *equal* to the developed countries of Europe" (S. Palmer 1992, 182, italics in original). Both Liberal ideology and the measures that accelerated market penetration of the most remote spaces remaining outside of the economy are clear precursors of the "development" that postmodernists such as Esteva claim emerged from a virtual *tabula rasa* on a single day in January 1949.

"Any aggressive North American," California traveler George Miller declared in his 1919 memoir, *Prowling About Panama,*

> looks upon the splendid areas of land, the fine rivers, the dense forests, and the
> other untouched resources of this rich country with amazement, and begins to

plan *development projects* and dream of organizing syndicates, but the native loses no sleep over such vain imaginings. If he dreams at all, it is of his food if he be poor, and of politics if he be rich. (135, emphasis added)

Miller's comment, brimming with the imperial arrogance of the nineteenth-century U.S. doctrine of Manifest Destiny, was a concrete expression of economic theories that view regions, peoples, and entire nations as bundles of resources waiting to be exploited in optimal fashion. Its notions of "development" and "backwardness" resemble those of Latin American Liberal modernizers. His mention of "development projects" (while undoubtedly understood differently from the way the term is used today) also highlights the key role that developmentalist ideology and practice played in legitimizing and solidifying the early stages of U.S. neocolonial expansion.[17] Particularly after the Spanish-American War, the U.S. interventions in Cuba, Puerto Rico, Haiti, and the Dominican Republic, and the U.S.-engineered secession of Panama from Colombia, North American construction of roads, sewers, water systems, and public-health facilities (and, of course, the Panama Canal) became an essential justification for the neocolonial project.[18] In Central America and Colombia, as well as in the Caribbean, U.S. banana companies dredged harbors, drained swamps, combated tropical diseases, built railways, and erected entire towns of "sanitary" workers' barracks on stilts in the middle of what had often been impenetrable jungle. This vast, early-twentieth-century effort to transform the tropics—at once a rationale and a strategy for securing U.S. domination—was, as the quotation from Miller indicates, permeated by a discourse about "development" and "underdevelopment" that resonates loudly in later discussions (M. T. Berger 1993; Black 1988). Aided and abetted by a bevy of diplomats and policy experts drawn from the leading universities, this developmentalist practice existed in a powerful synergetic relation with academic discourses that either echoed the racist Social Darwinism of late-nineteenth-century Liberalism or propounded early versions of modernization or stage theory, maintaining that Latin America would eventually "progress" economically and politically along the lines of North American "civilization." As Mark Berger concludes, in an astute study of early-twentieth-century Latin Americanist academics in the United States, "between 1898 and 1945 the connection between the practice of U.S. foreign policy in Latin America and the dominant professional discourses on Latin America was *even closer than in later years*" (1993, 1, emphasis added).

These precursors of contemporary "development" theory and practice were linked to emerging systems of domination, domestic (in the case of the Liberals) and foreign (in the case of the U.S. occupation forces and banana transnationals). In contrast, the debates between Latin American populists and Marxists in the 1920s and after were part of a growing counterhegemonic discourse that nonetheless considered development the fundamental social and political problem of the period. In a reflection on the Latin American contribution to development theory, Cristóbal Kay (1991, 32–35) points to the polemics between Peruvians José Carlos Mariátegui, a heterodox Marxist, and Víctor Raúl Haya de la Torre, a populist nationalist, as foreshadowing, respectively, the radical dependency and the reformist structuralist paradigms that shaped so many discussions of Third World development after 1950 (cf. Slater 1992, 291). I would add that the clash between Mariátegui and Haya de la Torre was emblematic of a broader Marxist-versus-populist struggle over development theory and practice which was played out with varying consequences in different Latin American countries after the 1920s.

The important point here is not to outline the 1920's and 1930's controversies between Marxists and populists, but rather to stress the centrality of notions of development and underdevelopment, both in their substantive theories and policies and in the passions that fueled their arguments and political movements (see Caballero 1987; Mariátegui 1979 [1928]; Vanden 1986). Haya de la Torre and Mariátegui shared a view of Peru as a semifeudal society and of the Peruvian capitalist class as so weak or so tied to foreign interests that it was incapable of assuming the progressive role historically played by European bourgeoisies. Both attributed Latin America's underdevelopment to the reactionary landlord class and to imperialism, and both advocated industrialization. Significantly, they emphasized that the dynamics of capitalist development were different at the center and at the periphery of the world economy (Kay 1991; Vanden 1986).

Haya and Mariátegui differed, however, in their opinions about what both saw as an inevitable, impending revolution. Haya maintained that the revolution had to be anti-feudal and anti-imperialist and that it was necessary to fully develop capitalism, albeit within a framework of national independence. Since the peasantry was too backward and the proletariat too small, the revolution was essentially a struggle for national liberation and had to be directed by members of the middle class. Mariátegui, in contrast, insisted that feudal and capitalist relations were elements of a single system of exploitation responsible for Peru's low level of development. He argued that the revolution had to skip the capitalist stage and be socialist right from the beginning. The peasantry was not only a revolutionary force but, with its community institutions rooted in pre-Columbian tradition, it contained as well the germ of the new socialist society (Godio 1983, 220–24; Kay 1991, 33–34; Mariátegui 1979, 76–79).[19]

In the Conclusion, I shall have more to say about some of the discussions over the peasantry's role as a political force in Latin America. Here, I wish merely to note that the populist regimes that came to power in Latin America in the early to mid-twentieth century—whether based on mass movements, charismatic leaders, or both—spoke a language of social reform and economic development, fused in some cases with anti-imperialism. Haya de la Torre in Peru, José Batlle y Ordóñez in Uruguay, Getulio Vargas in Brazil, Juan Domingo Perón in Argentina, and Rómulo Betancourt in Venezuela (to mention only the most important) all saw economic progress as their main challenge and geared their discourse to poor, multiclass constituencies that hoped to benefit from development.[20] The early-twentieth-century industrialization of the larger countries in Latin America, particularly Brazil and Argentina, owed much to import substitution and other incentive measures implemented under populist regimes. This populist trend in Latin American politics, social thought, and economic policy eventually had a profound impact on such influential individuals and institutions as Raúl Prebisch and the United Nations Economic Commission for Latin America, both central to the "development" debate after 1949 (Kay 1991; Sikkink 1988). In describing the post–World War II concern with "development" as a full-blown genesis (rather than as a discursive shift based significantly on much older ideas), the postmodernists' Foucauldian "archeology" appears to have barely scraped the surface.

Material Objectives and Identity Politics

This facile reinvention of "development" as a post–World War II phenomenon is important not just as an illustration of the shortcomings of the postmodernists' writing of intellectual history. It is basic to their understandings of collective action and social change in the Third World and their visions of what constitutes an emancipatory politics. Escobar, for example, hails the

> growing number of social movements that reject the economistic character of development, are deeply aware of other concerns (ecological, and those of peace and of women and indigenous peoples), and seek to use local knowledge to shift the existing architecture of power. It is in the vitality of these new movements

that the dissolution of a 40-year-old development apparatus, already beginning
to crumble but still in place, and the coming of a new era, more pluralistic and
less oppressive, can be visualized. (1988, 439)

One of the central themes of this book is that Third World social movements of recent decades, and the Costa Rican peasant movements in particular, have often been neither prototypically "old" nor "new," at least in
the sense in which this opposition is used in the "new social movements"
(NSMs) literature. Concern with NSMs dates to the late 1960s when a tide
of discontent swept over young people in diverse parts of the world—New
York, Berkeley, Paris, Tokyo, Prague, Mexico City, and elsewhere (including
Costa Rica [see González 1985, 267–68]). This worldwide political and cultural tumult—which some subsequently interpreted as a common howl of
protest against "bureaucratic organization . . . in the post-industrial age of
computerized identities and cold remote institutions" (Murphy 1991, 78)—
impacted social scientific thinking with the usual long lag time between
historical events and published analyses. Functionalist frameworks (Smelser
1962) that saw "collective behavior" as an irrational mass response to societal breakdown were clearly not up to the task of explaining major upheavals
in democratic polities during an age of unprecedented affluence. Rational-
actor approaches (Olson 1965) that viewed social movements as the sum
of participants' strategic, individually oriented choices could scarcely make
sense of why student protesters, in the pursuit of seemingly abstract common goals, would risk ruining promising careers or having their heads split
open by riot police.[21] And traditional Marxists, who saw the bourgeoisie and
proletariat as the main antagonists in capitalist societies, did not usually
know what to make of movements that often had largely middle-class leadership and multiclass constituencies (see Cohen 1985, 667–73; Eyerman and
Jamison 1991, 19–23; Gamson 1992, 58; Zald 1992, 330–32).

Alain Touraine (1974; 1981) was probably the first to articulate the out-
lines of what many came to consider the "new social movements" paradigm.
In Europe, growing numbers of social scientists began to study the environmentalist, peace and anti-nuclear, women's, gay liberation, minority rights,
and student and youth movements (Melucci 1989). Eventually, the approach
caught on in Latin America, which it entered first through Buenos Aires, that
most Europhile of Latin American cities.[22] There, the list of "new" movements grew to include those struggling for human rights and democratization, the rights of indigenous peoples, regional autonomy, the needs of urban
slum dwellers, and the creation of liberation theology–oriented Christian

base communities (Jelin 1989; Slater 1985).[23] As more social scientists began to focus on these movements, and as the list of "causes" grew, it became clear that a veritable "social movements 'industry'" was emerging in academia (Gledhill 1988, 257), though it was also increasingly difficult to speak of the NSMs framework as a coherent model.

Synthesizing what has become a rich area of discussion and debate entails obvious risks. Nevertheless, I think it is fair to say that proponents of new social movements approaches share several broad assumptions. First, they juxtapose the "classlessness" (Olofsson 1988) of the NSMs with the "old" labor or working-class movement for which class was the main social cleavage, category of analysis, principle of organization, and political issue. The "new" movements' rejection of class accompanies an aversion to seeking amelioration through existing institutional channels and a distancing from party politics and especially from the "verticality and sectarianism" of the traditional Left (Fals 1992, 304).[24] Social conflicts, rather than revolving primarily around a class dimension, proliferate in more and more areas of life, resulting in the politicization of more and more kinds of relations and in a blurring of public and private spheres (Laclau and Mouffe 1985). NSMs supersede parties and unions and become "the organic expression of civil society" (Vilas 1993, 42). Second, NSMs "emerge out of the crisis of modernity" and are engaged in "cultural struggles" over meanings, symbols, collective identities, and rights to "specificity and difference." Generally, these concerns are accorded more weight by both activists and scholars than those involving socioeconomic or political conditions (Escobar 1992a, 396, 412; Jelin 1990, 206; Melucci 1989, 20; Touraine 1985, 784). Movement participants, often termed "new social subjects," have multiple social "locations" or "positions" and their political activity cannot, therefore, be derived *a priori* from a single principle of identity or a particular structurally defined "interest," especially a material one (Laclau 1985, 27). Third, NSMs, while at times contesting state efforts to dominate the construction of cultural meanings (Touraine 1988), usually engage instead "in creating bits of social practice in which power is not central" (Evers 1985, 48), and these are "below the threshold where the systemic imperatives of power and money become so dominant" (White 1991, 107). Finally—and especially germane in the light of the discussion below—advocates of NSMs approaches have, with few exceptions (Calderón, Piscitelli, and Reyna 1992; Esteva 1988; León 1990; Starn 1992), devoted scant attention to rural politics or peasant struggles (Fox 1990).[25]

Despite postmodernists' adoption of "new social movements" as a political rallying cry and as both evidence of and explanation for the fragmented, contingent identities of "postindustrial"—or, contradictorily, "hyper-industrial"—society (Touraine 1988, 25), the term appears rather like a new "meta-category," subsuming many disparate phenomena under a single overarching rubric (Calhoun 1993, 391; Gamson 1992, 58–59).[26] The movements in question often tend to be highly critical of capitalism, and their activists, in many cases, are drawn from earlier anti-capitalist opposition movements. But the NSMs' versions of identity politics and postmodern scholarship nonetheless resonate with some of the more dehumanizing aspects of contemporary neoliberal economics. First, NSMs have "helped reproduce the fragmentation of the popular classes sought by the state and the market" (Vilas 1993, 42). The accentuation of difference and otherness that both their theory and practice imply is, in large measure, a reaction to rising inequality, economic insecurity, and competition (Burbach, Núñez, and Kagarlitsky 1997). It is also an adaptation to the "flexible accumulation" that characterizes contemporary capitalism—with its restless, profit-hungry investors roaming the world, electronic flows of information and money, and accelerated processes of technological and organizational innovation (Castells 1996). As David Harvey points out:

> The more unified the space, the more important the qualities of the fragmentations become for social identity and action. The free flow of capital across the surface of the globe . . . places strong emphasis upon the particular qualities of the spaces to which capital might be attracted. The shrinkage of space that brings diverse communities across the globe into competition with each other implies localized competitive strategies and a heightened sense of awareness of what makes a place special and gives it a competitive advantage. This kind of reaction looks much more strongly to the identification of place, the building and signaling of its unique qualities in an increasingly homogeneous but fragmented world.[27] (1989, 271)

Second, as Carlos Vilas indicates, the category "new social movements" implies a view of politics common to both postmodernism and neoliberalism in which civil society is "the result of an always circumstantial combination of . . . multiple identities, among which class is just one—and never determinant" (1993, 39). In other words, identities become potential resources in a resource-driven system, a part of human capital, rather like university degrees, skilled hands, or fetching looks. If it is true that what energizes "new" social movements is a sense of victimization, rather than the "old" movements' search for equality (Apter 1992, 142), then the pursuit of identity politics as an end in itself may contribute not to the alliance-building that might temper the most oppressive aspects of the market (and ultimately weaken the identities themselves), but to perpetuating the divisive processes that gave rise to those identities in the first place (Harvey 1993, 64; Castells 1997).

Critics of NSMs theory have questioned the assertions of "newness" that underlie the paradigm, as well as postmodernists' view of the "old" labor movement (and, more broadly, of "modernity" itself) as a coherent, unified entity with a single "master narrative" (Foweraker 1995, 40–45; Gamson 1992, 59; Gledhill 1988, 258–59; C. R. Hale 1997, 569; Hellman 1995, 171–74; Nash 1992, 292). Like the notion that two billion people suddenly became underdeveloped in a couple of days in January 1949, the "newness" claim rests on a kind of historical amnesia.[28] This, as Barry Adam points out, arises

> from two sources: (a) the current crisis in Marxism which has allowed leftist
> social theory to "see" movement activity around it which it had long refused
> to recognize, and (b) the upswing of many of these movements in their "second
> wave" after having declined in the 1940s and 1950s either due to Nazi extermi-
> nation, Stalinism, or McCarthyism. (1993, 323)

In a similar vein, Craig Calhoun argues that early workers' movements were, like the NSMs, "engaged in a politics of identity" and that, before the late nineteenth century, "class was seldom the self-applied label or the basis even of workers' mobilization" (1993, 398, 401). Indeed,

> there was mobilization over wages, to be sure, but also over women and children
> working, community life, the status of immigrants, education, access to public
> services, and so forth. Movement activity constantly overflowed the bounds of
> the label *labor*. Similarly, the categories of class and class struggle have been
> used far from the Marxian ideal type of wage laborers in industrial capitalist
> factories. Artisans and agricultural workers, white collar and service employees,
> and even small proprietors (not to mention spouses and children of all these)
> have joined in the struggles or been grouped in the category of the working
> class. Throughout the history of labor and class movements, there has been con-
> tention over who should be included in them and how both common and differ-
> ent identities should be established. Indeed, ironically, by leading to research on
> the protests of women, people of color, and other marginalized people, the re-
> cent growth of NSMs has helped to explode the myth that the narrowly white,
> male labor movement, against which NSMs were defined, was completely pre-
> dominant. (391)

Nor are contemporary NSMs as "classless" or as loath to confront state power and address material concerns as some theorists suggest; nor is the practice of the "old" labor movement as distant from that of the NSMs. Just as unions' demands for occupational health and safety are profoundly environmentalist, calls for equality, affirmative action, and nondiscrimination clauses in union contracts are profoundly economic, as are those for converting war industries to peaceful uses, moving toxic dump sites, or closing nuclear power plants (Adam 1993, 323–27). Many of the most significant recent struggles, especially in poorer countries, have occurred "precisely at the point of intersection between" class- and identity-based movements (Hellman 1995, 167).[29] And for the impoverished inhabitants of today's crisis-ridden Third World (or the scholars who work with them), the "postmaterialist," "classless" arguments of NSMs theorists ring particularly hollow.[30]

This critical appraisal of NSMs theory should not blind us, however, to its very positive contribution in highlighting aspects of popular movements that narrow, class-based interpretations often downplayed or missed. The NSMs theorists' views of social actors as bearers of multiple identities and of culture and politics as loci of contested claims constitute useful correctives to traditional understandings, as well as clues about where to look in understanding particular patterns of quiescence or processes of mobilization (see Chapters 2 and 4). But the replacement of "class reductionism with class rejectionism" (Vilas 1993, 40) often obscures more than it reveals and is part of a more general inattention to political economy and the workings of the state that often places social movements outside of history (Adam 1993, 317; Fox 1990, 2–3; Harvey 1993, 54–55; Williams 1983, 172–73). The triumphalism that marked the early NSMs literature had largely faded by the late 1980s along with some of the original NSMs themselves (Escobar and Alvarez 1992, 3; Foweraker 1995, 25). The sterility of the debate over "newness" becomes especially clear when researchers dig in the archives, trace organizational genealogies, or probe movement protagonists' political biographies and historical memories (see Chapter 2). Although some of these movements occasionally made alliances with wealthy groups (see Chapter 3), they drew their constituencies overwhelmingly from the poor and the powerless—not just the proletariat, of course, but from a wide range of social actors bearing various visions of a better, more just society.

The Costa Rican peasant movements that are the subject of this book coalesced in response to the eminently material forces of economic collapse that were then followed by stabilization and structural adjustment, but they appealed nonetheless to deeply held notions of *campesino* identity and to fears that the cherished "culture of maize"—and, by extension, *maiceros*, or maize producers—had no place in the new development model. In some regions a long-dormant indigenous identity even surfaced sporadically among the exclusively mestizo peasantry as a metaphorical reference point and a justification for militant struggle (see Chapter 4). The movements' roots are diverse and often go way back in time: from local-level struggles for land decades ago to Catholic liberation theology in the 1970s, from participation in banana workers unions to residence in urban squatter camps, from disappointed expectations raised by 30 years of social democracy to a leftist vanguardism that once inspired them but which they came to reject. The influence of environmentalism, one of the prototypical NSMs, also figured significantly in the peasant movement (Blanco and Campos 1988; Blanco 1991; Brenes 1988). To some extent this reflected a transparent "greening of the discourse," as cooperatives and other groups curried favor with international donors. But environmentalism also trickled down to and arose from grassroots practice, as agriculturalists who had no hope of ever securing foreign grants but who had seen drought wither their crops went, on their own initiative, into the few remaining primary forests to gather seeds to reforest their small plots with native tree species, which they preferred to the exotics touted by the state extension service. The Costa Rican movements are also characterized by debates over peasant identities, and inclusion and exclusion, that would be familiar to students of NSMs. Yet their participants and leaders are also acutely aware that the survival and reproduction of *the bearers* of these identities requires struggles around economic policy issues. In an era of crisis, abstract and distant forces—a World Bank structural adjustment program, for example—can become distressingly concrete even in the most remote rural areas, as interest rates soar, producer price subsidies vanish, and banks restrict credit. As peasant leaders came to grips with these complexities, they had to learn the language of bankers and politicians (and to master the latest computer and communications technologies), challenging in the process timeless images of rural people as unsophisticated rustics.

A History of the Book

Every new book has a history, and this one is no exception. I spent the 1980–82 crisis years in Costa Rica and found myself increasingly dismayed by the spiraling numbers of begging children, desperate mothers, and homeless families (as well as the acute anxiety of distinguished university colleagues whose salaries had plummeted from over one thousand to less than two hundred dollars per month). But although I was deeply shaken by these scenes of crisis, I did not see the economic collapse as a subject for in-depth study.[31] I was involved instead in a dissertation project on agrarian history and social change in the northwestern province of Guanacaste. My specific concerns centered on land tenure and land use, rural class relations, and the *latifundios*, large underutilized properties devoted primarily to livestock grazing which, despite the predictions of anthropologists, economists and other social scientists, had persisted in the midst of a modern, and until recently, dynamic, export-oriented economy (Edelman 1992).

In the course of this research, I also undertook a survey of peasant agrarian reform beneficiaries, many of whom had illegally rented or sold their land to large sugarcane and rice producers, only to become wage laborers, at times on the same lands they had received from the state (Edelman 1989). In Bolsón and Ortega, the two adjacent villages in Santa Cruz cantón where I carried out the survey, the problem of highly unequal land distribution seemed intractable; even well-intentioned reforms had, at least in this case, ended up with the dispossession of small producers and the formation of new large properties. More disheartening still was the peasants' seeming passivity in the face of this outrageous injustice and, more generally, the poverty and oppression associated with the ongoing dominance of *latifundismo* in the region.

The picture was not entirely bleak, however. Two years before my stay in Bolsón–Ortega, hundreds of cane cutters and mill workers had gone on strike at the nearby state-owned sugar refinery. Local people remembered with excitement how they had collected food and clothing for the strikers, and a few recounted in whispers how others had thrown tacks on roads leading to the mill to puncture the tires of company and police vehicles. Some pointed out the houses where "communists" who had participated in the strike lived; the "communists," for the most part, were reluctant to talk to me. The labor action at the refinery, led by a small, urban-based leftist party, lasted only a few weeks and failed to secure a serious commitment to collective bargaining from management. Within a couple of years, the cane workers union was dead and many of its activists were barred from virtually all employment in the region. But even then, around the same time as my fieldwork in Bolsón–Ortega, in an action for which nobody ever claimed responsibility, environmentalist saboteurs working under the cover of night rolled dozens of large logs onto the tiny Santa Cruz airstrip where the crop dusters took off that sprayed the large landowners' fields with "cocktails" of poisonous pesticides.

As I made the rounds of agrarian reform "beneficiaries" in early 1982, squatting on wobbly stools in dusty yards, breathing smoky air in dark kitchen shacks, jotting notes on my pad and listening to tales of despair and disillusionment, I gradually became aware that someone else was also "visiting" from outside. People would ask me, "Are you with the other *muchacho*?" One woman remarked curtly that she had already told my "*compañero*" everything she had to say and didn't see why she ought to repeat it. I think I convinced her that I had never even seen the "other kid," my supposed "companion" or "comrade," and we eventually had what was, for me, at any rate, a fruitful and interesting conversation. Only toward the end of my survey did the other fellow and I meet in the same backyard.

He must have been hearing about me, too, because we both grinned at each other with a look of instant recognition and relief at having finally met. I, of course, was more obviously the outsider, with my foreigner's Spanish, my recently acquired knowledge of local agricultural practices, my camera and tape recorder, and my sometimes awkward or silly questions. He, too, though, had a distinctly foreign appearance for the Guanacaste lowlands: hair that was almost blond, pale skin, and clothes and shoes that looked quite a bit better than those of the agrarian reform beneficiaries I had been interviewing, most of whom were dirt poor. We introduced ourselves, shook hands, and chatted briefly. He was distributing literature for "Pueblo Unido," a coalition of three left-wing parties that in February had garnered 3.3 percent of the vote for president and 6.1 percent of the congressional vote, which gave the Left four representatives in the 57-member Legislative Assembly. He told me he was from a community in the "high zone" in the nearby mountains; the place was so small that I had never heard of it and, when I looked later, I couldn't find it on the map. He gave a pamphlet to the man whose yard we were in, exchanged a few words with him, cheerily wished both of us good luck, and went on to the next house. The encounter seemed so insignificant that I made only the sketchiest entry in my notes and rapidly forgot about it.

In the next six years, I made only two very brief visits to Costa Rica. Finally, in June 1988, I was able to return with my wife and infant son for a longer stay. My main goal was to do whatever additional field and archival research was necessary to update, rethink, and rewrite the later chapters of my dissertation on *latifundismo*. I had envisioned a relatively tranquil ten weeks of talking with colleagues and old friends, visiting government offices and archives, some short field trips to a couple of different places in Guanacaste, and many days of writing on my new laptop computer. Events, though, got in the way of my plans, and therein lies the story of this book.

In June 1988, Costa Rican newspapers were full of news of peasant "strikes," highway blockades, and protest marches against the government's economic structural adjustment program. Just two weeks before our arrival, 200 agriculturalists had seized the municipal building in Santa Cruz, near where I had done fieldwork, and held it for two days. The police blamed a young peasant leader named Marcos Ramírez for the trouble and were holding him in jail at Liberia, the capital of Guanacaste province. National and regional agriculturalists' organizations were calling for freedom for Ramírez and those arrested in other parts of the country. They also demanded, among other things, that the government make public the texts of its agreements with the International Monetary Fund, the World Bank, and the U.S. Agency for International Development, which they claimed harmed the interests of large and small agriculturalists and undermined Costa Rica's sovereignty.

I couldn't help but be interested in what was happening with the peasant movement, especially since it appeared to be so different from the pervasive, depressing political passivity of many of the peasants I had known in the early 1980s. I was still trying to keep my nose to the grindstone, however, and while I did some fieldwork in the irrigation district in another part of Guanacaste, I deliberately—albeit reluctantly—avoided Santa Cruz, where I sensed I would be distracted from my "real work."

Shortly after our arrival, an old friend called and asked if I wouldn't like to speak to some of the leaders of the national peasant strike. I didn't consider this directly relevant to my research, but I decided to go along anyway and threw my tape recorder and some fresh batteries into my bag as I left the house. It was early in the morning and I recall being surprised when my friend told me to meet them at the headquarters of FESIAN, the rural union federation linked to the ruling National Liberation Party (Partido de Liberación Nacional, or PLN). Why, if the agriculturalists were locked in a bitter struggle with the government, were they having this meeting in the office of a group so closely identified with the party in power?

When I arrived at FESIAN, just south of downtown San José, I found the steel gate that covered the stairway on the front of the building bolted and it seemed nobody was inside. A small group of social scientists and journalists who had also been called to the meeting gathered on the sidewalk and we wondered what to do. Someone went off to look for a public telephone. After a few minutes, a short, intense man with a wiry frame and a scraggly beard showed up, nodded in our direction, and began to shout and bang on the gates. Someone said, "Ah, Ulises is here," as if I should know who Ulises was or why it mattered. When the gates still didn't open, the bearded fellow cursed and climbed with incredible speed and agility up the bars on the front of the building. When he reached the second floor and an entrance to a stairwell visible from the street, he squeezed his torso between two of the bars, winced, grunted, and began to bend the bars out with his arms. For a moment, he was poised there, hanging above the street, looking like a brash daytime cat burglar, or like Samson straining to push apart the columns of the temple. In a second or two, the bars—which turned out to be hollow tubular steel— gave way. He squeezed inside, then came downstairs, a mischievous grin on his face, to let us in the front gate.

Upstairs in the FESIAN building we found a large room filled with tables, ringing telephones, blaring radios, clanking mimeograph machines, and perhaps two dozen people running back and forth. The buzzer on the front door was broken, all the telephones were in use, and there was so much noise that nobody had heard our group banging on the locked front gate or Ulises' shouting. This was the temporary headquarters for the organizations that had staged the recent peasant strike; FESIAN was not actively involved, but it turned out that the problems of the rural sector had become so severe that even the ruling party's own union organization was sympathetic and had lent space to the independent groups behind the strike movement.

In the midst of this almost chaotic atmosphere, someone ushered the half dozen social scientists and journalists to a table in a corner. Ulises, who turned out to be Ulises Blanco, a leader of UPAGRA, the strongest of the independent peasant unions, sat down with us and launched into a long monologue, spinning the tale of recent events in a voice that was sometimes impassioned and engaging and sometimes plodding and a bit pedantic. "The crisis of the agricultural sector is a total crisis," he told us.

And it's most affected by free-market policies. So when the Central Bank assumes it's normal that it's impossible to produce in Costa Rica, that it's possible to import everything at lower cost, then all productive sectors are affected, especially basic grains producers. They are very preoccupied by the government's policy, because they don't have credits, they don't have guaranteed prices, now they don't have crop insurance. And they began to form organizations just to discuss their problems. And other sectors began to join them. . . .

As Blanco droned on, peppering his talk with mentions of new banking laws and Agriculture Ministry officials, and anecdotes about the disasters that had befallen peasants who had enlisted in the government-promoted, export-oriented "agriculture of change," I found myself racing to keep up, scribbling follow-up questions and long lists of unfamiliar Atlantic zone root crops in the margins of my notebook. Occasionally, he would be called away to the telephone and Carlos Campos, UPAGRA's secretary-general would wander over and pick up the conversation. Campos's manner was more animated and he projected a kind of alarmism and urgency unlike anything I remembered from even the crisis years of the early 1980s. When somebody asked if he could provide us with a written program detailing the organizations' goals, he responded:

> We don't have very profound written proposals because that scares us. Imagine with all that one says and all that they say about one what would happen if they found indications that one was seeking some profound modification in Costa Rican society. Well, we'd be there in boxes [dead]. It's better just to generate this type of debate. They say that we want power, but what we want is the power to live [Dicen que nosotros queremos el poder. Idiay, lo que queremos nosotros es poder vivir].

I later came to realize that Campos was probably the most articulate and certainly the most charismatic of the movement leaders. Part of his substantial personal magnetism derived from his capacity for convincingly mixing shocking touches of hyperbole with sophisticated and eloquently expounded analyses.

When the conversation with Blanco and Campos was over, someone who knew of my earlier work in the Northwest suggested that I meet Carlos Hernández, a member of ASPPAS, the new organization that was working in the area of Santa Cruz, Guanacaste. A quiet, serious man in his mid-twenties, Hernández struck me as somewhat shy, which at the time I attributed to his being a peasant (I later learned that, strictly speaking, he wasn't) or to my being foreign, older, and with more formal education. We talked for a moment, exchanged telephone numbers, and he promised to stay in touch. I didn't entirely believe him, since Costa Ricans—perhaps even more than harried urban North Americans—are much given to promising to call and then letting it slide (Edelman 1998b). But he seemed nice enough and sincere, so upon leaving I gave him copies of a couple of articles in Spanish that I had written about my research on "his" region (Edelman 1981, 1987).

A week later, Hernández called me. Marcos Ramírez, the Santa Cruz strike leader, had just been released after twelve days in prison. They had read my work and found it "very interesting, very agreeable [*ameno*]." Would I like to speak with Ramírez about the situation in Guanacaste? Flattered and intrigued, I could hardly say no. We arranged that I would take a bus to one of the working-class neighborhoods to the south of San José and get off at the end of the line, at a town plaza. After I hung up the telephone, I foolishly wondered how Ramírez would recognize me, or I him, in a crowded, urban park.

I descended from the bus at the appointed time and, almost immediately, a thin, smiling young man with a wispy moustache greeted me. We went to a nearby hamburger joint and sat at a rear table, away from the din of backfiring motorcycles and shouting peddlers in the street. I asked Ramírez a bit hesitantly if I could record our conversation. He seemed pleased and looked at me as if he were expecting it. As soon as I placed the tape recorder on the small Formica table, he launched into a lucid, blow-by-blow narrative of the peasant "strike" in Santa Cruz, complete with dates and times and an astonishing degree of other detail (see Chapters 3 and 4).

While Ramírez was highly personable, articulate, and seemed an ideal informant, I was concerned about one unstated aspect of his story. He spoke with the strongly articulated final "s" and the assibilated "r" that distinguish Costa Ricans in the central part of the country from those in Guanacaste, whose aspirated "s" and standard Spanish "r" make them sound more like Nicaraguans. He also had a remarkably light complexion, something unusual in rural Guanacaste, where the population is largely of mixed African and Amerindian ancestry. What was this "Cartago," as Guanacastecans called Costa Ricans from the central plateau, doing, representing himself as a "leader" (*dirigente*) of a Guanacastecan peasant organization?[32] At the time, this question took the form of a nagging curiosity related primarily to Ramírez's representation of self and secondarily to his personal trajectory as an activist. Eventually, when this conversation evolved into a research project, I came to realize that the issue of leaders' provenance had broader implications not only for my own study, but for the nature of peasant organizations in Costa Rica (and elsewhere).

At the conclusion of our near-three-hour interview, Ramírez invited me to accompany him to a series of "peasant assemblies" that ASPPAS was planning in various communities near Santa Cruz in late July and early August. The aim, he said, was to discuss strategy in the aftermath of the June strike, especially the issue of how to deal with the continuing local-level repression of rural activists in the region. Ramírez remarked that "several people like you" might also come along. I recognized that he was viewing me—with my background in "his" region, my anti-latifundist sympathies, my foreign ties, and my involvement in the world of writing and publishing—at least in part as a useful resource. I also anticipated that the planned assemblies would, like all good political meetings, be part theater, but with some of the drama directed at observers like me rather than the peasant participants. This issue, too, came to be more central to my research than I could ever have realized at the time.

The story of the peasant assemblies properly belongs in Chapter 4, where I discuss the aftermath of the rural upheaval of June 1988. Here, it should suffice to make two points: that the contrived, theatrical aspects of the meetings were considerably less coherent than I had expected and feared (the action at the assemblies was obviously and thoroughly spontaneous in almost all respects and the only "person like me" who came along was a sociologist who worked for a progressive Catholic magazine); and that the experience motivated me to begin a project on local-level reactions to and understandings of economic structural adjustment. I would be disingenuous if I did not acknowledge that I saw the almost millenarian fervor of the agriculturalists I met in July and August 1988—so different from the pervasive apolitical passivity of a half dozen years before—both as an inspiration and as an embodiment of a number of fascinating research questions. The appeal for me of carrying out research on these emerging political actors was not unlike that which Judith Adler Hellman describes for students of social movements elsewhere in Latin America:

> For some it is the excitement of witnessing the emergence of new identities
> and novel practices. What others find compelling is the activists' efforts to con-
> duct themselves in a genuinely democratic fashion within a broader context
> marked by authoritarian social customs. For some researchers, the study of
> Latin American movements is a page out of their own political autobiography;
> it permits them to relive a satisfying experience or rework an unsatisfying one
> from their own youthful days of militance in antiauthoritarian movements.
> (Hellman 1992, 54)

In addition to these motivations, all of which figured to some degree in my case, I also had a certain amount of "cultural capital" from my previous work in Guanacaste. I knew the names of landlords, politicians, trees, villages, and government agencies, as well as most of the regionalisms that rural people used to talk about agriculture, work, and indebtedness. I already had some entrée with the movement's leaders. And, although ASPPAS operated for the most part in a somewhat different area than where I had earlier done field-work, I still had a number of old friends and contacts nearby.

My emerging concern with the effects of structural adjustment on the peasantry was a natural outgrowth of my earlier work on agrarian problems. But it also touched on an even more fundamental concern. In the two years I spent in Costa Rica in the early 1980s, I unexpectedly became enamored of the Costa Rican social democratic development model. Despite the severe economic crisis of those years, the state still maintained a significant and generally very positive presence even in small communities. Many on the left, of course, viewed state efforts at community organization and provision of services as fundamentally "demobilizing," "paternalistic," or not address-ing the underlying causes of poverty and social pathology (and those on the right saw this as "stifling individual initiative" and "encouraging irrespon-sibility and waste"—cf., for example, Palma [1989] and Corrales [1981]). There is undoubtedly some truth to these assertions, in both their left- and right-wing versions. At the same time, it is also true that children need health care and good nutrition and to learn to read and that the Costa Rican state was fulfilling some of these responsibilities with considerable success, at least compared to other western hemisphere countries, including my own. Even in relatively remote communities in Guanacaste, I saw that dentists would come periodically to check people's teeth, that children ate hot meals provided by Asignaciones Familiares (Family Aid) programs in local schools, that elderly or disabled people often received pensions, and that even many small producers and day laborers enjoyed health and disability insurance through relatives who had regular jobs and were covered by the social secu-rity system. It is worth emphasizing that I saw these evidences of a benevo-lent state with the same eyes that had seen the abysmal health, education, and social welfare conditions not only elsewhere in Latin America, but in the marginal Latino, Chinese, and black neighborhoods of New York City, where children often have rotten teeth because their families are too poor or too disorganized to bring them to a dentist and because the state is too ineffi-cient, underfunded, or uncaring to bring a dentist to them.

My positive reaction to the Costa Rican social welfare state also reflected in another way what was happening in my own country. A type of economic structural adjustment had come to the United States at the beginning of 1981 with the inauguration of President Ronald Reagan and "Reaganomics." The so-called "free-market" policies implemented by the Reagan adminis-tration were more often than not a kind of Keynesianism for the rich and the military-industrial complex. They had tragic social consequences and brought greatly increased indebtedness, severe polarization among classes and ethnic groups, and a pervasive ethic of uncaring individualism and greed. In a well-known comment emblematic of the times, Reagan's Agriculture Secretary—seeking to drastically cut school lunch programs (that were rarely as good as Asignaciones Familiares programs to begin with)—had the temerity to suggest that the tomato ketchup and pickle relish that remained in the budget were nutritious "vegetables" (Tolchin and Tolchin 1983, 87). In the face of this kind of cynical, self-interested nonsense, the existence of a more humane social model (and in a relatively poor country at that), was something of an inspiration, albeit an obviously very imperfect one.

My interest in studying the consequences of economic structural adjustment in rural Costa Rica thus derived from broader preoccupations about the demise of the social democratic development model and the profound, probably irreparable, damage done to my own society by Reagan–Bush "free-market" policies, a model in some respects like that imposed on Costa Rica since the mid-1980s. I do not think it necessary to romanticize the pre-1980 Costa Rican welfare state or to deny its evident shortcomings—the swollen and maddeningly inefficient bureaucracies, the often mediocre provision of services, the astoundingly generous (for public-sector professionals) and economically unsustainable system of retirement pensions, to mention just a few. I do, however, consider it useful to see pre-1980 Costa Rica as a significant experiment and a historical alternative in a world in which there is now, for all practical purposes, only one economic model, and one that has yet to prove its worth for the great majority.

Another aspect of this book's history bears mention, if only because it suggests something about the ways in which researcher and research subjects are inextricably, and at times problematically, bound up with each other. Following fieldwork in 1988 and 1989, I wrote a lengthy paper for a conference in the United States in which I attempted to explain the peasants' shift from quiescence to mobilization and treated at length the seizure of the Santa Cruz municipal building and its aftermath.[33] Hoping for some comments from Costa Rican colleagues, I sent the manuscript to a few social scientists I knew who read English. Somebody—I never found out who—passed the manuscript along to the peasant groups that had organized the June 1988 strike. They, in turn, sought out a university English major who sometimes helped out in the San José office that the peasant organizations had opened in 1989. This young movement sympathizer, whom to this day I know only by his nickname, "Naíto," prepared a very competent translation of my paper, which was then read, apparently with considerable enthusiasm, by the organizations' leaders.[34]

In late 1990 I returned to Costa Rica to continue my research. I managed to get a call through to the one public telephone in a small town near Santa Cruz, where a neighbor then ran off and found Marcos Ramírez. I said I would like to see him, but he was going to Guácimo in the Atlantic zone for a day and then to Panama for a Central America–wide meeting of peasant organizations. Cryptically, he said that he hoped we could get together as soon as he returned, because "*I too* have some things to propose to *you.*"

A few days later I met Ramírez in the back of the drab, unmarked house in a working-class neighborhood of San José that several of the more militant peasant organizations now used as a headquarters. We spent some time catching up about personal and organizational questions. Then he came to his proposal. The organizations, he remarked, were tired of intellectuals who invited them to seminars and discussions and then just appropriated their ideas. CECADE and CEPAS, two of the leading NGOs with ties to the peasant movement, were, he claimed, now organizing well-funded programs around the idea of vertically integrated production for smallholders, a concept that they had taken from the organizations. I was different from these intellectuals because I wasn't trying to make a career for myself in Costa Rica or in one of the burgeoning number of academic or development-oriented nongovernmental organizations. Several of the *compañeros* had read my work on the 1988 peasant strike and on *latifundismo* and they wanted me to write a book on the history of their struggle for justice and the changes in their organization. This would be directed at two audiences: movement participants, on the one hand, and intellectuals and policymakers, on the other. The organizations would produce the book through their new publishing arm, ICODE (Iniciativas de Comunicación para el Desarrollo).

Ramírez's proposal left me elated, but with contradictory feelings. Not surprisingly, I was extremely flattered at the invitation to be a kind of official chronicler, to collaborate in giving "voice to the voiceless" (see Mintz 1989, 794). It seemed to validate my research, my ties with my informants, and my most deeply held professional and personal values. I thought almost immediately of how some of the works of anthropology and history that I most admired—Richard Price's *First-Time* (1983, 17) and Jeffrey Gould's *To Lead as Equals* (1990, 1–6), for example—had taken shape around similar requests.[35]

I was, nonetheless, hesitant about immediately assenting to Ramírez's proposition. My main reason for reluctance was a sense that, however problematical the notion of "objectivity" in the social sciences, a certain distance from my subjects' agenda was a virtual requirement of a responsible account of their history (and how "voiceless" were they, really, if they had such good connections to a publishing house?).[36] Ramírez and I already understood that we didn't agree on everything—indeed, friendly arguments had been part of our relationship for some time. But I knew that his organization had reached its peak strength around the time of the 1988 strike, and as its support subsequently ebbed and its goals changed, I suspected that his objectives and mine might diverge to a greater degree than they had in the past. I had come to appreciate that what I initially thought of (and what Ramírez still represented to me) as an "organization" was actually a fractious, disputatious composite of grouplets and individuals who had come together around certain shared strategic objectives. In addition, even if I were to accept being the peasant activists' official historian, I doubted that my work would be very useful *for them*, given the immediacy of their political needs and the inevitable long time between research and final publication of results.

Lastly, I hoped to analyze the peasant movement of the 1980s in relation to both earlier forms of resistance in the region and the political antecedents of its leaders.[37] Organization activists were loath to emphasize their previous involvement in a political Left from which they now desired to distance themselves (and which, for all practical purposes, no longer existed anyway). While I understood, respected, and sympathized with this wish, I also realized that key aspects of their practice (and of peasant militance in the region of study) were simply not comprehensible without reference to this now almost ancient history (and other, even older histories). Various movement leaders had spoken candidly with me about their earlier activities and allegiances, and organization documents occasionally pointed to past leftist ties as a troublesome legacy that was superseded with the move to organizational autonomy in the early 1980s (see Chapter 2). But I doubted that they would want this analyzed in any detail in an official chronicle of their struggles.

The significance of this political history was brought home to me in another small incident that had to do with my manuscript on the 1988 peasant strike. Not long after I met with Ramírez, I went to see Berta, an old friend, anthropologist, and former neighbor in Liberia, the capital of Guanacaste province. We went for a picnic and hike on the slopes of the Rincón de la Vieja volcano, where she told me that she too had obtained a copy of my paper. "Miguel and I were just reading your paper on the Santa Cruz strike," she told me with a grin, referring to another colleague and friend. "We were laughing, because you left out something very important." She pointed to the west, where in the distance we could see the long, jagged escarpment that rises from the plains in the center of the Nicoya Peninsula. "Those mountains there, that 'high zone' was one of the areas of influence of 'el M.'"

"El M" was shorthand among a generation of Costa Rican university students for "el Movimiento," which in turn stood for the Movimiento Revolucionario del Pueblo , or MRP. A small, romantically pro-Cuban organization that had disappeared by the mid-1980s, the MRP, like the rest of the Left in Costa Rica, never attained great size or influence. There were, however, two sectors where it did enjoy some strength in the 1970s. One was among agricultural laborers, poor peasants, and agrarian reform beneficiaries in a few parts of the Atlantic zone and in the area around Santa Cruz.[38] Several of the main leaders of UPAGRA, ASPPAS, and allied organizations had, in fact, cut their political teeth in "el M." The Movement's other key constituency was among college students and recent graduates, particularly those from the University of Costa Rica's School of Anthropology and Sociology.[39]

It was the MRP that had been behind the 1979 cane workers strike which I had heard about during my 1982 fieldwork in Bolsón–Ortega (see above and Edelman 1992, 280). Mario Sancho, the leader of the cane workers union, a ruddy-faced, serious young man in rubber boots and a broad-brimmed canvas hat, often dropped in at my MRP anthropologist neighbors' house on the outskirts of Liberia in 1981–82. When he came by, my neighbors would hurriedly drop the chess game, science-fiction novels, or rock music that often occupied their leisure time; they would all then joke anxiously about the visit from their "political superiors" and go out to the backyard, where they conversed in hushed tones. A half dozen years later, a long-time activist in Santa Cruz presciently remarked to me: "Mario Sancho is now totally blocked [from organizing] in Guanacaste. And if they investigate a little bit further back about Marcos Ramírez, I'm afraid they'll have him totally blocked here too."

I hadn't left the MRP out of my manuscript on the 1988 peasant strike in an effort to protect my informants.[40] Rather, at the height of the movement in 1988 and early 1989, the MRP simply didn't seem relevant in explaining rural unrest, especially since it hadn't even existed for several years and the more immediate effects of drought and economic structural adjustment were so visibly powerful. But as the Santa Cruz movement unraveled in 1989 and 1990, the issue of its leaders' old political histories surfaced with new intensity in local-level debates (see Chapter 5). When Berta told me that she had laughed at my failure to write about the "M's" legacy in the hills above Santa

Cruz, I had a flash realization that the "other *muchacho*" whom I had encountered distributing Pueblo Unido pamphlets in the lowland village of Ortega in 1982 (see above) was the same good-natured, marimba-playing, tomato-farmer militant I had spoken with several times in the "high zone" in 1988 and 1989. The older histories of rural activism were connecting to the newer ones in very concrete, personal ways.

My essay on the 1988 strike had one further effect on the course of my research and on the Santa Cruz peasant movement itself. In late 1990, shortly after Ramírez requested that I write a book on the peasants' "struggle for justice and the changes in the organization," one of the NGOs he had criticized for appropriating activists' ideas asked if I would be willing to have my paper discussed at a small roundtable. CEPAS (Centro de Estudios Para la Acción Social), despite Ramírez's criticisms of it, had a fine team of young sociologists who were doing some of the best academic work in the country on the peasant movement.[41] They promised to invite a dozen other specialists from the NGOs and universities and that everyone would have read my paper in advance. I had yet to receive any comments from the colleagues to whom I had originally sent the manuscript, so I excitedly looked forward to this opportunity to discuss my work.

I spent the two weeks before the scheduled roundtable in the Santa Cruz area, making the rounds of old friends and contacts. Marcos Ramírez was around for the first five days or so, and we spent much of that time together, but then he was off somewhere on organization business. It became clear that ASPPAS, the association that had led the Santa Cruz strike and that boasted 1,500 members in 1988, was essentially dead. Curiously, however, in the capital nobody seemed to realize that the organization had faded away. The CEPAS sociologists, for all their good intentions, rarely did fieldwork in the countryside, relying instead in their peasant movement research nearly exclusively on documentary sources and interviews with organization representatives in the capital.[42] In Santa Cruz, however, everybody knew of the organization's demise and many of its former activists had scathing things to say about the leadership and the new policy of adapting to, rather than challenging, the government's free-market policies (see Chapter 5). One disgruntled agriculturalist complained to me that "Marcos [Ramírez] makes it look very pretty, but hunger can't be made to look pretty. If one makes a situation like this look pretty just to save oneself, then we're really in bad shape." And another *campesino* from the "high zone" wondered bitterly about a visit by some French aid functionaries to a regional meeting of rural cooperatives. "I don't know what stories Marcos laid on those French people about ASPPAS. They went around asking, 'And ASPPAS? Where's this ASPPAS?' and he'd grab them by the arm, whisper I don't know what kind of nonsense in their ears, and pull them off somewhere else."

Just before the CEPAS roundtable began, one of my hosts informed me that "the organizations" were sending someone, too. She asked me if I knew Carlos Hernández, "the San José representative of ASPPAS." I told her I did and thought to myself how ironic it was that ASPPAS didn't really exist any more, that Hernández was acting as if it did, and that this otherwise well-informed scholar hadn't realized this. Hernández and the other guests took their seats. I spoke for about fifteen minutes, emphasizing the importance of empirical investigation in the countryside and of seeing political actors both in relation to economic forces and as constructors of an alternative, opposi-tional culture and of new rural identities. A lengthy discussion ensued, much of it about research methods and about how the CEPAS agrarian stud-ies team had, as one member put it, "failed to take advantage of various op-portunities over the past several years . . . to interview movement partici-pants and employ their own words in our analyses."

Then someone asked breathlessly about the current state of the peasant movement in Santa Cruz. I responded that I thought it necessary to speak frankly, that it pained me to say it, but that, as far as I could tell on the ba-sis of what I had just seen in Santa Cruz, ASPPAS didn't exist anymore. The CEPAS sociologists and most of their guests appeared startled and un-comfortable. Hernández was looking daggers at me. I pointed out that this shouldn't really be such a surprise, that peasant movements often rose and fell fairly rapidly or underwent radical shifts in ideology, and that many for-mer ASPPAS participants were now active in other kinds of organizations: cooperatives, community development associations, and cantonal agricul-tural centers. I suggested that this wasn't necessarily such a bad thing and that it might well have been one of the positive legacies of the 1988 strike.

When I finished, all eyes turned toward Hernández. He was still glower-ing at me and ventured a few terse comments about how my appreciation of the current situation of ASPPAS was "very subjective." I didn't take any joy in his discomfort or in having let the secret of the demise of ASPPAS out of the bag. On the contrary, I was saddened that it had fallen to me, of all people, to go out into the countryside and then return to the city with the bad tidings.

In early 1991, I saw Marcos Ramírez again. He confessed that when he heard what had gone on at the CEPAS roundtable he had at first been "quite upset." Then he told me that I had done the right thing to bring people up to date, to speak the truth. Just recently, he said, "the directors [of ASPPAS in

Santa Cruz] had managed with great difficulty to meet and agreed to dissolve the association." Shortly afterward, I spoke with three other members of the ASPPAS board, all of whom denied that such a meeting had even taken place. One commented that "the organization simply died."

It would, of course, be terribly grandiose of me to think that my paper on the 1988 strike or my comments at the CEPAS seminar had anything to do with the political death of the organization (on this, see Chapter 5). But my response to the question at the roundtable certainly contributed to spreading the news and probably to making it official. I couldn't help thinking that Ramírez's announcement of the dissolution of ASPPAS, in contrast to the demise itself, had a lot to do with my having spoken candidly, especially when I did so by contradicting one of the group's key protagonists and in the presence of the NGO and university scholars who were among the most articulate analysts of, and publicists for, the peasant organizations. The question remained, however, of why Hernández and Ramírez continued to project an image of ASPPAS as a vital organization well after it had ceased to be one (see Chapter 5 and the Conclusion).

Objective Researchers, Bad Data

Little had I imagined when I mailed Costa Rican colleagues my manuscript on the 1988 peasant strike that this would set in motion a chain of events that would lead key informants to announce the death of their organization (which, after all, was my "object of study"). It was difficult to conceive of any more effective demonstration that researcher and research subjects are entwined in a complicated, mutually influencing process of describing, analyzing, and constructing social reality. The saga of my paper and the CEPAS seminar inoculated me, I believe, against what Hellman (1992, 55) terms "the pitfalls of overidentification" and "the intensely protective attitude" displayed by many "nonactors" who study social movements (although, as I indicate in the Conclusion, I did not cease being a critical sympathizer). It also, inescapably, injected into my inquiry a preoccupation with reflexivity, although one that is somewhat different than the reflexive orthodoxy that has come to characterize much cultural anthropology in this era of postmodern sensitivities.

Reflexivity, Loïc Wacquant remarks, is a "label . . . vague to the point of near vacuity" (Bourdieu and Wacquant 1992, 36). He nonetheless points to three ways in which a "bending back" of science upon itself (in the tradition of Pierre Bourdieu) might contribute to a critical yet empirically grounded understanding of society: first, by examining "the social and intellectual unconscious embedded in analytic tools and operations"; second, by analyzing the researcher's insertion in an "academic field . . . , [an] objective space of possible intellectual positions offered to him or her at a given moment" and in a "field of [academic institutional] power"; and third, by butressing "the epistemological security" of the social sciences, rather than trying to undermine it, as is often the case "with phenomenological, textual, and other 'postmodern' forms of reflexivity" (36–39).

Two aspects of the latter point in particular deserve a brief comment in the context of the present discussion. First, many of the growing number of self-referential accounts of field research, rather than viewing the anthropologist's role primarily in relation to specific research problems, consider privileging the "authorial voice" as a paramount value in and of itself (see, e.g., Behar 1993, chap. 17; Jackson 1989). Critics of diverse viewpoints have accurately, if unkindly, characterized such reports as "narcissistic" (Ginzburg, in Luria and Gandolfo 1986, 103; Bourdieu and Wacquant 1992, 46) or, slightly more charitably, as "author saturated" or "even supersaturated" (Geertz 1988, 97). Second, concern about positioning the researcher is hardly new and is certainly not an invention or a monopoly of postmodernist writers. Numerous earlier scholars analyzed how both research and writing involve decisions about what is relevant and what is irrelevant, a process postmodernists "tend to stigmatize as 'occultation,' as if there were inevitably a dirty secret behind every attempt to say anything at all" (Launay 1992, 190; cf. Foucault 1972, 25). But the many pre-postmodernists who examined the problems of "values," "objectivity" or even "engaged" research steadfastly eschewed the currently popular "meta-skepticism" or "epistemological hypochondria" in favor of a reflexivity that saw the "social construction of reality" not only in history, culture, and daily life, but as an unavoidable and necessary accompaniment to the process of social scientific investigation itself (see Berger and Luckmann 1966; Lynd 1939, chap. 5; Mills 1959, chap. 4; Murphy 1971, chap. 3; Myrdal 1969, chap. 11; Novick 1988; Sartre 1968; Scholte 1972). Only another, usually subterranean tradition—explicitly nihilistic and with roots going well back into the nineteenth century—argued for the kind of extreme relativism and epistemological insecurity that characterize today's postmodernists (Nietzsche, for example, maintained that "it is precisely facts which don't exist, only *interpretations*" [1977, 458]).

In *The Death of Luigi Trastulli and Other Stories* (1991), Alessandro Portelli shows how these issues may be addressed *in practice* while making a related point about "objectivity" and ethnographic research on social movements. Trento Pitotti, an elderly cobbler in a central Italian hill village, obliged Portelli by allowing him to tape record an extensive collection of folk songs from the 1930s. While impressed with his informant's magnificent voice and enormous repertoire, Portelli was disturbed that two of the songs were "unmistakably Fascist." A year later, Portelli talked at length to the folk singer/cobbler and found out that, far from being a Fascist, he was a politically active Communist. Why, then, had he sung those Fascist songs? "'You asked for old-time songs, songs from when I was young,'" Trento told Portelli. "'That's what they used to make us sing in those days.'"

"Trento didn't know me, when I first recorded him," Portelli comments.

> His life experience had taught him that he would be safer singing religious, ritual, sentimental, humorous, or conservative songs to an outsider who didn't look or talk like working-class and who had said nothing about himself. I had thought I was not supposed to "intrude" my own beliefs and identity into the interview, and Trento had responded not to me as a person, but to a stereotype of my class, manner, and speech. I had been playing the "objective" researcher, and was rewarded with biased data. (1991, 30–31)

That members of subordinate groups tell social scientists, state authorities, and other outsiders what they think they want to hear is hardly remarkable enough to deserve much comment. The researcher unable to transcend a class- or nationality-stereotyped presentation of self in the field is especially likely to receive formulaic responses. To members of subordinate groups, even in democratic societies, a researcher's coming may portend anything from a mild bother, to an offensive intrusion (with the attendant lost time and potentially embarrassing questions), to a real threat of serious problems with the authorities. During my fieldwork in Costa Rica, for example, I several times arrived at locked and shuttered smallholders' homes only to be asked by apprehensive neighbors if I was there to serve a *"cobro judicial"*—the legal paper banks used to collect overdue loans.

If Trento reacted to Portelli "not as a person, but as a stereotype of [his] class, manner, and speech," North Americans doing research with highly politicized subjects in Central America in the 1980s sometimes faced more daunting hurdles. In the 1980s the region was racked by conflicts in which the United States was a key player: the genocidal counterinsurgency war in Guatemala, the civil war in El Salvador, the *contra* campaign against Sandinista Nicaragua, the long confrontation preceding the U.S. invasion of

Panama, and the use of Honduras and Costa Rica as rearguards and staging areas for the Nicaraguan and Salvadoran wars. In this atmosphere of violent geopolitics, radical nationalisms, social upheavals, intrigues, and treachery, exchanges between social scientists and their subjects were inevitably mediated with a kind of political currency and contingent on all kinds of implicit and explicit political tests. Researchers frequently had to prove their political bona fides to informants and colleagues suspicious of the pervasive and often covert U.S. intervention in the region. At the same time, too often they had to justify their concerns about human rights, repression, and violence to North American colleagues who saw these as partisan issues and whose conception of professional ethics was limited to narrow methodological questions such as informed consent, legal approval of research by host governments, and respect for traditional status quo institutions (Bourgois 1990).

A Coda on Methods and Sources

This study moves uneasily between global economic forces and poor rural families worried sick about crop failure and hunger, between grain prices and smug Central Bank officials, between interest rates and peasant movement strategists. Chapter 1 attempts to provide readers with some understanding of how and why a small, underdeveloped country could attempt to construct an advanced social welfare state. Chapter 2 discusses how agriculturalists began to mobilize in response to the erosion of the welfare state and the devastation that accompanied the severe economic crisis of the early 1980s and the subsequent years of stabilization and adjustment programs. In Chapter 3, I take a long view of peasant struggles in one region, the Santa Cruz–Nicoya zone of Guanacaste province, examining the diverse campaigns, ideological influences, and organizational efforts that informed the "strike" movement of 1988. Chapter 4 looks in detail at the 1988 agriculturalists' "strike," which marked the high point of peasant militance in the period under study; although the movement was nationwide, I give particular attention to events in Santa Cruz cantón. Chapter 5 analyzes the peasant organizations' shift "from confrontation to proposal" and their efforts, not always particularly successful, to implement concrete development programs that would serve the interests of their constituencies. In both Chapter 5 and the Conclusion, I pose the problems of the rise, fall, and reemergence of *campesino* organizations and of why weak or even "imagined organizations" can sometimes have real impact. The most telling fiction of late-twentieth-

century foreign aid discourse is not, I argue, "development" or "underdevelopment," but rather the existence of "organizations" without members
that nonetheless subsist through mutually reinforcing exchanges between
donors (and sometimes urban-based social scientists) and "leaders." But as I
have hinted above, this is not simply a matter of decrying some new kind of
rural Latin American Potemkin village. The mere fact (yes, fact!) that an organization is not all (or even anything) that its "leaders" claim does not necessarily mean that they cannot transform themselves into something else
and, paradoxically perhaps, be a fount of commitment, creativity, and solid,
practical ideas about development.

In the sections of the book that discuss macroeconomic policy, I have attempted to keep the human, political dimensions present as much as possible, in part by quoting key actors' written programs, spontaneous out-
bursts, and post hoc confessions, examining their visions of the future and
of what they did or thought they were doing in the past. This is not simply
a literary or stylistic device, intended to make palatable or entertaining an
otherwise dry, "dismal science" analysis. It stems instead from my conviction, which I hope to demonstrate more fully in the pages that follow, that
the politics of economic structural adjustment, too often studied as either a
dull sequence of high-level negotiations, lending-agency missions, and resulting policy shifts—or as purely reactive behavior by popular sectors—
is better understood as a complex and eminently *cultural* process of political and ideological contention within and between policymaking dominant
groups and popular sectors. The links between macroeconomic policy and
on-the-ground human beings are also something that the agriculturalists I
came to know would never let me forget, not simply in their laments about
being squeezed by the free-market scissors of falling crop prices and rising
input and credit costs, but in their anxious and often sophisticated questions
about what was in store for them. (*"Hola, Marquitos!"* one agriculturalist
friend called out to me from across a dusty street in the town of Filadelfia
in mid-1991, Hispanicizing and diminutizing my name at the same time.
"Tanto tiempo!" [Long time, no see!] *"¿Cómo le ha ido?"* Before I could
even tell him how I'd been, he began to gesticulate, flinging his hands around
in the distinctive, impassioned style of the Guanacaste lowlands and asking
me in an anguished tone if I knew whether "PAE III," the World Bank's third
structural adjustment loan, had been approved yet.)

In the sections of the book that are less global (or national) and more local, I rely heavily on in-depth interviews with peasant activists (and nonac-

tivists), attendance at their meetings and informal gatherings, and on the kind of primary documentary source materials that large research libraries typically discard as "ephemera"—leaflets, correspondence, pamphlets, and small mimeographed newsletters (and, to a lesser extent, on more conventional archives, press accounts, and secondary sources). I frequently used a tape recorder—always with permission, of course—and I generally found that after a very short time those I was with tended to forget about it and did not seem to experience it as an intrusion. Occasionally, however, when conversations shifted toward past or possible future acts of illegality—a land invasion, for example, or plans to release dozens of chickens in the lobby of the Central Bank in San José—I would be told in no uncertain terms to "Turn that thing off!" (*¡Apagá ese chunche!*). I have attempted throughout to subject oral (and other) evidence to tests of internal consistency and external corroboration and, where these have been lacking, I have tried to ask questions about the unconscious forces and the conscious personal and political agendas which account for the discrepancies. As Portelli comments: "The importance of oral testimony may lie not in its adherence to fact, but rather in its departure from it, as imagination, symbolism, and desire emerge. Therefore, there are no 'false' oral sources. . . . 'Wrong statements are still psychologically 'true,' and . . . this truth may be equally important as factually reliable accounts" (1991, 51).

I am naturally aware that oral sources have not escaped the embrace of the meta-skepticism long extended to "texts" (a category which in any case has attained such breadth as to be almost meaningless). James Clifford, for example, in an unacknowledged echo of linguist Roman Jakobson, declares that "quotations are always staged by the quoter and tend to serve merely as examples or confirming testimonies" (1988, 50).[43] I thought of this assertion several times in the field when, at one or another assembly or meeting, angry *campesinos* would approach me, spilling over with stories of the latest outrages to which they had been subjected, eager to have someone capture their words on a cassette and tell the rest of the world. In my account, I certainly "stage" the words of some of the protagonists, but they were also asking—indeed, demanding—to be "staged," to be subjects of history and of the history that I was writing. Their actions, experiences, and words, which I privilege in some portions of this book, constitute not only a necessary, key body of evidence for the story I have to tell, but a corrective to "inhuman" analyses of economic structural adjustment (and of social movements), the "fulfillment of a promise" to my Costa Rican interlocutors (as they themselves might put it), and a small effort to preserve or "to rescue" (*rescatar*, as they might say, implying also "to redeem" or even "to liberate") rich sources of popular memory and expression that might otherwise pass undocumented into oblivion. I have chosen not to dwell on peasant activists' "poetics" in this book, but I have often been forcefully struck by their insight, poignancy, and eloquence.

A final observation is perhaps in order about the thorny issue of "naming names." Anthropologists traditionally argued for disguising and "protecting" the identities of their informants and field sites, though the consensus around this practice has eroded somewhat in recent years. Historians, on the other hand, more concerned perhaps with being able to retrace each other's methodological footsteps or with their discipline's equivalent of "ethnographic authority," have generally required that even minor points based on oral evidence be footnoted with the source's full name and the date and place of the interview. Both disciplines have been enriched as their methods and concerns converge, but scholarly citation conventions and writing practices have become yet one more disputed gray area. I have had to balance several considerations in deciding what practice to follow here. When people expressed misgivings about having their names in print, when they were not public figures and their specific identity was not important to my account, or on those few occasions when I neglected to ask, I have used pseudonymous first names or simply described the individuals briefly. Costa Rica is a small country, where social networks are dense and flows of information—formal and informal—are remarkably developed. Disguising a locality where something dramatic has occurred or the identities of key individuals involved is virtually guaranteed to be unsuccessful. Many peasant movement activists are public figures who regularly grant interviews to print and electronic media. I sometimes employ published reports of these appearances on the public stage as sources, and cite them as any scholar should, yet they contain people's real names (as do the unpublished documentary sources to which I refer at various points below). And, finally, the question of naming names is tied to the issue mentioned above of *cumpliendo una promesa* (fulfilling a promise). Many of the protagonists of this history wanted their names to appear in what I was writing and would even be offended if they learned that they had appeared disguised with a pseudonym. If Costa Rica had not weathered the crisis of the early 1980s with its democracy intact, I would have been reluctant to honor their requests. But even at the height of the wave of arrests that followed the 1988 strike in Santa Cruz, the people who might conceivably have been most reticent about speaking frankly usually told me to go ahead and say who they were, that they had enough faith in the openness of their society, and that what they had done was right, so that they weren't worried. If they had to go to jail or be blacklisted, they knew it wasn't going to be because some gringo with a tape recorder interviewed them and years later quoted them in a "history book" or an obscure academic journal.

CHAPTER 1

The Rise and Demise of a Tropical Welfare State

The welfare state has failed in Latin America. That is a fact, and an important lesson taught to us by the past. . . . Statism as a form of comprehensive social policy only succeeded in eroding the very foundation of fiscal discipline, often making the State a source of inflationary pressures and intensified economic inequality.

—ENRIQUE V. IGLESIAS, *President, Inter-American Development Bank, 1989*

Costa Rica is not a country. It is a pilot project. It is an experiment.

—JOSÉ ("PEPE") FIGUERES, *former Junta Chief and President of the Republic, and founder of the National Liberation Party (PLN), 1982*

Better a bad agreement than a good fight. [Mejor un mal arreglo que un buen pleito.]

—*Costa Rican proverb*

How could a small, relatively poor Central American country—heavily dependent on coffee and banana exports, with a 1940 population of just over 650,000—successfully create and then maintain for some three decades an advanced social welfare state? How could one of Latin America's most notable instances of a state's support for its citizens' well-being and of state intervention in the economy metamorphosize in just a few years to become a darling of neoliberal proponents of the "magic of the marketplace"? Why did Costa Rica's social democratic party come to advocate and practice economic retrenchment and public-sector "downsizing"? To approach these problems it is necessary to outline, almost certainly (but unavoidably) in overly synthetic form, a broad sweep of history, ranging from the colonial era through the 1980s' economic crisis and its aftermath. In this chapter, I argue that whatever the shortcomings of twentieth-century Costa Rica's "statist" style of development, the apparent "success" of today's neoliberalism is due in

44

large measure to the high levels of human development made possible by earlier, interventionist reformisms.

Colonial and Ideological Heritages

Few countries have as beguiling an imagined past as Costa Rica. Traditional historians, politicians, and average citizens alike portray it as a redoubt of democracy and peace in a Central America forever plagued by tyrannies and internecine conflicts, as a bastion of egalitarianism and reformism surrounded by societies polarized between wealthy elites and impoverished masses, and as a "European" island and outpost of civility in an uncultured mestizo and Indian sea. These ideologized and even racist visions—sometimes termed the "white legend"—derive from a traditional historiography which, largely accurately, noted that colonial Costa Rica's tiny indigenous population, dearth of precious metals, and ephemeral export markets made the territory one of Spain's poorer possessions. Rather more fancifully, though, traditional historians presumed that this relative lack of dynamism meant that egalitarianism, shared poverty, isolation, stagnation, and social harmony prevailed throughout the colony's nearly three centuries of Spanish rule. And, in a seemingly endless recycling of imagined pasts and reinvented traditions, their fairy-tale vision of the colonial experience gave rise to two legendary approaches to the more recent period: for some, modern Costa Rica's democracy and stability were "natural" outcomes of apparently auspicious colonial antecedents; for others, who found fault with the "white legend"'s idealization of contemporary society, the conflicts and social inequalities of the late-nineteenth and twentieth centuries reflect a fall from grace brought on by the emergence and consolidation in the post-independence era of the coffee export economy. That even those critical of the fairy tale often ended up accepting its key assumptions has greatly complicated efforts to understand Costa Rica's history and contemporary culture.[1]

Over the past two decades, a new generation of historians has chipped away at this ideological edifice, questioning the empirical basis of both traditional writers' (e.g., Monge 1962) claims about colonial poverty and egalitarianism and the early critics' (e.g., Seligson 1980) assertions of sudden proletarianization during the rise of the coffee export economy in the decades after independence in 1821. It is now abundantly clear that colonial Costa Rica was not always harmonious (what society is?) and did not consist primarily of uniformly poor, dispersed and subsistence-oriented rural households.

Indeed, considerable commercial activity, economic differentiation, upward mobility, and conflict clearly took place in the villages and towns where most of the population lived, especially by the eighteenth century.[2] But at least in comparison with the rest of the region, the society was a "flexible" one, able to resolve most disputes more "through the force of law than the law of force" (Molina Jiménez 1991, 344). It had an early and fairly thorough process of *mestizaje* and little of the ethnically based legal stratification or coercive surplus extraction mechanisms that marked the northern provinces of Spanish Central America, New Spain, or Peru.

It is also evident that Costa Rica was not an economically dynamic province (though it was never as impoverished or stagnant as traditional historians maintained). Elites tied to the Church, Spanish bureaucracy or colonial-era export activities were not as numerically or politically significant as elsewhere in Central America (Cardoso 1975). Most historians of the region would now probably agree that this had two beneficial consequences: (1) Costa Rica largely (though again, not entirely) escaped the ongoing, fratricidal conflicts between secularizing, developmentalist Liberals and proclerical Conservatives that elsewhere often became a fount of despotism and that immersed the other countries of the isthmus in violence for much of the nineteenth and sometimes the early twentieth centuries; and (2) the absence of both ideological Liberal and Conservative parties and of intense, prolonged conflict between the types of social forces such parties represented elsewhere, permitted a more rapid modernization of the archaic, anemic economy inherited from the colony, as well as an earlier entrance into the lucrative world coffee market (in the 1830s and 1840s, as opposed to the 1870s and 1880s in Guatemala and El Salvador). Since this emergence as a coffee exporter occurred in a context of weak state and elite institutions, a small population, and abundant land, export income from coffee was somewhat better distributed than in countries where a greater proportion of production took place on large properties (Molina Jiménez 1991; Pérez Brignoli 1985; Williams 1994).

Were these conditions unique or sufficient for the appearance of democratic institutions? The agrarian structure of early independence Costa Rica was hardly extraordinary: Antioquia in Colombia, Andean Venezuela, and highland Puerto Rico, among other places, all had coffee export economies similarly dominated by small producers (Bergad 1983; Gudmundson 1986, 153; Roseberry 1993, 356). However, what *was* particular to Costa Rica was the centrality of this sector in both the national geographical space and historical experience (Molina Jiménez 1991, 348). Antioquia, for example, has long been a key pillar of the Colombian economy, but it is inserted in a vastly

larger, very different polity consisting primarily of distinct physical environ-
ments, and it did not, like Costa Rica's coffee-growing *meseta central*, contain
all of the main urban power centers or the bulk of the country's population.
In late-colonial Costa Rica's *meseta central*, prior to the coffee boom, the elite
and the poor were not estranged from each other to the same degree as their
counterparts elsewhere in the region. Iván Molina, author of one of the most
thorough recent analyses of the country's colonial heritage, observes:

> The cultural abyss which—in nearly all of Hispanic America—separated the
> direct producer from the wholesaler, from the bureaucrat and from the hacienda
> owner, did not exist in Costa Rica, with the exception of the indigenous and
> Guanacastecan peasantry. The *Meseta* was distinguished by the existence of a
> culture (secular and religious) shared by the agriculturalist and the merchant;
> with deep Spanish roots, it went from marriage to sin, from the imaginary to the
> attitudes about death, from the fiesta to literature. (Molina Jiménez 1991, 163)

In addition to this common cultural repertoire, colonial-era peasants and
members of the elite shared disappointment about the prolonged yet erratic
search for an export product which, many hoped, would bring economic
growth benefiting all strata of society (Ibid., 344). This inchoate sense of a
common destiny linking peasants, artisans, and dominant groups—rein-
forced by the social proximity that came with small scale (the population was
65,000 in 1824)—probably did not congeal in a coherent national identity
until the late nineteenth century, well after independence (Palmer 1993). It
nevertheless contributed early on to a more inclusive concept of what constituted the citizenry than in most other Latin American countries, where
pronounced ethnic distinctions, coercive forms of labor mobilization, and
great extremes of wealth and poverty were among the main colonial legacies
(Molina Jiménez 1991, 163).

Early Reformism

This greater sense of "citizens' equality" or *igualdad ciudadana* (Ibid., 349)
was obviously not sufficient to create or to account for the later development
of democratic institutions. It may be useful, however, to view it as a kind of
cultural substrate that contributed to a profoundly reformist, conciliatory
streak in Costa Rican politics, democratic or not.[3] The picture is by no means
a consistent one, since much of the nineteenth century was punctuated by
military conspiracies, violent coups and authoritarian regimes (Lehoucq

1993; Obregón Loría 1981). But countervailing tendencies often tempered these episodes to a significant degree, with military coup leaders generally abdicating power in favor of civilians, who then typically sought a legitimate power base through elections or popular acclamation (Acuña and Molina 1991, 203–4; Vega Carballo 1981a, 242–63). The longest of the nineteenth-century dictatorships—that of General Tomás Guardia during 1870–82— paved the way for a more democratic system and more orderly processes of regime succession. Guardia significantly strengthened the state's capacity to collect taxes and used the new revenue for an unprecedented expansion of the central government and the public sector (Yashar 1997, 51). He also un-dermined competing military and oligarchical groups, greatly expanded the public education system (which bolstered and broadened notions of civil so-ciety and national identity), and issued both the first modern constitution (in 1871) and an important "Law on Individual Rights." This, among other things, guaranteed the inviolability of Costa Ricans' lives, homes, and cor-respondence, established religious freedom, and assured that people could not be "harassed or persecuted for holding political opinions" (Guardia 1989 [1877], 59). In another move scarcely typical of nineteenth-century Latin American dictators—or indeed of most other governments at the time— Guardia abolished the death penalty in 1882 (Gómez 1985).

In 1989 Costa Ricans celebrated "one hundred years of democracy." This hallowed century began, so the official accounts go, with the 1889 electoral victory of opposition presidential candidate José Joaquín Rodríguez, who, de-spite considerable official fraud, achieved the unprecedented feat of routing the incumbent's hand-picked successor at the ballot box (Zelaya 1990). Ever since, Costa Rican heads of state have—with few important exceptions (see below)—been chosen in regularly scheduled elections (although these were hardly always clean, especially before the 1950s).[4] Political scientist Fabrice Lehoucq argues convincingly that this relative stability since the late nine-teenth century reflected the increasing institutionalization of mechanisms that compensated parties which lost presidential elections with greater rep-resentation in the legislative branch (1990, 1992a, 1992b). As electoral safe-guards (and the franchise) expanded during the first decades of the twentieth century, incentives diminished for illegally retaining executive power, hand-picking successors, and organizing coups.

This period of democratic institutionalization in the late nineteenth and early twentieth centuries was also the high point of Liberalism. But while Costa Rican Liberals shared the secular, developmentalist, free-market ide-ology of their counterparts in other Latin American countries, the policy problems they confronted and the solutions they advanced were, in some key respects, rather different. Perhaps most importantly, the matter of non-private property, at least in the *meseta central* (the main population center), had already been largely resolved (Gudmundson 1983). Church and community lands had, for the most part, passed into private hands much earlier, and to the extent that land was an issue at all, it involved settling a productive, commercially oriented peasantry on frontier or other available lands rather than expropriating a stubbornly subsistence-oriented one from its village commons (as, for example, the Liberals in El Salvador saw it). This gave Costa Rican Liberalism a decidedly interventionist bent that was somewhat at odds with the purer forms of laissez-faire doctrine (and which Gudmundson [1986, 155–56], Palmer [1996, 247] and Solís [1992, 88–102] rightly point to as a direct precursor of 1940s' social democracy).[5] Elsewhere, I have examined for one region and in some detail the ideological and policy dimensions of Costa Rica's early-twentieth-century agrarian reform (Edelman 1992, 167–80, 366–70). Here, the important point is that in the first half of the twentieth century the Costa Rican state implemented a significant series of land acquisition and redistribution efforts in the region (the Northwest) with the most skewed ownership patterns. While this produced mixed results, it had few parallels in other Latin American countries (outside of the more radical Mexican reforms).[6] The legislative debate around these mild, redistributive measures in the period 1900–47 was marked by frequent and intense expressions of reformist, conciliatory sentiment on the part of leading politicians and other members of the dominant groups.

It has become commonplace in Latin American studies to ascribe the rise of strong states—interventionist and reformist or dictatorial and repressive—to Liberalism's inability to deal with the economic collapse accompanying the worldwide depression of the 1930s (e.g., Bulmer-Thomas 1987, 68; Dunkerley 1988, 94; Salazar 1981, 19). These regimes—whether populist, authoritarian, or both—confronted a social crisis characterized by rising unemployment, plummeting prices for export products, falling tax revenues, and a lessened capacity for acquiring indispensable manufactured imports. Like the New Deal in the United States, their responses were interventionist and typically involved various combinations of Keynesian "pump priming," public works programs, protectionism, and import substitution in agriculture and industry.

In Costa Rica, however, this tendency toward state intervention in the economy was well developed substantially before the onset of the 1930s depression. A full discussion is not possible here, but it is still worth outlining some of the principal milestones, all indicative of a deeply rooted penchant for reform in the country's political life.[7] In 1913 the Costa Rican Congress attempted to resolve a deadlocked presidential election by appointing Alfredo González Flores chief executive. González Flores, who had not been a candidate, assumed office in 1914, just as World War I cut Costa Rica off from the main markets for its coffee in Europe. When private banks, cognizant of the growing fiscal deficit, refused to lend to the government, González Flores gained approval for a bond issue to fund a state-owned bank, which loaned both to the government and to small farmers. He then achieved passage of progressive income and property taxes, designed so that "the rich would pay like rich people and the poor like poor people" (quoted in Volio 1972, 51). In a move that further alienated powerful upper-class groups, he vetoed a petroleum concession granted to a foreign company that had managed to bribe key members of Congress (Salazar 1990, 33). In 1917, this reformist interlude ended when Federico Tinoco, González Flores's War Minister, overthrew the government and ushered in a 30-month dictatorship, one of two violent interruptions of the orderly succession of governments in the twentieth century (Murillo 1981). González Flores's banking reforms survived his ouster, though his efforts to tax the rich did not. The unseating of Tinoco in 1919 released a pent-up wave of popular ferment, including a major strike that won urban workers the eight-hour day in 1920 and compensation for work-related accidents in 1922 (Acuña 1986; Salazar 1987, 62).

One of the key figures in the movement that toppled the Tinoco dictatorship was Jorge Volio, a flamboyant priest, soldier, and politician, strongly influenced by European Social Christian doctrine, who founded the Partido Reformista and ran for president on its ticket in 1924 (see Volio 1972). Volio, who called for a wide range of labor, agrarian, housing, and education reforms, failed in his bid for the presidency but garnered sufficient support so that he served two years (1924–26) as second vice-president in one of the last Liberal administrations.[8] Most of Volio's goals remained unrealized until the 1940s, but the Costa Rican state did expand its reach in one very significant respect with the creation in 1924 of the national insurance monopoly that exists to this day. In the 1920s, Liberal governments established Ministries of Public Health and of Labor and Social Welfare, the latter charged with inspecting and improving workplace safety and health conditions (Salazar 1987, 63–64). One final example of this early penchant for state intervention in the economy and social welfare bears mention: the founding in 1930 of a national child welfare foundation (Patronato Nacional de la Infancia) which, despite its founders' sympathy for eugenics and restrictions on "undesirable immigration," eventually became quite effective in requiring errant fathers to make child-support payments (Murillo 1986, 292–94; Palmer 1996). This enlightened Liberal social policy was similar in its social work practice, pedagogy, and ideological tone to Progressive Era reformism in the early-twentieth-century urban United States. It arose at least in part from widespread elite concerns about high levels of infant mortality and disease among the laboring classes in a context—different from that elsewhere in Central America—in which labor was in perpetually short supply.[9] As historian Steven Palmer indicates:

> Institutions were created to mediate and diffuse class and political confrontation, accumulate knowledge on the conditions of the laboring poor to serve as the basis for anticipating and preempting social crises, and to further the state's capacity to educate the laboring groups in questions of moral decency, honest toil, racial hierarchies and national productivity. (1996, 247)

Similar reformist programs, while not uncommon in revolutionary Mexico or under populist regimes in South America during roughly the same period, were basically unknown elsewhere in Central America. Where some timid efforts occurred—as with Arturo Araujo in El Salvador (president in 1931) or the unionist party of the 1920s in Guatemala (see Kit 1993)—they suffered rapid reversals, with more bloodshed and longer-lasting repression than took place under the comparatively brief Tinoco dictatorship in Costa Rica.

The Crisis of the 1940s

The 1930s in Costa Rica were a turbulent decade, with the rise of the Communist Party, a major strike in 1934 by some ten thousand workers on United Fruit's banana plantations, and a growing sense of acute economic emergency occasioned by plummeting world coffee prices. State measures to cope with the crisis included temporary suspension of foreign debt payments, new consumption taxes, the institution of high tariff barriers against foreign livestock and agricultural products, minimum wage and unemployment insurance legislation, public works projects, and currency devaluations (Miller 1993). The state also established offices (in 1933 and 1940, respectively) to regulate and "defend" all aspects of the important coffee and sugar sectors. Significantly, despite the emergence in the 1930s of extremely dictatorial regimes in the rest of Central America, Costa Rica, even under the elected au-

thoritarian government of León Cortés (1936–40), retained sufficient political space so that emerging social groups could usually express their demands,
even when these were formulated by the Communist Party.[10]

The Social Christian reformism that had so influenced Jorge Volio also inspired other leading political figures. Clearly the most important of these was
Rafael Angel Calderón Guardia, elected president in 1940 after running virtually unopposed on the ticket of the National Republican Party (Partido Re-
publicano Nacional, or PRN) as the hand-picked successor of León Cortés, a
conservative strongman sympathetic to European fascism. Educated in philosophy and medicine at Catholic universities in Belgium, Calderón's commitment to European Social Christian doctrine marked a strong contrast with
both the authoritarian Cortés and the anti-clerical Liberals who had preceded him. His sensitivity to "the social question," intensified by the severe
crisis of the depression years, led him—"secretly and silently"—to plan a
social security program, which became law in 1941 (Rosenberg 1980, 53).
This move, initiated almost single-handedly and in the absence of any significant grassroots pressure, was not conceived solely as a politically rational
strategy for securing a constituency among organized labor, as some subsequent accounts (e.g., Rojas Bolaños 1979) have suggested. Instead, it reflected a paternalistic reformism that viewed the state as a mechanism for
harmonizing the conflicting interests of labor and capital (Rosenberg 1980).

Costa Rican capitalists never developed a coherent, unified position against
Calderón, despite the conventional scholarly wisdom (e.g., Rojas Bolaños
1979; cf. Vega Carballo 1981b, 15). Some of the new administration's policies—such as guaranteed coffee support prices and new tariffs on industrial
imports—clearly benefited important sectors of the upper class (Lehoucq
1991, 48–50). Nevertheless, Calderón's four years as president did see a
rapid erosion of what had been, in the election at least, near-unanimous elite
backing. At first, this upper-class opposition was likely rooted in a dispute
between the new president and his predecessor over the distribution of patronage posts to their respective factions (Lehoucq 1992a, 165–67, 195). But
Calderón's social security program also rankled his erstwhile upper-class
backers more than he initially realized. His support diminished further in
late 1941 with the Japanese attack on Pearl Harbor and Costa Rica's declaration of war on the Axis (Costa Rica's declaration of war against Japan actually
preceded the U.S. declaration, though obviously it was entirely symbolic).
Individuals of German and Italian nationality or recent descent were prominent in the coffee, sugar, banking, and retail sectors (as were pro-Franco
Spaniards in the latter). At the request of the U.S. State Department, many

were interned for the duration of the conflict in camps in Costa Rica or the United States (*Rumbo en Costa Rica*, Oct. 31–Nov. 6, 1985, pp. 6–7). Rapidly organized tribunals froze or seized many of their assets, often with little compensation or attention to due process. These measures alienated not only those directly affected, but many upper-class Costa Ricans who had moved in the same circles or had intermarried with the German and Italian families (Stone 1975, 299; Herrera 1988). Finally, Calderón made a move that both resulted from and exacerbated the waning of his elite support. In mid-1942, he solidified what some have called "the improbable alliance" (*alianza inverosímil*), seeking and obtaining the formal, active backing of Víctor Sanabria, the recently appointed archbishop—like him, inspired by Social Christian ideas—and of Manuel Mora, secretary general of the Costa Rican Communist Party (Stone 1975, 302).

The *calderonista*–Catholic–Communist alliance reflected a particular convergence of interests and individual political visions in an unusual historical conjuncture. Calderón sought out Archbishop Sanabria at a time when substantial segments of his original elite political sponsors and constituencies were deserting him. Sanabria, who shared the president's Catholic reformist sensibilities, hoped both to restore the Church's political influence after five decades of Liberal anticlericalism and to provide a reformist alternative to the Communists, whose strength had grown considerably during the Depression. Communist leader Mora secured added legitimacy with Sanabria's public statement that Catholic believers could support the Communist Party and saw in the alliance with Calderón a chance to realize social reforms that had been core party demands since its founding. The U.S.–Soviet alliance against the Axis, and the world Communist movement's Popular Front–era line of seeking unity with reformist moderates, provided a favorable international context (as did the 1943 dissolution of the Comintern and the Costa Rican CP's transformation into the Partido Vanguardia Popular, or PVP).

The social security legislation passed in 1941 laid the groundwork for a national medical care system and provided obligatory health, disability, retirement, unemployment, maternity, and life insurance for urban workers with monthly salaries below 300 colones ($53 in 1941) (Rosenberg 1980, 61–62).[11] The following year, Calderón obtained congressional approval for a series of constitutional amendments termed the "Social Guarantees." These included the formal creation of a national healthcare system, a broader system of retirement and disability pensions than that provided by social security, and a low-cost housing program, as well as guarantees of the right to strike and the incorporation into the Constitution of existing minimum-wage and workday legislation (Salazar 1981, 84–85). In 1943, he signed into law a new Labor Code, which required employers to make severance and disability payments to fired and disabled workers and protected the rights to organize, engage in collective bargaining, and strike. (The law, though, was weak on enabling measures and also protected employers' right to stage lockouts.) The Code created a joint minimum-wage commission (Comisión Mixta de Salarios Mínimos) with two representatives each from the government, unions, and employers' groups.

In the 1944 presidential elections, the *calderonista*–Catholic–Communist alliance backed Teodoro Picado, who defeated opposition candidate and former president León Cortés in a contest marred by fraud and violence.[12] In 1946 Picado added a mildly progressive income tax—with rates ranging from 2 to 20 percent—and a new property tax to the list of reformist laws passed under his predecessor (Dunkerley 1988, 127). Naturally, this further irritated upper- and middle-class groups, who had historically paid little in taxes.

This deepening series of reforms aroused antagonism in several quarters beyond those members of the old elite who felt Calderón had betrayed them. The opposition came to include a diverse assortment of groups: small business proprietors, hurt in their role as employers by the Labor Code; professionals who, especially after the end of World War II and the onset of the cold war, grew increasingly concerned about Communist influence in the government; and smallholding peasants in the *meseta* region, most of whom were vehemently opposed to any new taxes (Acuña 1987, 145) and who did not benefit directly from the social security or labor legislation (which did not cover most informal and agricultural sector employment). Anti-*calderonista* intellectuals who aspired to modernize their country's economy and political institutions clustered in two small organizations—Rodrigo Facio's Center for the Study of National Problems (Centro para el Estudio de los Problemas Nacionales) and José Figueres's Democratic Action (Acción Demócrata)—which merged in 1945 to found the Social Democratic Party. Throughout the Calderón and Picado administrations, the opposition's rhetoric grew more strident, focusing in particular on charges—often valid—of administrative and electoral corruption. As early as 1946, the Social Democratic faction of the opposition put forward the slogan "elections no, rebellion yes" (Dunkerley 1988, 129). By the time of the 1948 election campaign, the conservative opposition faction's slogan called for a total boycott of the official candidate's supporters: "If he's for Calderón, don't talk to him, don't buy from him and don't sell to him" (Cerdas 1991, 288). Opposition actions also became increasingly radical and included a twelve-day business shutdown in 1947 and preparations, principally by those around Figueres, for an armed insurrection.

In the 1948 presidential election Otilio Ulate, a conservative newspaper publisher, defeated Calderón's bid to succeed Picado. The *calderonista*-controlled Congress, however, refused to certify the presidential election results, alleging grave "irregularities." [13] In March, forces under José Figueres launched an insurrection, starting a five-week civil war that cost some two thousand lives and toppled Picado's government.

The complex political alignments, military campaigns, and diplomatic maneuvering of the 1948 civil war are beyond the scope of this book, as are the debates over the conflict's causes and whether it was inevitable (see Aguilar 1969; Lehoucq 1991; Rojas Bolaños 1979). The significance of the war for the purposes of the present discussion is primarily that it ushered in a relatively brief but crucial period of authoritarian rule by the social democratic faction of the victorious side. While the insurgent junta repressed the defeated Communists and *calderonistas*, as well as organized labor, it also institutionalized a deepening of the reform process and initiated a major qualitative and quantitative escalation in the state's involvement in the economy and social welfare policy.

In an agreement with his conservative allies, Figueres and his Junta Fundadora de la Segunda República ruled by decree for eighteen months before turning over executive power to Ulate, the candidate elected in 1948 but denied power by the *calderonista*-dominated Congress.[14] The Junta's key measures included the creation of a constituent assembly to draft a new constitution—which provided, among other things, for the creation of autonomous public-sector institutions outside the control of the executive—and of a fourth branch of government, the Tribunal Supremo de Elecciones, intended to insure clean elections. The new constitution also provided for tax breaks for capital goods imports, intended to stimulate industrialization; the founding of the public-sector Costa Rican Electricity Institute (Instituto Costarricense de Electricidad, or ICE), which gradually absorbed most existing utilities and telecommunications companies and provided highly subsidized services to industries and consumers;[15] the nationalization of commercial banks, which received the exclusive right to accept deposits from the public; a 10 percent tax on capital of over 50,000 colones (slightly less than $10,000); and the abolition of the army. Following on the heels of the seizures of German-owned properties, the bank nationalization, in particular, further weakened traditional upper-class groups; indeed, as sociologist Jorge Rovira observed, "The big bourgeoisie screamed to high heaven" (1982, 48).[16]

Both proponents and opponents of the new national banking system realized that it would permit channeling loans to economic sectors and regions of the country previously barred from receiving credit. This contributed to the social democrats' goal of economic diversification and to facilitating the ascendence of new social groups—public employees, industrialists, cattle ranchers, and sugarcane growers and refiners—that would come to be among their key political constituencies and that would compete economically with the traditional upper class of coffee exporters and large merchants. Together with the 10 percent tax on capital—necessary, as Figueres said, to "guarantee the stability of the remaining 90 percent" (Rovira 1982, 47)—the bank nationalization also gave the state, devastated by the inflation of the 1940s and the destruction wrought by the civil war, control of the funds necessary to rebuild and to initiate a wide-ranging public works program (Brenes 1990). The constitutional prohibition on a standing army both freed up resources for social spending and eliminated a potential tool for the restoration of conservative power. In the post-1948 period, despite a few abortive violent challenges to the constitutional order (Obregón 1981), governments controlled by opposition parties have for the most part alternated with those controlled by the social democrats, organized since 1951 in the National Liberation Party (Partido de Liberación Nacional, or PLN). During the three decades that followed the civil war, however, the PLN always retained sufficient strength—especially in the legislature and in the new autonomous public-sector institutions—so that the major programs of the emerging welfare state remained intact, even during periods when the conservative opposition controlled the presidency.

The Consolidation of the Welfare State

The evolution of the Costa Rican welfare state can, for our purposes, best be outlined by employing a periodization that corresponds roughly to each of the post–civil war decades. Two critical dimensions deserve particular attention: (1) the growing involvement of the state in the economy and social policy (sometimes described as a shift from "*Estado gestor*" [manager, or facilitator, state] to "*Estado empresario*" [entrepreneurial state]); and (2) the mechanisms it refined for meeting the needs and responding to the demands of subordinate groups and for local political-economic organization and control. The changing role of the agricultural sector in the new development model is also crucial to this discussion.

For the social democratic insurgents who won the 1948 civil war, electoral fraud, administrative corruption, and anti-Communism were almost certainly less important as motives for revolt than a desire to reshape Costa Rica's vulnerable and antiquated coffee- and banana-based export economy and to shatter the economic stranglehold of the powerful agro-export and banking families. As an essentially two-crop economy, the country's fortunes rose and fell with international market prices (particularly coffee prices, since bananas were produced primarily in coastal enclaves owned by foreign monopolies that could usually keep prices high even during economic downturns). Painful memories of these brusque fluctuations in export income and government revenues were still fresh from the depression of the 1930s. The lion's share of credit had historically gone to the coffee sector, in part because in good times profit rates were extraordinarily high and in part because export houses frequently had substantial stakes in the largest banks. The coffee sector's corner on available credit in effect blocked the emergence and rise of other social groups with interests in different economic sectors and geographical regions.

During eighteen months of rule-by-decree in 1948–49, the Figueres Junta began to address these concerns. Importantly, the Junta let stand the social security and labor laws, as well as the "Social Guarantees" which, along with the opening of the University of Costa Rica, were the most significant achievements of Calderón's administration. Little more than a month after taking power, Figueres outlined plans for building electric generators, a cement factory, a modern dairy plant, and low-cost housing. The Coffee Defense Institute (Instituto de Defensa del Café), founded in 1933 at the height of the Depression, was turned into a state-run Coffee Office (Oficina del Café), which not only set the prices processors (*beneficiadores*) had to pay producers, but also required the former to provide the latter with loans under favorable terms. The National Production Council (Consejo Nacional de Producción, or CNP) became a semi-autonomous state commodities board, responsible for stimulating food production for the domestic market by purchasing grain from farmers at guaranteed prices, storing surpluses, setting subsidized consumer prices, and running a series of retail outlets providing low-cost basic foods (Rovira 1982, 52–53).[17] For the grain sector, the CNP, together with the price-setting board in the Ministry of Economy, Industry and Commerce, largely replaced the market as the determinant of profit levels for private entrepreneurs at each stage of production, processing, and marketing.

Figueres and his allies had articulated a vision of a mixed economy even before coming to power, but they initially sought only a limited direct role for the public sector in the economy. Instead, they saw the state as a *gestor*, a "manager" or "facilitator" with responsibility for planning and—more importantly—for providing favorable conditions for private capital. In the 1950s, particularly during Figueres's first term as president (1953–58), this new state role included a greatly expanded road-building program (which doubled the length of the road network between 1950 and 1962), energy infrastructure construction, major efforts to raise productivity in the coffee and basic grains sectors, and the allocation of large amounts of National Banking System credit—often at artificially low interest rates—to new export activities, especially cattle and cotton. In addition, the nationalized banks became a key source of finance for the state itself, either directly or by serving as guarantors of loans from foreign banks (OFIPLAN 1982, 119; Sojo 1984, 49).

Figueres's first presidential term also saw the creation of some of the principal autonomous public-sector institutions, intended to address particular social problems while shielded from the political and budgetary concerns that periodically affected branches of the central government. These institutions—most importantly the National Housing and Planning Institute (Instituto Nacional de Vivienda y Urbanismo, or INVU), founded in 1954 to finance and build low-cost housing—became reliable bases of PLN power, patronage (in jobs, services, and contracts), and electoral support that persisted even in periods when anti-PLN presidents held power. The establishment of the *aguinaldo*, or "thirteenth month" end-of-year bonus, first for executive-branch workers, then for all public employees, and eventually for all salaried workers, further solidified PLN support within the growing bureaucracy and the population as a whole (OFIPLAN 1982, 168; Stone 1975, 330–34).

These narrowly partisan considerations and the state's growing role as a means of upward social and economic mobility for PLN supporters did not mean that the concern for social welfare which lay behind the founding of institutions such as the INVU was anything but genuine. Indeed, the reformist impulse was reflected in a range of other programs. Among the most significant in terms of widening popular participation in the economy were the measures (some actually enabling legislation for laws enacted during the *calderonista* years) passed to encourage the formation of cooperatives. The cooperative sector, which enjoyed generous tax advantages, assumed a wide range of functions, such as agricultural production, savings and credit, purchasing, transportation, and housing construction (Rojas Víquez 1990). The number and membership of cooperatives grew extremely rapidly until the mid-1980s, by which time nearly 30 percent of the economically active population belonged to one or another kind of co-op (Gallardo and López 1986, 123; Rojas Víquez 1990, 144). By the late 1970s, roughly one-third of all agricultural producers belonged to cooperatives, which were particularly important in the coffee sector; indeed, the far-reaching state effort to modernize coffee cultivation, channeled through a variety of public- and cooperative-sector research and extension institutions, gave Costa Rica the highest per hectare yields in the world and assured that coffee production remained profitable even in times of depressed prices (Raventós 1989, 15).[18] In agroindustry, co-ops accounted for 30 percent of the nation's output in coffee processing, more than half of all dairy production, 35 percent of the beef cattle slaughter, and 20 percent of refined sugar production (Salas U. et al. 1983, 140–41).

The 1960s, as economist Victor Bulmer-Thomas put it, appeared to be a "golden age" for Central America (1987, 175). Industrialization and intraregional trade advanced rapidly with the formation of the Central American Common Market (CACM) in 1960 (Costa Rica joined in 1963). President John F. Kennedy's Alliance for Progress channeled large amounts of U.S. aid to agrarian reform, road building, and other development projects. Traditional and new export sectors enjoyed generally good prices and rapid expansion. High growth rates for both total and per capita GDP suggested that the region was entering an age of economic dynamism and improved well-being.

Although Costa Rica was the last of the Central American countries to formally join the Common Market, it did so fully embracing the import substitution model that was at the core of the CACM's industrialization strategy. In essence, CACM planners adopted ideas propounded since the early 1950s by the United Nations Economic Commission for Latin America (ECLA). ECLA emphasized that if Latin America were to develop economically it had to produce a wide range of finished goods for domestic markets rather than just a few primary products for erratic foreign ones. Since domestic markets in Central America were small and the purchasing power of most of the population was quite limited, regional integration emerged as a way of expanding total demand. Manufacturers, primarily but not exclusively large multinationals, thus entered the region and, protected by high external tariffs, produced for a market stretching from Guatemala to Panama. Because the area between Guatemala City and San Salvador possessed

key locational advantages, especially access to the greatest geographical concentration of purchasing power, Costa Rica—near the opposite end of the
isthmus—had to develop other features that made it attractive to new industrial capital. In this, the Costa Rican state came to play a major role, providing extremely generous tax breaks, inexpensive credit, cut-rate electric
power and water, and establishing artificially low prices for other inputs (e.g.,
sugar for food manufacturers), as well as touting its new and rapidly length-
ening road network and the high levels of health and literacy of its population (both the result, of course, of extensive public investments in "human
capital").

In the 1960s, the state's extensive array of social programs expanded dramatically, with the establishment, among others, of the country's first modern agrarian reform agency (the Instituto de Tierras y Colonización, or
ITCO) and a major vocational training program (Instituto Nacional de
Aprendizaje, or INA). In 1963 a public-sector enterprise (Junta de Administración Portuaria y Desarrollo Económico de la Vertiente Atlántica, or
JAPDEVA) assumed responsibility for Atlantic zone regional development
and for administering the docks at Limón, the main Caribbean port. Public-
sector productive investment grew too, as the country's one oil refinery was
nationalized. In 1968 the National Community Development Directorate
(Dirección Nacional de Desarrollo de la Comunidad, or DINADECO) began coordinating associations in virtually every rural community that built
roads, water systems, clinics, schools, and nutrition centers for children, often by mobilizing the unpaid labor of local citizens (Mora 1989). Low-income
groups received greater access to credit through the Banco Popular y de Desarrollo Comunal, which made loans to DINADECO's community development associations and administered an obligatory (and thus at times distinctly *unpopular*) workers' savings program (OFIPLAN 1982, 125, 328).
Critics, however, later charged that both DINADECO and the Banco Popular exercised undue control over grassroots organizations and resources, thus
undermining autonomous initiatives for positive change (Palma 1980).

State control may have impeded the emergence of popular organizations,
but it is also clear that the economic benefits of the new state-directed development process were widespread in Costa Rica by the end of the 1960s.
During the 1950s and 1960s, Costa Rica's economic growth rates were the
highest in Latin America (and even during the 1970s they were still among
the continent's four highest [Rodríguez Céspedes 1988, 219]). Rapid economic diversification occurred, as industry and services accounted for a growing proportion of gross domestic product. Income distribution improved sig-

nificantly between 1961 and 1971, though it worsened somewhat during the 1970s (OFIPLAN 1982, 186); even in 1980, however, it was still substantially better than in the rest of Central America (Gallardo and López 1986, 157). The country's impressive social indicators—especially in rural areas—stood out in a region where Guatemala, El Salvador, and Nicaragua had also experienced rapid growth but without comparable investments in the well-being of their citizens (see Table 1).

The Costa Rican state reacted to the oil shocks and economic slowdown of the 1970s by greatly increasing its direct control over key means of production. Figueres, who had been president from 1953 to 1958, was elected again in 1970 and, when Daniel Oduber succeeded him in 1974, it marked the first time that the PLN had controlled the executive for two consecutive terms. This eight-year period of rule by the social democratic PLN, which was historically inclined to expand the public sector, saw both growing executive control over the autonomous institutions (the number of which continued to multiply) and the rise of the "entrepreneurial state." State involvement in the economy—which previously emphasized infrastructural and human capital investment, regulation of prices, and provision of financial and other services—now came to include ownership of a wide range of productive enterprises. To some extent, this enlargement of the state's role grew out of traditional PLN concerns about social welfare, particularly a desire to maintain acceptable levels of growth and employment (although feeding the party's vast patronage networks also clearly figured in this shift). During the eight years of PLN rule from 1970 to 1978, for example, the proportion of the population covered by the social security system expanded from 46 to 86 percent (Cerdas 1991, 318). The postsecondary educational system also developed rapidly in the 1970s, absorbing a significant share of what might otherwise have been surplus population; by 1980, a remarkable 27 percent of the population of university-student age was enrolled in 30 institutions of higher learning, almost all of them public and at least one of which provided correspondence courses available even to residents of remote areas (Mendiola 1988, 82). In this period, the government created a social aid institute (Instituto Mixto de Ayuda Social, or IMAS), charged with eliminating extreme poverty, and—within IMAS—a large-scale program of family assistance (Asignaciones Familiares) that, among other things, established preventative healthcare programs in rural zones and provided virtually all low-income school children with nutritious hot meals. It also established a National Basic Grains Program—emphasizing subsidized producer prices and generous crop insurance policies—which was intended to assure na-

TABLE 1
Central America: Some Basic Social Indicators, 1965–1985

	Life expectancy at birth, 1965–1970	Life expectancy at birth, 1980–1985	Infant mortality per 1,000 live births, 1970–1975	Infant mortality per 1,000 live births, 1980–1985	Doctors per 100,000 inhabitants, 1970	Rural illiteracy rate, 1970 (percent)	Rural population with access to potable water, 1969 (percent)	Primary school enrollment as percentage of primary school-age population, 1970[a]
Costa Rica	65.6	73.0	67.1	20.2	62	14.7	53.6	111.9
Guatemala	50.1	59.0	90.2	67.7	27	65.9	11.0	60.3
El Salvador	55.9	64.8	101.0	71.0	24	55.3	25.0	62.3
Honduras	50.9	59.9	110.7	81.5	25	54.4	18.5	87.3
Nicaragua	51.6	59.8	108.9	84.5	47	68.7	5.9	80.0
Panama	64.3	71.0	43.8	32.5	58	n.d.	6.7	102.0

SOURCE: ECLA data cited in Gallardo and López (1986, 191–92, 196, 200, 205, 215).

[a]Percentages over 100 reflect existence of adult primary education programs.

tional self-sufficiency in rice, maize, sorghum, and beans (Edelman 1992, 307–14). The rise of the *Estado empresario*, however, reflected not only traditional social welfare concerns but the power of groups linked to the PLN that saw direct state participation in the economy as a tantalizing new opportunity for upward mobility.

Most emblematic of the emerging "entrepreneurial state" was the Costa Rican Development Corporation (Corporación Costarricense de Desarrollo, or CODESA), founded in 1972 (M. Vega 1982; Sojo 1984). This massive public-sector holding company came to have investments in sugar and fuel alcohol refining; cement, fertilizer, cotton, and aluminum processing and distribution; and road, riverine, and rail transportation. CODESA also owned the national stock exchange (Bolsa Nacional de Valores) and participated in a variety of tourism joint ventures with private capital. Originally, CODESA was supposed to invest in economically or socially necessary activities that private capital avoided, either because of their high start-up costs or unacceptable risk levels. Once these vital programs were established and profitable, they were to be sold to private investors. This rarely occurred, though, and CODESA was eventually saddled with a number of very large—and very unprofitable—enterprises. In several sectors, CODESA established subsidiaries that appeared to compete with existing private companies, but which actually became new mechanisms for transferring public resources to affluent groups. CATSA (Central Azucarera del Tempisque, S.A.), for example, CODESA's giant sugar mill and fuel-alcohol subsidiary, drew its directors primarily from the ranks of private sugar refiners (Achío and Escalante 1985).[19]

This growing symbiosis between the public and private sectors gave rise to a significant new elite within the already bloated state bureaucracy. CODESA directorships and similar public-sector positions provided these high-level functionaries with lavish salaries, expense accounts, and free use of company vehicles, as well as insider knowledge and connections that frequently enhanced the performance of their private holdings. But as CODESA came to constitute a growing drain on the public-sector budget, much of the rest of the elite became receptive to neoliberal arguments that this deficit-ridden "white elephant" epitomized the evils of state involvement in the economy and social welfare.

Tables 2 and 3 provide a view of the rhythm of public-sector expansion in the period 1853–1979 and of the complexity of the Costa Rican state circa 1979 (see also Sojo 1991, 49–66). Until the social democratic victory in the 1948 civil war, the state's role in the economy grew slowly and remained small, with most public-sector functions concentrated in the executive branch

TABLE 2
Costa Rica: Evolution of Public-Sector Enterprises, 1853–1980

Year	Agriculture	Agroindustries, manufacturing	Electricity, gas, water	Commerce, tourism	Transport, warehouses, communications	Finance, insurance, development
1853	FNL					
1885						
1914					DNC	BNCR
1924						INS
1941			CNFL			
1943	CNP	CNP		CNP		
1948						BCR
						BAC
						BCAC
1949			ICE		ICE	
1950						BCCR
1953					ICPP	
1954						INVU
1959	ECR					
1961			ICAA			
1963					JAPDEVA	
					RACSA	
1964			JASEC			
1969						BPDC
1970						IFAM
						ASBANA
1971			JAAE			CODESA
1972		RECOPE				INFOCOOP
		CEMPASA				
1973		CATSA				
1975				DCC		
1976			ESPH		TFB	
					TRANSMESA	
					FECOSA	

1977		ALCORSA		CONAPE
1978		ALUNASA		
		CEMVASA		Corporación de Zona
		DAISA		Franca de Exportación, S.A.[a]
1979	Aquacultura, S.A.			
1980		CEPC	Inmobiliarias	
			Temporales, S.A.[a]	

SOURCE: Based on OFIPLAN (1982, 327–30).

Key to Abbreviations:

ALCORSA = Algodones de Costa Rica, S.A.[a]
ALUNASA = Aluminios Nacionales, S.A.[a]
ASBANA = Asociación Bananera Nacional
BAC = Banco Anglo-Costarricense
BCAC = Banco Crédito Agrícola de Cartago
BCCR = Banco Central de Costa Rica
BCR = Banco de Costa Rica
BNCR = Banco Nacional de Costa Rica
BPDC = Banco Popular y de Desarrollo Comunal
CATSA = Central Azucarera del Tempisque, S.A.[a]
CEMPASA = Cementos del Pacífico, S.A.[a]
CEMVASA = Cementos del Valle, S.A.[a]
CEPC = Consorcio de Exportación de Productos Costarricenses, S.A.[a]
CNFL = Compañía Nacional de Fuerza y Luz
CNP = Consejo Nacional de Producción
CODESA = Corporación Costarricense de Desarrollo, S.A.[a]
CONAPE = Consejo Nacional de Préstamos para Educación
DAISA = Desarrollo Agroindustrial, S.A.[a]
DCC = Distribuidora Costarricense de Cemento, S.A.[a]
DNC = Dirección Nacional de Comunicaciones

ECR = Editorial Costa Rica
ESPH = Empresa de Servicios Públicos de Heredia
FNL = Fábrica Nacional de Licores
FECOSA = Ferrocarriles de Costa Rica, S.A.[a]
ICAA = Instituto Costarricense de Acueductos y Alcantarillados
ICE = Instituto Costarricense de Electricidad
ICPP = Instituto Costarricense de Puertos del Pacífico
IFAM = Instituto de Fomento y Asesoría Municipal
INFOCOOP = Instituto de Fomento Cooperativo
INS = Instituto Nacional de Seguros
INVU = Instituto Nacional de Vivienda y Urbanismo
JAAE = Junta Administrativa de Acueductos de Escazú
JAPDEVA = Junta de Administración Portuaria y Desarrollo Económico de la Vertiente Atlántica
JASEC = Junta Administrativa del Servicio Eléctrico Municipal de Cartago
RACSA = Radiográfica Costarricense, S.A.
RECOPE = Refinería Costarricense de Petróleo
TFB = Tempisque Ferry Boat, S.A.[a]
TRANSMESA = Transportes Metropolitanos, S.A.[a]

NOTES: For English translations of enterprise names, see List of Abbreviations, pp. xv–xxii. Some state organizations were founded with slightly different names; the names here are those in use ca. 1979.

[a] Part of CODESA.

TABLE 3

The Costa Rican Public Sector, ca. 1979

Central government	Public-sector enterprises
National government[a]	Non-financial enterprises
Asamblea Legislativa	Acuacultura, S.A.[b]
Contraloría General de la República	Algodones de Costa Rica, S.A. (ALCORSA)[b]
Ministerio de Agricultura y Ganadería (MAG)	Aluminios Nacionales, S.A. (ALUNASA)[b]
Ministerio de Cultura, Juventud y Deportes	Cementos del Pacífico, S.A. (CEMPASA)[b]
Ministerio de Economía, Industria y Comercio (MEIC)	Cementos del Valle, S.A. (CEMVASA)[b]
Ministerio de Educación Pública (MEP)	Central Azucarera del Tempisque, S.A. (CATSA)[b]
Ministerio de Gobernación y Policía	Compañía Nacional de Fuerza y Luz (CNFL)
Ministerio de Hacienda	Consejo Nacional de Producción (CNP)
Ministerio de Justicia y Gracia	Consorcio de Exportación de Productos Costarricenses, S.A. (CEPC)[b]
Ministerio de la Presidencia	Corporación de Zona Franca de Exportación, S.A.[b]
Ministerio de Obras Públicas y Transportes (MOPT)	Desarrollo Agroindustrial, S.A. (DAISA)[b]
Ministerio de Relaciones Exteriores y Culto	Dirección Nacional de Comunicaciones (DNC)
Ministerio de Salud	Distribuidora Costarricense de Cemento, S.A. (DCC)[b]
Ministerio de Seguridad Pública	Editorial Costa Rica (ECR)
Ministerio de Trabajo y Seguridad Social	Empresa de Servicios Públicos de Heredia (ESPH)
Poder Judicial	Ferrocarriles de Costa Rica, S.A.
Inmobiliarias Temporales, S.A.	Instituto Costarricense de Acueductos y Alcantarillados (ICAA)
Tribunal Supremo de Elecciones	Instituto Costarricense de Electricidad (ICE)
	Instituto Costarricense de Puertos del Pacífico (ICPP)
Local governments	Junta Administrativa de Acueductos de Escazú (JAAE)
Consejos Municipales de Distrito	Junta Administrativa de Servicios Eléctricos de Cartago (JASEC)
Municipalidades	Junta de Administración Portuaria y Desarrollo Económico de la Vertiente Atlántica (JAPDEVA)
Public service institutions	Lotería Nacional
Caja Costarricense de Seguro Social (CCSS)	Radiográfica Costarricense, S.A.
Centro para la Promoción de las Exportaciones y las Inversiones (CENPRO)	Refinería Costarricense de Petróleo, S.A. (RECOPE)
Colegio Universitario de Alajuela	Tempisque Ferry Boat, S.A.[b]
Colegio Universitario de Cartago	Transportes Metropolitanos, S.A. (TRANSMESA)[b]

Comisión Nacional de Asuntos Indígenas (CONAI)
Compañía Nacional de Teatro
Consejo Nacional de Investigaciones Científicas y Tecnológicas (CONICIT)
Consejo Nacional de Rectores
Dirección General de Educación Física y Deportes
Consejo Nacional de Rehabilitación y Educación Especial
Escuela Centroamericana de Ganadería (ECAG)
Instituciones de Asistencia Médica Social
Instituto Costarricense de Turismo (ICT)
Instituto de Tierras y Colonización (ITCO)
Instituto Mixto de Ayuda Social (IMAS)
Instituto Nacional de Aprendizaje (INA)
Instituto Tecnológico de Costa Rica (ITCR)
Junta de Conservación y Vigilancia del Teatro Nacional
Junta de Defensa del Tabaco (JDT)
Juntas de Educación
Junta de Pensiones y Jubiliciones del Magisterio Nacional
Junta de Pensiones y Jubilicaciones del Poder Judicial
Liga Agrícola e Industrial de la Caña de Azúcar (LAICA)
Museo de Arte Costarricense
Museo Nacional
Oficina del Café
Orquesta Sinfónica Nacional
Patronato Nacional de la Infancia (PANI)
Servicio Nacional de Aguas Subterráneas (SENAS)
Servicio Nacional de Electricidad (SNE)
Universidad de Costa Rica (UCR)
Universidad Estatal a Distancia (UNED)
Universidad Nacional Autónoma (UNA)

Banking institutions
Banco Anglo Costarricense (BAC)
Banco Central de Costa Rica (BCCR)
Banco Crédito Agrícola de Cartago (BCAC)
Banco de Costa Rica (BCR)
Banco Nacional de Costa Rica (BNCR)
Banco Popular y de Desarrollo Comunal

Non-banking institutions
Asociación Bananera Nacional, S.A. (ASBANA)
Comisión Nacional de Préstamos para la Educación
Corporación Costarricense de Desarrollo, S.A. (CODESA) [b]
Instituto de Fomento y Asesoría Municipal (IFAM)
Instituto Nacional de Fomento Cooperativo (INFOCOOP)
Instituto Nacional de Seguros (INS)
Instituto Nacional de Vivienda y Urbanismo (INVU)

SOURCE: Based on OFIPLAN (1982, 306).

NOTE: For English translations of institutions' names, see the List of Abbreviations, p. xv–xxii.

[a] Legislative, Executive, and Judicial Branches, as well as the Supreme Electoral Tribunal.

[b] Part of CODESA.

of the central government. During the 1950s, however, the state created 13 new public-sector autonomous institutions; in the 1960s, it founded 36 new such entities; and in the 1970s, during the apogee of the *Estado empresario*, it established 50 (OFIPLAN 1982, 331). Together with the structures of the central government, the public sector was, by the late 1970s, what even Figueres termed a "veritable institutional archipelago" (Dunkerley 1988, 598) of some 185 distinct organizations, frequently with ambiguous mandates, overlapping functions, unclear lines of authority, and little coordination between them (Garita 1981, 11).

The State and Individual Well-Being

How did this statist development model affect the lives of individual Costa Ricans? Beyond the obvious, albeit uneven, improvements in living standards reflected in the social and economic indicators and the equally clear consolidation of a very substantial educated middle class, it is important to examine concretely some of the ways in which this giant web of institutions intersected with people's day-to-day lives and influenced their assumptions about social contract, legitimacy, and the appropriate bounds of state activity. For illustrative purposes, this is perhaps best accomplished by shifting from macro-level historical synthesis to a synchronic description relevant to the case at hand, the contemporary Costa Rican countryside circa 1979, just prior to the onset of the economic crisis.

As Table 4 suggests, state institutions came to permeate virtually every aspect of rural life and of agricultural and agroindustrial production. By the late 1970s, a medium-size (or even small) maize farmer might, for example, obtain subsidized credit from the National Banking System for renting land, planting, cultivating, and harvesting the crop, and perhaps for machinery or other capital investments. The bank would require him to purchase crop insurance from the National Insurance Institute. He could obtain inexpensive fertilizer from the nationalized fertilizer company, and technical assistance from the Ministry of Agriculture and Livestock or from one of the several other agencies that provided extension services. He would then likely sell most of the crop to the CNP at an artificially high price and, should he need maize for feeding poultry or for his family, then or later, he could purchase it at artificially low prices in a CNP retail outlet or a private grocery store (where maximum prices for staple foods were also set by a government board). If he were a member of an agrarian reform or other cooperative, he would have access to the extension and credit programs of the reform agency or the institutions serving the cooperative sector. Meanwhile, in his community, state agencies would be educating his children and, if he were not well-off, feeding them once or twice a day, as well as providing basic health services and at least occasional dental care to the entire population. Health Ministry clinics and Social Security hospitals in the towns and cities provided adequate to excellent care for more serious conditions. If covered by the social security system—either through a relative, participation in the formal labor market, or by paying individual or group premiums—he would have access to disability insurance and at least some retirement pension. The DINADECO-sponsored community development association very likely worked, at least occasionally, to improve the roads and water and sanitation systems and had probably built a large covered hall for meetings and festivities. And even extremely remote communities typically had at least one public telephone, installed by the ICE and generally administered by a local grocer, that connected everyone to emergency services and to relatives elsewhere in the country.

Obviously, this complex social safety net sometimes had holes in it or became hopelessly snarled as overlapping bureaucracies sought to provide similar kinds of services to the same groups and individuals. In my field work, for example, I sometimes encountered agriculturalists who complained bitterly of having received visits during the same growing season from extension agents attached to three or four different public-sector organizations, each of whom dispensed technical advice which contradicted that provided by the others.[20] Very commonly, too, the delivery of services from one part of the bureaucracy depended on having documentation obtained from other parts. Applying for an agricultural production loan, for instance, typically required, at a minimum, a valid property title (acquired at the Public Property Registry), an up-to-date identity card (from the Civil Registry), a notarized rental contract if the land was rented (necessitating a lawyer's services), a field inspection report (from the bank's own staff), and insurance certification (from the National Insurance Institute). If the crop was to be irrigated, scheduling would have to be coordinated with one or more of the relevant agencies, or permits might have to be sought for drawing river water. Delays with one bureaucracy inevitably caused delays elsewhere, something that was potentially disastrous in agriculture, where many producers could ill afford the extra time and money and where precise scheduling was usually essential for assuring good yields (and market access, in the case of new, perishable export crops).

TABLE 4

The Public Sector in Agriculture: Basic Organizational Structure, ca. 1940–1979

Public-sector activity	ca. 1940	ca. 1950	ca. 1960	ca. 1970	ca. 1979
Coordination	Consejo Nacional de Agricultura	Comisión Agrícola Nacional	Consejo Agropecuario Nacional		CAN
Sectoral planning					OPS, OFIPLAN
Scientific planning					CONICIT
Improved seeds					CIGRAS, ONS
Food technology					CITA
Agricultural production					CODESA
Social welfare					IMAS
Regulation of agrochemicals				MAG	MAG
Crop insurance				INS	INS
				DINADECO, CACs	DINADECO
Regional development				JAPDEVA	JAPDEVA
Land tenure			ITCO	ITCO	ITCO
Economic policy		MAI, CNP, BCCR, BNCR	CNP, BCCR, MAG, MEIC	MAG, CNP, BCCR, MEIC	MAG, CNP, BCCR, MEIC
				OFIPLAN	OFIPLAN
Water resources and irrigation	SNE	SNE	SNE	SNE	SNE, SENAS, CONARIEGO

Research and extension	UCR IDC	UCR MAI	UCR MAG	UCR MAG OFICAFE	UCR MAG OFICAFE ITCR UNA
Education	UCR	UCR	UCR	UCR MEP CITA INA	UCR MEP CITA INA ITCR UNA ETA ECAG
Marketing	JPC IDC	JPC CNP OFICAFE	JPC CNP OFICAFE JDT	CNP OFICAFE	CNP OFICAFE
Credit	BNCR	BNCR BCR BAC BCAC	BNCR BCR BAC BCAC	BNCR BCR BAC BCAC	BNCR BCR BAC BCAC IFAM CODESA INFOCOOP

(continued)

TABLE 4
(continued)

SOURCE: Salas U. et al. (1983, 147); SEPSA (1982, 27–30; 1985, 102–4).

Key to Abbreviations:

ASBANA = Asociación Bananera Nacional
BAC = Banco Anglo-Costarricense
BCAC = Banco Crédito Agrícola de Cartago
BCCR = Banco Central de Costa Rica
BCR = Banco de Costa Rica
BNCR = Banco Nacional de Costa Rica
CACs = Centros Agrícolas Cantonales
CAN = Consejo Nacional Sectorial de Desarrollo Agropecuario y de Recursos Naturales Renovables
CENADA = Centro Nacional de Abastecimiento
CENPRO = Centro para la Promoción de Exportaciones y las Inversiones
CIGRAS = Centro de Investigación de Granos y Semillas
CITA = Centro de Investigación y Tecnología de Alimentos
CNP = Consejo Nacional de Producción
CODESA = Corporación Costarricense de Desarrollo, S.A.[a]
CONARIEGO = Comisión Nacional de Riego
CONICIT = Consejo Nacional de Investigaciones Científicas y Tecnológicas
DINADECO = Dirección Nacional de Desarrollo de la Comunidad
ECAG = Escuela Controamericana de Ganadería
ETA = Escuela Técnica Agropecuaria de Santa Cruz
IDC = Instituto de Defensa del Café
IFAM = Instituto de Fomento y Asesoría Municipal

IMAS = Instituto Mixto de Ayuda Social
INA = Instituto Nacional de Aprendizaje
INFOCOOP = Instituto de Fomento Cooperativo
INS = Instituto Nacional de Seguros
ITCO = Instituto de Tierras y Colonización
ITCR = Instituto Tecnológico de Costa Rica
JAPDEVA = Junta de Administración Portuaria y Desarrollo Económico de la Vertiente Atlántica
JDT = Junta de Defensa del Tabaco
JPC = Junta de Protección a la Agricultura de la Caña
LAICA = Liga Agrícola Industrial de la Caña de Azúcar
MAG = Ministerio de Agricultura y Ganadería
MAI = Ministerio de Agricultura e Industria
MEIC = Ministerio de Economía Industria y Comercio
MEP = Ministerio de Educación Pública
OFICAFE = Oficina del Café
OFIPLAN = Oficina de Planificación Nacional y Política Económica
ONS = Oficina Nacional de Semillas
OPSA = Oficina de Planificación del Sector Agropecuario
SENAS = Servicio Nacional de Aguas Subterráneas
SNE = Servicio Nacional de Electricidad
UCR = Universidad de Costa Rica
UNA = Universidad Nacional Autónoma

NOTES: Dates refer to the period in which an institution became involved in the particular activity, not necessarily to when it was founded. For English translations on institutions' names, see List of Abbreviations, pp. xv–xxii.

[a] A public-sector holding company with various large agroindustrial subsidiaries.

Despite the inefficient, unsystematic, and frequently frustrating way many public-sector agencies provided services, most Costa Ricans derived at least some immediate, recognizable material advantages from this vast array of state programs. Certainly only a handful viewed the state as an implacable adversary, something that contrasted markedly with the situation elsewhere in Central America. While the Costa Rican social welfare state did not achieve any fundamental, progressive redistribution of resources, it did pay a "social wage" that by regional standards was extraordinarily high. That this was possible was due in no small measure to the overall prosperity of the country's economy during the three post–civil war decades (Dunkerley 1988, 607; Booth 1991). Not surprisingly, the Costa Rican state came, in this period, to enjoy a remarkably high level of legitimacy. This claim to represent universal interests rested to a significant degree on the concrete benefits that the social welfare system dispensed to large sectors of the population—the wealthy and middle class, as well as the poor. This was hardly just "socialism for the rich," as it has sometimes been unfairly labeled (Nelson 1989, 152). Not surprisingly, though, it did contain at least some of the seeds of its own destruction.

Crisis and "Recovery"

While signs of an impending crisis in this "statist" development model were present at least since the early 1970s, it was only in 1980–82 that the bubble really burst. The literature on Costa Rica's economic crisis is now vast, itself a sign of both fervent debate over its causes and potential solutions and widespread apprehension over its social effects. Rather than exploring these debates in detail, this section will outline in broad strokes the roots of the crisis and the about-face that led to the abandonment of "statist" economic policies in the early 1980s. It then looks at an issue not often examined in the huge outpouring of studies on the crisis: the extent to which the apparent "success" of free-market policies since the late 1980s resulted not only from the application of neoliberal measures, but from the legacies of the earlier, "statist" social democratic model.

By the early 1970s, and especially after the first oil price shock, the Costa Rican development model's deficiencies became ever more evident. The Central American Common Market was in disarray following the 1969 "soccer war" between Honduras and El Salvador, diminishing the size of the market and delaying payments for Costa Rican exports to the rest of the region.

Growth slowed and inflation reached unprecedented levels. The new industries, intended to produce at home goods previously purchased abroad, turned
out to be highly dependent on imports; indeed, for every $100 of manufac-
tured output, they imported $80 worth of inputs and machinery (González
Vega 1984, 356). Import substitution industrialization thus actually exacerbated a persistently negative trade balance. National Banking System loans
with interest rates that were often below the inflation rate, rather than encouraging production, diverted borrowed money to speculation and conspicuous consumption, which further aggravated the trade imbalance (low rates
for deposits also discouraged savings and fueled capital flight). Subsidized
prices for food staples combined with high farm support prices to fuel the
National Production Council's deficit. By 1980, the public sector employed
one-fifth of the workforce and accounted for nearly one-quarter of gross domestic product (OFIPLAN 1982, 319). But while the state's expenditures
rose from 15 percent of GDP in 1970 to 22 percent in 1980, its income remained constant at roughly 13 percent of GDP (Rodríguez V. 1990, 257). In
1976–77, following a major frost in Brazil, coffee prices soared, and with
them incomes and government revenues, but this constituted only a temporary reprieve from an inevitable reckoning.

The heightened social spending and the growing budget deficits of the
1950s and after had increasingly been financed with borrowing rather than
current revenues. In the late 1970s, commercial banks were recycling petro-
dollars accumulated after the sudden oil price hike of 1973 and offering easily obtained short-term credits. But the loans often had variable interest
rates that unexpectedly skyrocketed when oil prices jumped again in 1979.
Between 1977 and 1981, Costa Rica's terms of trade fell by one-third and its
debt service quadrupled. In the six years before 1981, the proportion of Costa
Rica's debt held by commercial banks more than doubled, from 23 to 47 percent. By mid-1980, dollar reserves covered only one week's imports and the
colón began a rapid downward spiral that in eighteen months resulted in
a 500 percent devaluation (Jiménez Sandoval 1990, 44; Nelson 1990, 183;
Rodríguez Céspedes 1988, 221).

Costa Rica declared a moratorium on debt payments in July 1981, over a
year before the famous "Mexico weekend" that is widely seen as marking
the onset of the Latin American debt crisis. Although the country had one
of the highest per capita debts in the world ($2,021 in 1980), as a "small
debtor" its problems attracted little attention or sympathy in the international financial community (CEPAS 1992, 18). Indeed, in their first post-
moratorium discussion with Costa Rican representatives, one of the bankers

initiated the proceedings by declaring bluntly, "We want you to give us our money back!" (Vargas Peralta 1987, 207). Given this initial intransigence, the IMF and the World Bank were virtually the only institutions that could mediate between Costa Rica and the private banks and that could assure flows of desperately needed fresh loans.

Small countries face special disadvantages in renegotiating debts. Their economies tend to be less diversified, so their ability to meet obligations is suspect. Measured in terms of their capacity to disrupt the international financial system, their weight is insignificant. Commercial banks were initially reluctant to negotiate at all with Costa Rica for fear of establishing precedents that might influence talks with Mexico and Brazil. Small debtors— including Costa Rica—thus received less favorable repayment terms in the first round of debt restructuring with private banks in the early 1980s.[21]

Small countries—and Costa Rica, in particular—also experienced earlier and more profound cross-conditionality in agreements with foreign lenders. Private banks tied further loans to the signing of a standby accord with the IMF. Disbursements of World Bank and USAID funds needed to pay the banks were then tied to timely fulfillment of IMF targets.[22] This linking of conditions complicated negotiations and absorbed the energies of economic policymakers needed in other critical areas. It also meant that different agencies often worked at cross purposes.[23]

Small scale has, however, another, arguably advantageous side. Modest transfers of funds from lending and aid agencies can have a significant impact. And—sandwiched between Sandinista Nicaragua and Noriega's Panama—Costa Rica combined small size with a pivotal position in Washington's geopolitical strategy for the region. Even before the country emerged from the severe economic crisis of 1980–82, it started to receive favored treatment from USAID, which began to provide large amounts of "economic support funds" intended to shore up its balance of payments (Table 5). As the decade progressed, this partiality was also at times reflected in the policies of U.S.-dominated multilateral lenders, especially the IMF and World Bank.

In 1980–81, two IMF accords with President Rodrigo Carazo's government broke down in the face of public opposition. But by late 1982, as inflation neared 100 percent and debt service obligations soared to nearly 70 percent of export earnings, the newly elected PLN government of Luis Alberto Monge had little alternative but to sign a $100 million IMF standby accord, committing itself to a package of measures intended to reduce inflation, cut the public-sector deficit, and bring order to the foreign-exchange market. To free up resources for paying the foreign debt, the IMF required Costa Rica to

TABLE 5
U.S. Aid to Costa Rica, 1946–1995 (millions of dollars)

Programs	1946–1961	1962–1981	1982	1983	1984
AID and predecessor agencies					
(a) Loans	10.9	126.0	9.7	20.2	11.6
(b) Grants	10.5	32.0	1.8	8.3	4.3
(c) Totals AID and predecessor agencies (c = a + b)	21.4	158.0	11.5	28.5	15.9
Food Commodity Assistance					
PL-480 "Food for Peace" Program					
(d) Loans	0	0	17.2	27.1	22.4
(e) Grants	1.1	20.5	1.1	0.2	0
(f) Total PL-480 Aid (f = d + e)	1.1	20.5	18.3	27.3	22.4
Agricultural Act of 1949, Sect. 416	0	0	0	0	0
(g) Total Agric. Act of 1949, Sect. 416	0	0	0	0	0
(h) Total Food Commodity Assistance (h = f + g)	1.1	20.5	18.3	27.3	22.4
Economic Support Funds					
"Projectized" and other					
(i) Loans	0	0	0	0	0
(j) Grants	0	0	0	0	0
(k) Totals: "Projectized" and other (k = i + j)	0	0	0	0	0
Balance of payments					
(l) Loans	0	0	15.0	118.0	35.0
(m) Grants	0	0	5.0	37.7	95.0
(n) Totals: Balance of payments (n = l + m)	0	0	20.0	155.7	130.0
(o) Total economic support funds (o = k + n)	0	0	20.0	155.7	130.0
TOTAL ASSISTANCE					
(p) Loans (p = a + d + i + l)	10.9	126.0	41.9	165.3	69.0
(q) Grants (q = b + e + j + m)	11.6	52.5	7.9	46.2	99.3
(r) Total all U.S. aid to Costa Rica (r = p + q; r = c + h + o)	22.5	178.5	49.8	211.5	168.3

SOURCE: U.S. Embassy, Costa Rica.

NOTE: Totals and subtotals reflect rounding.

1985	1986	1987	1988	1989	1990	1991	1992	1993	1994	1995
10.7	6.3	8.3	0	0	0	0	0	0	0	0
15.1	6.6	8.9	11.8	9.8	10.6	10.9	7.4	5.5	3.2	2.7
25.9	12.9	17.2	11.8	9.8	10.6	10.9	7.4	5.5	3.3	2.7
21.1	16.1	16.0	0	15.0	0	15.0	0	0	0	0
0	0	0	0	0	0	0	0	0	U	0
21.1	16.1	16.0	0	15.0	0	15.0	0	0	0	0
0	4.8	5.6	0	0	0	0	0	0	0	0
0	4.8	5.6	0	0	0	0	0	0	0	0
21.1	20.9	21.6	0	15.0	0	15.0	0	0	0	0
0	0	5.9	0	0	0	0	0	0	0	0
0	3.0	16.9	5.0	5.0	3.5	1.0	0	0.5	0	0
0	3.0	22.7	5.0	5.0	3.5	1.0	0	0.5	0	0
0	0	0	0	0	0	0	0	0	0	0
160.0	120.6	119.8	85.0	75.0	60.0	24.0	10.0	0	0	0
160.0	120.6	119.8	85.0	75.0	60.0	24.0	10.0	0	0	0
160.0	123.6	142.5	90.0	80.0	63.5	25.0	10.0	0.5	0	0
31.8	22.4	30.1	0	15.0	0	15.0	0	0	0	0
175.1	135.0	151.1	101.8	89.8	74.1	35.9	17.4	6.0	3.2	2.7
207.0	157.4	181.3	101.8	104.8	74.1	50.9	17.4	6.0	3.3	2.7

slash public-sector spending and investment, and to raise taxes, interest rates, and utility rates.

IMF actions in Costa Rica, however, suggested uncharacteristic sensitivity to the importance of political stability in the economic stabilization process. In a striking departure from monetarist orthodoxy, the IMF allowed National Banking System interest rates to remain below inflation and permitted the Central Bank to maintain a monopoly of foreign exchange transactions. Unification of the overvalued official exchange rate with the free market one was to occur gradually, rather than through sudden, disruptive "shocks."

Washington also set out to build a democratic, prosperous, and stable "showcase" next to Sandinista Nicaragua. Given the severity of the economic crisis, it had to move fast. Between 1983 and 1985, the $592 million in U.S. economic aid was equivalent to a staggering 35.7 percent of the Costa Rican government's budget, one-fifth of export earnings and about 10 percent of GDP. By 1985, Costa Rica was the second highest recipient of U.S. assistance in Latin America, after war-torn El Salvador, and the second highest per capita recipient in the world, after Israel (*Latin America Regional Report: Mexico and Central America*, Nov. 30, 1984; *Tico Times*, 1984 Review; U.S. Embassy 1985).

To stem "nonproductive" social welfare spending and losses from oversized publicly owned enterprises, USAID insisted on sweeping changes in the country's economy: an expanded role for private banks, the auctioning off of CODESA and other state companies, and the creation of new nonpublic organizations—from agricultural schools to export promotion offices—that intentionally duplicated functions of public-sector institutions, thus weakening the state, accelerating Costa Rica's embrace of neoliberalism, and establishing showcase projects that allegedly demonstrated the efficiency of private-sector initiative and the validity of a conservative vision of "civil society" (Macdonald 1994; Shallat 1989). Among the most controversial of these AID "parallel state" institutions was a lavishly funded private agricultural school with the catchy English acronym EARTH (Escuela de la Agricultura de la Región Tropical Húmeda), which duplicated many of the programs of the Costa Rican university system and of international organizations already established in Costa Rica, such as CATIE (Centro Agronómico Tropical de Investigación y Enseñanza) and IICA (Instituto Interamericano de Cooperación para la Agricultura). Other new AID-supported institutions competed with underfunded programs of the Ministries of Agriculture and Livestock and of Transport and Public Works (Gutiérrez 1993, 411).

U.S. demands on Costa Rica were accompanied by intense pressure (Sojo

1991, 1992). In 1984, for example, USAID said it was holding up disbursement of desperately needed funds until the legislature—sequestered during an exhausting twenty-hour debate—approved banking and currency reforms that permitted loans in dollars and that allowed private financial institutions to receive credit from the Central Bank.[24] U.S. money also went toward founding a new Coalition for Development Initiatives (CINDE)—staffed by Costa Ricans and North Americans, with offices in San José and several U.S. cities—which provided funds for nontraditional export projects, training, private-sector "educational" activities, and opening new markets abroad. CINDE, not coincidentally, duplicated—though with a vastly greater budget—many of the functions of the government export promotion office, CENPRO. CINDE and USAID, in turn, played key roles in establishing and staffing a new Ministry of Exports. In 1985 USAID created the Transitory Investments Trust (FINTRA) to support the buyout of state-sector companies.[25] Washington also pushed for and received reductions in Central American extraregional tariffs and generous incentives for producers of nontraditional exports. Meanwhile, the IMF, alarmed that Costa Rica was not fully complying with promises to slash public spending, conditioned continued support on the signing of a structural adjustment agreement with the World Bank.

In 1985 Costa Rica signed a new IMF standby accord, new agreements with the commercial banks and the creditor nations in the Paris Club, and its first World Bank structural adjustment loan (SAL I). Thanks in part to the huge flow of U.S. assistance, the economy had stabilized since the debacle of 1980–82: inflation had dropped below 20 percent, growth had been positive for two years in a row, and the public-sector deficit stood at about 6 percent of GDP—short of the IMF target, but less than half the 1982 level. The adjustment phase initiated with SAL I meant a continuation of measures adopted in the 1983–85 stabilization period. But it also portended a series of more profound, long-term changes in Costa Rican society.

SAL I—an $80 million, long-term loan from the World Bank—sought to redirect Costa Rican industrial development from domestic and Central American markets to new international ones.[26] According to World Bank officials, this shift would allow Costa Rica to sustain the recovery initiated in 1983. Lower tariffs would force local industries to be "competitive" and would facilitate the technology imports necessary for modernizing manufacturing; more tax breaks would encourage retooling and investment; and continued "mini-devaluations" of the colón would boost exports, dampen consumption, and keep trade deficits in check. In agriculture, the World

Bank program required the reduction and eventual elimination of crop price supports; subsidized production credit; restricted food, input, and machinery imports; and subsidized consumer prices for maize, rice, and beans. These measures were intended to bring domestic food prices into line with international prices, thus improving efficiency, and to reduce the large deficit of the state commodities agency (CNP). Discouraging basic food production was expected to free land, labor, and capital for agricultural export activities. The bank also called for a reorientation of extension and research away from food crops for domestic consumption and toward the "nontraditional" export crops that Costa Rican government officials dubbed "the agriculture of change": cut flowers, ornamental plants, coconut oil, citrus juices, tubers for the U.S. Latino market, macadamia and cashew nuts, mangos, melons and pineapples, cardamom, and winter vegetables. In order to encourage new exports—agricultural as well as industrial—producers were urged to take advantage of Washington's Caribbean Basin Initiative (CBI), which provided greater access to the U.S. market (Céspedes et al. 1985, 210–11; Fallas 1990; Martínez 1990; Torres and Alvarado 1990).

The World Bank also prescribed a fundamental transformation of the Costa Rican state. Rather than intervening directly in the economy, as in the 1970s, the state was to divest itself of unprofitable enterprises, slash its deficit, "downsize" its personnel roster, improve the efficiency of its administrative activities, and limit itself as much as possible to guaranteeing social stability and facilitating the activities of the private sector. The nationalized banks, which previously budgeted credits to meet the needs of specific economic sectors and social groups, were told to make loans only according to profitability—not social development—criteria.[27] Finally, the World Bank sought to reduce the growth of the foreign debt, to restrict new loans to those with favorable, "concessionary" terms, and to assure that "fresh" loans were not used for paying debt service.

SAL II, signed in 1988, was a $200 million loan agreement with the World Bank and Japan that contained an extensive list of measures designed to continue the "reassignment" of resources to the private sector and to export activities and the "reordering" and slimming down of the state that began under SAL I.[28] The accord committed the Costa Rican government to bringing domestic prices for basic grains into line with lower international ones, thus encouraging "efficiency" but also opening the market to a flood of imports and undermining many peasant producers. It also called for improving cold storage facilities, containerized ports, and transport and irrigation infrastructure, all necessary concomitants of the "agriculture of change." Public-sector services were to be transferred to the private sector when they were "not indispensable for the functioning of the government." Key policymakers, such as Central Bank director Eduardo Lizano, argued that state enterprises had to be privatized even when, as with the telephone company (ICE) and the oil refinery (RECOPE), they were running "healthy" surpluses (Lizano 1990, 46). New IMF accords in 1991 and 1992 kept the free-market juggernaut on track, committing the Costa Rican government to a complete liberation of exchange and interest rates.

The lengthy, heated discussions around SAL III—and its eventual cancellation by the World Bank—suggest that in Costa Rica it has not been easy to achieve consensus about the adjustment process. This $100 million World Bank loan, together with three additional agreements with the Inter-American Development Bank totaling approximately $150 million, called for a variety of measures that would further "modernize" the private sector and "adjust" the public sector by, among other things, dismissing eight thousand state employees. After several years of bitter legislative maneuvering, numerous amendments to the agreement, six extensions of the deadline, and several lobbying visits from important foreign functionaries, the Legislative Assembly finally approved the loan in 1994. Nonetheless, the World Bank rejected the accord in early 1995 because of Costa Rica's high budget deficit and its failure to reach a new agreement with the International Monetary Fund (Raventós 1995).

Despite the World Bank's wariness, Costa Rica managed in 1995 to cement a series of loan agreements with the Inter-American Development Bank totaling $250 million. The IDB accord was possible, however, only with the IMF's seal of approval, which required a series of commitments that included eliminating 2,000 government jobs and tightening monetary policy (*La Nación*, Oct. 18, 1995). Much of the IDB money was used to substitute low-cost foreign debt for high-cost internal debt. Even so, in 1996 interest payments still swallowed 30 percent of government revenue (*New York Times*, Sept. 30, 1996).

How Liberal Is Costa Rican Neoliberalism?

Measures to "privatize," "correct distortions," and "improve the allocation of production factors" have created new winners and losers and forced virtually every group in society to redefine its strategies for survival. Industrialists who produced goods for the domestic and Central American markets, large and small grain farmers, the urban poor, government employees, and students, faculty, and workers at the public universities have all been on the losing end. The political debates around SAL III notwithstanding, it has not been overly difficult to achieve a significant and rapid liberalization of Costa Rica's economy. While the inexorable march of economic globalization is certainly part of the explanation, two other determinants have also been important. First, the top-down character of Costa Rican social democratic reformism, and the absence of explicit multiclass, pro-reformist alliances such as those typical of European social democracies, facilitated the cooptation and/or conversion of political and business elites to the new free-market orthodoxy (Solís 1992). Second, Costa Rican neoliberalism has rarely been as liberal as it claims to be. This section raises the question of how closely structural adjustment actually conforms to neoliberal concepts and how effective it has been in meeting its professed goals.

The main beneficiaries of the rush to the free market have been the export and private banking sectors and foreign investors, especially those who have come to dominate key parts of the "agriculture of change" and the flourishing maquila assembly industry. By the late 1980s, almost half of Costa Rica's foreign exchange came from "nontraditional" exports—those other than the established mainstays, coffee, bananas, and sugar. Nonetheless, all the tax breaks, financial backing, new industrial parks and free-trade zones, and support for foreign marketing and promotion have not brought high-value-added industries or vertical integration of production to Costa Rica.

The key tax break did aim at generating more value-added, a necessity for a more dynamic and autonomous accumulation process. But it set the required level of value-added rather low and entailed a high price. Producers of nontraditional exports to non-Central American markets received tax-credit certificates called CATs (Certificados de Abono Tributario) if their output contained 35 percent national value-added in the form of local raw materials, labor, or energy. Established in 1972 during the heyday of the social democratic model, CATs cost the government $150,000 to $200,000 for each $1 million worth of exports. Because most taxes on exporters were abolished in 1984, holders of CATs sell them to other enterprises, which use them to pay their income taxes, thus depriving the state of revenue. Ironically, this statist subsidy has been crucial to the "success" of the new, supposedly free-market, strategy. But by the end of 1990, with the export fever generated by structural adjustment, CATs ate up 10 percent of the government budget and accounted for nearly one-half of the public-sector budget deficit, which in turn fueled rising interest rates, as the state issued new bonds to cover the shortfall (Franco and Sojo 1992, 68; Torres and Alvarado 1990, 18–19; CEPAS 1992, 58).[29] This exacerbated the difficulties that small producers faced in obtaining credit (see Chapter 3). In other respects as well, the distributional effect of CATs was highly regressive. In an eighteen-month period in 1988–89, 27 percent of the approximately $72 million in CAT subsidies went to only eight firms; a mere 26 companies received over half the CAT subsidies; and a single transnational—PINDECO, the pineapple subsidiary of Del Monte—received around 10 percent of the certificates (Franco and Sojo 1992, 72; Vermeer 1990b, 53–54). In surveys, a majority of exporters indicated that if CATs were eliminated, they would reduce or cease their activities (Román 1992, 20).

By the late 1980s, Costa Rica's export boom, based largely on tourism, maquila garment assembly plants, a resurgence of banana cultivation, and the new "agriculture of change," had brought respectable growth rates and better fiscal health (the trade balance, however, remained negative, largely because liberalized trade also had the less than salutory consequence of facilitating nonproductive consumption of luxury imports; see Table 6).[30] Costa Rica, along with Mexico and the Philippines, was among the first beneficiaries of the U.S. Treasury Secretary Nicholas Brady's debt-reduction plan and, of the three countries, received by far the most generous terms. In 1990, using foreign grants, it acquired and wrote off nearly $1 billion—or 63 percent—of its $1.6 billion commercial bank debt which, while it had much less favorable conditions than obligations to multilateral lenders, was selling at the time for only one-sixth of its face value on the secondary market (Robles 1990, 17–20).

A growing chorus of neoliberal economists and ideologues (see Introduction) described Costa Rica's economic "success" in glowing terms and ascribed it to what Ronald Reagan liked to call "the magic of the marketplace." However, the traditional neoliberal tools—lowered tariffs on imports, interest rate liberalization, privatization, and cuts in public spending—have been less important in bringing stability and fueling the export boom than a variety of non-market factors: the massive U.S. aid in the 1980s, the result of Costa Rica's strategic geopolitical position between Nicaragua and Panama; the new exporters' profiting from CATs subsidies, a program established under Figueres in the unabashedly statist 1970s; the expansion of U.S. quotas for key products under the Caribbean Basin Initiative; the constant currency devaluations demanded by the international lending institutions and pro-export lobbies in Costa Rica; and the decision of many foreign investors to locate in Costa Rica because of its well-developed infrastructure and its highly

Rise and Demise of a Tropical Welfare State

TABLE 6

Costa Rica: Basic Economic Indicators, 1980–1996

Year	Foreign debt (millions US$)[a]	Foreign debt to GDP (%)[a]	GDP Growth (%)[a]	GDP per capita (1988 US$)	Consumer prices (inflation)[b]	Real minimum wage (growth rate)[b]	Average real wage (growth rate)[b]
1980	2,737	54	0.8	2,394	17.8	n.d.	n.d
1981	3,222	82	−4.6	2,254	65.1	−19.4	n.d
1982	3,461	110	−7.3	1,517	81.8	8.1	−19.9
1983	4,177	122	2.9	1,513	17.8	19.2	10.9
1984	3,988	105	8.0	1,584	17.3	−1.5	7.8
1985	4,399	113	0.7	1,551	10.9	7.2	9.1
1986	4,576	105	5.5	1,590	15.4	−1.4	5.4
1987	4,721	102	4.8	1,618	16.4	−5.1	−1.3
1988	4,544	93	3.4	1,655	25.3	−7.2	−1.0
1989	4,603	86	5.6	1,668	10.0	9.3	5.9
1990	3,772	66	3.7	1,685	27.3	−2.5	−0.8
1991	4,026	68	1.0	1,664	25.3	−2.8	−5.8
1992	3,938	62	7.7	1,752	17.0	7.7	4.7
1993	3,850	56	6.3	1,812	9.0	1.4	10.2
1994	3,843	53	4.5	1,847	19.9	−0.2	5.3
1995	3,672	49	2.5	1,850	22.6	−2.0	−2.0
1996	3,667	49	−0.8	1,784	13.9	3.6	−1.9

[a] Inter-American Development Bank. Some data have been recalculated as 1988 dollars. Some 1996 data are preliminary.

educated, healthy labor force, both legacies of the social democratic model, not of neoliberalism.[31]

Economic recovery, and especially the balance of payments, has also benefited from Costa Rica's natural beauty and its sterling reputation as an international leader in environmental conservation, neither of course related to neoliberal prescriptions (though the privatization of some national park lands has been controversial—see Edelman 1995, 52). In 1994, tourism, largely directed to wilderness areas, surpassed banana exports as the country's leading source of foreign exchange.[32] Annual revenues are expected to reach $1 billion in the late 1990s (Edelman n.d.).

What have been the social costs of the apparent recovery in the late 1980s and 1990s? In Chapters 2 and 3, I examine this question in some detail, in relation to the rural poor. Here, it is worth noting some of the larger effects

Exports (millions US$)[a]	Imports (millions US$)[a]	Non-traditional exports (% all exports)[b]	Non-traditional exports (growth rate)[b]	Current account balance (millions US$)[a]	Central government deficit (% GDP)[a]	Per capita consumption (growth rate)[c]
1,002	1,375	38.0	—	−663	−8.2	−5.0
1,030	1,089	36.9	−2.4	−426	−3.6	−16.7
869	805	33.7	−21.2	−267	−3.2	−17.1
853	894	36.7	7.6	−280	−3.4	2.9
998	993	33.4	6.7	−151	−3.1	5.2
939	1,001	34.2	−0.9	−126	−2.0	−1.5
1,085	1,045	32.8	10.4	−80	−3.3	−0.8
1,107	1,245	38.2	20.2	−256	−2.0	3.4
1,181	1,279	41.1	15.7	−179	−2.5	0.1
1,333	1,572	46.6	27.7	−415	−4.1	2.1
1,366	1,833	48.1	7.4	−424	−4.4	2.9
1,487	1,680	52.8	3.8	−75	−3.1	−2.0
1,739	2,211	56.9	25.5	−370	−1.9	4.5
1,867	2,627	57.5	9.2	−619	−1.9	4.4
2,102	2,789	58.8	4.3	−463	−6.9	6.1
2,442	2,954	58.1	15.0	−152	−4.6	3.6
2,753	3,413	63.7	14.1	−142	−5.2	3.1

[b] Costa Rican government data; 1996 data are preliminary.

[c] United Nations Economic Commission for Latin America and the Caribbean.

on Costa Rican society as a whole. Both the state and the lending and aid agencies have attempted to blunt the negative social impact of structural adjustment policies. As Costa Rica's public sector shrank and the social safety net unraveled, foreign aid agencies, NGOs, and even the multilateral lenders began to provide "social compensation" funds to ease the crisis caused by large-scale dismissals of public employees, declining real wages, and cutbacks in state services. As early as 1983, USAID, European governments, and Catholic charities helped the government of President Luis Alberto Monge to begin indexing public-sector salaries to inflation and to institute a food distribution program that benefited 42,000 of the poorest families (Rovira 1987, 67–69). Soon after, the European Economic Community launched a major aid effort directed at the poorest sectors of the population throughout Central America (Cáceres and Irvin 1990). By the mid-1980s, NGOs and foreign-aid organizations proliferated in Costa Rica, incorporating personnel dismissed from the public sector and attempting, albeit with mixed results, to mitigate the negative social impact of the rush to the free market. Under the presidency of Oscar Arias (1986–90), the government built tens of thousands of low-cost houses, giving priority to the most militant urban squatter settlements. In 1990 the Calderón government introduced a "food bond" for needy families, which, despite its good intentions, reached less than half of those in the "extreme poverty" category. In the administration of José María Figueres Olsen (1994–98), son of PLN founder "Pepe" Figueres, anti-poverty strategy has targeted approximately one dozen of the country's poorest cantons. These efforts to absorb potential discontent among the poor were mirrored by efforts to garner support from disaffected sectors of the elite; industrialists, in particular, once adamant defenders of protectionism and overvalued exchange rates, were lured into backing the free-market model by generous subsidies for plant reconversion and export promotion and by the possibility of buying discounted CATs from producers of nontraditional exports.

In addition to "social compensation" measures and other steps that have blunted opposition to the new model, economic adjustment itself has had the "trickle down" effects that neoliberals predicted, but largely in the form of low-paying jobs in assembly industries or agroindustrial export enterprises. After a decade of stabilization and adjustment, per capita GDP, a key indicator of living standards, had not regained its 1980, pre-crisis level (see Table 6). The real minimum wage (i.e., adjusted for inflation), an important gauge of the living standards of the poor, jumped in 1983, as the country recovered from the devastating devaluation-inflation of 1981–82. But it has declined or remained stagnant every year since, with the exception of 1985, 1989, 1993, and 1994, all pre-election or election years, when governments in Costa Rica typically expand spending to garner votes and goodwill (knowing, too, that their successors will have to pick up the tab) (CEPAS 1992, 18; *Tico Times*, July 18, 1997).

Costa Rican macroeconomic policy has been characterized, since the mid-1980s, by cycles geared to electoral politics. Incoming presidents typically declare that the previous government has left budget deficits and other problems that can only be solved through urgent and drastic austerity measures and that necessitate postponing campaign promises to the poor. After some degree of stability has been achieved, the remaining two years of each president's term usually see more-lavish spending, intended to assure his popularity and the election of his party's candidate. This "vicious circle" from populism to austerity accompanies a downward spiral in the state's capacity to plan for the medium or long term and to implement social policies other than temporary "compensation" measures (Lara et al. 1995, 56–58).

And, to make matters worse, employers have increasingly flouted wage legislation, knowing that the state's enforcement capacity has been weakened by budget cuts and dismissals of public employees. By 1991, an estimated 37 percent of workers were paid less than the legal minimum (MIDEPLAN data cited in *Esta Semana*, May 24–30, 1991, p. 5). In agriculture, industry, and construction, the percentage of the workforce receiving below-minimum wages has risen well above 1980 pre-crisis levels; a particularly large number of complaints come from women employed in new garment assembly plants (CEPAS 1992, 26, 43; Sandoval 1997).

Average real wages since 1980 also show a periodicity geared to the rhythm of electoral politics. This indicator recovered to pre-crisis levels in 1986, but the gain largely evaporated by the time of the next election in 1990. Moreover, Planning Ministry specialists believe that the initial post-crisis rise in the average real wage likely reflects increased upward skewing of the income distribution (MIDEPLAN 1990, 14). Real private consumption per capita, often a better indicator than real wages of the burden of adjustment, plummeted during the 1980–82 downturn and, even after several years of growth in the mid-1990s, was still nearly one-fifth below its pre-crisis level (see Table 6).

Many categories of social spending fell sharply in the mid-1980s and some have since recuperated. Here, as in much discussion of the post-crisis years, the picture is clouded by differences over which indicators are most appropriate and meaningful. Measured as a percentage of GDP, the budgets of the ministries most critical to basic well-being remain considerably below 1980 levels. These include Health and Education, as well as the Family Aid (Asignaciones Familiares) Program (CEPAS 1992, 73). However, as a proportion of central government expenditure, IMF data suggest that these ministries' budgets are at levels broadly similar to those of the pre-crisis, late 1970s. Whether the quality of service delivery remains acceptable is a question much debated in Costa Rica. Affluent Costa Ricans' growing shift to private medical providers may suggest part of the answer.

Official poverty rates fluctuated during the 1980s and 1990s: 18.6 percent of the population lived below the poverty line in 1987, 24.4 percent in 1991, 20 percent in 1994, 14.8 percent in 1995, and 21.6 percent in 1996 (ECLA data in *Inforpress Centroamericana*, Aug. 13, 1992, p. 6; see also CEPAS 1992, 46–47 and *Tico Times*, July 18, 1997). Some prominent economists, however, argue that the decline after 1992 was an artifact of changes in how the government measures the "market basket" used to determine whether poor households are able to meet their basic necessities. In 1995 the official "poverty line" was a monthly income of 7,054 colones, approximately $39, per household member. The "low" poverty figures of the early to mid-1990s are controversial, however. Vice President Rebeca Grynspan estimated in 1994 that 30–38 percent of Costa Rican families live in poverty and 17–25 percent in extreme poverty (Lara et al. 1995, 70). The problem of poverty, however, is not simply an issue of how much of the population falls below an officially defined line; living in poverty is increasingly precarious in today's Costa Rica.

A recent International Labor Organization report which celebrates Costa Rica's adjustment experience notes that in 1980–90 the country conducted the second-sharpest reduction of public-sector employment in the hemisphere (after Chile). In contrast to the rest of Latin America, it claims, the expansion of the informal sector—street vendors, sidewalk food and shoe repair stands, and so on—has been negligible. The report lauds the large increase—from 14 to 22 percent of the urban workforce—in employment in "small private enterprises" (*Latin America Weekly Report*, Oct. 29, 1992).

These conclusions highlight one way in which changing, politically influenced definitions of key indicators have been used to cast a favorable light on troubling economic processes. The entrepreneurial energy embodied in "microenterprises" has been an article of faith for neoliberal theorists at least since the publication in 1986 of Peruvian economist Hernando de Soto's influential treatise, *The Other Path* (1989). *Microempresas* have also been a cornerstone of neoliberal strategies for economic recovery and growth. In Costa Rica, interest in charting this new sector led to changes in 1987 in the surveys used to measure employment, income, and living standards. After holding virtually constant between 1980 and 1986, the "self-employed" category was broadened to include more kinds of informal-sector workers and, not surprisingly, leaped 3.6 percent in 1987 to 22.9 percent of the labor force and climbed to 24.8 percent by 1991. Yet these "independent workers" were hardly something for neoliberals to crow about—53.5 percent were below the poverty line in 1991, in contrast to 39.8 percent of workers who were wage earners (CEPAS 1992, 41, 49).

Changes in definitions of other indicators have also affected understanding of the impact of adjustment. This is most evident in data on social spending. In 1987 methods were modified for recording some transfers of funds and services between public-sector agencies. These accounting shifts tend to "consolidate" certain kinds of public spending, an effect consonant with IMF and World Bank objectives, since funds sent by one ministry to another did not count twice as income. But some key kinds of social spending, such as the Family Aid program, which involved disbursements to numerous other public-sector organizations, continued to be counted with the old methods. This makes it difficult to tell to what extent the apparent recuperation of some kinds of social spending is real and to what degree it simply reflects accounting devices (Ibid., 91–92). In some cases, too, apparent fiscal health obscures disquieting realities. The budget of the social security system, for example—responsible for public clinics and hospitals, as well as old-age and disability pensions—recovered its pre-crisis share of GDP by 1987 and has retained it into the 1990s. The institution nonetheless increasingly suffers from severe shortages of equipment, medicines, and personnel, as the central government delays disbursement of promised funds in an effort to hold down its deficit (Ibid., 73; *Inforpress Centroamericana*, March 26, 1992).

As if the unraveling social safety net were not enough, the export boom also shows signs of considerable volatility—nontraditional export growth rates dropped precipitously in the early 1990s and then jumped in the mid-1990s (Table 6). The early-1990s slowdown was linked initially to the world recession, but it also arose from the temporary suspension and perceived imminent expiration of CAT subsidies, from Costa Rica's status as the adjustment "pilot project" for Central America, and from the type of comparative advantages it has been urged to develop. In February 1991 Costa Rica's Constitutional Court halted the CATs program, arguing that the subsidies violated "the principle of equality in public taxation" (*Tico Times*, Feb. 8, 1991, pp. 1, 22). Suddenly, a critical incentive for nontraditional exporters evaporated; although it was soon restored, no new CATs were granted after 1993. In 1991 the government promised to end the CATs program in 1996, but later it postponed the expiration date until 1999.[33] Nontraditional exports have clearly diminished the country's vulnerability to the brusque fluctuations that long characterized primary product markets, such as those for coffee and bananas. Thus far, though, they tend to be low value-added activities that generate low-wage employment and contribute only marginally to sustained and autonomous processes of accumulation.

Costa Rica's early "success" with nontraditional exports also paradoxically threatened its edge over neighboring countries in attracting new investment. The country's new insertion in international markets was based on abundant cheap labor and fertile soil, as well as on an institutional context that hindered labor organization, provided guarantees for capital, and failed to regulate the intensive agrochemical use that accompanies the "agriculture of change." But as other, lower-wage Central American countries followed Costa Rica's lead in the late 1980s and early 1990s, they competed to develop the same comparative advantages and to supply foreign markets with the same kinds of products. Instead of fostering comparative advantages based on human capital investment and the constant technical innovation necessary to survive and prosper in today's world, Costa Rica has become—at great cost to its people—a tragically passive player in an increasingly integrated and competitive world.

The crowning irony of Costa Rica's experience with neoliberalism is that—despite the 1990 Brady Plan arrangement—it has not brought more than a momentary reduction of total debt; indeed, overall debt is roughly the same in the mid-1990s as it was in the early crisis year of 1982. Clearly the country is now in a better position to meet its obligations. But faced with volatile markets for key nontraditional exports and an ongoing balance-of-payments deficit—themselves signs of the model's limits—Costa Rican governments have had to continue on the international financial institutions' treadmill, seeking new credits to cover old ones, promising new cuts in public-sector spending, and delivering only the most fragile and uneven of recoveries. Proponents of the new loans argue that most are low-interest, medium- and long-term multilateral credits, with generous grace periods. But with debt still at high levels, many macroeconomic targets unfulfilled, a majority with diminished access to social services, one-fifth of the population stubbornly mired in poverty, and erratic growth in the most dynamic sectors after more than a decade of stabilization and adjustment, Costa Rica is hardly an unambiguous free-market success story.

(*Above*) "Agricultural products are those that generate the country's foreign exchange." UPANACIONAL supporters, 1983. (Courtesy of the Centro Nacional de Acción Pastoral)

(*Below*) The 1986 peasant march turns into a riot. (Courtesy of the Archivo Nacional de Costa Rica)

(*Above*) Riot police attack the 1986 peasant march. (Archivo Nacional de Costa Rica)

(*Below*) Tear gas in the streets of San José, 1986. (Archivo Nacional de Costa Rica)

(*Opposite, above*) Demonstrators eat on the Cathedral steps following the 1987 peasant march in San José. (Centro Nacional de Acción Pastoral)

(*Opposite, below*) ASPPAS village committee representatives, 1988. *Left*, ASPPAS president Higinio Rodríguez; *standing*, in cap, Ezequiel Gómez; *right*, in striped shirt, Marcos Ramírez. (Centro Nacional de Acción Pastoral)

(*Above*) "Vertical production, horizontal organization." Cooperative members march in Santa Bárbara de Santa Cruz, 1988. (Centro Nacional de Acción Pastoral)

(*Below*) "For the right to production, labor, life." Blocking the highway in Santa Cruz, June 1988. (Centro Nacional de Acción Pastoral)

(*Opposite, above*) Blocking the railroad tracks in Guácimo, June 1988. (Centro Nacional de Acción Pastoral)

(*Opposite, middle*) Rural Guards advance on the "Muni," June 1988. (Courtesy of *La Nación*)

(*Opposite, below*) A peasant assembly in Veintisiete de Abril, Santa Cruz, 1988. (Photo by the author)

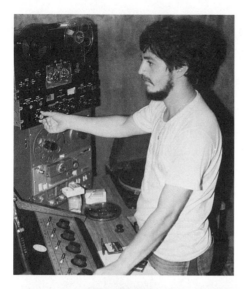

(*Opposite, above, left*) "In jail, we'll eat cement," 1988. (Photo by the author)

(*Opposite, above, right*) "Arrested for being an agriculturalist," 1988. (Photo by the author)

(*Opposite, below*) Cacao producers march for better production conditions, 1989. (Centro Nacional de Acción Pastoral)

(*Above*) "This is Radio Santa Clara. . . ." Broadcasting a *campesino* program, 1990. (Centro Nacional de Acción Pastoral)

(*Below*) Agriculture Minister José María Figueres addresses UPANACIONAL's 1989 Congress. UPANACIONAL leader Guido Vargas is in the white hat. (Centro Nacional de Acción Pastoral)

(*Above*) Payment for lost crops, 1990.
(Centro Nacional de Acción Pastoral)
(*Below*) Packing organic ginger for export,
1991. (Centro Nacional de Acción Pastoral)

CHAPTER 2

"Iron Fist in a Kid Glove": Peasants Confront the Free Market

We must stay the course, come hell or high water. . . . Every step back
sends the wrong message to economic actors, politicians and the general public. Certainly, we feel free to speak our minds in meetings, we
invite dialogue in seminars, we take part in roundtable discussions, we
smile and laugh, we tell jokes, and we even act very nice. Underneath
this smiling facade, however, we stand unshakable on our few selected
objectives and never think twice. The iron fist is always there, neatly
encased in its kid glove. In economic policy, unlike military strategy,
bridges must always be burned.

—EDUARDO LIZANO, *Director of the Costa Rican Central Bank, 1984–
90 (Lizano 1991, 26)*

In Costa Rica, as elsewhere, the rush to free-market policies caused a crisis
of legitimacy for the state and left opponents of adjustment policies grasping
for coherent political and economic alternatives. This chapter examines the
peasant movements that emerged in the era of economic stabilization and adjustment. It looks at how different regional and organizational experiences
eventually converged and converted the peasantry into the sector most active in the struggle against structural adjustment policies.

While Costa Rican political parties had long sponsored peasant federations that engaged in struggles for land, the crisis of the early 1980s fueled
the growth of new kinds of independent small producers organizations that
challenged key elements of the emerging economic model.[1] In contrast to the
older federations, these new groups went beyond the simple quest for land
to cultivate. The old agrarianism had emphasized "invasions," or "recupera-
tions" (as peasants often expressed it), of underutilized properties and insisted on attention from the state agrarian reform agency (IDA). The new
small producers organizations, in contrast, raised a broader and more sophisticated set of demands regarding price supports, input subsidies, inter-

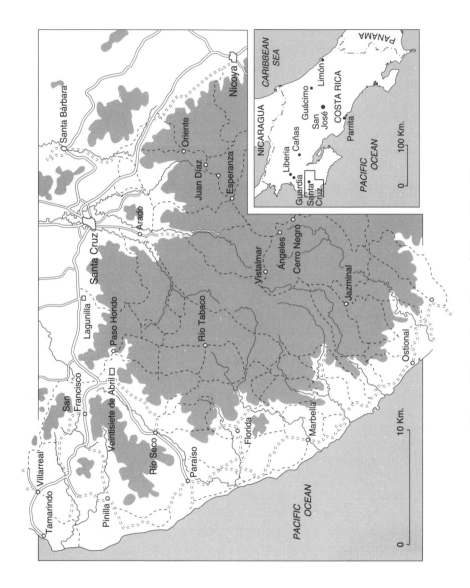

Map 1. Western Santa Cruz and Nicoya, Costa Rica

est rates, crop insurance, marketing mechanisms, and technical assistance, among others.

Initially, inflationary shocks played a pivotal role in the emergence of these new organizations, although by the mid- to late 1980s, when the peasant movement reached its peak, the inflation rate had subsided and was quite low by Latin American standards.[2] Between 1979 and 1981, however, prices for imported agricultural inputs skyrocketed by some 600 percent; this alone contributed to raising average production costs by 310 percent. During the same period, wholesale prices for food crops rose only 180 percent (Villasuso et al. 1984, 65). This "scissors crisis" most affected production for the domestic market, but it also offset significantly the gains that might otherwise have accrued to export producers from the currency devaluation.[3]

The First Protests

The first organized political response to this price squeeze came from small onion producers around Tierra Blanca, a community of some 4,500 inhabitants on the cool upper slopes of the Irazú volcano, 2,100 meters above sea level and a dozen kilometers up a narrow winding road from Cartago, Costa Rica's colonial capital. Rich soils deposited by the still active volcano, several large and small rivers, and abundant and reliable rain make the area extraordinarily well endowed for onion and potato production. In early 1981, as the value of the colón plummeted and inflation mounted, agriculturalists from Tierra Blanca and nearby communities traveled to the Panamanian border to physically prevent both legal and contraband onion imports, which they claimed would cause them further ruin. Like agrarian activists in the early stages of organization in other times and places, the protesters displayed a mixture of challenge to, and respect for, legal authority that complicates any characterization of them as radicals or rebels. Some dumped toxic agrochemicals into trucks, forcing importers to throw the onions away, while others marshaled supporters in the Civil Guard and the Judicial Police (Organismo de Investigación Judicial, or OIJ), who helped detect and arrest onion smugglers.[4]

By mid-1981, Cartago onion and potato producers, together with allies from throughout Costa Rica's central plateau, had formed the National Union of Small and Medium Agricultural Producers (Unión Nacional de Pequeños y Medianos Productores Agropecuarios, or UPANACIONAL) to pressure the overnment for relief. In August, the new peasant union marched on the Casa Presidencial in San José, calling for a refinancing of members' debts, more favorable terms for future loans, formal representation in the National Banking System, fertilizer and fuel price freezes, better quality control for inputs, provision of agricultural insurance for vegetable crops, and measures to end contraband onion imports (agrarian reform was conspicuously absent from the list, a reflection of UPANACIONAL's base among small proprietors). On October 1, the government increased fertilizer prices by 55 percent, and four weeks later UPANACIONAL staged another march on the capital with a wider list of demands. The day after the demonstration, as if to drive home the futility of peaceful protest, the government boosted fertilizer prices again, this time by 65 percent (Cartín and Castro 1986, 20–23). UPANACIONAL supporters then massed inside the Legislative Assembly, hoping to gain support for a reduction in the tax on earnings exporters received as a result of the difference between the free-market exchange rate and the overvalued official rate (a demand which ironically was not very different from subsequent IMF-sponsored measures to "unify" market and official exchange rates).

By December, with its key demands still unaddressed, UPANACIONAL's members decided to stage a producers' "strike" (*paro*).[5] On December 15, some 5,000 agriculturalists blocked eight key highways on the periphery of the *meseta central* and prevented food from reaching the urban areas until the government agreed to negotiate their demands for a fertilizer price freeze, improved credit conditions from the nationalized banks, and measures to regulate chaotic perishable produce markets.[6] "We had left everything prepared," one participant in the highway blockade remembered.

> Since we cook with wood, we left wood in the houses and a little money and some goods, rice and beans and potatoes and all those things. We were ready for sure, prepared to die. And the family was prepared for all that. But thanks to God it didn't happen that way. . . . The families sent us food at Ochomogo [near Cartago] where the blockade was. Many people supported us. They came in buses and congratulated us. Because they had to transfer buses there [from one side of the blockade to the other]. "It's a sacrifice," they said, "but we applaud you." And the teachers, some of the priests too, supported us a lot.[7]

Protesters went to the highway blockade ready to spend up to a month, but as it turned out the government agreed to negotiate after only five hours.[8] Almost immediately, the Legislative Assembly approved the changes in the currency law (Ley de la Moneda) that UPANACIONAL had demanded and the union then agreed to suspend its "strike," even though other issues remained unresolved (Cartín and Castro 1986, 23).

Despite these tumultuous beginnings, UPANACIONAL rapidly emerged as the most moderate of the new peasant organizations. It had its social base among a sector of peasants that had been, like those anthropologist Arturo Warman (1972) described in central Mexico, "the regime's favored children." Located in the densely populated central plateau, these producers had benefited more than most other rural residents from the tremendous social welfare advances of the previous five decades. As owners of small but highly productive properties close to urban markets, they did not have to rely for survival on stints of labor in the lowland banana plantations, and in general they had little experience with (or need for) unions or other popular organizations. Most of the leaders, however, and a large proportion of the membership, belonged to cooperatives, especially purchasing groups for agricultural chemicals and crop processing and marketing associations (Cartín and Castro 1986, 11). While the local focus, commercial nature, and legal charters of cooperatives impeded them from engaging in political action, thus requiring a separate union for any efforts to pressure as an interest group, the long history of state backing for the cooperative sector facilitated contacts with both public-sector institutions, such as INFOCOOP (Instituto Nacional de Fomento Cooperativo) and with local and national politicians.

Ideologically, most UPANACIONAL supporters were intensely anti-Communist. Although the union was nonpartisan and eschewed ties with organized parties, most of its members were enthusiastic backers of Costa Rica's social democratic development model.[9] Cartago, where the movement began, was historically the country's most conservative and devoutly Catholic province (and, characteristically, the individual usually credited with the idea of forming UPANACIONAL attributes his inspiration to divine intervention).[10] These factors ultimately made government functionaries somewhat less suspicious of UPANACIONAL, and more inclined to negotiate differences, than was the case with more militant peasant organizations (Román 1993, 188).

That this historically privileged sector of the rural population was the first to protest deteriorating conditions might be viewed as a measure of the severity of the economic crisis, as the result of a sudden fall from grace, or as a vindication of theories about the key role of "middle peasants" in agrarian movements (e.g., Wolf 1969, 289–94). While all these elements clearly came into play, it is probably more revealing to examine the particular factors that led the previously quiescent Cartago peasantry to mobilize. Prices for onions and potatoes, the Cartago agriculturalists' principal crops, unlike those for coffee and basic grains, were highly unstable; government intervention in the market consisted of occasional imports in periods of high prices rather than supporting producer prices.[11] Agriculturalists closely followed price variations in different regions and frequently traveled the length and breadth of Costa Rica in their own or hired trucks to take advantage of favorable conditions in distant markets. This pattern of geographic mobility, unusual for the more prosperous peasants in highland Costa Rica, gave the Cartago agriculturalists connections with counterparts throughout the central plateau. Since many small coffee producers also grew tomatoes, cucumbers, and other perishable crops, this regionwide network of contacts among vegetable farmers also linked the Cartago activists to Costa Rica's most important export sector, which was hurting after a sudden drop in world prices in 1979.

Many peasants viewed any union as a "dangerous, Communist thing," and the political conservatism of UPANACIONAL's constituency initially complicated organizing.[12] In Cartago, as elsewhere, new agriculturalists organizations eschewed the label *sindicato*, or union, in favor of other names not associated with the Marxist left, such as *unión* (not precisely equivalent to its English cognate) or *asociación*. Ultimately, tightly knit networks of relatives and close friends in the small, residentially stable villages around Cartago provided secure forums for discussion and sources of trusted recruits.[13] Priests sympathetic to the organization used the mass to allay political fears, and local radio stations spread the message of unity. The religiosity of UPANACIONAL's supporters appears to have infused the early movement with almost millenarian qualities. One organizer recalled arriving with a small group in communities in the western central plateau:

> It was like a party. They received us with pork tamales and music and many expressions of affection. They felt as if this was going to be the solution. It was like in the Bible when the Jews were told, "Here is salvation." We were part of the solution, and they gave us great demonstrations of happiness.

UPANACIONAL could not, of course, provide deliverance from the terrible uncertainties of the economic crisis, but it did achieve some notable successes, even in its first years. In 1981 the union circumvented intermediaries by purchasing wholesale large quantities of inputs (seed, chemicals, etc.) and selling them at cost to members. It also convinced legislators to allocate funds for a fertilizer subsidy and to authorize the creation of a peasant-controlled marketing company for perishable products.[14] Within two years, UPANACIONAL obtained social security coverage for its members, preferential loan rates for small- and medium-size agriculturalists, and reductions in fertilizer prices. By 1984, the organization had twelve thousand dues-paying members grouped in some 35 sections throughout the *meseta central*, as well as in some outlying zones in the north and south (Hernández Cascante 1990b, 12–15).

Militant Alternatives

While UPANACIONAL, centered in highland coffee and vegetable farming regions, came to be the country's largest peasant union, another type of organization emerged in the peripheral lowland zones.[15] Beginning in the mid-1970s, a trickle of urban-to-rural migrants, many children or grandchildren of *campesinos*, left the cities and took up residence in impoverished lowland regions distant from the central plateau. They were part of a generation that had experienced rapid geographical and social mobility and that was profoundly influenced by the anti-imperialism and internationalism of the Cuban revolution and the 1960s New Left. Many had participated in student movements, such as the massive demonstrations and riots against the bauxite concessions given to the aluminum multinational ALCOA that rocked San José in 1970.[16] Some who later came to be prominent leaders of agriculturalists organizations initially had ties to the Revolutionary Peoples Movement (Movimiento Revolucionario del Pueblo, or MRP), a small ultraleft party that, inspired by events elsewhere in Central America, sent cadres to build a base of support in the countryside.[17] In a few instances young migrants from central Costa Rica helped to found large and militant unions of agricultural laborers, small producers, and landless peasants.

Wilson Campos, a tall, sandy-haired activist, participated as a teenager in an UPANACIONAL chapter in the vegetable farming community where he grew up in the highlands above the city of Heredia. In a 1990 interview, he recalled his own political evolution and the more complex motives that led him to abandon the relative comfort of the central plateau for a difficult life in the northern Guatuso lowlands:

> It's a question of one's beliefs. I come from a *campesino* family and always worked a lot with my father. And I'm a Christian too. . . . So I was always a producer, of string beans, vegetables. My *papá* helped me to study and chose me to

go to the university, the only one of the children who was chosen. I spent two
years in the University of Costa Rica, part of a generation very involved in the
people's struggles. . . . We were linked to the left then and struggled against the
Somoza dictatorship in Nicaragua and the war in El Salvador. . . . Already in
high school I was very involved in the struggle. . . . Then I went north and my
compañeros in Santa Bárbara [de Heredia]—we had formed a group, planning to
all go to the north eventually—helped me a lot economically. . . . I took advantage of a government job, with the Health Ministry, when I first went. Guatuso
is a very marginal zone. The problems were serious: there wasn't even a road. . . .
For two thousand families there weren't even one hundred latrines. . . . I was 22
years old and I had married very young too.

The early and mid-1980s, apart from the severe economic crisis, were especially difficult years along the country's northern border. "I was marked as
a Communist leader," Campos commented.

At that time there was a terrible war in Nicaragua. To form a group of *campesinos* in Guatuso provided an argument for saying that we were collaborators of
the Sandinista Front, that we were Communists, that we wanted to mess things
up. . . . In Upala [a canton adjacent to Guatuso], one *campesino* leader, Antonio
Mendoza, was murdered by the *contras*. The cattlemen contracted a *contra*
group [to kill him]. In that time, when someone died violently in the northern
zone, it was said that it was because of a confrontation between the *contras* and
those who supposedly collaborated with the Sandinista Front. . . . Many times
we found abandoned [*contra*] camps, parachutes in the woods, it's very good
cloth. And I, at least, received various death threats. The *contras* would send papers which had a phrase "we're going to party" [*vamos de fiesta*], which signified an attack, a murder in this case.[18]

Campos survived the threats, participated in numerous land occupations,
and went on to found the Peasant Union of Guatuso (Unión de Campesinos
de Guatuso, or UCADEGUA) in 1985.[19] Within a year, UCADEGUA obtained social security coverage for its members and had a daily radio program on a local station belonging to the Catholic Church and administered
by a sympathetic priest of peasant origin. The organization continued to back
land invasions, but it also initiated a major program (with support from the
Canadian and Costa Rican governments) to build latrines and potable water
systems. It was, said Campos, "a more integral struggle: for land, for production, for marketing, for health, for *campesino* culture, and for a different
concept of solidarity."

The Struggle on the Atlantic Coast

The Atlantic Region Small Agriculturalists Union (Unión de Pequeños Agricultores de la Región Atlántica, or UPAGRA), led by Carlos Campos, a charismatic former engineering student from San José, was by far the most successful rural organizing effort initiated by the MRP.[20] Founded in 1978 in the Atlantic zone canton of Guácimo, UPAGRA first waged a concerted struggle with the national grain board (Consejo Nacional de Producción, or CNP) on behalf of maize farmers who sought higher prices, more timely payment, and an end to corrupt practices such as short-weighing and excessive charges for humid or dirty grain. This effort, which extracted significant concessions from the government, gained the union a wide constituency among smallholding peasants around Guácimo. Many of these peasants were workers who had been laid off from the region's large banana plantations and who, owning no land, had to rely on renting or squatting to survive as agriculturalists. In part to address the needs of these land-hungry peasants and in part, as some leaders subsequently conceded, to keep UPAGRA "alive" after the "euphoria" of the "triumph" in the struggle over maize prices, the organization began to study the possibility of occupying some of the unused properties in its area of influence.

In 1979 UPAGRA supporters invaded a large underutilized cattle ranch belonging to Ganadera Industrial Neguev, located precisely at the point where the union had its greatest concentration of supporters, in the village of El Hogar (Rivera Sánchez 1991, 30–31).[21] Initially, the police expelled the "invaders," burning their crops and huts. But within a year, the Neguev occupation led the state to expropriate and distribute parcels to many of the peasants. It also, however, brought UPAGRA into a long-term conflict with the agrarian reform agency, which tried to bar many peasants from receiving official recognition of the plots they occupied, or which required them to make sizable payments to cover titling, the cost of the land, and other agency expenses (see Anderson 1990a, 106–7). In 1982, the government charged, with little evidence, that the Neguev settlement had become an MRP guerrilla center (*La Nación*, July 15, 1982, p. 1).

Official hysteria about leftist peasant unions fed on stepped-up, though often uncritical, intelligence gathering, as well as on growing polarization and violence in Costa Rica and elsewhere in Central America. Nonetheless, it missed a central irony in the internal politics of the organizations. The leaders of the most durable MRP-sponsored groups, in particular UPAGRA, while originally countenancing the discipline of a centrally controlled party, invariably decided after having spent five or more years in the countryside that their constituencies' real interests could only be served by genuine organizational autonomy.

To some extent, the impetus for organizational independence derived from the long and bitter history of political parties' manipulation and control of popular movements. But it also reflected a realization that peasant organization representatives without political party loyalties would be in a stronger position in negotiations with the government. In any case, by the early 1980s, the organized Left began to disintegrate, despite the harsh economic crisis.[22] An official union history commented on this in 1985 with barely concealed disdain. UPAGRA, it said, was

> born in the heat of a struggle by five thousand maize agriculturalists in 1978. At that time, we had interference and recommendations from a political party [the MRP]. When in 1981 we opted for our total independence, our organization began to grow. Today we are proud of our political independence and of being builders of the future that we want. Our wish to do things well—well for the producers and for the people who believe in us—made the party's interests collide with those of the organization. We were warned that we had to have the guidance of a vanguard party, because without it we would lose perspective and disappear. Today the party has disappeared and UPAGRA exists.[23] (UPAGRA 1985, 2, quoted in Mora Alfaro 1987, 157–58)

Small Producers and the "Agriculture of Change"

Beginning in 1985, the government's economic structural adjustment program radically changed the macroeconomic rules of the game for agricultural producers, peasants and large farmers alike. In spite of official enthusiasm about "nontraditional exports"—which President Oscar Arias termed "the agriculture of change" (*la agricultura de cambio*)—most Costa Rican smallholders, lacking capital and technical and administrative expertise, found it difficult or impossible to participate in the new development strategy.[24] Those who did frequently experienced devastating losses when markets turned out to be glutted (e.g., with cassava, cardamom, and various root crops), or when crop diseases struck (e.g., with cacao). Indeed, Costa Rican capital in general faced stiff competition from transnational companies. A confidential 1988 report of the Banco Nacional de Costa Rica noted that foreigners owned 40 percent of the macadamia area, 80 percent of the citrus area, 46 percent of the pineapple area, 80 percent of the area in ornamental ferns, and 52 percent of the area in flowers (*La República*, Oct. 28, 1988, p. 2).

The stabilization and adjustment process of the mid- to late 1980s also coincided with vastly increased flows of U.S. food aid (Garst 1990; Garst and Barry 1990). Driven by both geopolitical and strictly commercial considerations, Washington began exporting grain to Costa Rica in 1982 under Title I of PL-480. This "Food for Peace" program, intended to win goodwill abroad and to reduce agricultural surpluses in the United States, provided soft credits to finance grain purchases. Importing countries not only benefited from balance-of-payments savings, but also resold the U.S. products at market prices to domestic agroindustries, thus generating local currency that became part of government budgets. PL-480 agreements, however, specified which agencies and programs could receive this budgetary support, thus in effect establishing a new kind of external conditionality like that of the World Bank or IMF.

The flood of "food aid" after 1982 had several deleterious consequences for Costa Rican grain producers: (1) consumers increasingly substituted products derived from imported wheat for domestically produced maize and rice; (2) U.S. "dumping" of yellow maize and sorghum led to the virtual elimination first of credit and then of actual production, even while demand from the poultry feed industry was expanding rapidly; (3) rice credit was restricted to irrigated farms (in part because of drought-induced crop losses); (4) credit for bean production also plummeted, dropping in 1989 to onequarter of the 1985 level (Torres and Alvarado 1990, 37); and (5) local currency generated by PL-480 sales to flour mills and feed concentrate factories went to programs that further advanced the export-oriented "agriculture of change" at the expense of domestic food production.[25]

In 1985 three key agreements sparked alarm among Costa Rican maize producers. In March the government presented a letter of intent to the IMF, one of the first formal steps in negotiating new short-term credits. In characteristically antiseptic language, the document specified that Costa Rica was "taking steps to adjust the prices of the basic grains purchased by the National Production Council (CNP), with the purpose of reducing to the minimum its internal financial needs" (in Céspedes et al. 1985, 231). The following month the government published the text of SAL I, Costa Rica's first World Bank structural adjustment loan program. Echoing the government's letter of intent to the IMF, SAL I committed Costa Rica to a "revision of the system of incentives . . . so that prices of agricultural products will approximate international [prices]." It also established that research and extension would be "oriented to support new export activities" (Ibid., 211).[26] Finally, in November, USAID and the Costa Rican government signed a new accord governing the sale to Costa Rica of 120,000 metric tons of U.S. wheat and flour and 10,000 metric tons of yellow maize.[27] The agreement required Costa Rica to adopt all possible measures to prevent the export of these grains or of any product derived from them. Like the IMF and World Bank pacts, it also committed Costa Rica to the elimination of all subsidies for basic grains. "Paradoxically," as one critic noted, "the Costa Rican government accepts an imposition that Reagan's own government is not willing to adopt, for fear of the political upheaval it could produce in North American society. Third world producers pay the political price of the subsidy given to the North American agriculturalists" (Gamboa 1986, 5).[28]

By July 1986, the implications of the IMF, World Bank, and USAID agreements became clear on the ground. Economy Minister Luis Diego Escalante announced the government's decision to diminish bean support prices by 25 percent and to eliminate completely the support price for yellow maize for the remainder of 1986 and for 1987. The white maize support price would be maintained as long as any losses resulting from export sales of excess production at lower international prices were shared between the CNP and the producers. Eventually, however, Escalante noted, all subsidies for the agricultural sector would have to go. These would be compensated, he claimed, by making available new loans for small producers of nontraditional export crops and by opening new markets abroad (Gaete, Garro, and Rivera 1989, 20–21). Nonetheless, the share of bank credit to the private sector channeled to agriculture dropped from 16 percent in 1985 to 12 percent in 1987, while the share for "small producer" loans, with lower interest rates, plummeted from 4 to 2 percent (BCCR 1988). The nominal total allocated to small agriculturalists had diminished only slightly since the beginning of the decade—from 3,645.6 million colones in 1980 to 3,381.4 million colones in 1985; but in dollar terms this represented a decline from $346.5 million to $66.6 million (BCCR 1986, 21).[29] To make matters worse, bank estimates of operating costs failed to keep pace with inflation, in effect requiring loan applicants to have other sources of capital.

Increasingly, in the maize producing regions of Costa Rica, disincentives for basic grain production led smallholding agriculturalists to link the threatened peasant objective of producing the household's food with national food security, or "food sovereignty" (*soberanía alimentaria*). The nation became, in the eyes of many, a rural household writ large, unable to meet its consumption needs, with its survival in jeopardy.[30] The conspicuous foreign presence in the new export sectors and the knowledge that painful economic shifts resulted in part from the demands of international lending and aid agencies generated additional resentment. The reformist state derived part of its legitimacy from protecting smallholding grain producers with subsidized credit, guaranteed purchase of crops at supported prices, and generous technical assistance programs. With "the agriculture of change," it betrayed expectations of benevolence developed over more than four decades.

UPANACIONAL, the politically moderate smallholders union, issued a joint statement in mid-1986 with several large producers organizations (*cámaras*) that reflected these concerns: "Nobody can guarantee that if we stop producing foodstuffs that in the future we will be able to obtain them at prices lower than our production costs or, even worse, if there will be a secure supply" (quoted in Vermeer 1990, 53).

Ten other organizations, led by the radical Atlantic zone union UPAGRA, presented a petition to President Oscar Arias demanding that cuts in support prices and in credit for maize and beans be rescinded and lamenting "the absence of the most minimal orientation in agrarian matters, as well as the effects of the profound economic crisis which batters our people" (quoted in Sibaja 1986, 17). They closed saying that they would come to San José on September 17 to receive the president's response in person, revealing at once both their desperation and their tacit assumption that Costa Rican politicians were at least somewhat open and accessible, even in times of crisis.[31]

On September 17, 1986, some one thousand members of UPAGRA and allied groups, including many women and children, marched on San José, calling for better production conditions and for "the right to continue being producers."[32] Specifically, they demanded government support for raising the productivity of small producers, a guaranteed profit margin that reflected their higher costs, increased allocations of affordable credit, and changes in the CNP's "punishment table" (*tabla de castigo*), which enumerated the penalties assessed for grain with high levels of moisture or contaminants. Initially, the marchers headed toward the Casa Presidencial in the southeastern barrio of Zapote, hoping to be received by the president, but police blocked their way. They then turned toward the center of San José and sat down in the middle of the Avenida Central, across from the Central Bank. There, inside, as one march leader put it, was bank director Eduardo Lizano, "one of the people responsible for imposing the policies of the International Monetary Fund, which crush [*estrujan*] the neediest classes" (quoted in *La*

Nación, Sept. 18, 1986, p. 10A). Riot police ordered the marchers to disperse, and after a three-hour standoff they attacked with clubs and tear gas.

Célimo Vargas had come to the march from Río Jiménez, an UPAGRA stronghold on the outskirts of Guácimo. "At first everything was very nice there in the march," don Célimo remembered.

> Then suddenly the gases came, at the corner of [Radio] Monumental, and I became frightened, because I thought that they were shooting, because a gas grenade struck a window above me and glass was falling all over. I started to run, everyone was running. And there were two huge clouds of smoke, smoke here and smoke there. We had to run toward the ice cream store, but they were also shooting [gas grenades] at the corner of the ice cream store. . . . I remembered that I had an orange in my shirt pocket, already peeled, so I grabbed it, dried it on my handkerchief and I put it on my eyes. I crossed toward the park and I ran into another group [of demonstrators] and they said to me, "Let's go to the Cathedral."

After the first onslaught, some demonstrators responded by throwing rocks and sticks at either the police or the Central Bank.[33] The police arrested thirteen. Most, though, simply ran and sought sanctuary in the Cathedral. One young *campesino* from Limón who took refuge in the Cathedral recalled:

> We were there three days and they jerked us around. . . . They made a book there, which I still have, called the Maize Development Plan, *El Plan de Fomento Maicero* was born there.[34] And the truth is I was really enthused, because . . . the Bishop committed himself to the *campesinos*, that he was going to resolve the problem, and Margarita [Penón de Arias, the first lady] arrived speaking very nicely. But she said one thing that I have never forgotten. She said, "Oscar and I are good people, we want to help you, but we can't." So in other words she said a lot: that they aren't the ones in command of this country.

The brutality of the police action, mild by Central American standards but drastic for Costa Rica, as well as the news media's pictures of peasants forced to seek sanctuary in the Cathedral, shocked even those Costa Ricans unsympathetic to the agriculturalists' demands. For the peasants, the assault on the march and the broken promises made in the Cathedral became key symbols of their new adversarial relation with the government. The largely accurate perception that even a well-intentioned president was helpless in the face of the international financial institutions contributed to a growing sense of desperation and rising militance.

Negotiating Agrarian Questions

President Oscar Arias found addressing the agrarian question in many ways more intractable than resolving military conflicts in the rest of Central America—for which he won the 1987 Nobel Peace Prize. Indeed, Arias's close advisors have pointed out that his administration could not simultaneously oppose Washington's free-market economic policies and its war against Sandinista Nicaragua. Arias stood firm against the Reagan administration's determination to base thousands of Nicaraguan *contras* on Costa Rican soil. But he had to attempt to mollify U.S. policymakers by accepting their economic policy recommendations, including the banking, pricing, and budgetary reforms that had so angered peasant maize producers (Honey 1994, 89–90).

In Arias's four-year term he had three ministers of agriculture, each articulating a greater commitment to economic liberalism and taking a more intransigent stance toward peasant organizations. The agriculture portfolio became known as the "*quema-ministros*" position in Arias's cabinet, a phrase roughly equivalent to "hot seat," but which literally means "minister-burning." [35] Shortly after the September 1986 attack on the peasant demonstrators, the first of these ministers, Alberto Esquivel Volio, granted concessions, canceling planned cuts in support prices for rice and white maize, while maintaining those for yellow maize. He then issued a program for the agricultural sector entitled "A Permanent Dialogue," which declared:

> It is the sacred duty of governors and governed to assure the independence of Costa Rica and the sovereignty of its decisions. The uncertainty that Central America experiences today does not exclude the threat of war. Today, more than ever, it is necessary to jealously guard the independence needed to make decisions based on patriotic values. The country's capacity to supply local consumption strengthens the independence of its decisions. The government's objective, therefore, is to see that all the foodstuffs that Costa Rica might need be produced locally. (MAG 1986, 1)

This discourse of patriotism and self-sufficiency, characteristic of a "neo-developmentalist" current within Arias's cabinet, was coupled with calls for greater efficiency, more exports, and privatization of public-sector companies. It nonetheless did not sit well with advocates of orthodox adjustment policies, particularly Eduardo Lizano, the English-trained economist who was Central Bank director and a favorite of the international lending institutions and USAID. Tensions between neodevelopmentalists and orthodox neoliberals provoked a crisis within the administration that led to Lizano's resignation in March 1987.[36] When Minister Esquivel, apparently victorious, derided "coffee house economists who believe they can fix all the country's problems, but who don't take into account the real social and political situation," the rest of the government's economic team threatened to leave (quoted in Vermeer 1990a, 55). Within weeks, Lizano, a clear target of Esquivel's impolitic outburst, was back in his position and Esquivel was on the street. The neoliberal faction had won the day, very likely with the help of foreign pressure.

Antonio Alvarez Desanti, Esquivel's replacement as agriculture minister, was a young lawyer, with little experience in the countryside, who was still somewhat heterodox in comparison with Lizano and the rest of Arias's economic team. In a 1987 speech entitled "Neoliberalism versus Agricultural Development," he noted that Costa Rica had the sixth highest per-hectare rice yields in the world, and he ridiculed the free marketeers' notion of efficiency.

> They pretend to define efficiency as a function of international prices. We are efficient if we sell cheaper here than abroad and inefficient if it is cheaper to import. This means that the New York or Chicago [Commodities] Exchange determines our efficiency and that Exchange price fluctuations can make us efficient and inefficient various times in a single day. (Alvarez Desanti 1988, 61)

While Alvarez Desanti's sarcasm about neoclassical price theory surely won him no friends among economic policymakers, his real undoing was his aggressive approach to the peasant organizations' demands. On September 15, 1987, on Central American independence day and one year after the police attack on marchers in San José, peasants staged a new demonstration against economic structural adjustment. This time the demonstrators demanded that

> the agreements signed with international financial institutions be reviewed [publicly], because they are an obstacle that prevents the government from meeting its obligations to us and to the Costa Rican people. We Costa Ricans have the right to know to what Costa Rica has committed itself and if that affects our children's future of peace and labor (Comisión Campesina 1987).[37]

The march transpired peacefully, but demonstrators camped out in San José's central park and on the steps of the Cathedral, where some began a hunger strike to protest the government's "lack of seriousness" in negotiations. Something of Minister Alvarez Desanti's manner was suggested by a letter six organizations addressed to the President of the Republic just days after the march. The Minister, they complained, had referred "to peasant leaders in offensive terms, calling them 'ingenuous fools.' His whole style has been absolutely disrespectful, offensive and arrogant (*prepotente*). We consider," they said,

> that the Minister nearly declared war on the peasant organizations in conversations of recent days. When one peasant leader told the Minister that if nothing was achieved in negotiations it would no longer make sense to demonstrate in the capital, the Minister, in what may indicate a lack of self-control inappropriate for someone of his rank and functions, practically challenged (*retó*) the peasant organizations to fight, saying that then they should go to the mountains [like guerrillas] and that the problem could be resolved on that terrain too, because the government was also ready to confront them there. (UNAC et al. 1987)

Despite this inauspicious beginning, negotiations between the Agriculture Ministry and the *campesino* organizations continued in the weeks following the march. The presence of hunger strikers and other demonstrators camped out in downtown San José, as well as brief occupations of the National Production Council's (CNP) offices and the municipal building in the northern canton of Guatuso (CENAP 1988, 20), kept the pressure on the government.[38] By the end of September, Alvarez Desanti announced an agreement with the peasant organizations that would (1) strengthen and make more efficient agricultural sector institutions, such as the CNP, the Agriculture Ministry (MAG), and the agrarian reform institute (IDA); (2) institutionalize the participation of peasant organization representatives in the planning and program implementation of all three organizations; (3) augment the amount of National Banking System credit at subsidized rates for small- and medium-size agriculturalists; (4) commit the MAG to gathering information about drought losses, so that agriculturalists could obtain compensation from the National Agricultural Contigencies Fund (FNCA); (5) take measures to facilitate the acquisition by peasant organizations of a majority of shares in the public-sector fertilizer company (FERTICA); and (6) request from the government copies of all accords with international financial institutions, which would be made available to peasant leaders, whose comments and recommendations would then be conveyed by the Agriculture Minister to unspecified "high functionaries" within 45 days (*La Nación*, Sept. 30, 1987, p. 5A; Primer Encuentro Campesino 1987). This apparent victory for the peasant organizations did not, however, augur well for a solution to the crisis, since both sides recognized that the Agriculture Minister had made commitments that he was not empowered to carry out.

Allies and Adversaries

Planning for the 1986 and 1987 marches had involved growing levels of coordination between peasant organizations in different parts of the country, as well as with urban supporters in the unions and universities, many of whom hawked 10-colón "bonds" to support the protests. While the 1986 demonstration had been largely limited to UPAGRA and its close allies, the following year saw the participation of a broader range of organizations, including FESIAN, the rural workers union linked to the ruling social democratic National Liberation Party, or PLN (CENAP 1988, 51), and many other groups that one organizer said "we had never even heard of before."

UPANACIONAL, however, with its ten thousand members in the central plateau region, had remained officially on the margins (although many of its members marched as individuals in the 1987 protest). Indeed, invoking traditional Latin American notions of gender roles, some UPANACIONAL leaders impugned the masculinity of UPAGRA activists who had placed women and children in harm's way by bringing them to the 1986 San José demonstration. But even though UPANACIONAL had not participated in the 1987 demonstration, it nonetheless took advantage of the government's apparent weakness in the post-march period to negotiate reductions in the taxes levied on small coffee producers (Hernández Cascante 1990, 17–18).

This continuing split between UPANACIONAL and UPAGRA and its allies went beyond negotiating tactics and vying for the attention of government officials to a broader contest over authenticity which employed potent symbols of rusticity and traditionalism. UPANACIONAL's general secretary, for example, always appeared in public wearing a white, wide-brimmed canvas hat of the kind that Costa Rican newspaper cartoonists invariably placed on "genuine" peasants. This not only symbolized his own rural roots, but served as a silent rebuke to rival organizations' leaders, who in the city sported designer jeans and bomber jackets and whose credentials as agriculturalists by implication were "less authentic." UPANACIONAL leaders' frequent references to themselves and their organization as "democratic," while at face value innocuous, employed a code word that is immediately understood in Costa Rican political discourse. These remarks claimed legitimacy by identifying with hallowed Costa Rican liberal democratic traditions,

while at the same time insinuating that other leaders were po,
pect ("not *campesinos*, nor agriculturalists," as editorialists of th
tial daily *La Nación* put it on Sept. 19, 1987).

If UPAGRA's relations with the moderates in UPANACIONAL we.
a long time fraught with tension and distrust, those with organized la
producers paradoxically proved easier, at least in late 1987 and 1988. Crisis
induced indebtedness and decapitalization had not only affected smallholders, though the consequences of crop loss and tight credit were most drastic
for this sector. Large ranchers and rice growers had also suffered huge losses
and defaulted on loans. Dryland rice farmers had found their access to credit
slashed in favor of a tiny number of producers with irrigated land, and ranchers—caught in the crunch of stagnant prices and rising interest rates and
production costs—were slaughtering the herd faster than it could reproduce.
Traditionally, large producers groups, or "chambers" (*cámaras*), organized
along narrow sectorial lines, had wielded tremendous influence in the Costa
Rican political system.[39] But with the advent of "the agriculture of change,"
the Federation of Chambers of Cattlemen (Federación de Cámaras de Ganaderos) and the Rice and Basic Grains Chambers (Cámara de Arroceros and
Cámara Nacional de Granos Básicos) found that their traditional methods of
exercising influence were insufficient, and they began to cast around for new
allies.

Both large and small producers stood to gain from any accord with the
banks that would reschedule debts and increase credit to the grains sector, or
from "indemnification" of drought losses.[40] They also had complementary
capacities as pressure groups: the *cámaras*, while representing relatively
small numbers, had long-standing connections in the state and were expert
at political wheeling and dealing, whereas the small agriculturalists' organizations were capable of mobilizing large numbers for marches or other shows
of force. Though agrarian reform constituted an area of potential discord and
mutual suspicion between the two groups, it was not uppermost on either's
political agenda. Moreover, the possibility that large agriculturalists might
pay debts with land that could then be made available to small agriculturalists, through the agrarian reform agency or the banks, reduced tensions
around even this inherently conflictive issue.

Surprisingly, the catalyst for this improbable cross-class alliance was
Agriculture Minister Alvarez Desanti, who once again had misread the extent of rural discontent. In January 1988, he called a meeting of agricultural-
sector representatives, both large producers and peasant organizations, to
present the government's credit program for the coming year. But the in-

vited representatives, instead of accepting the Minister's report, decided then and there to form a pressure group, or "front," that would include the entire agricultural sector. One peasant participant in this meeting, accustomed perhaps to the harsh cane liquor called *guaro*, or to the homemade fermented maize beverage *chicheme*, recalled with amazement the opulence of the conference setting and the minister's ingenuousness: "There, in the office of the Minister of Agriculture, surrounded by cups of wine and whiskey and all the things that they drink, the Minister, together with the large agriculturalists, and the small ones, impelled the formation of the National Union of the Agricultural Sector [Unión Nacional del Sector Agropecuario, or UNSA]."

A few days later some 1,500 agriculturalists gathered for UNSA's first assembly at the Capulín Exhibition Field on the outskirts of the northern town of Liberia, a site that the powerful Guanacaste Cattle Producers' chamber frequently used for livestock shows. UPANACIONAL representatives attended, as did a wide range of producers groups from throughout the country (*La República*, Jan. 8, 1988, p. 4). Less than a week later, 500 delegates from the same producers groups convoked a meeting with Alvarez Desanti at a large restaurant in a San José suburb. When the Minister arrived four hours late, irate agriculturalists prevented him from entering and insisted that he provide immediate information about credit availability and agricultural pricing policy, as well as commit himself to naming a joint UNSA-government task force to find solutions for the crisis. The organization representatives warned him that their members would suspend food shipments to the capital and surrounding cities if the government refused to negotiate issues of debt rescheduling, credit, and support prices. Alvarez Desanti, having underestimated the agriculturalists' rage, beat a hasty retreat. One week later the Guanacaste Chamber of Cattle Producers cut off meat supplies to urban central Costa Rica for three days to demonstrate what might happen on a larger scale if UNSA carried out its threat.

UNSA, though it ultimately proved to be a short-lived marriage of convenience of some thirty large and small producers' organizations, served during the first half of 1988 as a significant pressure group and arguably as a partial, momentary check on government plans to impose further austerity measures (Román et al. 1988). Discrepancies between the diverse forces in the coalition were nonetheless evident from the beginning. UNSA's public declarations and letters to government negotiators veered erratically from the conciliatory tone usually favored by the large producers chambers to the confrontational rhetoric characteristic of UPAGRA and its allies. On June 3,

1988, for example, as tensions heightened throughout the country, UNSA wrote to President Arias:

> Heeding your requests for constructive, Costa Rican–style dialogue, we had set aside any attitude of struggle and pressure, hoping for joint, serious, constructive solutions. Today we are ashamed to see that while we sought such a solution, you and your government redoubled your efforts to assure that current policy would not change, in your eagerness to transform Costa Rica into a domain of the transnationals and big capital. (quoted in Román 1993, 138)

On another occasion, UPAGRA leader Carlos Campos, also a key figure in UNSA, reportedly threatened to march on and "take" San José, a bit of bravado that provoked nervous disavowals from *cámara* representatives (*La Nacion*, Sept. 20, 1988, p. 5A). Eventually, large producers organizations, particularly the cattlemen, found they could still negotiate individually with government and withdrew from UNSA. By the end of 1988, this cross-class coalition, which had inspired so many hopes, was basically moribund.

The perceived commonality of interests between large and small cultivators, however short-lived, nonetheless triggered a politically inspired change in the self-identification of many smallholders. Instead of describing themselves as *campesinos* (peasants), a term that implied small-scale, precarious production conditions and a "rustic" world view, the more politicized smallholders increasingly adopted the scale-neutral and less culturally loaded appellation *agricultor* (agriculturalist). But what began as a neutral label that facilitated an interclass alliance became in a brief time a politically charged badge of pride as the agriculturalists' movement spread to other regions of the country and again confronted the state.

CHAPTER 3

Organizing in "The Cradle of Maize"

The northwestern province of Guanacaste was one region in Costa Rica where the confrontation between the peasants and the state over economic structural adjustment became most acute in the late 1980s. A decade or so earlier, Guanacaste seemed a promising place for establishing a new *campesino* organization. The region had some of the worst poverty and problems of landlessness in the entire country. Squatters frequently invaded cattle ranches and unused *latifundio* properties, hacienda peons and sugarcane cutters formed a huge and destitute rural proletariat, and thousands of Guanacastecans migrated each year to the banana zones, where they participated in Communist-dominated labor struggles (Edelman 1992). Moreover, in the central Costa Rican imaginary, Guanacaste was not only close to, but a lot like Nicaragua, where in 1978–79 a violent revolution against the Somoza dictatorship was under way.

George Rudé, in a discussion of popular protest that has particular resonance in the Guanacastecan case, distinguishes "inherent," or "mother's milk," ideology—based on direct experience or folk-memory—from "derived" ideas, borrowed from others, that "are often a more sophisticated distillation of popular experience and the people's 'inherent' beliefs" (1980, 28–29). The "mother's milk" ideology of Guanacastecan smallholders included an intense commitment to maize culture, and more broadly to the "right to cultivate," as well as a powerful longing for land, particularly among those who were renters, sharecroppers, or squatters rather than proprietors. Nevertheless, as agriculturalists began to organize in the 1980s, land did not figure as a major issue, primarily because the perceived threat to their way of life was not, in an immediate sense, directed at their land but at their ability to make the land produce. Also important, in an alliance that briefly came to include representatives of all strata, from impoverished sharecroppers to millionaire rice farmers, was the fact that land was a distributive and ultimately class-based issue that could only have a divisive impact.

Varied sources of "derived" ideology, some decades old and others more recently arrived, combined with the "mother's milk" attachment to the need and right to cultivate maize and other food crops. In this chapter, I outline the complicated interplay of "inherent" and "derived" ideologies, the age-old "culture of maize," and the terrible synergy between a newly savage market economy and a degraded and increasingly erratic physical environment. I contend that, here at least, peasant mobilization must be explained through precisely this combination of autochthonous hopes and expectations, diverse "outside" ideas and individuals, ecological catastrophe, and free-market onslaught. Naturally, the complexity of this case should suggest, as well, the limitations of relying too closely on narrow "grand theory" paradigms for explanations of how and why real people form social movements.

The Left, Old and New

The peasant movement in Guanacaste had links to the broader *campesino* struggle developing in Costa Rica, but it nonetheless had particular dynamics rooted in regional history and culture and in a multiplicity of organizing efforts. In the mid- to late 1970s, the Revolutionary Peoples Movement (MRP) had devoted considerable resources to unionizing workers on the large sugar plantations in the northwestern province of Guanacaste. Before "the party disappeared" (as UPAGRA's official history, quoted above, put it), its organizers also targeted peasants in the nearby Santa Cruz–Nicoya highlands (see below and Introduction). Attracted by the area's rough terrain, economic marginality, and absence of government authorities, MRP leaders apparently considered the Santa Cruz and Nicoya highlands a promising place to recruit without attracting the attention of elites or security forces. Many high-zone inhabitants worked periodically in the lowland sugar plantations, which the MRP was trying to organize. And—for a group that romanticized guerrilla warfare, engaged in various kinds of quasi-military training exercises, and sent cadres to the Sandinistas' campaign against the Somoza dictatorship—the high zone's proximity to Nicaragua gave it a certain strategic significance if major fighting were to break out in northern Costa Rica (a possibility which might seem outlandish, but was not at all far-fetched in the late 1970s). While few highland residents signed up formally with the MRP, many undoubtedly acquired at least some familiarity with Marxist ideas from the organizers who crisscrossed the area in the years before the MRP's demise in the mid-1980s.

The MRP's efforts built on other militant traditions, some recent and some a half century or more old. Squatters from Costa Rica's central plateau region first settled the forested, uninhabited highlands of Santa Cruz and Nicoya in the 1920s, engaging over the next several decades in protracted struggles with the Sobrados, a family of powerful Spanish landowners who claimed much of the area (Edelman 1992, 269; Schmais 1991). Hamlets with whimsical names—such as Vistalmar ("Sea View"), La Esperanza ("Hope"), and Cola de Gallo ("Rooster's Tail")—had, since the 1940s, struggled independently and through government-organized community associations to have roads built and improved, and to obtain schools and basic services. And even if services remained inadequate and, as residents were prone to remarking, even if the roads were repaired "only every four years during the election campaign so the politicians can come in their Mercedes Benzes," the experience of organized effort had left a body of practical skills and a residual sense of empowerment.

Long before the MRP's organizing drive in the lowland sugar fields and mills, another tendency of the Marxist left had achieved a more profound impact on Guanacaste's rural poor, especially several generations of late-adolescent and young-adult men. Since the early twentieth century, so many Guanacastecan men had migrated to work in the banana regions of Limón and Puntarenas provinces that they and their families and neighbors referred to the plantations familiarly and simply as *"la zona"*—the zone. For some fifty years—from the 1934 banana workers strike until the 1983 division in the Costa Rican Communist Party—the banana plantation unions were among the country's best-organized and most militant. Not surprisingly, the Nicoya Peninsula in Guanacaste, home to so many banana worker migrants, was an area of Communist strength in the 1940s. The village of Ortega de

Santa Cruz and the town of Nicoya were important centers of Communist organizing, as was Las Juntas de Abangares, a mining center in the non-peninsular part of Guanacaste (De La Cruz 1986, 368; Edelman 1992, 177–78). In 1946 the Communist Party (Partido Vanguardia Popular) consisted of eleven geographical "sections," seven of which corresponded to the country's provinces. The canton of Santa Cruz, Guanacaste, merited one of the remaining four, as did the canton of Cañas, near Las Juntas, in the nonpeninsular zone (Miller 1993, 524). In the 1948 civil war, many banana workers from these and other communities fought in the Communist-controlled militias that tried to no avail to defend the government of Teodoro Picado against the insurgent army of José Figueres.

It would not be accurate, however, to assume that participation in Communist-dominated banana workers unions or even the militias of 1948 necessarily produced high levels of political militance among peasant migrants who returned to Guanacaste. For some, long-term work in the banana zones was motivated largely by individualistic dreams of accumulation, by the desire to return home with capital for land, a small store, or a business. For others, driven by concerns with simple survival, migration was a temporary seasonal or life-cycle phenomenon that did not permit their full identification as workers or union members while in "the zone." Few Guanacastecan migrants ever remained active militants on their home turf. In addition to the nonproletarian aspirations which led to their leaving for the plantations, once back home many felt the weight—"the conformism," as they often put it—of small-town life and the immediate pressure of family obligations.

In the mid-1980s, the United Fruit Company closed down its banana operations in southern Puntarenas, generating increased return migration to Guanacaste. This brought large numbers of under- and unemployed young men, many with union experience, back to small villages throughout northwestern Costa Rica. Many, however, were disillusioned and bitter about the organized Left and the unions that had hurled them into poorly prepared, easily defeated strikes. Nevertheless, Guanacastecan peasants' long history of labor movement participation in the banana zones demystified the sources of power and provided the returnees with tools of organization and struggle.

In the mid- to late 1970s, progressive Catholics influenced by liberation theology also came to the Santa Cruz–Nicoya highlands. The Catholic hierarchy in Costa Rica, despite its embrace in the 1940s of progressive Social Christian ideas (see Chapter 1), was skeptical of—and at times distinctly hostile to—the notion that the Church should become actively involved in combating oppression. Following the 1968 Latin American Bishops' Conference at Medellín, Colombia, a number of parish priests, lay activists, and Catholic intellectuals tried nonetheless to exercise the "preferential option for the poor," using the Bible as a guide for understanding contemporary reality and as a goad to action against injustice. In the Santa Cruz–Nicoya high zone, one promoter of this *concientización* process was a young politician who years later became a dogged adversary of the very peasants he had helped to train (see Chapter 4). Jorge Eduardo Pizarro recalled that in the mid-1970s,

> I belonged to the Courses of Christianity movement [Cursillos de Cristiandad], and the Nicaraguan situation was very much in vogue, producing a change of consciousness in Latin America and a different attitude. A group of priests and I, as director of the group, created a change of consciousness in those people up there. With those priests, we trained "delegates of the word," five hundred, more or less. Those are fighting people, capable of entering into combat, into struggle.

While Pizarro's estimate of the number of delegates of the word trained in highland Santa Cruz in the 1970s is almost certainly exaggerated, his appreciation of the change of consciousness of at least some leaders in the small mountain communities is basically accurate. Today, few employ biblical imagery to describe their plight or their organized efforts for change. But the agriculturalists' language—replete in many cases with references to the sanctity of the "humble people" and the suffering that is the destiny of the poor—still betrays a familiarity, however indirect, with liberation theology's dream of realizing God's kingdom on earth.

Middle-Class Farmers Mobilize

Middle-class farmers also organized in Santa Cruz in 1979 and 1980 (Pizarro joined them, too, indicating that, at least in his case, activist energy could be directed in more than one direction). With rising costs for equipment, inputs, insurance, and credit, and stagnant official producer prices, many of these more prosperous agriculturalists were behind in paying off bank loans and were thus unable to obtain new financing that might permit them to continue growing rice, sugar, and other cash crops. Frequently, they were part of, or had close ties to the small-town elites of Santa Cruz and surrounding communities. Like their peasant neighbors, they combined farming with other activities, although these tended to be skilled professional or artisanal work rather than day labor. When they organized a Committee of Guanacastecan Agriculturalists (Comité de Agricultores Guanacastecos) in late 1979, their board of directors included a veterinarian, an agronomist, a saddle maker, and a high school teacher. Only 3 of the Committee's 113 members were women (CAG Actas, Jan. 28, 1980, 18–19); two, however—one a prominent local politician—later headed the new organization's "Sub-Committee on Press and Propaganda."

The Committee's first public action was to place an advertisement in *La Nación*, Costa Rica's largest daily, announcing its formation and making a series of demands on the government. Paid for with dues assessed on a sliding scale, as well as with funds raised from raffles of hens and a heifer, the ad—datelined "Santa Cruz, Folkloric City"—called for refinancing outstanding farm debt at an interest rate no higher than 4 percent and for having the government guarantee loans for those lacking sufficient collateral, something that had earlier been granted to cotton growers.[1] In internal discussions, recorded in a meticulously detailed minutes book, Committee members proposed further demands, including higher subsidies for inputs, improved government technical assistance (especially regarding herbicides for rice, some of which "burned" the crop as well as the weeds), measures to break the "monopoly" of fumigating enterprises, and modification of the state insurance institute's policy of restricting full coverage for rice crops to irrigated zones (see Edelman 1992, 308). Several members made repeated calls for a "general strike," and some described with considerable anguish calls on imprisoned friends and relatives serving long sentences for inability to pay debts.

Although the Committee was resolutely "apolitical," eschewing involvement in elections and ties with organized parties, it nonetheless sought a variety of local and national allies and directed most of its appeals to state functionaries. At the local level, it planned an ambitious schedule of "visits" to outlying communities to inform people of its goals and recruit members. Some participants wanted to enlist support as well from the Catholic bishops and from "the students," who, they said, could be counted on to back any effort to stage a "strike." In March 1980 the group received a high-ranking representative of the Central Bank and Rafael Cordero Croceri, the Minister of the Presidency, who committed himself in writing to a number of steps to facilitate refinancing of debts, insuring of rice crops, and purchasing of fertilizer and fuel at cost. The Minister also promised to bring complaints about poor quality rice seed to the National Production Council and to seek limits from the Ministry of Economy on the profits that could be made from agricultural machinery sales (CAG Actas, Mar. 13, 1980, 85–86).

Around the same time, the Committee established contacts with the radical peasant union UPAGRA, whose secretary general, Rafael Angel Murillo, visited Santa Cruz, seeking support for members arrested in the Atlantic zone (CAG Actas, Mar. 16, 1980, 86–87). Committee President Eduardo Morales Parrales also attended an event in San José called the Assembly of the People (Asamblea del Pueblo). "El Nica" Parrales, as he was always referred to around Santa Cruz, nonetheless reported with chagrin that this "degenerated into an activity of the Communist Party, for which reason he was obliged to retire from the event" (CAG Actas, Mar. 17, 1980, 92).

The Committee of Guanacastecan Agriculturalists ultimately proved to be short-lived, succumbing by mid-1980, several months before the full onset of Costa Rica's economic collapse, to political factionalism, personal jealousies, and accusations of financial malfeasance. Indeed, eight years after its demise, almost everybody in Santa Cruz had largely forgotten about it (except, perhaps, "El Nica" Parrales, veterinarian Frank González, and a few other of its erstwhile leaders). There are several reasons for recalling it briefly here. First, the Committee's experience suggests that while many social movement organizations fall into oblivion, their demands and tactics are often taken up later by new groups. Second, the vehicles for this transmission of social movement practices are frequently individual activists who join one effort and then re-emerge as participants in other, related struggles (only after a close reading of the Committee's 1979–80 minutes did I realize that several of its members were people I met eight years later who were involved in the struggles analyzed in Chapters 3 and 4). Finally, the history of "failed" social movements constitutes a reservoir of experience that marks the tactics and world view informing future efforts, such as the practice of organizing "visits" to outlying villages, the attempts to catch the ear of high-ranking cabinet ministers, and the group's underlying assumption that the state not only should, but *could*, provide amelioration to the agricultural sector. Even when the specific experiences of a particular organization are largely forgotten, individuals' conceptions of how to carry on a struggle often bear their imprint.

The MRP Again

When the Revolutionary People's Movement (MRP) began to organize in the northwest, it doubtless hoped to replicate its earlier success in the Atlan-

tic zone, where UPAGRA had enjoyed startling growth in impact and support. Although the MRP could build on previous activist traditions in Guanacaste, and on contemporary social tensions, it also faced a widespread, vis-
ceral anti-Communism like that manifested in "El Nica" Parrales's remark
about how he had been fooled into attending "the Assembly of the People."
The MRP's greatest accomplishment in Guanacaste was unionizing CATSA,
the state-owned sugar mill near the town of Filadelfia, just north of Santa
Cruz. The MRP-directed cane workers union (Sindicato de Trabajadores de
la Caña, or SITRACAÑA) staged a bitterly fought strike at the height of the
1979 harvest season. Led by Mario Sancho, an MRP organizer from Alajuela
province, outside the region, the labor action at CATSA ultimately gained
little for the workers. The mill's management tripled the number of guards
it employed and acquired mechanical harvesters that constituted a tacit reminder to cane cutters of how dispensable they were and of the futility of
any future work stoppages. After firing the main union activists, it also
founded an employer-worker *solidarista* association, part of a growing movement in Costa Rica that stressed the common interests and interdependence
of labor and capital, while providing employees some concrete benefits in the
form of housing and low-cost loans. Within a couple of years, the cane workers union was dead (Edelman 1992, 280).

The militant SITRACAÑA may have been a flash in the pan, but it reflected an investment of organizational resources that scattered a small but
dedicated corps of political activists—most locals and a few originally outsiders—around central Guanacaste. In one case, a young man who had arrived as an MRP labor organizer in a village near Filadelfia in the late 1970s
settled down and married a local woman, starting a family and participating
in the community development association and a local agricultural cooperative. A number of area residents who had been high-profile SITRACAÑA
supporters either returned to nearby farms (as did the Pueblo Unido organizer I briefly encountered in 1982—see Introduction) or found themselves
blacklisted for years and prevented from obtaining employment in the region.

In most cases when the MRP sent cadres to the countryside, however, its
urbanized intellectuals and activists were unable to withstand the rigors and
tedium of rural life or to rally the peasant masses to their organizations.
Elsewhere in Guanacaste, for example, a young anthropology student acquired a small farm on a back road in the lowlands along the east bank of the
Tempisque River and, after a disappointing experience attempting to organize the local peasantry, returned to the city. The property became a place for

weekend excursions and occasional retreats by groups of recent graduates of the University of Costa Rica's School of Anthropology and Sociology.

The experience of rural cadre building in Guanacaste seemed to come to a grotesque end in 1985, several years after "el M" had disbanded, when a team of its former activists staged an abortive stickup at the Filadelfia branch of the Banco Nacional.[2] After that, the movement was "burned" in the area and its former adherents had to lie low and avoid open involvement in politics.

Even before the bank robbery, however, many peasants' views of the Left parties had already soured. This was not just a result of the defeat of Communist-led strikes in the banana zones in the early 1980s. One Santa Cruz agriculturalist remembered years later (in 1991) that some of the main Guanacaste activists of the 1970s and 1980s had been MRP members and that "when those [MRP] people were involved in the SITRACAÑA business, they did things we didn't think were right. Whenever there was a big assembly, they would go to one of the big farms and steal a steer to roast. 'They're just going to lend us this,' they would say and they would laugh. But we knew that this wasn't right."

Paradoxically, however, the *campesinos* most hostile to, or disillusioned with, the organized Left sometimes became sentimental, recalling earlier experiences as militants and pining for new channels of collective action. Even those who had participated in conservative organizations, such as evangelical churches or the employer-organized *solidarista* associations (see Blanco and Navarro 1984) that largely replaced unions in the banana zones after the early 1980s, frequently drew lessons about the benefits of unified struggle and either ignored or explained away the ideologies that had given rise to and imbued those experiences. Pedro Ruiz, a young agriculturalist from the village of Florida who spent several years in "the zone" in Limón province, commented (in 1988) in this vein on his transformation from Communism to *solidarismo*: "In the [banana] zone, to be honest, I've been in more than one organization. And I've seen movements. I was a big Communist in the zone. Well, afterwards they washed my 'coconut' [brain], and I went over to the other side, to the *solidarista* association. But I do know what organization is, and it's a good thing. What we need here is to organize ourselves."

Ruiz's remark, echoed by many others, occurred in a context of heightened struggle that was a long time in building and that briefly excited intense hopes among the peasants of Santa Cruz and Nicoya. Despite his apologetic confession about having "changed sides" and having been "brainwashed," he clearly yearned again for the exhilaration of unified action and the concrete gains that it might achieve.

An Activist Resurgence

Marcos Ramírez, a son of a shoemaker and a domestic worker who had been a high school MRP activist in San José, began to come to the Guanacaste lowlands in the early 1980s, after SITRACAÑA's failed strike at the sugar refinery. Eventually, he settled in Santa Cruz, on the northern end of the Nicoya Peninsula, a canton with an area of 1,331 square kilometers and a 1984 population of 31,133, of which 79 percent was rural. With some large and many small properties, the hot Santa Cruz lowlands constitute a transitional zone between the smallholding Nicoya Peninsula and the large haciendas to the north and east (Edelman 1992). In the small but rugged mountains that run from Santa Cruz south into Nicoya—beyond reach of the national electric grid and many government services, where roads and telecommunications are poor—smallholders predominate, many traditionally involved in coffee production.

Coincidentally or not, Nambí, the small community where Ramírez first spent time, was on the highway right at the turnoff of one of the dirt roads leading to the mountainous Santa Cruz–Nicoya "high zone," where the MRP had tried to organize peasants in the 1970s. Like other activists, though, in recounting his decision to move to the countryside, Ramírez downplayed the role of party discipline, stressing instead a mix of family and economic motivations fused with almost utopian sentiments about rural life. "I have a crazy uncle," he explained, "an uncle on my mother's side."

> My uncle lived in the United States and came back at the beginning of the 1980s and bought a farm here in Guanacaste. My grandparents in Atenas [Alajuela province] had a farm and my uncle too. My uncle bought a farm here with the goal of becoming a cattleman. He brought my grandfather to that little farm. In the end, though, my uncle was a lazy bum. He just departed again for the United States and left my grandfather on the finca. Since then I began to come to Guanacaste, to my grandfather's. I was around nineteen. My grandfather planted crops . . . I would come to help in the dry season. Not to plant, because in the dry season you can't plant anything, but to help him a little with the fences and that sort of thing.

Life in the countryside agreed with Ramírez, especially when compared with the difficulties faced by a young, working-class father in the capital.

> I saw that form of living as very healthy and interesting, that one could live from one's own production, without killing oneself too much and without many

anxieties in life. I especially began to see the relation with the neighbors, of having a cow, having the milk, all those things that in the city you have to kill your-
self to obtain. Then it occurred to me to see how it would be to accompany my
grandfather on the farm. Because I had the experience of working in a factory,
in Productos de Concreto, as an electrician's assistant, and then in another factory. I had started a vocational high school and studied to be an electrician, but
I never finished. . . . So I saw that the most feasible option was to come here and
I began to come much more often, at the beginning of '82. . . . But then at the
end of '83 my grandfather left. I kept my family [in the capital], I hadn't brought
them because I wanted some economic stability for my wife and daughter. I only
had one [child] then. When my wife came, she was pregnant with my son. When
she came, four months didn't pass before my uncle sold the farm and told me
we had to leave.

Ramírez spent a year in precarious circumstances, living with friends near
Nambí or at his in-laws' house in the capital, where his wife had returned
with the children. During this difficult time, he also sought out the handful of
MRP members in the Santa Cruz area (although it was years before he conceded this to me).[3] Eventually, he managed to rent a 6-hectare farm nearby
in the tiny community of El Rincón de San Vincente, which he worked with
sporadic help from his *concuño* Carlos Hernández and from Francisco Sánchez, a sometime sociology student, both of whom had, like him, grown up
in Desamparados, a working-class neighborhood to the south of San José.[4]
The neophyte agriculturalists did not have an easy time and low maize prices
and the harsh climate of lowland Guanacaste, in which crop losses are frequent and severe, exacerbated their difficulties. When the money ran out and
they had nothing with which to pay their hired peons, they proposed that
everyone—employers and employees—work the land together, as a cooperative, and share equally in whatever profits it might generate. They called
their new experiment "Cooperincón" (for Cooperativa del Rincón de San Vicente), even though it was never formally incorporated as a cooperative and
even though most of its members had joined primarily because the remuner-
ation promised them had not been forthcoming and it was their only hope of
recovering what they were owed.

Efforts to obtain legal status for "Cooperincón" never bore fruit, primarily because the participants were working rented land. In 1987, following a
meeting of local cooperatives and rural development organizations, several
participants in "Cooperincón" joined a legally constituted cooperative called
"Coopeasab" in Santa Bárbara, a nearby town not far from Santa Cruz, the

cantonal seat. Coopeasab (Cooperativa Autogestionaria de Santa Bárbara) had lost several associates and was in danger of losing its 45-hectare farm if it did not recruit new ones. The fusion of the two "*coopes*" permitted the Santa Bárbara group to retain its land, while the Rincón group gained access to land and legal status. Not long after, Ramírez, who had managed, with the help of a Catholic NGO, to obtain a 1 million-colón soft loan (approximately $15,000) from the German organization Bread for the World, became administrator of Coopeasab.

Culture of Maize, Culture of Survival

The difficulties of the novice agriculturalists who formed Cooperincón and who then joined Coopeasab were not due simply to inexperience. Guanacastecan peasants have long faced daunting obstacles in their struggle to survive and prosper. Land is scarce, agriculture is risky, work is poorly paid, families divide when men migrate to distant banana plantations or women leave for the cities to work as domestic servants, and the heat of the lowlands is enervating, even for those whose workday ends at noon and who know enough to remain in the shade until late afternoon. For maize, beans, and rice—the main smallholder crops—a successful harvest depends on an annual precipitation of between 1,500 and 2,000 millimeters, well distributed over the May-to-November rainy season. While there has been a pronounced decline in annual precipitation since 1950, almost certainly related to the severe deforestation in the region, annual and monthly variation is still very high (IMN n.d; Hagenauer 1980; Fleming 1986).

Guanacastecan agriculturalists are thus not inexperienced when it comes to drought, flooding, and crop loss. In some years the poorest or least fortunate harvest only "handfuls" that do not even provide their households' consumption or seed for their next planting. Nevertheless, the widely articulated expectation of the annual cycle is to harvest at least the "household's expenditure." In order to obtain this minimal security, many small producers trade labor "shoulder for shoulder" with neighbors and cultivate plots with their own resources—or, as they say, with their "pulse." But many also incur significant cash costs, renting land (generally for about 3,000 colones [about US$38.00 in 1988] per hectare for each four-month production cycle), taking out bank loans, hiring peons, and purchasing expensive inputs.

Peasants in many parts of Costa Rica grow maize, and maize was traditionally a major item in their diet. But in most maize-producing regions, such as Limón province, even if maize was consumed in the household, it was primarily a cash crop. Guanacaste, in contrast, still has a full-blown culture of maize, much like that of peasants further north in Mesoamerica, but unlike anything elsewhere in Costa Rica. Only in Guanacaste does the diet include such a rich variety of maize recipes: the beverages *pinolillo* and *chicheme*; the cereal dishes *atol* and *pozol*; the sweet *yol tamal* and numerous other *tamales*; and the baked *tortillas* and *rosquillas*, among others. Significantly, *"maicero"* (maize producer) and *"frijolero"* (bean producer), virtually synonymous with "hick" in coffee-growing central Costa Rica, are simply descriptive labels in this region.

Contemporary Guanacastecans' enthusiasm for maize dishes grows directly out of pre-conquest Mesoamerican traditions. The area that became Guanacaste was, in pre-Columbian times, one of the southernmost places under Mexican influence. Administered for much of the colonial period as a *partido* separate from both Costa Rica and Nicaragua, or as part of Nicaragua, its culture and speech are still heavily influenced by Costa Rica's northern neighbor, and its people—descended from the indigenous Chorotegas, African slaves, and Europeans—at times speak of themselves as having a "physiognomy" different from the largely European-descended inhabitants of central Costa Rica. These cultural and historic ties to Mesoamerica—and more immediately to Nicaragua—form part of a regional Guanacastecan identity that, for the smallholding peasant, is expressed in a deeply felt attachment to maize culture. Manuel Morales, a young agriculturalist from the mountain village of La Esperanza, expressed this widely held sentiment, albeit more eloquently and passionately than most:

> Guanacaste is the cradle of *atol* [a thick mush made from boiled corn powder], of maize, and we Guanacastecans have to continue with the traditions of our ancestors. For thousands of years [we have done this] and we wouldn't ever be able to restore it [if it were lost]. Maize is one of the most vital products for the country's diet. Food. The bread of the poor. If we don't produce what we eat, what the hell are we going to do? We're not going to eat coffee—yes, I grow coffee, I drink it, but I'm not going to eat it. As a Guanacastecan I would never accept that the government offer me the possibility of growing something else for money if I had to stop cultivating maize. I don't know if someone else would accept, but I wouldn't.

Morales's comment about the possibility of having to stop cultivating maize, assertive and defensive in the same breath, suggests outrage at the threat to an entire way of life, legitimized and ennobled by references to thousands of years of history. Interviewed in his carefully tended, irrigated garden of coffee seedlings, he was clearly no enemy of change nor a risk-averse, subsistence-oriented atavist. At the core of his analysis and tone—and central to the predicament of Santa Cruz's small agriculturalists in the mid- to late 1980s—was the near-simultaneous challenge to several historically conditioned expectations. These included dramatically worsened weather conditions, shifting state policies, and a growing urgency that led to political mobilization and a change in the "conformist" self-image of the region's peasants.

Subsistence Crisis and Economic Crisis

Before the mid-1980s, drought years—with annual precipitation of less than 1,400 millimeters—were almost always followed by years of adequate or high rainfall.[5] But in the years 1985–87, very low rainfall produced a "subsistence crisis" (Scott 1976, 16–18) that unexpectedly confronted the poorest of Guanacaste's agriculturalists with the threat of imminent ruin. By the May 1988 planting season many had sold their remaining pigs and poultry and had eaten or sold the maize and beans that were to have served as seed. The resulting desperation was summed up by one erstwhile agriculturalist from the dusty lowland village of Veintisiete de Abril:

> Right now I'm not planting anything because I don't have anything with which to do it. Because of being poor, I lost a hectare-and-a-half of maize and three of rice and I sold everything I had, one little animal, to continue feeding my children. And we're living from that. We spent last year floundering too, selling any damned thing.

To term such environmental disasters and the resulting social upheavals "subsistence crises," however, may obscure the extent to which even small agriculturalists were producing for more than their own consumption and were involved in complex commercial and financial relations. This dimension of the crisis, as well as something of the consumption expectations attached to "normal" times and the anguish of recent disasters, were encapsulated in the comments of a father of six, the oldest only fourteen, also from Veintisiete de Abril:

> Three years ago [in 1985], seeing myself pressed and unable to feed my kids, I contracted a debt in the bank. I said to myself, "I'll plant three *cajuelas* [one

cajuela = 32 pounds] of beans to see if I get something, if the wet season is good. If it's good, I'll buy the kids clothes, shoes, some things." Of the three *cajuelas* of beans—two that I planted in my own little plot, about a hectare—from those two I got one *cuartillo*, eight pounds. And from the other *cajuela* I had on rented land I got one kilo. In '86 the wet season was bad, in '87 also. So I couldn't pay and now I plant absolutely nothing because I have the doors closed at the bank. Sometimes [in the past] I've grown watermelon, melon, green beans, squash, various things, but damn—without a centavo in my pocket how am I going to get a peon to help irrigate the watermelon or to help me work?

Having "the doors closed at the bank" was becoming a familiar experience, even for those who had been able to pay back earlier loans. The economic structural adjustment programs that began in 1985 sought to make the public-sector National Banking System more efficient by permitting pri-

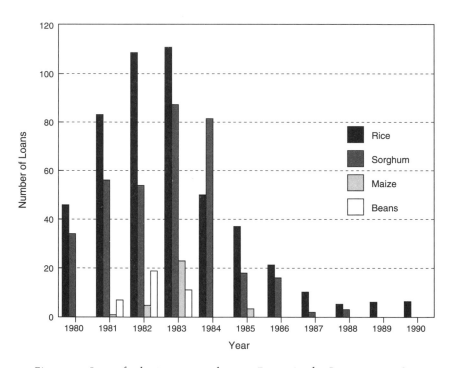

Figure 1.   Loans for basic grain production, Banco Anglo-Costarricense, Santa Cruz, Guanacaste, 1980–1990, adapted from data supplied by BAC Santa Cruz office.

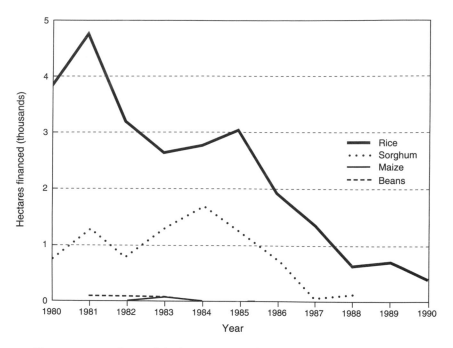

Figure 2. Area financed for basic grain production, Banco Anglo-Costarricense, Santa Cruz, Guanacaste, 1980–1990, adapted from data supplied by BAC Santa Cruz office.

vate financial institutions to compete in offering an increasing range of services and by introducing stricter profitability criteria for making loans. At the local level, in Santa Cruz, this meant severe reductions in credit for basic grains production and significantly higher interest rates for those loans that were available.

Figures 1 and 2 suggest how rapidly credit for basic grains production disappeared in the Santa Cruz area. The Banco Anglo-Costarricense (BAC), one of the country's four main public-sector banks, was the second largest lender in the region after the Banco Nacional de Costa Rica (BNCR). BAC data suggest that both the number of loans made and the total hectares financed dropped precipitously after the mid-1980s. The BNCR's Santa Cruz branch, which in any given year typically conducted several times as many credit operations as the BAC, did not provide comparable data, although a Bank functionary assured me that the downward tendency in basic grain loan activity was the same as that at the BAC.

A Movement Forms

The Guanacastecan peasants had a vast reservoir of frustration over lost crops and expensive credit. Their diverse organizational experience and aspirations, as yet largely untapped, had parallels in other regions of Costa Rica. Initially, the development of a group consciousness among Santa Cruz's small agriculturalists owed less to their local struggles than to an increasing awareness of events elsewhere in the country, where the peasant movement had been growing in militance, visibility, and sophistication since 1986. In September of that year, the Civil Guard dispersed peasant protesters in San José with tear gas and truncheons. Few Guanacastecans made the long trip to San José for this event, but for many of them, as for other Costa Ricans, the police attack seemed to violate their traditions of tolerance and free expression and galvanized opposition to government economic adjustment policies (CENAP et al. 1988; Reuben 1988; Rivera and Román 1988). The following year, Co-operincón sent a dozen members from Guanacaste to San José to join UPAGRA and other organizations in another peasant march.[6] This protest did not bring forth significant police violence, even though some marchers ended up occupying the atrium of the capital's cathedral and staging a hunger strike in the central plaza (see Chapter 2). In Santa Cruz, the process of first observing and explaining, of assuming a new consciousness, and then of holding forums and establishing committees, fed on the presence of community activists, delegates of the word, would-be *campesino* leaders, and others who were attuned to these and other national events. But the peasants' redefinition of political possibilities also grew out of new alliances that brought a sense of strength and efficacy.

In Santa Cruz, the peasants' most immediate expectation of the state, and the proximate cause of their first steps toward organization, involved the National Agricultural Contingencies Fund, which was supposed to "indemnify" agriculturalists in regions suffering widespread crop loss. In "normal" times, agriculturalists viewed the Fund, financed by a 3 percent tax on grain sold to the CNP, as a costly inconvenience and, like the National Emergencies Fund (Fondo Nacional de Emergencias) that was the center of a scandal involving a former president and vice-president, a possible source of political "sausages" (*chorizos*), as corrupt deals are called in Costa Rica. Few smallholders believed that the tax, which they termed a "punishment" (*castigo*) along with CNP charges that "punished" their grain's excess moisture or dirt content, would ever benefit anyone other than *"los grandes"*—the large, politically connected rice growers whose representatives sat on the Fund's board of directors. But after three years of drought losses, the Fund appeared to be one of the few possible solutions for an increasingly indebted, decapitalized, and desperate peasantry.

In October 1987, following a month of negotiations between government agencies and agriculturalists' organizations in other parts of Costa Rica, the MAG began to gather information about that year's drought losses in Guanacaste.[7] In response to this show of interest from above, peasants began to organize—"spontaneously" as several recalled—to coordinate collection of data on production costs and losses. Cooperincón and the Santa Bárbara community development association convoked a meeting of cooperatives and agriculturalists and community groups to inform people about September's march and the peasant movement in general, as well to "detect necessities in terms of land, production and technology" and "to orient a process toward the consolidation of coordinated work to find solutions to these necessities." Specifically, the organizers hoped to present a unified position to the government concerning crop losses, as well as their needs for credit, irrigation, and better price guarantees. Groups from six nearby villages sent representatives, as did the Guatuso Peasant Union (UCADEGUA) from northern Alajuela Province, on the other side of the volcanic cordillera. A Catholic NGO, the National Center for Pastoral Action (CENAP), provided economic and technical support for the get-together (Primer Encuentro Campesino 1987).

The last months of 1987 saw a flurry of activity. Organizers from several cooperative, community, and religious groups visited communities all over Santa Cruz cantón and in adjoining areas of Nicoya and Carrillo. Local broadcasters, particularly Church-owned Radio Chorotega, encouraged residents of remote communities to discuss their own losses and needs, and informed them about regionwide meetings.[8] By December, agriculturalists from over twenty small villages had formed committees that agreed to meet together each Sunday at noon, "since these matters are something that must be resolved with the utmost urgency" (Agricultores del Distrito 1987, 2). They appointed a "press attaché," a three-person committee charged with drafting a press release, and two representatives to collect precise data on crop losses to be presented to the local Agriculture Ministry representative. ("This must be done seriously and responsibly . . . , so that the data are accurate and credible," a record of the meeting reads [Ibid., 3].) Most village representatives who attended the Sunday meetings were not ideological in the sense of having a strongly held, coherent political orientation. Nevertheless, the emerging organization was clearly ecumenical, including both erstwhile leftists and supporters of FESIAN, the rural union federation linked to the ruling National Liberation Party (PLN), which had a center of strength in Cartagena, a village north of Santa Cruz. The Sunday meetings, as Marcos Ramírez later recalled, sparked a process that the government "knew how to promote, but didn't know how to control."

With three years of drought-damaged crops, large debts, and little prospect of obtaining credit, many Guanacastecan peasants viewed a prompt "indemnification" by the Contingencies Fund for the previous season's losses as their only hope of obtaining capital to plant. On February 27, 1988, over two hundred met in Santa Cruz to found the Association of Small Producers of the Dry Pacific (Asociación de Pequeños Productores del Pacífico Seco, or ASPPAS). Higinio Rodríguez, a coffee and vegetable farmer and community leader from the high zone village of Vistalmar, was elected president; Marcos Ramírez, then 26 years old, was chosen as secretary. As its first act, ASPPAS presented a document to the local Agriculture Ministry functionary describing drought losses and detailing members' needs for irrigation, technical assistance, and credit. The Ministry representative promised a response in two weeks. Ramírez recounted what happened next: "We waited a month, then two months, and [heard] nothing. We sent telegrams, letters. The peasant[s] felt betrayed. In Guanacaste we have to plant before May 20. We can't just plant whenever we want."

Increasingly, the movement's development in Santa Cruz became entwined with the national *campesino* movement and national politics, particularly the ongoing discussions between public-sector agricultural officials (from the MAG, CNP, and IDA) and the multiclass coalition called UNSA (see Chapter 2). The leisurely pace of these conversations, however, clashed with the agriculturalists' growing sense of urgency as the first rains and the planting season drew near.

Although the government had acceded in February to UNSA's demand for an UNSA-government negotiating commission, this recognition of the coalition's legitimacy was not accompanied by steps toward resolving the agriculturalists' pressing problems, even after two months of discussions. On April 18, only weeks before the expected beginning of the rains, UNSA gave President Oscar Arias a document outlining the problems facing the agricultural sector and proposing a series of short- and medium-term solutions. Given the imperative of the approaching planting season, the organization requested an answer within ten days. Exactly one month later the

Agriculture Minister made public the government's response, which UNSA members, especially the small grain producers, considered totally inadequate (Román et al. 1988).

The "Strike" in Santa Cruz

ASPPAS in Santa Cruz was not yet part of UNSA, but its members and leaders closely followed national-level events. Increasingly, negotiations between UNSA and the government shaped local political mobilization, as the agriculturalists realized that effective pressure tactics required linking their efforts to those of their counterparts in other regions. On April 22, for example, shortly after UNSA submitted its position paper to President Arias, several hundred ASPPAS members marched through Santa Cruz in support of their "right to cultivate." They staged brief "symbolic takeovers," lasting one or two hours each, of the offices of agricultural sector agencies, the IDA, CNP, MAG, and Banco Nacional, and provided functionaries in each with documents outlining specific needs. Their last stop was the Santa Cruz municipality, where they requested the support of the local government.

On May 9, still without any response from President Arias, peasant organizations in several parts of the country demonstrated and blocked highways to protest government inaction. In Santa Cruz, the highway blockade lasted three hours before the protesters, numbering in the hundreds, decided to leave. It was, some later commented, a "warning" of their desperation and what could happen if they did not have resources to plant. In late May and early June, ASPPAS leaders consulted with assemblies in 36 communities around Santa Cruz to decide what steps to take. Some of the leadership's more creative ideas, such as releasing dozens of chickens in the San José offices of the Central Bank to dramatize the peasants' inability to produce yellow maize, were rejected outright by the assemblies (these ideas were "*babosadas*," some *campesinos* later told me, employing a term that connotes the silly things that a drooling baby might do). Instead, ASPPAS members opted for joining UNSA in a nationwide "strike" that would establish a "definitive blockade" of highways for an indefinite period of time.

On the morning of June 8, agriculturalists in several grain-producing regions of Costa Rica blockaded highway bridges to demand payment for drought losses, better credit availability and conditions, and "just" producer prices.[9] The multiclass nature of the protesters and their distinct capacities for mobilization were reflected in the character of the demonstrations in different parts of Guanacaste. In Santa Cruz, smallholding peasants held the highway just outside town, while to the north in Guardia de Liberia, an area of large properties, a few of the province's wealthiest farmers achieved a similar effect by parking tractors and combines on the bridge over the Tempisque River. This contrast, between those who blocked bridges "with their bodies" and those who did it "with their employees' bodies and their machinery," symbolized the strains inherent in the UNSA coalition, as well as the different personal risks faced by the smallholders and *los grandes*.

Twenty-four hours later, at 5 A.M. on June 9, the Rural Guard, one of Costa Rica's two main police forces, sent several hundred heavily armed men to the Santa Cruz bridge and threatened to launch tear-gas grenades. The Guards, one protester said later, were dressed in camouflage uniforms, "a color that wasn't either green or blue." Another remembered that they "were ready with grenades and things—like the devil himself!"

Johnny Brealey, a politically well-connected rice grower active in UNSA who had helped block the Guardia bridge, appeared with a message from the government saying that the Agriculture Minister had agreed to meet with a delegation from each region. With the threat of tear gas, an offer of talks from the government, and their allies, the large growers, driving tractors and harvesters off the Guardia bridge, the Santa Cruz protesters agreed to lift their blockade. Two ASPPAS leaders, Marcos Ramírez and Ezequiel Gómez, departed for San José in Brealey's plane to meet with the minister, while the rest of the protesters regrouped at the local Chamber of Cattlemen's office.

"We didn't have enough experience in this type of action," Ramírez remembered. "When we arrived in San José we realized that we had been betrayed"—not by Brealey, but by the government. When the Guanacastecan representatives arrived at the Agriculture Ministry, nobody was there to meet them. They then traveled to Guácimo, Limón, where some 1,500 peasants had sealed off the roads and railway tracks. Unknown to the Guanacaste protesters, agriculturalists in Guácimo and Parrita had rejected the dialogue with the Agriculture Minister, arguing that he had no real power of decision. They also chided the ASPPAS representatives for lifting the blockade.

Guácimo, however, was the only place in the country where the "strike" continued. In Guanacaste, protesters had lifted the blockades in Santa Cruz, Guardia, and Cañas. In Parrita, on the central Pacific coast, the protesters stopped blocking the road when the Rural Guard arrested two local leaders. In the agriculturalists' eyes, this appeared to be another indication of government inconsistency or bad faith. "How were we going to negotiate with *compañeros* in jail?" asked one ASPPAS leader.

After Ramírez and Gómez flew to San José in search of the Agriculture Minister, the Santa Cruz protesters in the Cattlemen's Chamber office heard Radio Chorotega report on the arrests in Parrita, the "betrayal" by the minister, and the weakening of the strike in the rest of the country. The mood was melancholy. It was also raining heavily, an unpleasant reminder for many of their lack of resources for planting, as well as a practical obstacle to sustained outdoor protest.

CHAPTER 4

"In Jail, We'll Eat Cement": Finale to a Peasant Strike

"I don't know how many there were, a lot, since through the windows I saw their heads everywhere."

—*Witness's deposition, June 15, 1988*

Shortly after nine o'clock on the morning of June 10, a large canvas-covered truck—its license plates covered with brown paper and bunches of plantains protruding from the tailgate—sped past the Rural Guard contingent still watching the highway and hurtled through the gate of the Santa Cruz municipal offices. There it disgorged a cargo of several dozen angry peasants who immediately entered the cavernous building, announced a "takeover," and secured the doors with sturdy wooden poles—"sealing them hermetically," as the local prosecutor put it (JISC, Sumaria de Anabelle Cabalceta Aguilar, June 10, 1988). Within minutes, before the Rural Guard arrived, others joined those who came in the truck, bringing the total number of protesters to around two hundred. The truck raced off and vanished.

What occurred next is the subject of contradictory and often diametrically opposed accounts. The contending versions illustrate, however, how the reconstruction of events is, for protagonists on both sides, intensely influenced by political and personal agendas.

"I'm not a peasant," Municipal Executive Jorge Eduardo Pizarro—"taken hostage" in his office by the protesters—later remarked in an interview. "I don't cultivate the soil, nor am I a cattleman. I am from a family of musicians, businessmen, and politicians . . . that has lived here for 250 or 300 years, that built this town. My roots are here. For that reason I know the people."

When the agriculturalists seized the building, Pizarro was in his office with two guests, one "a North American who had come to invest" in the canton. After securing permission from protesters in the yard for his visitors to exit through a side door, he faced those inside with what he subsequently described as "valor":

> I closed my door and went to see what was happening. They pushed me and yelled at me whatever they wanted. I told them to go to hell and warned them that the country's situation couldn't take this. We had the Panama conflict on one side and the Nicaragua conflict on the other, and we couldn't provoke a situation with the peasants in this country because it was extremely dangerous, it threatened the country's stability. I told them that they had to be men, that they were a herd of cowards and sons of whores. I told them I wasn't going to accede to what they wanted, which was for me to bend my knees, that they had to kill me first. And I told one of them, "When this is over, look for me in the street and we'll settle it with blows. But don't be a faggot here in the office with that pack of dogs that you have here." . . . What they argued—their suffering, their pain, their necessity—we agree about that, it exists, and the government has been responsible, short-sighted. But that didn't mean that it wasn't a very dangerous situation for the country.

The situation calmed down, Pizarro noted, when ASPPAS secretary Marcos Ramírez returned from the failed negotiating mission to San José and Guácimo. Together with Ezequiel Gómez, an older agriculturalist from Veintisiete de Abril, Ramírez had arrived on a bus from the capital, disguised with sunglasses and a big hat. The police boarded the bus at the nearby bridge, but as Ramírez recalled, "Fortunately they were from Nicoya, not from here, so they didn't recognize us."

The two ASPPAS leaders exited the bus, crept along the wooded bank of the Río Diriá, and slithered on their bellies through a muddy sewer that went from the river to the municipality's yard, eluding the Guard cordon around the building and dashing inside. One town employee later recalled in a deposition that this had been around noon, or slightly after. "I found out that he had arrived because the agriculturalists began to applaud, and that Señor Marcos Ramírez took the megaphone and told them that he had conversed, or rather that he hadn't been able to negotiate, that they had been betrayed by the government" (Denuncia de Luis Humberto Santamaría Ruiz, JISC, June 30, 1988).

The peasant protesters then allowed women municipal employees, as well as visiting functionaries from the National Controller's office (Contraloría General de la República), to leave, and the two sides agreed to permit each to use the telephone. The women who left returned a short time later and began passing crackers and soft drinks to the male "hostages" inside until several of the protesters ordered them to stop. Pizarro, confined to his office with three peasant guards, recalled planning to escape with his assistant by attacking the protesters and jumping through a plate glass window, the only one that did not have bars on the outside.

In the afternoon, the municipal council went into session just outside the building and, angered that they could not enter their usual meeting room, agreed to press charges with the local investigative judge (Juez de Instrucción), Ricardo Guevara, who had also come to the scene. "We arrived at the Municipality for a two-o'clock meeting," one outraged council member stated. "But on arriving we found the building invaded by the workers (agriculturalists), the same ones who in recent days have been on strike because of the losses they have had in agriculture and as a protest and to exercise pressure to get the government to help them solve their problems" (Denuncia de Mario Villafuerte Villafuerte, JISC, June 10, 1988).

Other witnesses Judge Guevara examined identified a handful of the participating agriculturalists by name, and several blamed the occupation on Marcos Ramírez, variously identified as Marcos Ramírez Ramírez [sic] or Marcos Ramírez, "second [i.e., mother's] last name unknown." The indictment drafted at the scene added to this somewhat mysterious quality, noting that Ramírez's *"calidades"*—marital status, occupation, and identity card number—and his "domicile" were unknown. Another witness, however, declared—accurately—that Ramírez "apparently now lives in Santa Bárbara, of this canton, although he is not from there" (Denuncia de Fredy Obando Granados, JISC).

At 4:30 P.M., the judge gave the protesters one hour to "release" the eleven municipal employees still inside and at 5:00 P.M. the employees left the building. The question of whether they were liberated "hostages" or simply completing their work day, however, remained disputed, with peasants insisting that they asked the employees to leave and that they did not want to go, and others, such as Pizarro, insisting that they were held against their will.

The peasants who occupied the municipality adduced a variety of reasons for the action, ranging from the assistance they had traditionally received there, to the need to take shelter from the rain or to revive a flagging "strike." However, Municipal President Pizarro, they agreed, "behaved with us like a true gentleman."

"At first," one agriculturalist noted, "he began to tremble and asked us please not to do anything to him. He got all nervous. He thought we were going to attack him. The truth is that our goal wasn't to attack anybody. We came with another objective."

When the peasants explained their demands for credit and payments from the National Contingencies Fund, the municipal executive "agreed [to work] with us. He continued collaborating with us. He would come to communicate with us, [asking] if we were well, if we needed something. . . . At no time did he ask permission to leave. He didn't say to us, 'I want to leave.' Nobody said that to us. We spoke with the employees and the workers there. He continued with his work, received telephone calls and everything."

These protesters' version of events could not be more different than Pizarro's portrayal of his own violent machismo and homophobic, confrontational rhetoric. But another peasant recalled that the executive also tried to enlist them in an action to call attention to the province's neglect by the national government.

> Before leaving, he met with us and said that they had petitioned the government [and] if before July 25 [the anniversary of Guanacaste's 1824 annexation to Costa Rica] it hadn't complied, then they had decided—the league of municipalities of Guanacaste—to seize the Río Lagartos bridge [linking Guanacaste to central Costa Rica on the Pan-American Highway]. Then he asked for our collaboration . . . in taking the bridge. We said "agreed," as long as he went at the head and [with] all the municipalities, we would accompany them.

Finally, before departing, Pizarro and his assistant reportedly offered help if there were problems with the Rural Guards: "They said that if the Guard bothered [us], if it wanted to break down the door, to call them. They would come back immediately to accompany us. With them inside, it would be impossible for the Guard to break in." When the two functionaries left, the agriculturalists ruefully recollected, "There was applause and everything for the executive."

That night, after the municipal employees departed, the agriculturalists remained inside the building. While the taking of the municipality had in some respects been well planned, the protesters had neglected to bring food, thinking that someone outside would deliver it later. This hardship apparently occasioned a certain amount of bravado. One witness outside the building reported hearing someone inside haranguing "his *compañeros* with a megaphone, asking if they were afraid, and they answered 'no,' asking if they were hungry, and they answered 'no.' They were playing guitars and singing until around eleven at night" (Denuncia de Omar Matarrita Durán, JISC, June 20, 1988).

The Rural Guards refused to let anyone enter or leave, including two protesters inside who had fallen ill. Only after the intervention of the Archbishop of Tilarán, at around 11:00 P.M., did the Guards permit ASPPAS supporters to bring in *gallo pinto*—rice and beans—that had been prepared that morning and that by then tasted "bitter and horrible." Finally, in the evening, the telephones, electricity and water were also cut.

The following day, June 11, pressures mounted on both sides for a resolution of the standoff. The protesters stated that they would not leave until the government agreed to appoint a commission to settle the issues raised not only by the "strike" in Guanacaste, but in the rest of the country as well. The cantonal and departmental Rural Guard directors requested to enter the municipality to see if the protesters were armed, to gather information, and to verify if the protesters had damaged the facilities during the occupation. The agriculturalists agreed on condition that the Guards enter unarmed. The Guard officers also requested the names of all those inside, and the agriculturalists, feeling they had done nothing wrong, agreed, though some refused or cautiously provided false names. Once inside, cantonal Guard Director Saúl Briceño reportedly told the occupants not to be afraid, that the situation could be settled peacefully. But he also informed them that the little spheres the guards had on their belts were grenades that caused vomiting, dizziness, and diarrhea. "If it were a question of removing you, we'd take some of these bombs and we'd get you out in fifteen minutes. You'd go to hell [*al carajo*]."

"At that point," one protester said, "the situation had changed and the people were a bit afraid." But the occupation's end was not simply a matter of a Rural Guard show-of-force. On the morning of Saturday, June 11, the government offered to send a car to bring the protesters' representatives to a meeting with a technical commission in Guácimo, a five-hour drive away in the Atlantic zone. The agriculturalists agreed, but declared they would not leave the building until their representatives arrived in Guácimo. By afternoon the mood inside the municipality was less spirited. "We gave permission for people to leave," one of the last holdouts stated. "And when we finally left [at around 5:00 P.M.] we were only about thirty, all the rest had gone."

Carrots and Sticks

Once in Guácimo, ASPPAS leaders joined other agriculturalists organizations in meeting with the commission and then with the president's wife, Margarita Penón de Arias, who had been sent to negotiate on the government's behalf. Doña Margarita promised the protesters a meeting with her husband and that there would be no reprisals. On June 16, President Oscar Arias, in a meeting with 26 UNSA representatives, agreed to form commissions to study support prices, credit, access to land, "indemnification" for crop losses, and other issues raised by the "strike." One week later, the government announced that it would not increase prices for maize or beans, but that it would provide low-cost inputs through the Cantonal Agricultural Centers (Centros Agrícolas Cantonales). It also promised more funds to the IDA, the land reform agency, and expansion of bank credit offerings.

While negotiations continued at the national level, Santa Cruz judicial authorities proceeded to gather information to bring the peasant protesters to trial. For two weeks, the local prosecutor and investigative judge gathered depositions and issued subpoenas, attempting to identify the individuals who occupied the municipal building and to establish the precise criminal charges that could be brought against them. One subpoena ordered Radio Chorotega, the local Catholic station, to turn over copies of all the personal advertisements broadcast in recent days, since that could help "determine who is participating in the strike movement and who is the leader" (JISC, Guevara to OIJ, June 15, 1988). Others requested affidavits from the employees of the National Controller's Office who had returned to the capital following their release from the municipality. Finally, on June 27, the court issued an order to arrest Marcos Ramírez and charge him with "inciting to riot, usurpation of public property, and extorsive kidnapping in violation of public tranquility." The warrant specified that Ramírez was to be "captured and sent to any prison in the country by order of this court." As to where the suspect might be found, the judge advised that "he could be located in the strike movements carried out by the agriculturalists."

That same day, several hundred ASPPAS supporters, unaware of the outstanding arrest warrant and heartened by the government's announcement of expanded agricultural credit offerings, assembled in Santa Cruz's one movie theater to discuss their next move. In order to test the government's word about the newly available loans, a contingent of about one hundred went to the nearby Banco Nacional to apply for credit for the second production cycle that would begin in August. There Bank officials said the only lines open under the small agriculturalists program provided 10,000 colones (about US$143) per hectare of maize or beans—approximately one-third of average actual operating costs. Another group went to the IDA to apply for plots that were supposed to be available as part of a "new" one hundred million colones agrarian reform appropriation. IDA personnel informed them that the funds were already committed to a program for which there was a six-year waiting list. The matter of drought losses was still being studied by a government commission.

As Marcos Ramírez left the movie theater, a Rural Guard patrol surrounded him, handcuffed him, and whisked him off to jail, where he was formally accused of kidnapping, usurpation of public property, and instigating a public disorder, charges which potentially carried a combined sentence of ten to fifteen years. Dozens of peasants, in town for the assembly, approached the Rural Guards asking that they too be taken prisoner because they were guilty of the same thing. A small crowd followed the Guard patrol to the local lock up. Juvencio Matarrita, 80 years old, recalled how he responded then when he tried to visit Ramírez in jail and officials asked him, "Who is he to you?" "I'm an agriculturalist, one of those that produce so that all of us may eat. So that the policeman may eat, so that the judge may eat, so that the lawyer may eat. And I want to see Marcos Ramírez, who is imprisoned for us, the agriculturalists."

Others kept up the pressure by milling around the jail and sending telegrams to government officials. "We, the small agriculturalists of Veintisiete de Abril," one typical message declared, "members of the Association ASPPAS, deny the accusation made against Marcos Ramírez that it is he who forces us to take these measures to exert pressure. This is not true. We agriculturalists as a whole, that is ASPPAS, have taken these measures." Heidi Arce, Ramírez's wife, remembered:

> After they took him prisoner, the people went to the jail. The people wanted to stay put in front of the Santa Cruz jail, near the market. Our people were spread out in the market, all around, and they hadn't lost their will, their desire to fight. They were waiting, but the atmosphere was dangerous, there could have

been a very aggressive, very violent response [from the Guardia]. So it wasn't convenient that the people stay there. We didn't know how the thing was being handled legally, at the level of the people who had brought the charges, or at the level of the people of [the town of] Santa Cruz.

At his arraignment Ramírez declared that he had no economic resources and was assigned a public defender, Primo Chacón Barquero. "The lawyer," Heidi Arce said, "comported himself very well. It turned out that Primo had gone to high school with [UPAGRA leader] Carlos Campos, he wasn't from Santa Cruz, and he identified with us and our struggle."

Ramírez provided the court basic information about his *"calidades"*—his date of birth, identity card number, address in Santa Bárbara and his landlady's first name ("He does not know her surnames"), Heidi Arce's name (his *compañera* in "free union"), his parents' names and occupations ("shoemaker" and "housewife"), and that he had completed most of high school and considered himself an electrician by trade. Then he exercised his right to abstain from testifying and the judge denied the first motion for bail. Shortly after, as Arce remembered,

> they began to take other *compañeros* prisoner. Then they moved Marcos at dawn to the prison in Liberia [the provincial capital, an hour's drive away, where a well-defended, fortresslike penitentiary lies just off the central plaza]. They feared that the people would go and spring him from jail. Well, our people, some said "yes" about that and some said "no." The [Rural] Guard, the police were feeling a lot of pressure, so that's what they feared. And I suppose too that the other, powerful people who were handling this from behind the scenes felt the pressure, since now they had taken other prisoners and I suppose that to have Marcos there in the jail didn't seem like a good idea. So they moved him to Liberia at dawn, handcuffed, at dawn so nobody would find out. They would never have taken him out in a car during the day with all the people there. It would have created a huge ruckus, ten thousand ruckuses [*diez mil escándalos*].

Primo Chacón, Ramírez's public defender, continued efforts to secure his client's release on bail. He also asked the court to obtain depositions from people who could testify that Ramírez was in the capital, San José, more than three hours drive away, at the time the peasants seized the Santa Cruz municipality. These individuals included Agriculture Minister Antonio Alvarez Desanti, millionaire rice farmers Johnny Brealey and José Miguel Brenes, both UNSA representatives involved in the failed negotiations at the Ministry of Agriculture, a TV journalist who broadcast an interview with Ra-

mírez on Thursday evening, and a newspaper reporter and a functionary of
the National Center for Pastoral Action (CENAP) who had both spoken with
him on Friday morning, at almost the same time the peasants had stormed
the municipality. Testimony from these people would, it was hoped, establish
an alibi for Ramírez. It would also make it possible to suggest that Ramírez
had been surprised by the peasants' action. Indeed, when I first spoke with
him about the June "strike," he hinted that while he had been away from
Santa Cruz on the negotiating mission, things had gotten out of hand. "We
movement leaders had been overtaken by the agriculturalists," he told me.
"We had been displaced."

More Arrests and More Warrants

Twelve days after Ramírez's early morning transfer to Liberia, Johnny
Brealey, together with some other large farmers who had blocked the bridge
in Guardia with their tractors and combines, contributed 30,000 colones (approximately US$430) bail to secure the young leader's release from prison.

The day after he was freed, however, his lawyer informed him that warrants
had been issued for 60 other agriculturalists, most ASPPAS village committee leaders.[1] During the last week in July, Rural Guards seized several peasants in the lowland village of Veintisiete de Abril, caught others while they
were working at odd jobs in downtown Santa Cruz, and pulled four more off
buses coming from the highlands. A few of the "most wanted" fled to San
José for several days to lie low. Most of those named in warrants, however,
remained in highland communities where the Rural Guard had no permanent posts and where local committees stationed lookouts to watch for entering police vehicles. Less than one-quarter of those sought spent any time
in the tiny Santa Cruz jail, most for only one or two days.

The arrests, however, were carried out with an aggressiveness that heightened peasants' anger at the government. Elder Gómez owned a small store
where he administered Veintisiete de Abril's one public telephone. He knew
from "half hearing" others' phone conversations that arrest warrants had
been issued for many of his neighbors but not for him, even though he had
participated in a few demonstrations during the peasant strike.

> I was still worried and I asked my wife to run an errand for me in Santa Cruz,
> since I feared they might capture me there. . . . One is the foundation of the
> household. If one goes inside [to jail], who's going to earn anything? So I was in

the house alone with my mother-in-law, who is a *señora* of 80 and a bit more years. She doesn't see, she's blind. And this Señor shows up, Ramón Vallejos, the Guard from here in Veintisiete, the Guardia Rural. "The *delegado* [cantonal police commander] wants you," he told me. "He wants to speak with you." "Yes, sir. What can I offer him?" "Walk to the police station!" I told him, "One moment, I have to lock the house." I was in shorts, working around the house. I asked the chief of the patrol for permission to change, he could even send a Guard to watch me change. He didn't want to. I was just in shorts, barefoot, and that's how I went to jail.

The Guards' reluctance to let don Elder change his clothes stemmed in part from the escape of other suspects. Sixty-three-year-old Ezequiel Gómez (a neighbor and distant relative of Elder) recounted what occurred on the Tuesday afternoon when the Rural Guards came looking for him.

We took a chance, we took off down there [pointing to the fields and woods behind the house]. They didn't arrest us. They said we had the face of leaders, ringleaders (*cabecillas*). Supposedly we were going to fall. So before they arrived for us, we made the decision to flee. . . . Then I went out and I saw the patrol there. "The *delegado* is calling you." I say, "I'm coming." Then I left through the kitchen, grabbed my machete, and put it like this [next to the thigh] so they wouldn't see it. And I managed to go into the bedroom. And then the one who represented the *delegado* said to me, "*Idiay*, Señor, hurry up!" "I just told you that I'm coming." So then I left the back way and there [at the barbed wire fence] I tore my pants to shreds. Of course I left with the machete. You can't go in the woods unarmed, because a viper, anything, could attack you.

The Guards did not follow Gómez in time and he was able to elude capture and catch a bus to San José. One of the Guards on the patrol, interviewed later, excused Gómez's escape, claiming that he had threatened to kill them with the machete. Asked about this, Gómez was vehement in his denial: "Never! That's a big lie! That Señor [the Rural Guard] has a school for liars there and they're learning well. They're studying hard and graduating some very intelligent pupils."

Other agriculturalists were enraged because they believed President Arias had reneged on his promise to halt the harassment. Teodoro Mena, a soft-spoken *campesino* from Oriente de Juan Díaz, had traveled to San José in late June as part of an ASPPAS negotiating mission. This was the second time he had met with Arias, itself a remarkable indication of both the accessibility and legitimacy of Costa Rica's high-level officials, and of the widespread perception that they actually listened to the poor and humble. "When we were in the Casa Presidencial," Mena recalled, "it was about two weeks after we took the '*muni.*' I addressed myself to don Oscar, asking him to remove the charges against those of us who participated in taking the municipality. And he told us, '*Yes,* of course, yes, yes, yes.' I also told the [Agriculture] Minister, and he too said 'Yes.' But these were only words, nothing more."

In late July and early August, as news of the arrests spread, peasants began to hold strategy meetings in small villages throughout the Santa Cruz–Nicoya highlands and in a few of the larger lowland communities, such as Veintisiete de Abril, where many ASPPAS supporters lived. Because so many people were named in outstanding arrest warrants (the more intimidating Spanish term is "*orden de captura*," or "capture order"), these "assemblies" had to be held in a kind of semi-clandestinity that was highly unusual in democratic Costa Rica. Often they were organized almost on the spur of the moment and advertised in hastily coded personal messages broadcast over Santa Cruz's Radio Chorotega. As in many rural areas with poor roads and few telephones, the local radio transmitted a steady stream of folkloric-sounding personal messages to alert residents of outlying hamlets that relatives were arriving, that Mamá was delayed in Liberia or San José, that a mass would be held for the departed soul of Juan Pérez, or a wedding celebrated in the village hall of Vistalmar or at the home of the bride's parents, 200 meters east of the large *pochote* tree near the turnoff to Cola de Gallo. In the countryside, women often left radios on and half attended to this torrent of trivia as they went about their work, sending a small child to run to the men in the fields or to a neighbor's if they heard anything significant. In late July and early August, however, attentive listeners would have noted a sudden and peculiar increase in the number of "packages" (*encomiendas*) arriving throughout the highlands, often at curious hours when there were no public buses scheduled.

The "packages," naturally enough, were ASPPAS leaders or messengers. Sometimes the "*cuñas*," or ads, were ordered from public telephones at rural grocery stores only an hour or two before a planned meeting. Mobility, though, was a problem, since the organization did not have any vehicles. Short distances, especially in the high zone, could be covered on horseback, but in the lowland plains, villages were too far apart and certainly too distant from the mountains. One ASPPAS supporter, known by the quintessentially Nicaraguan nickname "Paisa," owned a motorcycle, which he used to locate and excavate "*huacas,*" or pre-Columbian archaeological sites, and to traffic in artifacts.[2] Taking a break from this dubious and unlawful trade, Paisa and his bike did heroic duty on rough trails throughout the highlands, carrying messages for ASPPAS, struggling, as he put it, to sustain his other calling, that of agriculturalist. And for a time, a Costa Rican sociologist who worked for the progressive Catholic magazine *Aportes* managed to borrow an old jeep from a Canadian NGO and put it at the service of the Association. It was in this ailing vehicle with "M.I."—Misión Internacional—license plates that I managed to reach the more remote peasant assemblies.

The settings for the assemblies ranged from tiny stores (*"cucaracheras,"* or "cockroach nests," as one fretting owner described his bankrupt business), to houses at the end of long footpaths that wound through woods and pastures, to airy *salones comunales*, or village halls, in the mountains. Everywhere, Ramírez and other ASPPAS leaders instructed people on how to handle the legal situation. "If the Guards come to your house, ask them for a search warrant." "If they have a search warrant, but no arrest warrant for you, run to your neighbor's house. They can't take you out of there."

> Those of you who were in the municipality—you know who you are—we ask you please not to go down to Santa Cruz until we let you know about the situation. . . . Some people have now spent three nights in jail there. We want to do things in an orderly way. We'll take groups of ten, ten at a time, to the judge, so that he can take their declarations, so that there's no problem. If they put ten in that jail at once, for them it's a mess.

Elderly people who had not participated in the strike were a frequent presence at the peasant assemblies. Several invoked Guanacastecan identity and the region's fabled indigenous past as reasons for standing firm against the government in distant, "European" San José. One septuagenarian *campesina*, for example, exhorted her neighbors, "Don't falter, don't be afraid! The Guard is applying pressure to see if it can make us afraid. But why should we fear if we are *guanacastecos*? We are Indians and we aren't capable of fear!"

In Veintisiete de Abril, several dozen men and women gathered furtively in the back yard of a large wooden house painted with broad red and blue stripes, the colors of the Costa Rica's Social Christian party (whose brief alliance with the Left in the 1940s is described in Chapter 1). There, a local musician strummed a battered guitar and sang folk melodies about Guanacastecan *sabaneros*, or cowboys, and about how the people are the source of all wealth (*"Pueblo, fuente de riqueza . . . "*). Three young girls with ribbons in their braids and long ruffled petticoats sang along and danced, whirling around and around. At one point, a titter passed through the crowd as a couple of men showed up who were being sought under outstanding "capture orders." They had fled to San José, walking miles across the highlands to the south and then taking a bus from a town where nobody knew them. Now they had come back, disguised with floppy hats, fake mustaches, and spectacle frames with no lenses. They explained the precaution as necessary because the San José bus stopped right in front of the house of a Santa Cruz *regidor,* or councilman, who happened to be one of the key complainants in the legal case against the peasants who had seized the municipality.

As I departed the assembly in the jeep, together with Marcos Ramírez, another ASPPAS activist, and the sociologist from the magazine *Aportes,* an elderly woman flagged us down next to the dusty central park of Veintisiete de Abril. "You just came from the agriculturalists' assembly, right?" she asked in a conspiratorial tone. "Don't turn that way, leave the other way. The *delegado,* Saúl, is waiting there with that Ramón and his other men to arrest you!"

In a flash, Ramírez vaulted over the seat into the rear cargo compartment, pulled a greasy tarpaulin over his body, and flattened himself against the floor. The other ASPPAS activist squeezed into the space behind the front seat and tried to conceal himself with our backpacks and duffle bags. My sociologist colleague and I drove out to the highway and sped past the police by the side of the road, two light-skinned, bearded guys in a Canadian "M.I." vehicle, trying to look as if they had just made a foolish wrong turn on their way back from the beach.

Outrage and Disappointment

Peasants at the assemblies in July and August expressed intense and often highly articulate outrage at the government's structural adjustment policies and repression of the agriculturalists' movement. Indeed, as part of this break with the Guanacastecan peasant's traditional "conformism," the label *agricultor* increasingly took on a new meaning in local discourse. From a class-neutral category that included everybody from the wealthiest farmer to the most marginal sharecropper, the term suddenly was being asserted in a new adversarial context, assuming connotations of persecution and dignity, and becoming almost synonymous with a punishable offense.

The change was exemplified by the remarks of María Bonifacia Mena, a 54-year-old grandmother from Oriente de Juan Díaz, who had been on her way to Nicoya to sell beans and *pipián,* a kind of squash, when the Rural

Guard arrested her and accused her of being a "follower" of Ramírez. Recounting the experience, her speech trailed off as she pondered whether it had been her "destiny to be arrested for being an agriculturalist or for being humble. . . . " When asked why her son had been seized as well, her voice rose as she bridled at the patent stupidity of the question: "Also for being an agriculturalist!" (*¡Pues por agricultor también!*).

Another protester, asked if he thought he had committed a crime in occupying the municipal building, responded simply, "No, the way I see it, it's not a crime. To be an agriculturalist, as they say, isn't a crime, because all of us do it, like the poor people that we are."

Others, like Iris Matarrita, who had not participated in the takeover, expressed anger at the authorities' vilification of her neighbors: "I'm indignant, because I know these people very well, they're humble people. I've never known them to be thieves, to be dangerous. They didn't go take the municipality or the streets as a lark or to show they had balls. I don't like that they treat the agriculturalists like an old rag, like something worthless, just because we're agriculturalists."

Several older women had played visible roles in mobilizing their communities. Perhaps because of their age, their participation did not clash with *machista* notions about appropriate feminine behavior and they had been welcomed by the largely young, male protesters. When women were arrested, however, *machista* ideas were invoked to denounce the government. In an assembly of three dozen peasants, one young organizer reported on recent arrests, juxtaposing highly respectful terms for women with off-color slang references to men: "You heard that two women (*compañeras*) fell [were arrested] and two guys (*carajos*) more. It's not that we don't value the male, but when a male (*compañero*) goes inside [to jail], well, he endures it. But for them to arrest a woman—a *señora* like doña Ramona [Briceño], who is a grandmother—that they take her prisoner, for us that's insulting."

Briceño, however, weathered her day in jail with aplomb and recalled lambasting her much younger uncle, the cantonal Guard director who had ordered her detained. "I told him if we were without means to eat, no doubt because of government orders, we would eat brush like worms, as long as there was brush, and when the brush was finished, we'd eat dust, and in the jail we'll eat cement, I told him."

Several peasants, citing a recent radio report on a new environmental law, also compared agriculturalists to animals, specifically to endangered species: "They're letting the agriculturalists fall like wild animals. As far as I know, there's a law that protects animals. In other words, there's more protection now for animals than for the agriculturalist. How is that?! The government wants the people dead of hunger."

While anger at the government's stance gave rise to heated commentaries, negotiations continued between the Agriculture Ministry and the nationalized banks, on the one hand, and ASPPAS and the agriculturalists organizations, on the other. The two sides achieved a first set of accords less than a month after the June strike. The Agriculture Ministry and the banks agreed to suspend collection of agriculturalists' outstanding debts for 30 days, to facilitate payments by the National Agricultural Contingencies Fund (FNCA) to the banks, making it possible for agriculturalists "indemnified" for crop losses to receive fresh credits, and to have the National Production Council (CNP) provide loan guarantees for groups of small agriculturalists that had joint projects but who had not been able to pledge sufficient collateral (BNCR et al. 1988). But government concessions, even if well intentioned, fell victim to the inertia of bureaucrats oblivious to the urgency felt by the agriculturalists, who could not just plant any time they wanted.

By late July, the national-level accords trickled down to the local level. The government agreed to provide up to 700 agriculturalists in the Santa Cruz area with an "emergency" credit of twenty thousand colones per hectare for bean cultivation, which generally begins in August. The loans, however, were conditional on the CNP's serving as guarantor, which required inspections of applicants' fields. ASPPAS recruited 115 agriculturalists who planned to grow beans to apply for the new credits. Throughout August, CNP specialists crisscrossed bean-growing areas of Santa Cruz and Nicoya checking fields and speaking with loan applicants. But, on September 23, when the CNP finally sent the banks its list of approved agriculturalists, the banks refused to provide loans, citing the fact that the second planting period was almost over. "Those fifteen days went by us," said a once hopeful Pedro Vallejo, referring to the last two weeks in which it was possible to plant. "Time is going by and now it's impossible to plant even if they would give the money, because the time is finished."

"Hoaxes" and "Dirty Trifles"

At the end of this failed second planting season, when those who cultivated maize and beans did so almost exclusively with their own resources—"with their pulse," as the *campesinos* said—the government began paying "indemnification" for the previous year's losses. This might have represented a victory, since payment from the Contingencies Fund for crops lost to drought had been one of the main demands of the June "strike." But if the money arrived too late to pay for seed and fertilizer or to hire peons, the peasants saw even less rhyme or reason in the way it was distributed. Agriculture Ministry officials had inspected the fields of those claiming drought losses, and agreements had been reached on who was to be paid and for how many hectares of damaged crops. Yet when checks were issued, the 4,200 colones (about US$60) that were supposed to be paid for each hectare of lost maize or beans, was halved in some cases, doubled in others, or never arrived at all.[3] In every community where the government paid "losses," politically connected individuals who had not planted anything were said to have received checks. Those claimants most active in the June "strike," with few exceptions, received nothing at all.

Six months after the municipal building takeover, many peasants saw the "payment of losses" as their movement's greatest success. Some, though, viewed it as a "hoax," a "dirty trifle," or "candies" that did nothing to solve their long-term problems and that the government was "throwing" to the peasants to "tranquilize" them. "They played with the agriculturalist like a toy," one resident of the village of Florida declared in a rather typical expression of bitter disappointment. "They took him for a fool" (*"Al agricultor lo agarraron como un juguete, lo agarraron de maje"*).

The June 1988 agriculturalists' "strike" in Santa Cruz was an unprecedented movement for this region of Costa Rica, as both participants and government officials realized. Octogenarian Juvencio Matarrita chuckled about this with the satisfaction and wonder of having waited for something a long time: "Never in my life before this damned thing (*carambada*) had I seen these mobilizations, not until now. It's the first time I've seen this thing, and I have been living for more than 80 years. We've never paid attention to these issues. . . . [But] now it's a new world."

Yet although the terrain contested was clear to all involved, it was also a movement that most agreed had no real winners or losers. Geared to an immediate sense of desperation and an urgency tied to the planting season, its strength ebbed once the hope and possibility of planting had passed and once the government disbursed nominal payments for the previous year's losses. Protest leaders had built what seemed like a powerful organization, but its consolidation remained largely beyond their capabilities, in part because of lack of resources for communicating with a widely dispersed constituency and in part because of the basic, time-consuming imperatives of production and survival. The "new world" was not a world of peasant pride and power, as don Juvencio may have dreamed, but one of intra-organizational feuding and conflict.

The state had played its hand well, reacting to the agriculturalists' mobilization with a classically Costa Rican combination of prolonged negotiations, minor concessions, vague promises, and sudden—yet basically sporadic and mild—repression. Certainly its benevolent image eroded, but by making payments—however inadequate—for crop losses, it reasserted itself in the role of provider, reinforcing expectations derived from decades of living in a social welfare state.

An Informant's Trial and an Ethical Dilemma

The polarized atmosphere of Central America in the 1980s and early 1990s highlighted for many foreign social scientists the problems of fieldwork in conflictual situations where vast disparities in power separate elites and subalterns (and to a lesser degree, anthropologists and their usual objects of study). Philippe Bourgois (1990) has pointed out that the established ethical concerns of anthropology—informed consent, compliance with host-country laws, not doing anything against the "good of the community," protection of informants' confidentiality and anonymity—are sorely tested and generally found severely wanting in contexts where state repression and human rights violations force citizens and foreign social scientists alike to choose sides and take public stands. While Costa Rica was far from a repressive society by Central American standards, the wave of arrests in Santa Cruz in 1988 and the trial of Marcos Ramírez in 1990 nonetheless raised issues that were not easily resolved within the overly abstract, value-free framework of the American Anthropological Association's Principles of Professional Responsibility.

ASPPAS leader Ramírez faced a possible prison sentence of ten to fifteen years for his role in the municipal building occupation. He was charged, among other things, with kidnapping Municipal President Jorge Eduardo Pizarro. I had a tape on which Pizarro told me in no uncertain terms that it was only thanks to Marcos Ramírez that the irate peasants who seized the municipality had calmed down and not harmed him. I was, in effect, in possession of exculpatory evidence in a trial where a conviction could bring a very long prison sentence to a key informant and friend. A strict constructionist interpretation of the AAA ethics code would perhaps require me to hold onto the cassette and its contents in order to "protect" informant Pizarro's right to confidentiality. The possibility that such "protection" could result in serious harm—specifically, a criminal conviction and imprisonment—to another informant simply isn't contemplated in the profession's ethical code. The vague standard of "community good," of course, assumes not only an overly traditional anthropological focus on a single place, but a homogeneous, undifferentiated "community" in which a social scientist's unethical act would somehow harm all members more or less equally. A "greater good" interpretation—choosing between the conflicting right to confidentiality of one informant and the well-being of another—depended on what was, from the highly formal point of view embodied in the official Principles of Professional Responsibility, a dubious ethical relativism. As Bourgois points out: "The problem with contemporary anthropological ethics is not merely that the boundaries of what is defined as ethical are too narrowly drawn, but more importantly, that ethics can be subject to rigid, righteous interpretations which place them at loggerheads with overarching human rights concerns" (1990: 45).[4]

Ramírez's trial took place before a three-judge panel in Liberia, the provincial capital, on October 2, 1990. This was more than two years after the municipal building occupation, when tempers had cooled considerably in Santa Cruz. Several plaintiffs and prosecution witnesses, as well as the investigative judge who initiated the inquiry in the case, had been implicated in scandals that ranged from minor episodes of corruption to cultivating marijuana on an isolated mountain farm. Their credibility as investigators, witnesses, and "victims" was potentially compromised. One of the departmental Guard commanders, another important witness, had recently died in an automobile accident.

As it turned out, the tape of my conversation with Pizarro was never played at the trial. Indeed, as Ramírez wrote to me the day after the verdict, "The testimony of Quirindo [Jorge Eduardo] didn't differ much from what he said in the interview on your cassette."

When the judge and the lawyers for each side grilled Pizarro and the other complainants, they received such inconsistent testimony that the prosecutor himself ended his summation with a request for an acquittal (and an admission to the defendant, after the decision, that the charges had been politically motivated).[5] Ramírez reported that he felt "tranquil" during the trial, but in his letter this steely political commitment was mixed with palpable relief.

> I went to trial without a single witness in my favor, because all those who could have gone were from the Organization and in the event that I were found guilty, they too would have been implicated. I was accompanied only by the certainty of what is right and the justice of an authentically peasant struggle. . . . How do you like that? We were acquitted, they declared us innocent! It is important to clarify, though, that this sentence was not for free. It was necessary to apply political pressure at the highest levels.

I next saw Ramírez about five weeks after the trial. He seemed relaxed, optimistic, and even ebullient (though before long we would have a temporary falling out, as a result of my critical remarks about ASPPAS at the CEPAS roundtable described in the Introduction). When I pressed him for details about "the high-level political pressure" that had contributed to his acquittal, I found him uncharacteristically tight-lipped and enigmatic. President Arias and doña Margarita (de Arias), he reminded me, had promised on several occasions to halt prosecutions of peasant activists. "Yes," I replied, "but Arias had also stated repeatedly that the executive branch could not interfere with the judicial branch. And in any case, he was no longer in power," having turned over the presidency in May 1990—five months before Ramírez's trial—to his elected successor from the Social Christian Unity Party, Rafael Angel Calderón Fournier.

While I never learned from Ramírez or anyone else what, if any, political influence had been brought to bear in the trial, the acquittal did permit a more candid discussion of what *campesinos* throughout the region increasingly viewed as "history" or "the past." This new frankness often fueled bitter polemics, as people tried to make sense of their movement's successes and failures, their own participation and sacrifices, and their dashed hopes and continuing aspirations (see Chapter 5).

The Costa Rican criminal code's "double jeopardy" provision, which guarantees that a defendant cannot be tried twice on the same charges, also allowed Ramírez to indulge in confessions that would earlier have been imprudent, if not downright perilous. Up until then, I had thought of the municipality occupation as a spontaneous, late-twentieth-century *"tumulto,"* or riot, carried out by members of an organization—ASPPAS—but broadly comparable nonetheless to the *"tumultos"* that have punctuated the agrarian and small-town history of Latin America since the colonial period. I had formed this impression from numerous conversations with, and extensive observation of, leaders and participants, as well as "hostages" and Rural Guards. I had heard indiscreet, revealing remarks about all kinds of sensitive issues, including people's past involvement in land invasions, strike-related sabotage, left-wing parties, guerrilla movements, extramarital affairs, embezzlement of funds, rustling cattle, cultivating marijuana, and pillaging archaeological sites. I naively assumed that if the *"muni"* takeover had been anything other than an unrehearsed explosion of *campesino* anger, I would surely have heard about it.[6]

"Now that the trial's over, there are some things that can be said about what happened," Ramírez acknowledged one day, demolishing in one breath my assumptions about late-twentieth-century *tumultos* and *campesino* spontaneity. "The taking of the *'muni'* was planned with precision, like a military operation, by people in the movement with military experience, some from the [Sandinistas'] war [to topple Somoza] in Nicaragua and others from the [Costa Rican civil] war of '48."[7]

He then returned to the moment during the June 1988 "strike," when he was on the road to Guácimo and hundreds of ASPPAS members were waiting at the Cámara de Ganaderos (Cattle Producers Chamber) in Santa Cruz. Placing local events in their national context and defending the *"'muni'* operation" as a crucial piece of a broader peasant movement strategy, he reminded me that, then,

> there was a very tense situation. The communications media reported that in the entire country the movements had voluntarily agreed to negotiate and that only Guácimo [in Limón province] was a point of conflict, because there, really subversive, belligerent people were at work. The situation in Guácimo was very dangerous. Most of the public force [Civil and Rural Guards] was concentrated in Guácimo. A huge number of military troops, with heavy weapons, rifles, machine guns, because it was rumored that our people were armed, which wasn't true. We're accustomed to mobilizations of police with clubs, with revolvers, but that kind of weaponry we hadn't seen before. They allowed us to enter Guácimo because of orders from the Minister of Agriculture, but we had passed four roadblocks and we saw that the town was totally surrounded by military troops. The situation was very delicate and it was necessary to act—and rapidly.

Ramírez had gone to Guácimo after his trip to San José, where he had hoped to participate in negotiations with the Minister of Agriculture. Back in Santa Cruz, the agriculturalists had lifted the highway blockade and were simply waiting, holed up in the headquarters of the Cámara de Ganaderos, trying to decide what to do next.

> It was said that in Guanacaste there was practically no movement, the same in Parrita [in Puntarenas province]. The Minister of Security was creating an atmosphere, influencing public opinion, so that a violent action could take place in Guácimo to repress the movement. . . . So we called Santa Cruz and our people, well, we had established our system and the people simply acted. Because everything, public opinion, the news media, everybody was focused on Guácimo, that the agriculturalists' struggle at the national level had been resolved and only those people in Guácimo were subversives and didn't want to accept dialogue. It was necessary to break that climate of tension, to reassert the national struggle. So on that day, June 10, our people took the municipality. Don Ezequiel [Gómez] and I already knew when we were on our way back to Santa Cruz. . . . Later that day the *compañeros* from Guácimo called us at the municipality to tell us that the level of tension there had declined and that it had been a very important action that we had taken.

Transforming a Movement

The 1988 "strike" and the occupation of the Santa Cruz municipality might have been "very important" actions, but they also marked a significant turning point for the peasant movement. In succeeding years, movement leaders increasingly suggested that the price of such confrontational tactics had been exceedingly high. Vast amounts of energy, and a substantial proportion of the movement's scant resources, had been expended in marches, highway blockades, and pressure tactics. These activities, as well as related arrests, beatings, jailings, and trials, had economically exhausted the organizations, upset the lives of hundreds of families, and disrupted the productive activities of numerous small farms and other rural enterprises. All of this contributed to fatigue and growing discord among the movement's grassroots supporters. The personal and organizational costs of continuous protests, the leaders said, greatly outweighed the meager gains won at the negotiating table.

Following the 1988 "strike," and especially in 1989 and 1990, a shift began to take place that movement leaders summed up in the phrase "from protest to proposal" (*de la protesta a la propuesta*). The slogan encompassed several interrelated dimensions of peasant political practice. It reflected leaders' conviction that *campesinos* were capable of administering their productive, commercial, and financial activities more effectively in order to survive the free-market onslaught. This would mean organizing peasants around productive goals rather than protest activities, and presenting policymakers with concrete economic, agronomic, and organizational proposals instead of staging costly confrontations or making "unrealistic" or utopian demands. The turn "from protest to proposal" also suggested movement leaders' belief and hope that they themselves were in the struggle for the long haul, that they had real alternatives to offer their constituencies and their country, and that this was not a movement that would disappear—as so many before it had—like a flash in the pan.

CHAPTER 5

Movements Evolve, Organizations Are Born and Die

Al principio pensábamos que teníamos lo mejor para los campesinos
entonces les informábamos . . . y yo me sentía muy bondadoso.
Cuando teníamos algunas dudas les consultábamos . . . y yo me sentía
democrático.
Para mejorarlo pedíamos sugerencias a los campesinos . . . y yo me
sentía más democrático.
Pensábamos que era mejor para nuestros objetivos contar con algunos
delegados campesinos . . . y yo me sentía muy participativo.
Ahora todo lo decidimos juntos campesinos y técnicos . . . y me doy
cuenta que fue recién empezamos a comunicarnos.
Me pregunto: ¿Qué hacíamos realmente al principio?

*(At first we thought that we knew best for the campesinos, so we
informed them . . . and I felt very generous.*
When we had some doubts, we consulted them . . . and I felt democratic.
*To improve things, we asked the peasants for suggestions . . . and I felt
more democratic.*
*We thought it was best for our objectives to have some peasant delegates
. . . and I felt very participatory.*
*Now we decide everything together, campesinos and técnicos . . . and I
realize it's only recently that we began to communicate.*
I ask myself: What were we really doing at the beginning?)

— *Anonymous poem on the wall at the Consejo Campesino Justicia
y Desarrollo (Justice and Development Peasant Council), 1993*

"In the last eleven years, we've had seven ministers of agriculture,
each one with his own silly obsession (*cada uno con su tontera*)."

—JORGE HIDALGO *of the Mesa Nacional Campesina, 1997*

156

The shift "from protest to proposal" did not occur overnight.[1] While the peasant movement eventually did become much more "democratic" or "participatory" than it had been "at the beginning," the process was hardly as painless and automatic as the self-congratulatory poem above seems to suggest. Moreover, while greater internal democracy and more genuine participation may have been intrinsically praiseworthy values, they were not unambiguously positive from the point of view of building a strong movement. Open discussion, accountability and "transparency" could and did also lead to processes that would weaken, or at the very least, profoundly transform, the peasant movement.

In this chapter, I describe how conflicts over money and political vision constituted a frequent source of tension in the top leadership and at the grassroots. Both local organizations and, eventually, national-level coalitions disintegrated under these pressures. Even though the peasant movement emerged weakened from factional infighting, its leaders continued to manifest considerable creativity in lobbying and in devising economic-productive strategies that would permit their supporters to survive the free-market onslaught. But the institutionalization of *campesino*–government negotiating processes and of new "productive projects" often led organizations to focus on serving their existing constituencies rather than on their original objective of building a powerful movement for fundamental change.

The National Movement

The organizations that launched the 1988 "strike"—UPAGRA and its closest allies—continued to rely heavily on a small core of charismatic leaders representing—or claiming to represent—constituencies in different parts of the country. Privately, among themselves, and only partly tongue-in-cheek, they referred to each other as "the group of six" (*el grupo de los seis*), echoing with intentional irony the designation widely used for "the Group of Seven" industrialized nations. Soon they found that it was easier to forge unity at the top and at the grassroots when organizing marches and "strikes" than in the prolonged negotiations and organizational transformations that followed the upheaval of June 1988.

Part of the problem was that the government, and particularly the executive branch, displayed little interest in discussing and negotiating *campesino* demands, at least during the administration of President Oscar Arias.

The 1988 protests had demonstrated to public opinion the near universal loathing of both large and small grain producers for Agriculture Minister Antonio Alvarez Desanti and the "agriculture of change." But the negotiations that followed the protests seemed to confirm the peasant leaders' claim that the minister had no real decision-making power.[2] During the June "strike," President Arias, instead of sending his agriculture minister to discuss the protesters' demands, directed his wife to represent the government side. This was widely interpreted as a slap in the face of Minister Alvarez Desanti and, even worse, one with potentially emasculating implications. Two months later, the humbled Alvarez was kicked upstairs to become Costa Rica's representative to the Central American Economic Integration Bank.

Arias's appointment of José María Figueres as the new minister of agriculture was a last-ditch attempt to recapture rapidly eroding support in the rural areas. An experienced agricultural entrepreneur who had previously served Arias as foreign commerce minister, Figueres did not suffer from the obvious lack of political and practical background that had hobbled his predecessor. In addition, he had "the right name." His father, senior statesman José ("Pepe") Figueres, had led the social democratic insurgents that triumphed in the 1948 civil war, and he had served three periods as head of state or president. Among the most beloved figures in Costa Rica, the elder Figueres embodied, for many, democratic politics and social reform. And, for the younger Figueres, if an illustrious father and practical experience were not sufficient to recoup flagging backing among agriculturalists, the new minister's reputation as a tough former Civil Guard officer who had graduated from West Point could help intimidate restive elements.

The new minister soon let it be known that he would brook no complaints from producers unwilling to participate in "the agriculture of change." "Here we don't have the time nor can we afford the luxury of negotiating continuously," he declared. "Things are clear. What remains is to implement what has been agreed. We all have to work and move forward" (Molina 1988, 17).

More than either of his predecessors, Figueres's discourse employed almost all of the subtle and not-so-subtle elements that figured both in official attempts to impugn the legitimacy of the peasant organizations' leadership and in disputes between and within the organizations themselves. It also displayed the inconsistent twists and turns of an erstwhile social democrat freshly converted to free-market orthodoxy. Shortly after assuming his new post, he signaled his support for economic adjustment policies by denying ever having spoken in favor of agricultural subsidies, even though his pro-subsidy remarks had appeared in the country's largest circulation daily barely two months before (*La Nación*, Sept. 11, 1988, p. 10A).[3] When asked whether his ministry would treat some agriculturalists' organizations differently than others, he replied: "It's probable, [because] there are all kinds of organizations. Democratic ones interested in solving the peasants' and agriculturalists' problems, and another kind interested only in taking advantage of conflictive situations for mounting political platforms and for creating a spirit of chaos and disorganization." Questioned about which organizations he meant, Figueres hinted darkly that the more militant groups were foreign-inspired and unpatriotic: "We Costa Ricans will recognize which are which" (Molina 1988, 17).

This public acknowledgment of differential treatment for peasant groups coincided with a far-reaching covert effort to define the necessary political criteria. An extensive confidential report that the Security Ministry prepared for Figueres shortly after he became agriculture minister classified virtually every rural organization in the country and its leadership according to "political position" and "affiliation" (see Appendix). In the case of groups aligned with the governing National Liberation Party (Partido de Liberación Nacional, or PLN), referred to as "democratic," the report generally noted that the peasants' concerns were "real" and "justified."[4] Groups and leaders labeled as "leftist" were listed as having "external" financing and inspiration or as being "peons" of particular Communist union functionaries. One individual linked to the Social Christian opposition party was described as "dancing with whomever plays him the best tune" (*baila con él que le toque el mejor son*).[5] Another local union head, characterized as "demanding, but tolerable," was said to "speak a lot but say nothing." The report warned that "care" had to be taken even with the politically moderate founders of UPANACIONAL in Cartago, whom it termed "agitators" known for their "violent reactions."

The contempt and fear reflected in the Security Ministry report and in Figueres's public statements naturally colored his relations with peasant organizations. One leader of a small producers association allied with UPAGRA recalled that when Figueres encountered him during a discussion with local agriculturalists, he hissed aggressively, "Who sent you here?"[6] The intention was, as the target of the challenge indicated later, "to tag me as an outsider, an impostor, in front of the peasants, with no right to lead."

Carlos Campos, UPAGRA's secretary general, asserted that among the "death threats" he had received was one from the Minister of Agriculture. He claimed to have learned from a disgruntled functionary that "in a meeting where all his deputies from the Ministry of Agriculture and from other institutions were present, José María Figueres told them, [referring to UPAGRA leaders and allies], 'You tell me where they are and I'll fire the shots.'"[7]

Even if apocryphal, this account was indicative of the deadlock separating the government and the agriculturalists. On the one hand, key officials increasingly viewed rural activists as illegitimate interlopers or incurable atavists intent on stirring up trouble and preserving "backward, inefficient" kinds of production. On the other hand, peasant organizations argued that their livelihood was threatened and that the government had undermined sovereignty and national values by acceding to the dictates of international lending and aid agencies.

NGOs, Social Scientists, and Peasants

Economic disruption and political upheaval in rural areas brought increased attention from nongovernmental organizations (NGOs) and social scientists. While the IMF, the World Bank, and AID went about creating a framework for the "agriculture of change," European and church aid programs and NGOs (e.g., Bread for the World, Caritas, the various national branches of Oxfam, and many others) sought to cushion the shock, providing grants and soft loans for food production cooperatives and small agroindustrial projects.[8] These funds also fueled a profusion of Costa Rican NGOs, many of which carried out studies of, or provided training and technical assistance to, peasant organizations. Ironically, in the midst of a generalized rural crisis, money could be had for those with the skill and contacts to pursue it.

Some peasant leaders complained that social scientists had "appropriated" their ideas about alternative production strategies, written large grant proposals, and then spent the funds on salaries, foreign trips, and well-equipped NGO offices in the cities. They frequently cited the example of what they called "vertical integration of production," that is, the linking of peasant farms with small rural agroindustries controlled by cooperatives or agriculturalists' associations. These small agroindustrial projects—grain milling and drying facilities, coffee processing plants, cellophane snack packaging machines, among others—not only permitted peasants to "capture" value-added that previously accrued to wealthy entrepreneurs, but also facilitated control of marketing. While surely not an invention of peasant organizations, the way in which some NGOs became advocates of this development strategy—of controlling a larger portion of the "commodity chains"—appeared to peasant leaders at the very least somewhat opportunistic.[9]

Even when *campesino* leaders acknowledged the "good, healthy intentions" that often lay behind such projects, they increasingly charged, in indignant tones, that "the great intellectuals of this country, who would be without jobs" if not for the NGOs, viewed peasants as exotic, helpless rustics. UPAGRA Secretary General Carlos Campos, for example, told how one academic "think tank" sent a letter "all worried because we were going to buy some computers. They said that's not logical for the *campesino* and it's not logical that we have a two-story building. But we're in another moment now. Now we have to have a telephone, a fax, a modem. Without them we can't compete."[10]

In 1989, after "years of depending on those organizations," leaders of UPAGRA and allied groups sought meetings with representatives of the principal NGOs involved in the agricultural sector. The encounters were anything but cordial. Peasant leaders charged that they had been "utilized" and that the aid they had been given had become an "invoice" which they were expected to pay by continuing to be compliant "objects of study" or "guinea pigs."[11] They demanded access to "all the information" about relevant grants and criticized as "corruption" the "rich salaries" of NGO directors. Caught off guard, the social scientists and NGO personnel, who considered themselves sympathetic to the peasant organizations, bore the attacks with a stoic calm that nonetheless often hid underlying resentment.[12] But one agriculturalist association member who participated in the talks remembered: "When we spoke of those things, their hair stood on end. Nobody had ever questioned them on this and they had thought they were above it, that everything was cool (*pura vida*)."

The erstwhile militants whom the MRP had dispatched to the countryside had, after years among the peasantry, apparently learned their lessons "too well" and broken with the "vanguard" party that sent them. Almost a decade later, after years of association with NGOs and academic specialists, they felt they had mastered another sort of lesson and were again ready to declare independence. Even Costa Rican NGOs that had provided essential logistical and economic support to the peasant movement in its early days, such as the National Center for Pastoral Action (CENAP) and the Center for Studies of Social Action (CEPAS), came under fire.

A New Coalition for "Justice and Development"

In 1989, after the collapse of UNSA's efforts to forge unity between large and small agriculturalists, UPAGRA and several associated organizations founded a new group, the National Council of Small and Medium Producers "Justice and Development" (Consejo Nacional de Pequeños y Medianos Productores Justicia y Desarrollo). The Council was a coalition of around two dozen local and regional groups from throughout Costa Rica but was dominated by UPAGRA and its allies. It was directed by the self-described "group of six": Carlos Campos and Ulises Blanco (both from UPAGRA), Wilson Campos (from UCADEGUA in Guatuso, northern Alajuela province), Pedro Alvarez (from Coope Llanoazul in Upala, northern Alajuela), Marcos Ramírez (from ASPPAS in Guanacaste), and Carlos Hernández (who until 1991 claimed to be "the San José representative of ASPPAS").[13]

Headquartered in a drab, unmarked house in the gritty Barrio México neighborhood of San José, the Council's offices were sparely furnished with a mixture of knotty pine tables and chairs and mattresses on back-room floors for when visitors from out of town had to stay the night. The internal patio contained some wire clotheslines and a covered outdoor cooking area with a battered propane burner. Tattered posters from the United Nations and other international agencies adorned the walls. A gated carport on the street was usually empty, but occasionally someone would park a dilapidated motorcycle or a rusty pickup there, more often than not using the opportunity to change a worn tire or perform an urgently needed oil change or repair. The place was near the seedy bus terminals that served outlying regions, which both made it convenient and marked it as an organization of people with few resources. When somebody donated a burnished hardwood boardroom table, it appeared incongruous alongside the cheap pine furniture—in a setting where the offices' occupants never seemed to really settle in, constantly rotating instead between the city and the countryside.

The Barrio México headquarters also housed a new NGO, which the Council founded to seek support for its member organizations' agricultural development projects. The "Our Land National Agricultural Development Fund" (Fondo Nacional de Desarrollo Agropecuario Nuestra Tierra) quickly proved to be a canny competitor with the established Costa Rican NGOs.[14] Many funders, particularly European-donor NGOs and governments, looked favorably on Nuestra Tierra because its leaders were articulate and even charismatic, its participants belonged exclusively to small producers associations, and its overhead expenditures were, as the Barrio México house suggested, a fraction of those of the academic and development-oriented NGOs situated in downtown San José and the more upscale neighborhoods around the University of Costa Rica. Nuestra Tierra also proved adept at "greening" its discourse, declaring in an early mission statement that it "elaborates integral proposals that constitute a real option for the economic, social and political development of the *campesinos*, promoting at the same time the use of alternative technology without altering [their] cultural identity, and guaranteeing an adequate and efficient protection of natural resources" (Nuestra Tierra n.d.).

This "green" sensitivity was only partly attributable to good grantsmanship, however. Awareness of environmental problems was widespread at all levels of Costa Rican society and, if anything, was greatest in the countryside, where drought, soil erosion, and agrochemical poisoning were commonplace. The Fund's "green" image and its new foreign NGO contacts allowed participating groups to begin exports of organically grown produce—particularly ginger, peanuts, and cashews—to European niche markets through "Productico," a peasant-controlled exporting company. Within a short time, Nuestra Tierra had hired an agronomist, an animal husbandry specialist, and an accountant to provide technical assistance to member groups and to help administer the grants and merchandise orders. Several other *"técnicos"* worked full- or part-time on writing and overseeing project proposals. An experimental organic garden next to UPAGRA's headquarters in Guácimo served not only to identify promising export crops, but also as an obligatory stop on the *giras*, or tours, given to environmentally minded European (and other) funders. Ironically, not long after the peasant organizations initiated their attack on "parasitic, opportunistic" NGOs, they not only established their own NGO, but also found themselves caught up in the dynamic of seeking out and appealing to funders. In effect, *campesino* leaders were saying to the Europeans, "Fund us, not them."

"The Riches That We Produce"

Even after the economic adjustments of the 1980s, the state continued to set producers' wholesale and retail prices for a number of basic foods, most importantly vegetable oil, liquid milk, and rice. This, in effect, established profit margins by decree and tended to favor agroindustrialists, in the grain sector in particular. Indeed, the largest rice growers cultivated rice (often year-round, with irrigation) not so much because it was especially profitable, but in order to assure a constant flow of raw material to their highly lucrative, giant modern mills (Edelman 1992, 309–13). Peasant leaders, appropriating the prevailing neoliberal discourse much as they did environmentalism, charged that agroindustrialists had accumulated fortunes without facing competition in a genuinely free market. They argued for limiting or eliminating intermediaries' and agroindustrialists' large profits and for creating conditions in which small agriculturalists could process and market their own output. The organizations' first "proposals" were thus aimed at permitting small producers to "appropriate the riches that we produce."

These were hardly novel concepts in rural development, but the suggestion that such ideas could find expression within the ongoing process of imposing "free" market relations and an export-oriented "agriculture of change" did appear new. The peasant organizations were calling for the abolition of privileges and saying that, given a level playing field, they were prepared to compete with anyone, especially with those who had not really had to compete in the past.

In the Northwest this ostensible embrace of free-market ideology and the shift "from confrontation to proposal" seemed to get off to a propitious start. In 1989 ASPPAS acquired a small electric rice mill, a Japanese-made "*piladora*," that would permit transforming "vertically integrated production" from theory into practice. The fact that UPAGRA had loaned funds for the mill was known to the top ASPPAS leadership, but it was only talked about *sotto voce*, since the national news media continued to portray UPAGRA as a "subversive" organization and many peasants were viscerally opposed to anything smelling of "Communism." The mill was installed in a small shed on the property of Coopeasab in Santa Bárbara, next to the road, a twenty-minute ride from Santa Cruz. Marcos Ramírez was ecstatic:

> If we were to succeed in covering the whole productive process in rice, we'd be generating 75 percent profits. The [agro]industrialist makes a 25 percent profit, that's his right according to law. The industrialist sells to the wholesaler with 5 percent more and the wholesaler sells to the retailer with another 5 percent, who sells it to the consumer with another 15 or 20 percent. The industrialist makes 25 percent on his investment, but it's not 25 percent annually, but a 25 percent markup in a month, which in a year is an incredible amount. Supposedly the agriculturalist makes a 25 percent profit when he sells to the industrialist, but it's over one productive cycle [of four months]. Everything depends on the velocity, on how fast it moves. And in rice, beans and maize processing

the velocity is very rapid. So our idea is to not sell to the industrialist or the wholesaler, but to industrialize [grain] ourselves and transfer those profits to the producers.

During and just after the harvest months—in November, December, and January—a steady stream of small producers came by the new mill, some with a truckload or two of unhulled grain, others with just a couple of ragged burlap bags tied to the saddles of emaciated horses or donkeys. The rice went in one end of a large chute, passed through a six-foot-tall device to the pounding beat of the electric motor, and appeared at the bottom husked and clean. The bran and the "*semolina*," or gluten, which could be used for poultry and animal feed, came out separately. Those using the mill's services could, for a slightly higher processing fee, retain these byproducts, though most opted to pay less and leave them to the organization. Much of the industrial rice processors' large profits derived from appropriating and selling bran and "*semolina*," the prices of which were not controlled, to feed concentrate factories. ASPPAS had now "captured" this part of the commodity chain and had begun selling rice byproducts at below-market prices to small-scale poultry and pig producers throughout the surrounding area.

The little rice mill generated high profits around harvest time, but its flow of clients slowed to a trickle by March, when it processed only the occasional couple of sacks that somebody had stored in a barrel or neglected to bring in earlier. From the middle or end of March until November, the mill simply sat unused, gathering dust. One way to achieve greater profitability would be to expand the market for milling services. The possibility of organizing a "coordinated" grain production program, with credit "directed" through the Association, seemed to be a promising way of jump-starting the local peasant economy and assuring the viability of the new mill.

"With Repression or with Money"

"There are two ways to kill a movement," leaders of the Justice and Development Council were fond of remarking in the late 1980s, "with repression or with money." The truth of this adage would be borne out sooner than they realized. And money, naturally, would prove to be a much greater factor in the disruption and demise of organizations, since repression in Costa Rica, such as that which followed the occupation of the Santa Cruz municipal building (see Chapter 4), was, at worst, mild and sporadic.

The success of the Nuestra Tierra Fund caused money-related and other tensions within the peasant movement to come to the fore. To some extent, these strains were similar to those affecting peasant organizations elsewhere: co-optation, accusations of corruption, leaders' upward mobility, differing strategic visions, and the conflicting demands on people's time and resources of production and mobilization (Landsberger and Hewitt 1970). But in important ways the specific problems of Nuestra Tierra's achievements also grew out of fundamental disputes over the markers of peasant identity. The notion of small agriculturalists managing their affairs with computers and making deals over fax lines challenged widely held images of peasant rusticity. But the peasant-as-rustic, both within and outside the movement, remained an important element of authenticity and legitimacy. The Fund's directors sought to break with this legacy and to establish the "dignity" of a "modern" small producer in place of sentimental, demeaning stereotypes of the unsophisticated *campesino*. At the same time, however, their effectiveness as leaders of pressure groups depended on their ability to mobilize large numbers of rural residents who conformed to the image of broken-down, endangered peasants. One former ASPPAS activist from near Santa Cruz commented scathingly on this contradiction and on the growing gulf between leaders and constituents:

> When there's an activity in San José, [the leaders] begin to scour the country to bring the peasants. "You!" they say. "Bring that old hat so that you're seen looking really like shit (*hecho mierda*)." And to you [in the city] they say [in a solemn, sonorous voice], "These are the campesinos." But when someone has to go to Europe to represent the organization or the peasant, only the [leaders'] group goes.[15]

Bitter discussions over authenticity and "the right to lead" took place at the grassroots, at least in the Northwest, some time before they affected the "group of six" that led the Justice and Development Council. This suspicion of leaders fed upon the new grants and loans channeled through the Council's Nuestra Tierra Fund. It also grew out of efforts to expand the initial experiments with vertically integrated production, such as the ASPPAS rice mill in Santa Bárbara.

In 1989, not long after installing its tiny rice processor, ASPPAS received approximately US$12,000 through Nuestra Tierra to establish a rotating credit fund for rice, maize, sorghum, and bean producers. In addition to providing an alternative to the National Banking System, which had little or no affordable credit for small producers, the project would, it was hoped, allow the rice mill to operate closer to its full capacity. The Association selected several dozen program participants, including both individuals and organized groups that cultivated collectively. Members of its board of directors, who now had added administrative responsibilities, received larger loans, in theory so that they could use earnings from extra output to cover the cost of travel to meetings.

As had often occurred when peasants borrowed from the banks, this new money didn't arrive by the beginning of the planting season. ASPPAS organizers, and Marcos Ramírez, in particular, insisted that a check in dollars was already in Nuestra Tierra's San José account waiting to clear and be converted into colones. Hearing this, many project participants took out loans from local agricultural supply houses and began to plant, anticipating that the promised funds would arrive any day. When the project money did finally arrive, it was distributed by organizers carrying wads of cash in their pockets, and this often without securing collateral or even receipts. ASPPAS leaders kept a box of index cards with data on each loan and exhorted loan recipients to be scrupulous about repayment and about spending the monies for the intended purposes. But extending credit without requiring collateral or even signed contracts, a striking contrast with the bank loans to which the peasants were accustomed, made many think that the basic grains project was "almost like hitting the lottery." It seemed a bit like in years past, when the region's agriculturalists had at times received "soft" loans that weren't closely monitored, that didn't really have to be repaid or that were subject to eventual debtors' amnesties.

Some agriculturalists used the "bonanza" to buy clothes, shoes, and small household appliances, rather than to plant or hire peons. In the tiny community of Cola de Gallo, loan recipients repaired to the local cantina as soon as the ASPPAS representative was seen heading downhill. There, they had a fiesta, toasting their luck with cup after cup of *guaro* and terming each shot a *"mazorcazo"*—translated roughly, a blow from a corn cob—an ironic reference to the "maize program" in which they were supposed to be participating.[16]

Because ASPPAS did not have legal status and could not open a bank account, it placed undisbursed funds in the account of Coopeasab, the cooperative directed by Marcos Ramírez. Not surprisingly, this hastily organized effort, managed from another organization's bank account, turned out to be a bookkeeping nightmare—a confusing "mixture of pineapples and mangos," as one project committee member put it. (Later, the rice mill was also found to have suffered from similarly muddled accounting.) As the growing season came to a close, it became clear that the goal of vertically integrated production—with finance and milling provided by the organization—had not been achieved, in part because small rice and sorghum producers depended on, but did not own, mechanical harvesters. Even though loan recipients had promised to process their crops at the ASPPAS mill, many were only able to rent harvesting machinery if they sold their output to the combine owners. To delay and seek better rental terms was inconceivable, since the rains were about to begin and a wet crop would command lower prices or could even be lost altogether.

Moreover, the low level of loan repayment did not permit establishment of an ongoing, rotating fund. Part of this was due to the irresponsibility of those who drank up their loans or used them to buy clothing for their children rather than to plant. But to some degree failure to repay simply reflected the prevailing low prices for basic grains and the high risks of virtually all crop agriculture in Guanacaste. One disillusioned project participant recounted how, after harvesting his sorghum he had taken it to Liberia, the provincial capital, to sell: "And when I returned from Liberia with the cash, I had them call Marcos Ramírez to my house and I told him, 'Marcos, take out my [loan] card, how much do I owe? Here it is.' And [after I paid him] I drank a Coca-Cola with the *compañero* who had helped me with the truck. That's what the sorghum gave me. A Coca-Cola! That took all of my [remaining] cash."

Even worse than only gaining a Coca-Cola, however, was the dissipation of the dream of a rotating credit fund. "If I pay," declared another of the "more responsible" agriculturalists, "I automatically have a right to [borrow from] that fund. I want to know what happened to my money, to see where it is, to maybe borrow for the next [agricultural] cycle. When we realized that in the fund there wasn't any money, we sat down and began to talk. We began to say, 'Well, so-and-so paid, so-and-so paid, and so-and-so *didn't* pay. . . .'"

While several participants in the basic grains program, including the largest cooperative in nearby Carrillo canton, managed to repay the loans, many had no ability to cancel their debts, and an undetermined number had no interest in doing so. Several made promises of future payment in cash or in kind, occasionally saddling the Association with unannounced deliveries of lumber, grain, or other goods that then had to be stored and sold. Project committee members began to accuse one another of carelessness, deceptive accounting, and, worse, embezzlement. The San José office of Nuestra Tierra promised to send a *fiscal*, or auditor, to probe the many bookkeeping irregularities. The Nuestra Tierra emissary turned out to be Francisco Sánchez, a sociology student and boyhood friend of Ramírez, who had collaborated sporadically in Cooperincón and in early ASPPAS organizing efforts. Sánchez's arrival attracted the attention of state security forces which, convinced that he was fomenting land invasions or other trouble in the area, contacted agricultural sector agencies to alert them to his presence.[17] By the end of Sánchez's stay, moreover, he was convinced that the basic grains project had been severely mismanaged, and he held Marcos Ramírez responsible. Their lifelong friendship dissolved in mutual suspicion and recriminations.

This "cannibalistic fight," as Ramírez later called it, coupled with the disastrous results of the loan program, virtually destroyed ASPPAS, which only one year before had boasted more than one thousand members.[18] In small communities where peasants had received project loans, rumors abounded that the money really did not have to be repaid, that it had come from the Sandinistas or from Cuba, that it was a personal gift from Ramírez, or that it was a *partida específica*, the patronage-like appropriations that Costa Rican legislators receive to spend in their districts or dispense to their constituents.

In the atmosphere of attacks and counterattacks, of distrust and even hatred, that the basic grains project left in its wake, the issue of ASPPAS secretary Ramírez's extraregional, urban origins surfaced with new intensity. One project participant recalled the manner in which he had interrogated Ramírez, whom he confessed he still "loved and appreciated":

> We questioned everything, from his arrival here, to how he joined the cooperative, to how he obtained the one million pesos [approximately $10,000] from Bread for the World that allowed him to be named cooperative director. And what happened to the one million, because that cooperative is now belly up, one of the worst off of any. . . . We told him we knew that they [the MRP or UPAGRA] sent him here, because that's the truth, even if he says otherwise. And we said if they sent him here, at least they could have sent him with something, like a motorcycle [for organizing].

This questioning, in its skepticism about leaders' motives and abilities as producers, frequently echoed aspects of the elite, anti-peasant invective that was emanating from Arias's Ministry of Agriculture. But because it originated among rural producers and derived from their own experience and observations, its effect on the strength and credibility of the local organization was undoubtedly much greater. While ASPPAS supporters generally excused Ramírez's inattention to production as part of the cost of directing the group, they were less forgiving of his meager productive background. One agriculturalist mimicked both Ramírez and his critics, asking:

> What am I doing telling you, "Look, come, agriculture has to be done this way. We have to pressure for credits. We're suffering because we don't have aid from anyone." And you've never seen me plant even a daisy. What are people going to think of that? "What's that jerk (*jodido*) talking about? That damned guy (*carajo*) doesn't know anything, I've never seen him work." How is someone going to become the people's savior if he doesn't save himself?

Ramírez did, in fact, work, often very hard, in the sorghum and maize on Coopeasab's property and, somewhat later, with a large herd of scraggly goats, whose milk he hoped to market to hotels that catered to health-minded tourists at the nearby beaches. Like many other agriculturalists, he also had a modestly lucrative business on the side, repairing radios, blenders, and other household appliances. The problem was that he tended to disappear for days or even weeks at a time, leaving others to watch over his "productive activities." In the minds of many local peasants, a true agriculturalist was someone who accorded top priority to production, even staying in the fields at night as the crop matured to ward off birds, rodents, and thieves (which some, in a bit of Spanish doggerel, dubbed *las ratas de dos patas*— "the two-legged rats").

Ramírez replied to the attacks on his authenticity with a well-practiced discourse that denied any lack of autonomy in his decision to settle in Guanacaste and that stressed his recent or distant peasant origins and his hard life since opting to go to the northwestern lowlands almost a decade before. Facing the "interrogation" described above, Ramírez replied that when he first came to the Northwest he had lived without electricity or running water and had had to walk several kilometers through the mud to reach the nearest store. "The Guanacastecan isn't only he who is born in Guanacaste," he declared. "It's he who shares her happy moments and her pain" (*sus alegrías y sus penas*). Responding to regional Guanacastecan prejudices against "Cartagos" (people from central Costa Rica), he emphasized that even though he had spent most of his life in the capital, both sides of his family had been agriculturalists from remote rural zones, and his father was from nearby Nicaragua. Even the urban experience assumed bucolic qualities in his account:

> My father is Nicaraguan and feels very identified with his roots, with Guanacaste. Because here also people eat fresh curds, tortillas, plantains. I lived a time

in Nicaragua at my grandparents when I was a kid, so I experienced that too and feel very close to this [regional] culture. . . . My father is a shoemaker, but he always dreamed of having his parcel [of land]. So much so that his yard [in the capital, San José] is practically a small farm. On the slope by the river he has maize, squash, vegetables. He was always saying, "When I have my parcel . . . , when I have a piece of land, I'm going to raise pigs, I'll have chickens."

This defense frequently came up in Ramírez's discussions with other agriculturalists, but typically it was only partially successful in convincing skeptics. Some agriculturalists maintained that peasant ancestry did not confer any special insight:

There are agriculturalists' sons who grow up in school, in high school, in the university, and then become representatives of the people in the Legislative Assembly, all without knowing what it is to be an agriculturalist. But someone who has always soiled his hands with the earth, a "dirty paws" (*patasucias*), that's someone who's worth something, who can be trusted.

Others mocked Ramírez's assertion that experience in the countryside even qualified someone to direct a movement:

"I'm so and so. . . ." "I have tractors, so I have the right to speak in the name of the *campesinos*. . . ." "I go to this meeting and that one, so I have the right. . . ." "I came here all broken down (*hecho leña*), I spent a year in the middle of nowhere, I got screwed (*me llevé puta*), so I have a lot of consciousness and the right to lead."

Who Will Lead?

Increasingly, in 1989 and 1990, agriculturalists around Santa Cruz were losing interest in organizations and in being led. In January 1989, I accompanied Ramírez as he canvassed a dozen small communities, attempting to "diagnose" their needs and ASPPAS's possible role in addressing them. He was also trying to recruit participants for a two-day workshop to be held in Río Seco, a tiny community near the coast, that would develop a detailed regional "diagnosis" and plan what steps to take.

In this period, which took place before the debacle of the basic grains project, it was clear that the charismatic Ramírez still commanded extraordinary respect from a wide range of people throughout the area. Once, for example, arriving at midday in the small hamlet of La Florida, on the edge of the high zone, he asked a local contact's whereabouts of four young men who were busy imbibing cold beers in a corner of a cavernous community hall. "Why does our visitor wish to see him?" one of the mildly inebriated men asked with a smirk. Ramírez offered a long, vague, and convoluted explanation, intended, I thought, to protect the confidentiality of organization business. Exasperated, one of the drinkers exclaimed, "Get to the point, buddy" (*¡Vaya al grano, maje!*). "Who are you, and why do you want to see Raúl?"

When the ASPPAS secretary said matter-of-factly, "My name is Marcos Ramírez," a look of astonishment came over the men's faces. "*¡¿Vos sos Marcos Ramírez?!*" one asked incredulously, switching to the familiar second-person form and simultaneously pulling out chairs for us to sit on, waving excitedly to the bartender for more beers, and beaming at the celebrity who had unexpectedly showed up in this remote place. But after more than an hour of animated conversation about past struggles in Guanacaste and the banana zone, the need for future organizing, and many warm expressions of agreement and goodwill, none of the men—all unemployed—could be convinced to take a day off, all expenses paid, for the planned meeting at Río Seco.

Despite Ramírez's visits and attempts to recruit in a dozen communities where ASPPAS committees had existed, the only *campesinos* who showed up for the Río Seco meeting, apart from the half dozen members of the Association's board of directors, were a gregarious octogenarian who arrived on horseback from the nearby village of Paraíso, and a couple of fortyish day laborers from the outskirts of Veintisiete de Abril, whom Ramírez and Ezequiel Gómez had met long before at some now forgotten assembly. A sympathetic social worker from the agrarian reform institute led the event, although not in her official capacity, using felt-tip markers and a large newsprint pad on an easel to elicit problems that would be included in the "diagnosis" (technical assistance, credit, land titling, out-migration, etc.). This methodology, so highly dependent on the written word and so reminiscent of the authoritarian relations of an elementary-school classroom, would have worked well in most places in highly literate Costa Rica. As it turned out, though, the two day laborers did not know how to read, and merely pretended, with ill-concealed embarrassment, that they were following the growing list of topics on the easel. I was the first to detect this, several hours after the meeting had begun, and during a coffee break I managed discreetly to convince the social worker to modify her routine. The impact on don Félix and don Facundo, however, was already clearly negative. Upon leaving at the end of the next day, don Facundo turned to me and plaintively lamented, "Here, there's a lot of *diagnóstico* and everything else, but there [where we're from], there's a lot of hunger" (*Aquí hay mucho diagnóstico y toda la cosa, pero allí hay mucho hambre*).

The "hunger" around Veintisiete de Abril, and elsewhere in Guanacaste, was certainly not as widespread or severe as the long-term calorie and protein deprivation that existed in rural Honduras or Guatemala, but it was almost as grotesque, given that it existed in "affluent" "progressive" Costa Rica. Don Facundo's ironic parting aside also highlighted the difficulties that a dwindling peasant association faced in mobilizing a disheartened constituency and in confronting the continuing crisis in the agricultural sector. The desperation that had sparked an almost millenarian upheaval in 1988 had, less than a year later, become an element in the demobilization of the movement.

In 1990 a major shift occurred in the tense relations between the state and the peasant organizations. Free-market policies had been the main point of confrontation since the mid-1980s, and—if anything—the May inauguration of President Rafael Angel Calderón Fournier, an advocate of orthodox structural adjustment, portended accelerated economic liberalization.[19] Calderón, however, while proceeding apace with economic "reform," appointed as agriculture minister a leader of the National Agriculture and Agroindustry Chamber (Cámara Nacional de Agricultura y Agroindustria), Juan Rafael Lizano, who was personally sympathetic to the small grain producers' plight and to the goal of national food security. The new minister immediately began meeting with diverse agricultural sector groups.

Even though ASPPAS was already little more than a shell organization, Ramírez threw himself into a flurry of activity, hoping to capitalize on the government's new openness to the peasant organizations. Shortly before the new administration took office, he participated in a meeting among fourteen Santa Cruz cooperatives and local agriculturalists' committees in the coastal village of Brasilito. The result was a list of demands for the government, ranging from the titling of several properties held by *campesino* groups to financing for cooperatives that wished to acquire CNP retail outlets about to undergo privatization. The meeting included a tense confrontation between Ramírez, who insisted on addressing all the groups' concerns through ASPPAS, and representatives of other organizations, who either viewed ASSPAS with suspicion or now perceived it as indistinguishable from Ramírez himself. "Marcos got angry and yelled," one Santa Cruz cooperative member reported afterwards.

> He kicked and kicked some more and finally ended up on the planning commission, but it didn't really seem to interest him. His thesis was that everything had

to be called ASPPAS, but we thought the important thing was to sit down together, all the groups in the region and get something going, call it what you may. If it's called ASPPAS, okay, but let the people decide, not one *carajo* who's pressuring, who doesn't have any right to speak in my name.

Despite the friction at the Brasilito meeting and his increasing isolation at the grassroots, Ramírez managed to invite several high-ranking officials to Santa Cruz, including the new agriculture minister, to whom he presented a long letter detailing the concerns of the region's cooperatives and the steps that ought to be taken by the relevant state agencies. The letter's final demand—and the only one to be met almost immediately—was for the transfer of the Santa Cruz IDA coordinator who, "because of his character and way of being, has had many disputes with our organization, as well as with other groups, [and] in a move that we consider dishonest has gone so far as to collect signatures among [land reform] beneficiaries asking that he remain in his post" (Ramírez 1990).

The incongruity between ASPPAS's sudden access to the highest levels of the political system and its lack of backing among the peasants at the bottom was all the more notable, since it coincided with concrete efforts that were enjoying considerable popularity. In Santa Bárbara and Cola de Gallo, the Association had opened small retail outlets that sold basic foods and agricultural supplies at cost, and Coopeasab had started a small plant for making concrete blocks. Even these demonstrations of entrepreneurial initiative and the Association's proven access to national-level politicians were not enough, however, to overcome many peasants' qualms about joining a small group of "leaders" who wanted to "direct" them, but who sometimes preached more effectively than they listened.

The decline of ASPPAS was so rapid that Ramírez conceded in early 1991 that "the directors had managed with great difficulty to meet and agreed to dissolve the Association." Around the same time, I spoke with three other members of the board of directors, all of whom denied that such a meeting had even taken place. One commented starkly that "the organization simply died."[20]

The reasons for the death of ASPPAS were not hard to divine. Ramírez and the small group around him were overextended and often isolated from their constituents. The demands of administering their ambitious "proposals"—the rice mill, the basic grains project, the little retail outlets—were sometimes beyond their capabilities. At the local level, these projects, especially when combined with the leaders' often brash speechifying—"*la filoso-*

fada bonita," or "the pretty philosophizing," as one disillusioned *campesino* put it—raised tremendous expectations that could hardly be fulfilled, especially in the short run.[21] The projects also gave rise to suspicions that ASPPAS leaders were, at best, incompetent and, at worst, corrupt. The ensuing conflicts also suggested that, despite the peasant organizations' modernizing ideology and practice, some version of rusticity still figured in the rural poor's own understanding of authenticity and legitimacy, just as it did in national politics. Finally, in a province with pronounced regional sensibilities, an organization led by a "Cartago" aroused anxieties that were linked to Guanacastecans' long and too often negative experience with natives of central Costa Rica, whether politicians, landowners, or the myriad other scoundrels who appeared from time to time, making fantastic promises but later vanishing with the peasants' money, women, and dignity.[22]

This sense that Guanacastecans had not been sufficiently represented in their own organizations induced yet another group to try to fill the vacuum left by the disintegration of ASPPAS. "El Nica" Parrales, who ten years earlier had founded the short-lived Committee of Guanacastecan Agriculturalists (see Chapter 3), attempted in December to launch a new Civic-Agricultural and Integral Development Association of Guanacaste (*Asociación Cívico-Agropecuaria y de Desarrollo Integral de Guanacaste*). Resurrecting his decade-old dreams of organization, Parrales and his small group of largely middle-class agriculturalists held a "founding assembly" in an airy wooden house in downtown Santa Cruz. Beginning at 9 o'clock on a bright Sunday morning, the meeting started off with flowery regionalist oratory from a local high school teacher and an announcement that the assembly was short of the twenty members needed to register officially under Costa Rica's Law of Associations. Finally, at 10:15, the meeting chair began to collect the signatures and identity card numbers needed to register the Association. But at 10:30, he announced that they were still three short of the needed twenty members. Two of those present were sent into the street to recruit passersby, but only one returned, along with a few new recruits, some of whom quickly drifted out. At 11:30, nineteen people were waiting impatiently on the hard wooden benches, casting anxious glances toward the street, apparently hoping either that they could escape or that newcomers would miraculously appear and create a quorum. The aversion to organization seemed to be such that assembling the required twenty warm bodies proved elusive. Only in early afternoon did the organizers succeed in keeping twenty people in the room at once. And most of these fled once their names and *cédula* numbers were affixed to the petition for legal status. This new Association was essentially stillborn, a victim of the tremendous disillusionment with leaders and organizations that had seized the region's agriculturalists over the preceding year.

Factionalism and Unity at the Top

Divisions such as those that ravaged ASPPAS took longer to appear at the national level, though here too it became apparent that "money" could destroy—or at least, radically shake up—an organization. The advent of a seemingly more receptive national administration in 1990, the accumulation of successful and failed grassroots production and organizing experiences, the continuing availability of European "cooperation" funds, and even the crumbling of the socialist bloc and the end of the cold war led the directors of the Justice and Development Council to reexamine and debate past practices and future directions. In the process of "adjusting to adjustment," as some described it, they attained a new level of legitimacy with the political elite and new resources for the base organizations. But access to resources also exacerbated splits within the leadership, just as it had between the leadership and agriculturalist association members in the countryside.

After many years of trying to defend the state's role in the agricultural sector, the leadership of the Justice and Development Council grew increasingly critical of both particular government agencies and of the idea that the public sector could effectively meet their constituents' needs in areas as diverse as setting prices and interest rates and providing technical assistance. They continued to negotiate with the agriculture ministry around these and other issues, and occasionally attained significant concessions, but they also manifested a new appreciation of entrepreneurialism and the free market.

Part of this was the kind of quixotic bravado that had led ASPPAS leaders to think that their tiny rice "peeler" could compete with the giant industrial rice mills like those that dotted the outskirts of Liberia, Puntarenas, and other northwestern cities. On another level, however, the shift reflected a more profound understanding of the relations between international lenders and the Costa Rican state. "The World Bank doesn't come and say, 'We don't want you to provide credit to the maize producers of Guácimo,'" Carlos Campos explained, referring to the canton where UPAGRA had its headquarters.

That's something that our government defines. The World Bank says, "We want you to reduce the public-sector deficit, we want economic recovery, to cut infla-

tion." It says, "We have to reduce the size of the state," but it never says, "let's
close down agricultural research." . . . It's not right to say "IMF, get out," as we
used to do. It's not possible. But we have to insist that the IMF not govern here
and that there be better negotiations with the IMF. . . . The sad truth is that
those who govern don't know how to negotiate and the World Bank has cor-
rupted them. With these policies, they're creating excess labor that will work at
[low] wages and be competitive within Central America. And they're trying to
guarantee that all lands belonging to small producers pass into the hands of
transnationals, where our rulers then become partners.[23]

Attributing the negative effects of economic structural adjustment not to
all-powerful, distant institutions, but to "corrupt rulers who did not know
how to negotiate" made the situation appear manageable, especially since
the new agriculture minister, presumably not "corrupt" himself, had manifested willingness to entertain the organizations' recommendations. In shifting from "confrontation" to "proposals" and in embracing the free market,
the agriculturalists' organizations accorded new legitimacy to the state and
the international lending and aid institutions. In doing so, they were able to
make new allies, both among the powerful and among conservative rural organizations. They nonetheless alienated that large part of their constituency
which had not benefited from NGO-funded programs and for whom conditions had not improved. "From one minute to the next," complained one
irate Guanacastecan who was in sporadic contact with people at the Nuestra
Tierra Fund,

from May 8 [1990, inauguration day] on, everyone is kissing ass with people
from the state, for political strategy reasons. This left me numb, because I was
going along that line—that state policies have to change, that we have to fight,
to struggle to make those people understand. Well now, I don't see the government letting up and the organizations are nice and quiet. No, now "everything's
fine" and nobody wants to march in the street.

The perception that the Justice and Development Council (and its associated NGO, Nuestra Tierra) constituted a unified, harmonious coalition was
hardly accurate, however. Personal jealousies, disputes over decision-making
procedures and political strategy, and conflicts over funds produced a split in
the "group of six" that came to a head in 1992. Much of the conflict revolved
around Carlos Campos, UPAGRA's secretary general. Campos had long enjoyed a much higher profile in the news media than other leaders, partly because he was extraordinarily charismatic and eloquent and partly because

UPAGRA was unquestionably the largest and most thoroughly consolidated of the organizations in the Justice and Development Council. His public prominence required frequent extemporaneous pronouncements in the name of the group and at times made him a kind of lightning rod for elite anger. According to several individuals close to the Council's internal discussions, Campos's public stature accustomed him to making decisions individually that others felt were beyond the competence of any single leader.[24]

Campos had also taken an extremely belligerent attitude toward the politically moderate small producers in UPANACIONAL, whom he frequently disparaged as a collection of "sellouts" or "appendages" of the National Liberation Party (PLN).[25] This injected a note of tension into the joint negotiations that the Justice and Development Council and UPANACIONAL initiated with Agriculture Minister Lizano and hampered the budding alliance between the Council and Costa Rica's largest agriculturalists' union.[26] More importantly, it made it possible for government negotiators to play off against each other the "good" peasants in UPANACIONAL and the "bad" ones in the "subversive" Justice and Development Council.[27]

When a showdown finally occurred within the Council, several leaders took Campos to task for his "autocratic obsession" with being a "*líder máximo*" and for his "verticalist" approach to the organizations' members, whom he was said to consider "masses who needed to be directed" (rather than people who ought to be consulted). Several instances came to light in which funds lent or donated to UPAGRA and Nuestra Tierra had been employed for his own pet projects—"to curry favor with the political fauna of this country," as one of his opponents expressed it. Other criticisms leveled at Campos included his efforts to involve Justice and Development in founding a new agrarian political party to field candidates in the 1994 elections, and his having represented himself to various donor NGOs as speaking for the entire Council leadership when actually he had not consulted them.

Outnumbered four-to-two in the Council's "group of six" and under increasing fire within UPAGRA, the base organization he founded, Carlos Campos withdrew to his pig farm near Guácimo, leaving *campesino* politics to a cohort of younger leaders who, despite everything, had been profoundly influenced by him over the years.[28] Some of those who stayed remembered him with marked ambivalence as "a real bastard, but one who at least lived from his own production." Ulises Blanco, who left the Council at the same time as Campos, was remembered more affectionately, as "an excellent leader, a real pioneer in the area of *campesino* forestry."

In 1992, in the aftermath of Campos's expulsion from the Justice and Development Council, the organization entered into an internal evaluation process that seemed to suggest that some important lessons had been learned. The organization also renamed itself the Consejo Campesino Justicia y Desarrollo, dropping the phrase "pequeños y medianos productores" (small- and medium-size producers) which, some said, was insufficiently "peasant" and overly suggestive of openness to cross-class alliances. The newly named Council moved its office from the working-class Barrio México to the upscale neighborhood of Los Yoses, near, as it turned out, to most of the European embassies that were providing growing levels of "cooperation" funding to grassroots development groups throughout Central America. With the exception of Carlos Hernández, an erstwhile member of the "group of six" who remained the Council's San José coordinator, most of those involved in day-to-day operations and in the coalition's governing committee were people who just a few years earlier had been middle-level local leaders. Unlike most members of the "group of six," they were unambiguously of rural extraction and generally enjoyed good working relations with Nuestra Tierra's staff of *técnicos*.

This appearance of calm did not last long, however. By 1995, tensions were building again over issues of money and leaders' accountability. Several of the Consejo Campesino's base organizations began to question why so few of the grant funds administered by Nuestra Tierra made it to the countryside. European donor NGOs also pressured for a more rigorous reporting of expenditures. Audits of both the Council and Nuestra Tierra suggested that the peasant leaders and *técnicos* were, at best, lousy bookkeepers. While the examination of the organizations' books was not conclusive, some NGO officials and leaders of *campesino* base organizations were certain that at least one member of the Council leadership had embezzled funds. Faced with the imminent withdrawal of both its main funders and of a large portion of its membership, the Justice and Development Peasant Council, along with its associated NGO, Nuestra Tierra, closed its doors.

This denouement, the end of a long chain of factional disputes that began in the countryside, later fractured the "group of six," and now finished off one of the principal national-level peasant organizations, gave rise to new enmities, realignments, and reconsideration of strategy. Several local organizations that had participated in the Council now severed all ties to the national peasant movement. Others, along with what remained of the Council's top leadership, affiliated themselves directly with the Mesa Nacional Campesina (National Peasant Roundtable), an outgrowth of the negotiating coalition between UPANACIONAL and the Justice and Development Council. A few small cooperatives and local associations formed a new Rural and Peasant Council (Consejo Rural y Campesino, or CORYC), grouped around the figure of Wilson Campos and headquartered conveniently in the capital of Campos's home province of Heredia. The peasant movement was not dead, but its organizational composition had shifted, and what its followers once referred to as its *capacidad convocatoria*, or "capacity to convoke," was much diminished.

The State Disengages

Intermittent negotiations with the government in the early 1990s produced some significant gains for the peasant organizations. But negotiations also caused considerable frustration and depleted the groups' energies and resources (as did the factional battles). The very fact that the government recognized the organizations as valid interlocutors and institutionalized formal mechanisms for consultations about macroeconomic and pricing policies, extension programs, marketing, and agrarian conflicts was perhaps the groups' most important gain in this period. A new bipartite, *campesino*–government Land Commission, in particular, managed to resolve a number of contentious squatter disputes by having the government acquire lands for the occupants or move them to nearby state lands. Shortly thereafter, though, the agrarian reform agency shifted gears, letting it be known that it would no longer purchase lands for distribution, but would henceforth limit itself to titling smallholders' farms and to acquiring house lots for members of its existing projects. Similarly, the peasant organizations made little headway in securing commitments about production credit or adequate prices for domestic consumption food products, especially basic grains. And, finally, as peasant leaders frequently pointed out, "consultation" was not the same thing as genuine *participation* in decision making.

In this highly discouraging context, the peasant organizations began to demand that the government start a program for "the reconversion of production." During the 1980s, as Costa Rica was shifting from a protectionist to a free-market economic model, the state had buffered manufacturers with a variety of subsidies. *Campesino* leaders now hoped that they could force the state to soften this transition for small-scale agriculturalists as well. "Reconversion," as the peasant organizations understood it, included a wide range of demands: (1) the creation of joint public sector–peasant organization enterprises for marketing basic grains and perishable vegetables;

(2) efforts to strengthen the entrepreneurial and technical capacity of both individual producers and their organizations; (3) continued public-sector investment in infrastructure, technical assistance, organizational training, and market intelligence; (4) provision of seed money for a *campesino*-administered credit system; and (5) reform of diverse laws regarding privatization of state agencies and enterprises.[29] More broadly, demands for "reconversion" implied state commitment to national food security (which peasant leaders increasingly termed "food sovereignty"), basic grain production, and agroforestry and soil conservation projects that might permit the long-term survival of small-scale agriculture and small-scale agriculturalists.

By the mid-1990s a few tentative bright spots appeared on the otherwise dismal scene. In 1995 the government promised (though, as often happened, it did not actually disburse) 3 billion colones (approximately $20 million) of "seed capital" for financing programs that were part of the peasants' proposals for "the reconversion of production." More concretely, in late 1995, the Legislative Assembly appropriated 8 million colones (about $4 million) toward the creation of an innovative "Bean Consortium" (Consorcio Frijolero) with participation of the state commodities board (CNP), the National Cooperative Union (UNACOOP), and several of the organizations in the Mesa Nacional Campesina (Hidalgo 1997,53–57; Román 1997a,42–44).[30] In the process of privatizing public-sector entities, the CNP had withdrawn from the business of buying beans from producers. The Bean Consortium was to fill the CNP's shoes, assuring the national supply of this key staple food by purchasing producers' harvests or arranging for imports if domestic output proved insufficient. In its first year, the Consortium bought and distributed approximately 60 percent of the 1996 harvest, paying market prices to some eight hundred small agriculturalists and premiums to those supplying high-quality or seed beans. It rented storage facilities no longer needed by the CNP and also imported 6,000 metric tons of beans from China, Canada, and Argentina (about 37 percent of total bean imports). Later in the year, when the Consortium turned a profit from the sale of the beans, it distributed dividends to participating producers.

After a decade of demanding "food sovereignty," the peasant movement had become the central player in a business that, as one of its main activities, imported a crop that had been the major means of livelihood for some of its most militant supporters, the *frijoleros* of the north-central part of the country. Now, at least part of their income would derive from importing the same food that they produced. This irony highlighted one of the chief transformations of the peasant movement since the first, mid-1980s confrontations over economic structural adjustment. From demanding fundamental changes in the economic model which might benefit the peasantry as a whole and assure national "food sovereignty," the *campesino* organizations had gradually shifted to an entrepreneurial approach that sought to deliver benefits to a more narrowly defined constituency, the participants in a new mixed-capital consortium. Seeking to demonstrate a capacity to move from "protest" to "proposal," as well as newly acquired administrative abilities, it had managed to wrest from the state the legal endorsement and the economic support needed to "verticalize" production and reap at least some of the riches that its supporters produced.

The initial success of the Bean Consortium sparked interest in applying the model to other crops, such as basic grains and vegetables, and to other activities, such as finance and supplying agricultural inputs. Peasant leaders' enthusiasm, however, masked a troubling paradox. Their more sophisticated proposals had finally borne some fruit, but their organizational capacity—the ability to mobilize large numbers of followers around a shared political project—was much reduced. The government had adopted the peasants' "reconversion" program because it was a low-cost way of assuring that some significant economic functions were fulfilled at a time when the state was withdrawing from the market. At the same time, the "reconversion of production" could contribute to quieting historically restive elements in a period when the government had few resources for engaging in more traditional forms of patronage and co-optation, or for continuing the types of programs that were emblematic of the largely defunct social welfare state. Inertia and a policy vacuum also contributed to the convergence between peasant organizations and the state. As one *campesino* strategist remarked:

> The reconversion of production is a proposal that we made to the government at a time when there was absolutely no policy defined for the agricultural sector. [Minister] Mario Carvajal was leaving the MAG and almost the only thing he did was to reduce the payroll. Reconversion was the proposal that the organizations put in the government's hands and which it in some way adopted. (Hidalgo 1997,56)

The government and the peasant leadership may have seen eye to eye on the question of the Bean Consortium, but it remained difficult to reach consensus on larger issues. Increasingly, *campesinos* began to assimilate in practice the overwhelming realities of the new Costa Rica. In the countryside, most small-scale agriculturalists had little idea of what the "reconversion of production" might mean. But they were acutely aware of the impact of the new magic of the marketplace and the new liberal economic model. The budget of the public-sector agricultural agencies, for example, plummeted by over 50 percent in real terms between 1991 and 1995 (Román 1997,45). State institutions simply ceased carrying out their traditional functions: the agrarian reform agency no longer distributed land, the commodities board no longer purchased crops, the public-sector insurance company no longer insured peasant food production, the agriculture ministry no longer offered technical assistance, and what was left of the national banking system provided little or no credit for anything other than nontraditional export crops. Levels of protection for most peasant crops also dropped precipitously as Costa Rica entered the GATT and then the WTO, and, even more, as a result of its adherence in 1993 to the Central American Tariff System (Sistema Arancelario Centroamericano), which instituted free trade in basic grains throughout the Isthmus. In several areas of the country, smallholders were selling their properties to transnational banana companies, ecotourism and conservation projects, and a variety of large-scale export enterprises.

The peasantry was not dead—indeed, more than 50 percent of the country's people still lived in rural areas. But a smaller and smaller proportion of them worked in agriculture, the area in basic grains production dropped each year, food imports continued to soar, and the growing number of rural people who had to buy staple foods now paid market prices for beans, rice, and maize—that is, prices that were no longer cushioned by public-sector subsidies.[31] The "fruitful soil"—hailed in Costa Rica's national anthem as giving "sweet shelter and sustenance"—no longer exercised the same hold on the country's "simple and laborious sons and daughters" as it had even in the recent past.

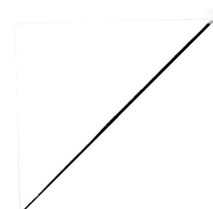

Conclusion: Peasant Movements
of the Late Twentieth Century

> The group image is a mystification. In real social movements, involve-
> ment ebbs and flows, coalitions form and dissolve, fictitious organiza-
> tions loom up and fade away, would-be leaders compete for recognition
> as the representatives of unorganized constituencies, leaders make
> deals with police and politicians. At the extreme . . . professional social
> movement organizations manage to keep movements going despite
> little or no contact with the publics on whose behalf they claim to be
> acting; they manage by finding elsewhere the resources to sustain a
> challenge. What is more, organizers, brokers, some participants, and
> some authorities commonly know that they are not dealing with a
> group durably organized around a well-defined interest. Yet they
> collaborate in maintaining the illusion. Why?
>
> —CHARLES TILLY *(1984, 311–12)*.

Books have an end, but histories do not. The temptation is to strive for narrative closure, even though the processes and struggles analyzed here are
ongoing and incomplete. Many of the people who have appeared in these
pages are still organizing, marching, negotiating, quarreling, scheming and
dreaming, still weeding the rice, injecting the livestock, spraying the water-
melons, and mulching the beans. They are still searching—sometimes successfully, sometimes not—for land, credit, fertilizer, seed, good prices, and
prompt machinery services, and for the knowledge that might allow them to
reap better harvests and defend themselves against the invisible hand of the
market. The most to which a conclusion can aspire is to say something about
the significance of their history so far, both for them and for the broader
study of rural people and of collective efforts for social change.

Simple Models, Complicated Movements

Perhaps the first lesson of this continuing saga is to fully appreciate the het-
erogeneity, complexity, change, and contradiction that characterize the contemporary peasantry and its organizations (in Costa Rica and elsewhere [see
Edelman 1998a]). This is not a history easily pigeonholed in an arid taxonomy
of "identity-based" versus "class-based" movements, nor does it describe a
single *thing*, prototypically "new" or "old," in the ways in which social movements theorists have employed these designations. Indeed, even as scholars
of collective action turned their gaze on the "new" ethnic, women's, peace,
environmental, and gay and lesbian movements, their analyses of these supposedly novel objects of study too frequently resembled the very meta-
narratives about allegedly unitary "old" movements which they sought to
subvert and transcend. Phrases such as *"the* indigenous movement," *"the*
anti-nuclear movement," and the like were redolent of those hoary old anthropological entities, *"the* Nuer" or *"the* community." They could and did
shift easily and imperceptibly from convenient shorthand expression to bed-
rock analytical category, often concealing in the process the disputes, the divisions, and the dropouts (for, in contrast to the epic accounts that peppered
the literature of the 1980s, most movements lose adherents along the way,
sometimes faster than they gain new ones). As John Burdick points out, one
of the "blind spots" of collective action scholarship has been "a striking skit-
tishness about dealing with discursive, ideological, and practical variation
within social movements" (1992, 184).[1]

Another aspect of the heroic, or at least Whiggish, accounts of contemporary social movements has been their relatively unproblematical view of
how organizing takes place. Stories about *"the* movement" (whichever one
it was) tended to assume high levels of agreement among leaders and con-
gruence between the aspirations of leaders and grassroots participants (cf.
Rubin 1998). They also often took for granted an almost Pavlovian conception of how mobilization takes place (whether the stimulus is a threat to an
identity, the pursuit of resources, or an offense to an historically acceptable
standard of living or moral economy). In this reactive conception of human
agents, the role of organizing as a purposeful, deliberate, long-term process
can slip out of view, as can the very important part that organizations play
in social movement activity (Foweraker 1995, 15). This occurs, to some extent, because scholars have accepted uncritically organizers' downplaying of
their own impact and their related efforts to represent movements as spon-

taneous expressions of popular discontent. If I have devoted considerable attention in the preceding pages to intra- and inter-organizational politics, it
has been to redress this imbalance in scholarly thinking and to suggest how
movement activists often spend their time and expend (or even exhaust) their
political energies in factional struggles that sometimes have little immediate
relation to the broader objectives they claim to pursue.

Fortunately, activists and scholars of social movements increasingly appreciate that real episodes of collective action are vastly more complicated
than is suggested in some of the more celebratory portrayals of such phenomena in the academic—and especially the early "new social movements"—literature (Burdick 1992, 1995; Hellman 1995, 1997; Rubin 1998).
This probably reflects a longer acquaintance with movements themselves, as
well as a greater willingness in the less polarized post–cold war era to eschew
the earlier overidentification with, and romanticization of, both "insurrec-
tionary others" and "everyday" resisters. Whatever the reasons, though, this
sound, overdue shift in approaches to understanding actually existing movements is necessarily unsettling for established scholarly conceptions and
practices, since it juxtaposes complex empirical referents with overly simple
abstract categories and explanatory frameworks and finds the latter greatly
wanting. In other words, when social scientists examine specific movements
and find them overflowing the grand theoretical categories—of "old" and
"new," of "class" and "identity," of "ameliorative," "resource-driven," or
"utopian"—it is only a short distance further to questioning the very paradigms that gave rise to these exceedingly abstract and often sterile labels.

What, however, can be put in their place? If the experience of the Costa Rican movements analyzed here suggests anything, it is certainly that greater
caution is in order when it comes to constructing and then reifying categories of analysis. In a complaint that is at least as relevant today as it was
forty years ago, C. Wright Mills declared that "when we descend from the
level of grand theory to historical realities, we immediately realize the irrel-
evance of its monolithic Concepts" (1959, 44). Charles Tilly, similarly, maintains that "recognition of the historical specificity of the forms of collective
action is the beginning of wisdom" (1984, 305). This, of course, requires a
scaling back of theoretical pretensions and a capacity, as Mills put it, "to
shuttle between levels of abstraction" (1959, 34). Whether or not we believe
a unified theory of social movements—or even peasant movements—is possible or desirable, it is clear that many of the key concepts and approaches employed in generalizing about contemporary collective action require both a
greater degree of confrontation with their concrete referents and a more skep-

tical treatment as tools of analysis. The history of the Costa Rican movements has, I hope, demonstrated that "new" and "old," "identity-" and "resource-oriented," "post-materialism" and "post-development," "collective" action and "movement," and certainly "peasant" itself are intensely problematic notions that need to be taken as such rather than as *a priori* givens. More-over, leaders' claims about their autonomy, objectives, constituencies, and personal political trajectories need to be persistently interrogated. It may well be that middle-range generalizations are the most that can come out of a con-frontation between the received models and a series of difficult-to-classify cases.

What, then, might some of these middle-range generalizations be? Here, I will merely sketch out some suggestions that grow out of the experiences of the Costa Rican peasant movements (and, to some extent, out of subse-quent research on related movements elsewhere in Central America [Edel-man 1998a]). First, even after more than a decade of neoliberalism, state agencies remain absolutely central points of reference, foci of demands, and sites of struggle, despite the undermining of traditional power centers that accompanies economic globalization and the by-now old assertions of "new social movements" theorists that emancipatory politics takes place primar-ily in spaces outside or at the margins of the state. The state may have di-minished its size and the scope of its activities, but it still remains a fount of resources in a situation of extreme scarcity, a potential source of ameliora-tion for specific problems, and an essential element in the political legitima-tion—as well as the certification, licensing, even incorporation—of "new so-cial subjects" who seek to survive by engaging the market.

Second, this central role of the state necessarily makes social movement assertions of "autonomy" highly problematic, whether they originate with organization leaders or with those who study them. State agencies, in Costa Rica and elsewhere in Latin America, have demonstrated that the historic practice of co-opting, or "mediating" (as people in the region say), popular movements is still alive and well, in spite of ongoing fiscal austerity (cf. Landsberger and Hewitt 1970). When Tilly asks, in the passage quoted in the epigraph above, why state authorities collaborate in maintaining the illusion that fragmented or even fictitious social movements are durable, it is neces-sary to pose the question of what the alternatives are from the point of view of the key players within the state. Government officials are perhaps more cognizant than most social scientists of the dangerous potentials of charis-matic leaders and the notorious tendency of social movements—and of peas-ant movements, in particular—to rise and fall, to manifest sudden shifts of ideology and practice, and to grow virtually undetected in distant, marginal areas where the state's presence is weak. In Chapter 5 we saw how a moribund ASPPAS organization actually enjoyed a higher profile among high-ranking government officials, who were naturally aware of the previous years' upheaval, than when it was capable of mobilizing hundreds of activists. As the confidential report reprinted in the Appendix also suggests, in situations of crisis state agencies and functionaries (in this case, the Security Ministry reporting to the Minister of Agriculture) may devote considerable attention to identifying "soft targets" among the perceived opposition and to estimating the minimal material or political investments required for assuring an acceptable level of quiescence. Both state officials and movement leaders may stand to gain by the substitution of prolonged negotiations for militant actions and threats of disturbances.

Part of the reason why organization leaders may stand to gain less from immediate results than from the never-ending "give and take" (*toma y daca*, as Costa Ricans call it) of negotiations with the state has to do with a third aspect of contemporary social movement practice that is increasingly widespread in Latin America and elsewhere. Social movements are frequently "mediated" not only by the state, but by the vast numbers of nongovernmental organizations (NGOs) that now pervade the Third World landscape, some effectively building new civil society structures, others assuming functions that used to be carried out by government, others simply providing a more-or-less comfortable living for their staffs and directors, who are typically professionals "downsized" or "retrenched" from public-sector agencies with the implementation of economic adjustment programs (Alvarez 1998; Macdonald 1994). Social scientists concerned with collective action need to take seriously—as part of their research program—the peasant movement adage of the late 1980s that there are "two ways to kill an organization, with repression or with money." When movement leaders collect salaries paid through NGO grants, or when base organizations receive "soft" loans from international "cooperation" agencies (as we saw in Chapter 5), it is hardly surprising that militancy subsides and grassroots activists disperse (hoping at times to establish their own, independent channels to the seeming cornucopia of outside resources).

A fourth and final middle-range generalization may be ventured on the basis of this study. We are in an age when *campesinos* routinely use computers as political and economic tools, when indigenous people attend universities, when the discourses (and sometimes the practices) of environmentalism penetrate to remote rural regions, and when poor rural people rooted in particular places have nonetheless traveled and lived elsewhere. Much of the discussion in anthropology of such "hybrid" phenomena comes perilously close to making peasants or Indians with computers, camcorders, or law degrees a new kind of exotic "Other" that embodies a charming combination of sophistication and primitiveness. Nevertheless, it remains true that today's forms of organization and resistance, and today's peasant movement leaders, will only occasionally and partially resemble the peasants we have known, or thought we knew, in the past. Their lack of fit with the received images and models requires not so much the coining of clever neologisms— Michael Kearney's "polybians" (1996, 142), for example—as an effort to take seriously their histories, as well as their own definitions of self and their framing of their past and present struggles.[2]

Peasants and Modernity

Thus far I have held in abeyance what is, for some scholars, a key question. Does it make sense to speak of "peasants" or "peasant movements" in the late twentieth century? If we ask social scientists, a number of the answers we receive are emphatically negative. Kearney, for example, in *Reconceptualizing the Peasantry*, argues that "the peasant is no longer an identity supported by contemporary social conditions" (1996, 65). Several considerations underlie this assertion: (1) the poor rural people traditionally called "peasants" depend on nonagricultural activities for a significant and growing portion of their income; (2) this, together with accelerating migration out of rural communities, has created multifaceted, often transnational, identities that now generally supersede the rural poor's old, primal identity as "peasants" rooted in particular places or "communities"; and (3), the rural poor of today typically participate in a range of cultural practices—from dress to music, from technology to the imaginary—that implicate them in a thoroughly modern, or even postmodern, world. The very classification "peasant," Kearney affirms, originated as an oppositional category replete with meanings that contrasted it with everything modern. "Anthropology," he contends, "invented the peasant," at once engaging in a new form of "othering," or stigmatization, and also assuring its survival as a discipline in a period when its traditional "primitive" objects of study were approaching extinction (1996, 39, 119).[3]

Situated between the "primitive" and the "modern," however, the "peasant," in Kearney's view, became a "troublesome" category, "disruptive" to the neat binary modes of thinking that pervade anthropology. This concern with the term's imprecision, while reminiscent of Teodor Shanin's discussion of the "awkward class" (1972), or Anthony Leeds's "unpleasantries on peasantries" (1977), assumes a more extreme form in the 1990s. Neither Shanin, who in the 1970s emerged as an energetic advocate of a new comparative and interdisciplinary "peasant" studies, nor Leeds, an acerbic critic of his colleagues' casual use of this ill-defined term, denied that "peasants" existed. Shanin merely noted that the category did not lend itself to traditional sorts of class analysis, while Leeds insisted that since it confused "persons" and "roles" it ought to be eliminated from social scientific discourse.[4] Kearney, on the other hand, seems to seriously think that the "peasant" is solely a kind of anachronistic, essentialist mystification.[5] While Kearney's provocative reconceptualization of peasant studies has much to recommend it, his notion that it is no longer useful to speak of "peasants" or "peasantries" would be problematical if we were to employ it in making sense of the Costa Rican rural movements of the 1980s and 1990s.

What, for example, are we to do in the field when we confront interlocutors who stubbornly assert their "peasant-ness"? How are we to understand their discussions (see Chapter 5) over "who is" and "who is not" a "peasant" (which, unlike most of our own arcane social scientific debates, frequently have immediate, real-world political consequences)? The Costa Rican movements' embrace of the label "campesino"—in its organizations' names and in its participants' definitions of self—is suggestive of an identity with profound historical roots. It also points to that identity's "reinvention" in the midst of the contemporary crisis as a statement about political and economic marginality which, among other things, opened doors to international recognition, alliances, and funds (cf. Brysk 1996). The experience of the Costa Rican movements is indeed "troublesome" for "post-peasant," "post-development" and "new social movements" frameworks, especially given the insistence of leaders and activists not just on their "peasant" identities, but on their aspirations for improved economic and social well-being, which they happen to call "development" (cf. Warman 1988, 657–58). One need not share Shanin's preoccupation with defining generic peasant attributes to recognize the validity of his assertion that peasants "are not only an analytical construct, not only 'bearers' of characteristics . . . , but a social group which exists in the collective consciousness and political deed of its members" (1990, 69).[6]

This, though, is not the only reason for retaining at least some limited, critical use of the "troublesome" term. I pointed out in Chapter 3 that in probing the self-identification of the protagonists of the Costa Rican movements, or in simply listening to them speak to each other about their lives and work, a variety of more-or-less essential categories emerge—*"campesino"* certainly, but also *"agricultor"* and *"productor."* Clearly, "peasant," or its Spanish equivalent, "exists in the collective consciousness of its members," although many, not surprisingly, would also point out that it is but one aspect of their livelihood or being. This self-identification alone would argue for taking the term seriously, as a significant cultural category, even if it is not a very serviceable analytical one. Listening to the subjects of this history also, however, highlights another problematic, contested aspect of the "peasant" label. Orin Starn has noted that in Peru the use of the term *"campesino"* can be a strategy for village elites' "'euphemization' of their real economic position" (1992, 96; cf. Seligmann 1995, 115–16). While this obviously occurs in Costa Rica, too (Edelman 1992, 395), the history of the Costa Rican movements suggests that "peasant movement leaders," and not just "village elites," engage in this type of "euphemization," assuming a political and cultural stance which sometimes is only arguably theirs and which may consequently become a source of discord and organizational division.

Kearney's argument that the "peasant" category ought to be jettisoned rests ultimately on a "binary semiotics of identity" (Nelson 1996), which holds that an individual cannot be both a peasant and sophisticated or modern at the same time. This antinomy has, of course, a long history in the social sciences (and an even longer "folk" tradition). It was strikingly and appallingly present at the very founding of North American anthropological peasant studies, when Robert Redfield (1930, 209–20) nonchalantly labeled residents of the outlying barrios of Tepotzlán *tontos* ("fools"), thus uncritically accepting the derisive category employed by his middle-class informants (*"los correctos"*) from the center of town. Later, social scientists felt free to make generalizations about peasants that would have been viewed askance if they had referred to almost any other human group. Some, as Redfield had, posited "low cognitive capacity" as a "universal" peasant "trait" (Singelmann 1974, 48), while others suggested that peasants were "out of touch with the modern trends of [the] nation" (Wagley 1964, 21).

Kearney rightly faults this "peasant versus modern" opposition as emblematic of the thinking of elites and romantic 1930s and "modernist left-wing" anthropologists, but he accepts nonetheless that a sophisticated, cosmopolitan peasant is a contradiction in terms. In this respect, his argument advances little beyond those of the predecessors he criticizes. With "peasants," as with other timeless anthropological taxa, the supposedly "generic" features of particular human groups often prove to be historically specific and contingent, if not simply reflections of outsiders' own psychological projections or analytical limitations.

The old "modernist left-wing" anthropology, Kearney says, "emphasized relations and forms of production in shaping identity, [whereas now] consumption of material and especially symbolic artifacts and information is of central concern in the global discourse" (Kearney 1996, 132). What this perspective misses is that production and consumption are inextricably linked in the practices and aspirations of poor rural people—whatever they choose to call themselves and however we end up describing them. The encounter with modernity, which Kearney views as undermining "peasants," has also, paradoxically perhaps, permitted them to redefine their conception of the social world and their place *as peasants* in it. As geographer Anthony Bebbington points out:

> Agrarian technology is not merely an instrument for environmental manipulation, but is a symbol speaking to rural people of their social history and relationships, a sign by which they read their identities and their relationships with past, present, and future. Similarly, when peasants incorporate new ideas and material technologies into their practices, this can become a sign that the group is now more distant from a past when they were socially dominated, that their relationship with other social groups is changing, and that they now are claiming rights of access to resources and knowledges previously closed off precisely because of this domination. In short, the incorporation of modern technologies can be a sign of being liberated from a past of domination, even if this may imply new dependencies. It may be that incorporating modern techniques may be politically empowering rather than culturally disempowering. (1996, 91–92)

The Costa Rican *campesinos* we have encountered in the preceding pages have had to adapt to major technological changes in agriculture (first, "green revolution" input "packages" for rice and maize, and then, delicate, high-risk "non-traditional" export crops). They have also had to navigate the labyrinthine financial, marketing, extension, cooperative-sector, and land-tenure institutions which for decades have sought to govern every aspect of smallholders' productive activities. Urban and rural culture have also converged. This is not just because of rural-urban migration or electronic media reaching into the countryside. (For example, televisions powered by automobile batteries bring national newscasts and images of San José's stylish Avenida Central into candlelit homes in remote zones of Costa Rica, beyond the electric grid.) As is the case elsewhere in Latin America, a significant proportion of the economically active population in agriculture now resides in urban areas, and a growing portion of the economically active rural population is engaged in nonagricultural activities (Ortega 1992; Román 1997). A profusion of pro-peasant, nongovernmental organizations has imparted courses on topics as varied as accounting and entomology, communications software and marketing intelligence, forestry and soil chemistry. It is no wonder that today's movement activists aim to "struggle against discrimination," to replace the image of "peasants" as atavistic rustics with that of "peasants" as the politically savvy, dignified, and efficient small producers which they believe themselves to be (Vargas Artavia 1997).

But Are the Leaders Really Peasants?

A different and thornier question of authenticity must also be raised in relation to the movements discussed here. Often their most articulate and charismatic representatives have significant ties to urban society and culture and shallow roots, if any at all, in the countryside. As we saw in Chapters 4 and 5, these issues are rarely uppermost in the consciousness of movement participants, but they can and do surface at moments of crisis, often with devastating political effects. In the critiques directed at failed leaders during intra- and inter-organizational clashes, urban origins and habits become yet one more shortcoming, heaped on top of, and perhaps explaining, other real and perceived defects.

Social scientists disagree about the role of charismatic leadership in contemporary social movements. Gavin Smith, for example, in a stimulating study of an agrarian movement in Andean Peru, maintains that

> the importance of charismatic leadership (often by outsiders) has been exaggerated largely because of the requirements of post hoc account-giving, which tends to conform to the structural requirements of narrative over and above the structural requirements of the movement being described. Whether or not peasant rebels actually require charismatic leaders may depend on many factors; the fact remains, however, that good narrative does indeed so require at least some such equivalent of the hero. (1989, 27)

Gerrit Huizer, on the other hand, has asserted that "in general, peasants seem to need a leader who through his personality gives to his disciples a sense of strength, discipline and bravery for overcoming the great evils that afflict them." He notes, however, that while "these charismatic elements can be useful in the initial stage, when movements later begin to develop and gain strength, they can be counterproductive" (1973, 274–75). Joe Foweraker, similarly, in a masterful synthesis of the recent social movements literature, argues that "just as the theorists may have overestimated the spontaneity of social movements . . . , so they have underestimated the importance of external leaders to movement emergence and success" (1995, 52). Charles Brockett forthrightly states that "significant peasant mobilization seldom is self-generated. Outside organizers, including religious workers, union organizers, revolutionary guerrillas, political party activists, and development workers, have been especially important to the political changes of recent decades in the Central American countryside" (1988, 6).

This is, I hope, a book without heroes. The process of researching and writing it has, to some extent, involved the uncomfortable task of unmasking would-be heroes and toppling them from their pedestals, or at least watching them as they fell of their own accord. I have tried to suggest how, for the movements' constituencies, one day's hero may become the next day's scoundrel, and how the contested lines between "external" and "internal" are not to be taken for granted (as both Smith and Foweraker appear to do). Still, it seems apparent that the history of the Costa Rican movements bears out Huizer's, Foweraker's and Brockett's position on the importance of leaders more than Smith's. As I indicate in the Introduction and various other places in the text, the "narrative requirements" of movement leaders and protagonists, as well as those of almost all the Costa Rican activist-scholars who "accompany" them, are decidedly "anti-hero" in nature, minimizing the role of movement "*caudillos*" (authoritarian leaders), downplaying long processes of building cadre networks and organizations, and soft-pedaling ideological commitments, past and present, in the interest of effective image management. Smith's methodological prescription, that "fieldwork done during rather than after resistance provides an opportunity" to test whether charismatic leaders are products of real movement activity or post hoc narratives (1989, 27), ends up, in this case at least, disconfirming his hypothesis. Indeed, it is possible to conclude that charismatic leadership has been virtually a "structural requirement" of the Costa Rican peasant movements, since without it they would have found it difficult or impossible not only to mobilize followers, but even more to negotiate with politicians or make their voices heard in the news media.[7]

It is hardly news that social scientists are divided over the issue of charisma, given the debates between Weberians and Marxists which reach back to the early twentieth century. More surprising is that those collective action theorists who have seen fit to address the problem of "external" leaders appear to have achieved a consensus unusual in this congenitally fractious area of scholarship. Of course, some substantial portion of the literature simply ignores the issue, commonly as a result of authors' overidentification with, or advocacy for, the movements they study. Ironically, these scholar-activists sometimes collaborate with the leaders themselves, with varying degrees of intentionality, in maintaining the fiction of a "leaderless" movement. Those who have grappled with the question of "outsiders," however, generally agree that their significance is considerable.

Several of the prototypical "peasant wars" of the twentieth century were rife with "outside agitators." In early-twentieth-century, pre-revolutionary Russia, for example, "hundreds upon hundreds of college students, doctors, nurses, [and] university teachers . . . quit their urban life and attempted to 'go to the people'" (Thorner 1986, xi). The Chinese peasant leagues which eventually fueled the Nationalist and Communist movements included workers, students, and even affluent landowners (Wolf 1969, 138–43). Historian Alan Knight notes that the Mexican Revolution was similar in this respect and provides a set of useful general guidelines:

> A 'peasant movement' does not, of course, have to consist entirely of peasants. It does not have to be led, in all cases, by peasants. Rather, across a range of indicators, it must be shown to elicit the spontaneous (not coerced) support of peasants in pursuit of objectives that the peasants voluntarily—indeed, eagerly—endorse. . . . Leadership must be judged in light of support, program, and achievements. (1994, 37)

Knight goes on to say, much as I have suggested earlier, that "style and culture" also matter greatly if non-peasants are to lead peasant movements. These criteria constitute, in my opinion, a commonsensical answer to social scientists who disingenuously profess distress about the "authenticity" of peasant leaders or peasant movements, and to the Costa Rican elites and media editorialists who cavil about "*dizque campesinos*" ("so-called" or "putative" peasants). Notably, though, Knight, like Foweraker, Smith, and Brockett, appears to accept an unproblematical, sharp division between "peasant" and "non-peasant." This distinction, as I argue in a number of places above, is never carved in stone and is not serviceable without reference to specific social contexts and political conjunctures. Rather, the challenge for researchers is to treat "peasant-ness" as a claim loaded with political and cultural significance, to examine the biographies, activities, and motives of those making the claim, and to analyze the moments in which the claim is largely accepted and those in which it becomes the focus of contention.[8]

Social Movements' Support, Programs, Achievements, and Potential

If we are to take Knight's directive seriously, to evaluate peasant movements in terms of "support, program, and achievements," we need first to apply it to the specific struggles that are the subject of this book and then to ask what implications our findings might have for social movements in general. Judith Adler Hellman points out that statements about the achievements and potentials of social movements generally fall into three categories: "the first is that they transform the consciousness of participants; the second, that they win concrete concessions for movement activists; and the third, that they play a key role in the process of democratization that is supposed to be unfolding throughout Latin America" (1995, 174).

The issues of "support" and "consciousness" are, of course, inextricably bound up with each other. Social movements typically obtain the backing of only a small part of their potential constituency. As John Burdick notes, "This disproportion between participants and nonparticipants is quite obvious, both to people at the local level and to anyone who has been in the field. Yet, its empirical and theoretical implications have not been explored systematically" (1992, 183). Moreover, many social movements, and peasant movements in particular, experience rapid growth and disintegration, or oscillations between reformist, radical, and conservative positions (Piven and Cloward 1977; Zamosc 1989). Peasant movements employ a bewildering range of tactics that may span the spectrum from "weapons of the weak" to "peasant wars," but are generally more likely to include petitions, land occupations, meetings, demonstrations, and time-consuming but vital negotiations with state officials over such issues as support prices, interest rates, the cost of fertilizer and pesticides, or the pace of agrarian reform.

Peasant movements, like most kinds of collective action, are frequently neither unambiguous successes nor failures (and any evaluation in the latter terms depends mightily, of course, on the criteria and time frames used). Sometimes, too, participants in unsuccessful struggles repress painful memories of defeat, obscuring experiences that researchers might otherwise uncover and analyze (Bozon and Thiesse 1986). One aspect of the Costa Rican movements—their periodic tendency to crumble and lose support—is clearly a broader phenomenon, as Hellman points out:

> The outcomes of social movements are not always positive. . . . Disempowerment may occur when a movement is coopted or repressed. But it may also occur when participants grow discouraged and disillusioned with the dynamics of group participation, the behavior of their co-activists who rise to leadership positions, or the bossiness of foreign or middle- and upper-class NGO workers—to cite but a few negative possibilities. . . . Such movements decline not only in response to repression or co-optation, but to loss of enthusiasm for collective activity itself on the part of burnt-out social activists. (1997, 16)

This "disillusionment," however, is only part of the picture. In the Costa Rican case examined here, movement activists drew inspiration from age-old attachments to maize agriculture, "modern" aspirations for development, and "postmodern" sensibilities about threatened identities. Sometimes, as I have discussed above, these inspirations live on in the accumulated experience of peasant movement participants even after the movements themselves have faded away. These "enduring activist subcultures" (McAdam 1994, 43) are a widespread phenomenon (and one which tempers Hellman's pessimistic observations about activist "burnout"). A noted economist has observed that leaders of grassroots development efforts share

> one striking characteristic: . . . most of them had participated previously in other, generally more "radical," experiences of collective action. It is as though their earlier aspiration for social change, their bent for collective action, had not really left them, even though the movements in which they had participated may have aborted, petered out—or perhaps ended successfully. Later on, this "social energy" becomes active again but likely in some very different form. (Hirschman 1988, 8)

This, indeed, is a common thread running through the history of the Costa Rican peasant movements of the late twentieth century. On the one hand, it describes a figure such as Carlos Campos, who went from being an urban cadre of the Marxist–Leninist MRP, to founding the radical peasant union UPAGRA, and then to participating in the staid National Chamber of Pork Producers and the conservative Social Christian Unity Party. On the other, it fits as well the uncounted former ASPPAS activists around Santa Cruz and Nicoya who say they are too *resquemados*—implying both "burned" and "embittered"—to join another *campesino* association, but who continue to work quietly in cantonal agricultural centers, community development associations, new and old cooperatives, and a variety of other groups which provide hope, real benefits, and a channel for their irrepressible "social energy." It even applies to Marcos Ramírez, whose efforts to form a durable *campesino* organization in Santa Cruz failed and who was ultimately cast out of the national peasant movement, but who acquired a small farm further south on the Pacific coastal plain, joined a local agriculturalists' association, and continues to hatch plans for obtaining low-cost loans for organization members and for exporting organic coffee to the United States.

This kind of long-term commitment to change, whether or not we call it "social energy," is also useful for considering the concrete achievements of the Costa Rican peasant movements over the period since their rise in the late 1970s and early 1980s. "Concessions," as Hellman astutely remarks, are "the area of organizational achievement that receives the least attention because it appears to be the one that most embarrasses social movement analysts" (1995, 176). She rightly recognizes that movements often obtain concessions, if they do at all, by compromising their autonomy vis-à-vis the state, and that material demands are commonly the aspect of most importance to movement participants. To acknowledge either of these things may be disconcerting for those committed to working within an "identity politics" or "new social movements" framework, since collective activity is supposed to occur at a distance from the state and without material needs as a central focus. My discussion above of ASPPAS and the struggle for payment for drought losses in Santa Cruz, and of the national peasant movement more generally, bears out Hellman's assertion about the centrality of material demands; the experience of the national organizations also validates her observation about the potential loss of movement autonomy. Like her, I have noticed, and sought in a small way to break, the silences in the literature regarding "concessions" won as a result of movement activity (and I have tried to move beyond "embarrassment" in the process).

I have, of course, referred throughout my account to specific accomplishments, large and small, and it is perhaps worth summarizing a few of them here, particularly given the less than heartening tone of much of what I have had to say so far about both the peasant movements and social movements in general. First, the post-1948 Costa Rican state, while it enjoyed considerable peasant support, did not generally give rural, informal labor or small independent entrepreneurs coverage under its social security system. For agriculturalists, this began to change in the 1980s, as UPANACIONAL, and later UPAGRA, UCADEGUA, and other groups, pressured successfully for the inclusion of their members (and members' families) in this national health and pension system. Around this time, the social security system entered a profound crisis, linked to the free-market transition and the growing disengagement of the state from social welfare activities (Castro 1995, 81–84; Valverde 1993, 53–58). But obtaining coverage nonetheless signified a strengthening of social protections for a previously marginalized sector. Second, the movements secured a host of conjunctural gains, including "indemnification" for drought-induced crop losses, concessions in negotiations over prices, settlement of land occupation and agrarian disputes, occasional emergency production credits, and programs—typically short-lived—that provided inputs at or even below cost. A third kind of achievement of the Costa Rican peasant movements has been in the area of enhancing their constituents' entrepreneurial capacities. Bookkeeping disasters, unintentional and deliberate, have played a formidable part in the disintegration of a number of national and local peasant organizations. But it is also the case that *campesinos* have begun to administer new varieties of enterprise, from small purchasing cooperatives and marketing companies to major sectoral players such as the Bean Consortium. Fourth, and finally, the peasant movements achieved a startling degree of legitimacy and political recognition. Even the "bad," radical leaders of the late 1980s now sit alongside the "good" *campesinos* from UPANACIONAL when they face government negotiators. And negotiations continue to take place within a variety of agencies in the executive and legislative branches of government and in the remaining autonomous public-sector institutions. At a time when students, intellectuals, and organized labor have been in retreat, in terms of presence in public debates and media attention, *campesino* activists have been among the most prominent, outspoken, and articulate critics of the new economic model.

These accomplishments have occurred, however, against a background of diminishing militancy and grassroots support. Collective action theorists sometimes argue that a movement's failure to obtain a material response for its activists may lead to demobilization (Foweraker 1995, 78). I have suggested above, particularly in my discussion in Chapter 4 of the struggle for "indemnification" for lost crops, that *obtaining* a response may also have that effect, precisely because many movement participants are motivated primarily by material concerns. Probably a more useful way of looking at the problem is to suggest that demobilization may reflect not only inactivity or defeat, but an inability to balance constituents' different objectives, as well as those which may or may not be shared between leaders and movement participants. As political scientist Vincent Boudreau indicates, in a comment derived from experience in the Philippines but which applies squarely to the Costa Rican peasant organizations, "direct socioeconomic relief can convert protest organizations into collectivities geared mainly to provide services to constituents" (1996, 185–86; cf. Piven and Cloward 1977).

Social movements' achievements, as I suggested (following Hellman) at the beginning of this section, should be considered at both the most tangible level of material "concessions" and at the more impalpable, complicated level of the transformation of consciousness. This terrain is, of course, less amenable to traditional social scientific forms of analysis and description than is the question of "concessions" or movements' concrete achievements. In delving into the intricate recent histories of the Costa Rican peasant movements and their relations to the consciousness of participants and leaders, I have had two principal objectives. First, I have tried, particularly in Chapter 3, to examine the diversity and distant historical roots of collective struggles that preceded, yet still informed and shaped, the "new" peasant movements of the 1980s and 1990s. While I have not quite managed to attain here the century-long "frame of reference" which historian Steve Stern (1987, 13) recommends in his superb methodological treatise on peasant rebellion, I have sought to give an account of the varied political currents—"mother's milk" agrarianism (to use Rudé's memorable term), radical Christianity, "old" and "new" Marxisms, banana worker unionism, and even student anti-imperialism—that constitute the historical experience of the activists and the direct antecedents of the struggles central to this book. Second, in keeping with my concern that human agents and organizing processes not be given short shrift, I have focused attention not just on diffuse ideologies, but on the people who were bearers of these currents. I have asked how particular individuals conceived of their own situation as historical subjects and how they acted in light of, or in spite of, those conceptions.

Did the Costa Rican peasant movements of the 1980s and 1990s achieve significant and lasting changes of consciousness in the people they professed to represent? It is hard to provide a definitive response to this question, both because this work has not pretended to be so comprehensive in scope as to "cover" all the constituencies the movements claimed to represent and because consciousness, especially in a tumultuous period such as the one analyzed here, can only be the product of a combination of influences (which are unlikely to be the same for each group or individual). The pages above nonetheless contain some suggestive grounds for at least a tentative affirmative answer. It is worth recalling the dramatic contrast, to which I alluded in the Introduction, between the surface passivity of many Santa Cruz peasants in 1982 and the combativeness, again of many, in 1988. More relevant per-haps—because the contentiousness of 1988 proved to be ephemeral—is the ease with which rural people throughout Costa Rica now converse, critically and with sophistication, about economic structural adjustment, inflation and devaluation, the effects of the growing export orientation of the economy, and the disengagement of the state from the countryside.

Can this shift in awareness, though, be attributed to the movements' ef-forts, or must it be seen as the product of a wider economic and political con-juncture? Both clearly played a role, and in weighing their relative contri-butions some caution is in order, not least because of the ever-present and conspicuous disparity (noted above) between leaders' claims to represent others and the frequent indifference or hostility of those others about being "represented." The experience of living through the crisis of 1980–82 and the subsequent neoliberal transition brought Costa Ricans—in the country-side and the urban areas—face to face with market forces against which they had long been cushioned by an interventionist state. This stark confronta-tion required virtually all sectors of society—and all individuals—to re-define their survival strategies and their relation to an external political and economic world that they increasingly realized shaped their present and fu-ture possibilities. A surprising number of poor rural people came to grasp the rudiments of macroeconomics, if only to comprehend what was happen-ing to interest rates, their currency, and the prices which they paid for their equipment and clothes and those which they received for their crops. For many—probably most—this undoubtedly occurred in the absence of direct contact with the peasant organizations. The awareness that others like them were marching and being tear-gassed in the streets of San José, however, brought a much larger number to the point where they at least attended to the movements' message, distorted though this was by the glib and conser-vative communications media. And for some small portion of the rural pop-ulation, the lived experience of crisis and the passionate, exhilarating sense of engagement that came with activism combined to form an ongoing "en-ergy" and commitment, accompanied by more profound learning processes, that persisted even when the movements they belonged to disappeared or metamorphosized into businesses, NGOs, or service organizations.

The contribution of social movements to democratization is often consid-ered a criterion by which to measure "success" or "achievements." At first glance, it might seem peculiar to examine this question in Costa Rica. After all, the country has long enjoyed extraordinary prestige as a political democracy, where representative government and human rights are respected and honored. How could Costa Rican democracy possibly be any better?

A thorough answer to this question is beyond the scope of this discussion, although I have alluded in the chapters above to a number of the limitations, in theory and practice, of Costa Rica's democratic model. For my purposes here, the key contribution of the peasant movements of the 1980s and 1990s has been to advocate forcefully on behalf of small agriculturalists at a time when elites and development planners have been largely hostile, or at best indifferent, to peasants and their concerns. For peasants, it was a new and unprecedented kind of participation and representation to be part of bipartite commissions, to sit in the same room with cabinet ministers and presidents, and to hash out the details of payments for crop losses, a joint *campesino*-public sector marketing consortium, procedures for resolving a land occupation, or any of the myriad other issues that have been on the table. In a narrow sense, these encounters—frequently frustrating and inconclusive—grew out of the peasant organizations' flexing their muscle, out of demands for material concessions and for the negotiation of differences. More generally, they can be seen as a broadening of conceptions of citizenship, the claiming of new political spaces, and "the invention and creation of *new* rights" (Dagnino 1998, 50, italics in original). That these "new rights" are, however, fragile, precarious, and only the fruit of intense and continuing struggle is suggested in the anguished and angry comments of UPANACIONAL leader Guido Vargas to a 1997 meeting of peasant leaders:

> It is often said that now we have representation. But that is false. It is true that now we can sit at a negotiating table, just as we can block a highway. But it's very hard to get those who govern to fulfill negotiated commitments. We've made some progress, because now we *campesino* agriculturalists do not believe that we are different, just as women now do not believe that they are inferior to men and blacks do not believe that they are inferior to whites. But those who discriminate haven't yet changed. The rest of society, and especially those who govern, continues to believe that we are inferior. They continue deceiving us and lecturing us. (Vargas Artavia 1997, 16)

The peasant movements have managed to gain a modicum of participation, to contribute to transforming consciousness, and to wrest significant material concessions from the state. With the aid of foreign "cooperation" agencies, the movements have guaranteed their own survival, at least for the foreseeable future. A different question is whether they have assured the survival of the peasantry, those on whose behalf they claim to struggle.

Will Peasants Survive?

In the 1970s, in a debate with continental reverberations, Mexican social scientists clashed, often bitterly, over the ultimate fate of the peasantry.[9] Observing the unprecedented penetration of the countryside by large agribusiness, one side in the polemic argued that the peasantry was undergoing a process of proletarianization and would soon disappear as a distinct social group. Unable to compete with capitalist agriculture because of problems of productivity, scale, and access to capital, markets and technology, peasants would find no alternative but to abandon the land and become wage workers or part of the unemployed "reserve army" of labor. These *descampesinistas*, generally sympathetic to the Mexican Communist Party, believed this imminent melding of the peasantry into the working class was a political step forward, since most of Latin America still had many more peasants than proletarians and the newly proletarianized would presumably recognize their "true," revolutionary class interests, something impossible as long as they retained access to land and "petty bourgeois," entrepreneurial values and dreams. Anthropologist Roger Bartra even went so far as to suggest that "the Mexican peasantry, as we know it today, is an invention of the bourgeoisie, which engendered it in its own image and likeness" (1975, 321).

On the other side of the discussion, a diverse group of *campesinista* social scientists rejected the unilineal evolutionism and the implications of inevitability that characterized the orthodox Marxist position. Several pointed out that capitalism, at least in Mexico, required a large peasantry. The cost of reproducing the labor force could be borne by small farms instead of becoming part of capitalists' wage bill. Self-provisioning or petty commodity production during part of the year or part of the incompletely proletarianized peasant's lifetime constituted a subsidy to capitalist entrepreneurs, who could feed their employees low-cost foodstuffs and would not have to pay a high social wage as long as peasant households absorbed the costs of rearing children and of sustaining the unemployed, disabled, and elderly. Some *campesinistas* indicated that women were disproportionately responsible for generating this subsidy, through unwaged household, artisanal, and subsistence production which permitted men to temporarily leave farming and enter the labor force (Deere 1979). Other transfers of "value," or "surplus," from small farms to capitalists—via unequal exchange, intermediation, loan sharking, and so on—made it "logical" to maintain *campesinos* in the countryside. Key *campesinista* theorists emphasized that while peasant households did not operate according to the same profitability criteria as capitalist firms, they nonetheless employed creative and flexible methods of allocating scarce resources. In an incisive study of rural Morelos, Arturo Warman, for example, described what he called the peasants' "devilish dialectic":

> To satisfy the demands of "growth and development" the *campesinos* have intensified their activity, making it more diverse, complex and arduous to meet a rate of exploitation that is higher, and more ubiquitous and harsh. To be "modern"—to graft fruit trees, to fertilize with chemicals, to harvest products that are too expensive for them to consume—the *campesinos* have had to become more "traditional." They have to plant the maize that they are going to eat . . . [and] establish reciprocal relations for the direct, non-capitalist exchange of labor and resources. They have had to reproduce themselves and expand the size of their surplus labor force. (1976, 15)

Other *campesinistas*—Armando Bartra (1985) and, to a lesser extent, Gustavo Esteva (1983)—argued that it was primarily through political struggle, rather than through the "logic" of the rural household or the larger economic system, that peasants had historically guaranteed their survival. The upsurge of new peasant movements in Mexico in the late 1970s and early 1980s seemed to suggest that this dynamic would persist well into the future (Gordillo 1988; Moguel, Botey, and Hernández 1992).

The adversaries in the *campesinista–descampesinista* debate engaged each other on various levels. *Descampesinistas* (e.g., Feder 1977, 1444) marshaled census data that showed a rapid growth of the "landless peasantry," while *campesinistas* (e.g., Warman 1980, 173–74) argued on the basis of their field experience that apparently landless people frequently had access to land through family members or informal tenure arrangements. By the mid-1980s the discussion had subsided, unresolved. Much of it, as William Roseberry (1993, 334–35) has observed, was in effect a somewhat sterile replay on Mexican soil of an old polemic between Lenin and Chayanov over the nature of social classes in the Russian countryside. If the *campesinistas* had failed to interrogate the Chayanovian vision of the peasant household as a self-contained unit, it was also true that the Leninist *descampesinistas* had greatly underestimated peasants' capacity to hold off proletarianization by increasing their involvement in the informal, nonagricultural economy.

Probably more significant in curtailing the discussion, however, than this jousting over "sacred" texts and models was what Cynthia Hewitt de Alcántara termed the "embarrassingly persistent failure of the peasantry to disappear" (1984, 185). Gustavo Esteva put it more bluntly when he ridiculed "the radical failure of long-nurtured predictions that the *campesinos* would fade away. The fact is that they do exist and their numbers increase daily" (1983, 206).

The *campesinista–descampesinista* debate, after a nearly decade-long letup, re-emerged in the early 1990s with the reforms to the Mexican Constitution's Article 27, which permitted privatization of agrarian reform lands (Appendini 1992). A few years later, the North American Free Trade Agreement exacerbated the problem of U.S. dumping of "surplus" grain, already a significant difficulty for Mexican maize producers, large and small. Much as was the case in Central America, it appeared to many that *this* time the peasantry really was going to succumb to a free-market onslaught far more ferocious than that which had provoked the debate nearly twenty years earlier. Michael Kearney, for example, generalizing from his rather peculiar vision of Mexico to the rest of the agrarian world, asserted that "peasants are mostly gone" and that "global conditions do not favor the perpetuation of those who remain" (1996, 3).

The first round of the Mexican debate had reverberations in Central America, but these were ultimately faint in comparison with the louder and more pressing polemics that polarized the entire region during the civil conflicts that racked the region—touching even peaceful Costa Rica—from the late 1970s to the early 1990s. As peace returned to the isthmus, and development was once more on the agenda, the debate over the fate of the peasantry resumed (Rodríguez Solera 1992; Arias 1989).

The "failure" of the peasantry to disappear, as well as the end of the cold war and the crisis of Marxism, made it difficult to carry out the discussion in the sweeping, unconditional terms that had characterized the debate of the 1970s. Nonetheless, several tendencies appeared undeniable to those on both sides: (1) in Costa Rica (and in most of the rest of the region as well), the proportion of the economically active population working in agriculture was declining; (2) the percentage of rural household income derived from agriculture was also falling; and (3) migration from rural to urban areas was accelerating (Rodríguez Solera 1992; Román 1997). Yet, while these processes would seem to confirm the old predictions about the demise of the peasantry under capitalism, several countervailing trends were also evident. First, rural households were diversifying their already diverse survival practices, com-

bining artisanal, rural and urban, informal and proletarian labor, and producing a bewildering mix of agricultural products, often for both household
consumption and for high-priced markets, domestic and foreign. Second,
migration to cities often figured in overall household strategy not as a permanent transition for the entire unit, but as a temporary expedient for one or
a few of its members and intended to generate remittances for maintaining
a base, however tenuous, in the countryside. This reflected the widespread
realization that living standards and social status for the poorest of the poor
in the cities—those sleeping in the streets, in the squalid markets, or in
shacks on the urban periphery—compared unfavorably with those of the
poor rural dwellers. And, finally, capitalism could be cruel to capitalists, too,
which sometimes redounded to peasants' advantage.[10] In areas where large,
modern farms had failed, such as United Fruit's vast properties in southern
Puntarenas, for example, thousands of squatters—many, former Company
laborers who, though proletarianized, had never lost their hopes of becoming smallholders—moved in and carved peasant farms out of abandoned banana plantations. Sociologist Carlos Rodríguez Solera observes of this region: "There, where they used to produce for export, they now produce for
self-consumption; where they once utilized tractors, they now use wooden
ploughs; and where the great proletarian masses were concentrated, we now
find only *campesino* producers" (1992, 211).

Rodríguez Solera's research—based, inevitably, on census data—is one of
the most detailed empirical contributions to the debate on the future of the
peasantry.[11] While the focus on Costa Rica may attract little attention in
Mexico, still at the forefront of the debate, this careful study does draw several conclusions of considerable significance here. Most importantly, Rodríguez Solera suggests that processes of *"descampesinización"* and *"recampesinización"* are occurring simultaneously in different, often adjacent, zones
of the country. If the overall tendency was of *descampesinización* during the
1950–73 period, "this halted completely by 1984 as a result of the economic
crisis." Moreover, while the relative importance of the peasantry in the economically active population fell throughout the 1950–84 period, its absolute
size continued to grow (Rodríguez Solera 1992, 200). For Costa Rica, as for
Gustavo Esteva's Mexico, the peasants "do exist and their numbers increase
daily."[12]

What aspects of peasant production, agrarian society, or the broader economy explain this dynamic mix of contradictory processes and tendencies? In
attempting to answer this question it is useful to distinguish between two
broad groups within the landed peasantry. Following economist Alain de

Janvry and his colleagues, I may characterize these as (1) peasant units capable of accumulating capital and competing in commercial agriculture, even though the institutional context may not be highly favorable for them, and (2) "sub-family" units which function as a "refuge sector" and whose number varies inversely with economic growth (de Janvry et al. 1989, 105–6). The survival of the first group, which is well represented in the Costa Rican peasant organizations, especially UPANACIONAL, depends not only on favorable market conditions, but on creating a more favorable "institutional context"; indeed, this has been a major focus of the movements discussed in this volume.[13] The second, "refuge" group tends to expand and contract, depending on the availability of other options. Economists might describe these peasants as having to estimate the tradeoff between the potential income generated from their parcels and the opportunity cost of their labor. This invocation of a coolly calculating *homo economicus*, however, conceals more complicated cultural, psychological, and even economic dimensions of the problem. In contemporary Costa Rica, as in other times and places (cf. A. Bartra 1985, 13), the lack or instability of waged employment keeps alive and strengthens *campesino* aspirations. *Campesino* migrants, and the working-class and informal-sector descendants of *campesino* parents or grandparents with an insecure and perpetually subordinate position in the urban labor market, are less likely to develop a proletarian consciousness than to crave the self-sufficiency and autonomy which they imagine, rightly or wrongly, they or their ancestors once enjoyed. Until the Costa Rican model of development demonstrates that it is capable of offering these people sustained employment at adequate wages, or a stable and remunerative insertion in the urban informal sector, their dreams will, during economic contractions, at least, often focus on land and on the countryside (cf. Hewitt de Alcántara 1984, 191).[14]

Cultural Specificity and the Free-Market Onslaught

In the Introduction and in several other places in the text, I have communicated my view that economic structural adjustment, typically represented as an effect of overwhelming and inexorable global forces that homogenize everything in their path, might better be understood as a profoundly *cultural* process of contention between dominant and popular sectors (and their respective allies, at home and abroad). Even a cursory consideration of Costa Rica's transition from a statist to a free-market economy suggests that to speak of the imposition of a single, uniform neoliberal model is fraught with problems. The country's indulgent treatment at the hands of the international financial and aid institutions, its persistent and continuing failure to meet key macroeconomic targets (particularly in the area of fiscal deficit reduction), the elite's enthusiastic embrace of free-market ideology, and the government's ongoing—albeit inconsistent and inadequate—efforts to maintain some semblance of a social safety net are all suggestive of specificities that need explanation. To some extent, I have sought to outline the relevant aspects of the historical and political context in Chapter 1. Here, I will simply restate some of the principal points.

The politics of economic structural adjustment—and free-market transitions, more generally—is too often portrayed as a dry sequence of high-level negotiations and policy shifts followed by purely reactive behavior on the part of the popular sectors. This picture misses at least three kinds of striking variation: (1) the distinct demands the international financial institutions make upon different countries and their inconsistent enforcement of those demands; (2) the specific policies governments implement in their efforts to meet (or to give the appearance of trying to meet) those demands (when negotiating over how to reduce a budget deficit, for example, do they first offer to slash spending for security forces, highway maintenance, or primary education?); and (3) the varied political practices of non-elite groups which, as we have seen, draw heavily on long historical experiences of struggle and highly specific sorts of assumptions about political possibilities.

It is important to keep in mind that states—and not just the people who form social movements—have "action repertoires" (to use Tilly's suggestive term [1984, 307]). The Costa Rican peasant movements might block an avenue or a highway, but not by burning old automobile tires (as might occur in Mexico) or building defensible stone barricades (as might occur in Nicaragua); they might place an advertisement in a newspaper, but would be unlikely to carry out a letter-writing campaign (as might happen in the United States). Similarly, the Costa Rican state—largely demilitarized and with a legacy of reformism—might threaten to clear a blocked street or road with tear gas or even truncheons, but using fire hoses or rubber-coated bullets—implements not in its normal toolkit of repression—would be highly unusual (although Costa Rican security forces have, on rare occasions, shot squatters during evictions [Edelman 1992, 259]). Both sides bring to the fray expectations and practices developed over historical time and not just as the product of particular "political opportunities" or conjunctures. The now extensive literature (e.g., Brockett 1991; Tarrow 1994) that sees "political opportunities" as central to the formation of social movements rightly points to the critical importance of moments of state or elite vulnerability. But for this potential to be realized or even recognized, grassroots organizers need already to be in place or, alternatively, to emerge quickly; in either case, they have to undertake a great deal of analysis and very hard work. And "opportunities" may be lost, as we have seen above, if organizers do not succeed in moving—in both senses of the word—potential movement participants.

Economic structural adjustment has also had culturally specific features because the reproduction of difference—and not just the homogenization of differences—is a crucial part of contemporary capitalism. This is not to attribute any kind of teleological agency or volition to an abstract capitalism, but simply to point out, as others have in much greater detail (e.g., Castells 1996, 106–15), that spatial and class inequalities, while constantly shifting, are a necessary feature of globalization. For a Costa Rica that is moderately prosperous by Central American standards, having an impoverished Nicaragua next door provides a ready source of inexpensive, unskilled labor for the booming tourism and banana industries. For consumers in affluent countries, the Central American maquiladora assembly factories—those contemporary "satanic mills" (to cite Polanyi's [1944] famous description of the textile plants of early-nineteenth-century England)—turn out vast quantities of affordable, fashionable garments. Our clothes, our tropical desserts, and much else are products of this unevenness in the world economy—and of the sweat of small and large producers and their hired laborers. In the same way, local and national struggles have distinct "rules of the game" and contenders whose historical and individual experience informs their political imagination, ideas, and practices. These particularities continue to shape the reproduction of small spaces, such as that erstwhile "pilot project" called Costa Rica.

Final Reflections

Speculation about the "invention" of "peasants" is one of the curious undertones in recent anthropological literature about agrarian societies. Did anthropology "invent" or "engender" the "peasant," as Michael Kearney asserts? Or did the cold war (as he also insists)? Did the Mexican (or some other "populist"-minded) bourgeoisie "invent" the Mexican peasantry, as Roger Bartra argued in the 1970s? Did Mao Tse-tung's Communists create backward "peasants" out of people previously called "farmers" in order to underscore the evils of pre-revolutionary society, as China scholar Myron Cohen (1993) maintains? These conjectures indicate that, in much of the world, the term still carries an intense political charge, even in the late twentieth century. They also suggest that social scientists attribute to themselves and to the realm of high politics a great deal of agentive power.

For the rural poor, in contemporary Costa Rica at least, the proposition that *campesinos* are an invention of a distant, unseen force, of the upper classes or of foreign anthropologists, meets with bemused incomprehension or, occasionally, hilarity. Writing in *Pig Earth*, his lyrical paean to rural France, John Berger captures better than many of the theorists encountered above the core dilemmas of a social group that struggles to reinvent itself in every generation. "The peasantry everywhere," he says, "can be defined as a class of survivors. . . . The word *survivor* has two meanings. It denotes somebody who has survived an ordeal. And it also denotes a person who has continued to live when others disappeared or perished" (1992, xi, xiv).

In the face of the invisible hand of the market, peasants have had to learn to manage their microeconomies in spite of all the economists who surround them.[15] This management—this reinvention—occurs in complex, dynamic interactions with all of the elements that have traditionally affected survival—soils, water, seeds, animals, pests, and pathogens—as well as with state agencies and banks, non-peasant citizens groups, the urban informal sector, the news media, outside agitators and foreign NGOs, and with—and sometimes in spite of—their "own" organizations and leaders. Berger's appreciation of how the rural poor see what is to come is as germane in 1990s Costa Rica as it was in France three decades earlier:

> How do peasants think or feel about the future? Because their work involves intervening in or aiding an organic process most of their actions are future-oriented. The planting of a tree is an obvious example, but so, equally, is the milking of a cow: the milk is for cheese or butter. Everything they do is anticipatory—and therefore never finished. They envisage this future, to which they are forced to pledge their actions, as a series of ambushes. Ambushes of risks and dangers. (1992, xvii)

It is this combination of future-oriented action and vision—so different from both "culture of poverty" and "post-peasant" conceptions of the rural poor—that makes this a story as yet without a conclusion. In their organizations, in their dreams of autonomy and security, in their often agonizing physical labor, in their protests and negotiations, Costa Rica's *campesinos* have their sights set on survival—and, they hope, survival with dignity.

Many of the risks and dangers are clear to them, but they also know there will be unanticipated ambushes. Steeling themselves to weather this onslaught is the stuff of everyday activity, a process of constantly reinventing themselves in new situations, natural and human-made. And it also means assuring in large and small ways—as *campesinos* continue to proclaim in the Legislative Assembly and at the Casa Presidencial, in the Agriculture Ministry and at the Central Bank—that "they won't take away our future": *¡No nos arrebatarán el futuro!*

REFERENCE MATTER

APPENDIX: THE COSTA RICAN SECURITY
MINISTRY'S VIEW OF THE AGRICULTURALISTS'
ORGANIZATIONS IN 1988

This secret document, leaked to the author by an official of the opposition-led (PUSC) administration that took office in 1990, provides a unique look at the surveillance capabilities and ideological concerns of what is usually considered an ultrademocratic state. During the 1988 rural upheaval described in Chapters 3 and 4, Costa Rican security forces carried out extensive undercover work and catalogued numerous agriculturalists' organizations, sometimes in quite piquant terms, according to political orientation, number of members, and the real or potential "threat" each posed to the state. The Ministry of Public Security then provided this material to Agriculture Minister José María Figueres, who frequently had to travel to different rural zones and meet with peasant organization leaders. The document also suggests the tremendous variety of agriculturalists' organizations that existed in 1988. Women are nearly entirely absent in the groups' leadership ranks; several organizations, primarily cooperatives, are headed by individuals with university degrees (*licenciados* ["Lic."] and agronomists ["Ing."]); some appear as leaders of more than one organization. In translating the document, I have left organization names in Spanish; material in parentheses appears as such in the original; I occasionally use brackets to provide additional information or original Spanish phrases. The document's authors made a number of errors of substance and form. I have not bothered to indicate these, although I have corrected some minor typos found in the original. Some organizations, generally cooperatives or local affiliates of national *cámaras*, or producers' "chambers," are listed, but appear not to have been targets of serious intelligence gathering. The frequent "n.d."'s appear in the original (*"no hay datos"*). ASPPAS, discussed above in Chapters 3–5, appears first in the original document, suggesting perhaps that it was a focus of special concern at the time. The Atlantic zone groups that also preoccupied the Security and Agriculture Ministries are listed at the end.

Ministry of Agriculture and Livestock [MAG] Directorate of Planning
Basic Information for the Office of the Minister
(**Confidential Information**)

Name	Location	Area of influence	Leaders	Number of members	Objectives	Political position
DRY PACIFIC REGIONAL DIRECTORATE						
Santa Cruz						
Asociación de Pequeños Agricultores de Santa Cruz [ASPPAS]	Santa Cruz	Santa Cruz	Marcos Ramirez J.	1,500	Collect payment for losses, maize, beans and rice.	n.d.
Sindicato de Trabajadores de Guanacaste (SINTRAG)	Santa Cruz	Santa Cruz	Francisco Gómez	n.d.	Seeks land and credit.	n.d.
Confederación Auténtica de Trabajadores Democráticos (CATD)	San José	Santa Cruz, Nicoya	José J. Meléndez	400	The acquisition of land.	n.d.
FESTANO	National	Cartagena, Santa Cruz	Carlos L. Andraneto, Francisco Cortés C.	150	To obtain land.	n.d.
Upala						
in formation	Upala	Upala	Pedro Alvarez, Erasmo Aragón	n.d.	Agricultural and livestock production.	n.d.
Filadelfia						
Grupo de Agricultores de Belén, Grupo de Agricultores de San Blas	Filadelfia	Filadelfia	None	both together 125	Payment for crop losses.	n.d.
Oficina del Arroz						
Cámara de Productores de Caña						
Cámara Nacional de Granos Básicos						

Affiliation	Reason for which it arises	Economic activities in which it participates	Surface area [of its lands]	Observations	*Observations*
UNSA	Because of interest in securing payment for crop losses in 87–88.	Rice, maize, beans	n.d.	The leader(s) seek to consolidate the organization on a more permanent basis.	The leader probably receives additional economic support.
n.d.	Need for land and credit for agriculture and livestock production.	n.d.	n.d.	Despite their many efforts, they haven't been able to satisfy their needs.	The problems they face are real. It's not known if they have goals beyond their immediate objectives.
n.d.	The acquisition of land for agricultural and livestock production.	n.d.	n.d.	Includes groups from Santa Cruz and Nicoya, such as the Asociaciones de Pequeños Agricultores de Nicoya, Ortega, 27 de Abril, San José de la Montaña, Huacas y Caimital.	The problem which gives rise to the union is real.
n.d.	The acquisition of land for agricultural and livestock production.	n.d.	n.d.	At the local level, it is not a dynamic organization.	The justification for its existence is real.
n.d.	Unite all forces in the canton in the area of production.	n.d.	n.d.	Form a united front in the entire canton.	The best known external leader Carlos Campos.
n.d.	Support in determining crop losses from 87–88.	n.d.	n.d.	These groups organized in coordination with the Ministry [MAG].	Groups are temporary and have no relation with other organizations.

Name	Location	Area of influence	Leaders	Number of members	Objectives	Political position
CENTRAL PACIFIC REGIONAL DIRECTORATE						
Garabito						
Campesinos de Playa Hermosa y Garabito	Garabito		Hubert Madrigal	24	Obtaining land.	Democratic
Grupo de Campesinos de Garabito y Quebrada Amarilla	Garabito	n.d.		32	Obtaining land.	n.d.
San Mateo						
UNASANA	San Mateo	Oricuajo, Labrador	Jorge Rodríguez	18	Securing credit.	n.d.
Grupo de los 12	San Mateo	Oricuajo, Labrador	Fernando Herrera	12	Organization for credit.	Democratic
Asociación de Pequeños Productores de Labrador	San Mateo	Labrador	Eladio Umaña	19	Organization for credit, housing, basic services.	Democratic
Empresa Autogestionaria Campesina Pozo Azul	San Mateo	Jesús María	Julio Alfaro Sibaja	21	Organization for production and marketing.	Democratic
Chomes						
Asociación de Pequeños Productores de la Zona Norte de Puntarenas	Puntarenas	Sardinal, Guacimal, Pitahaya, El Roble, San R. de Sardinal	Efraín Ramírez Garita, Hernán Cruz (secondary), Ramón Castro (secondary)	144	Purchase and distribution of land.	Right-wing
Comité de Abangaritos	Puntarenas	Abangaritos, Manzanillo, Coyolito, C. de Pájaros	Orlando Jiménez Mendoza, Domingo Rojas, Arnulfo Jiménez Mendoza	40	Generate sources of jobs.	Democratic
Monteverde						
Comité de Agricultores de Santa Elena de Monteverde	Puntarenas	La Cruz, Catitas, San Bosco	Hernán Brenes, Jimmy Alvarado, Carlos Abarca	n.d.	Diversification of production.	n.d.

Affiliation	Reason for which it arises	Economic activities in which it participates	Surface area [of its lands]	Observations	*Observations*
n.d.	Obtaining land.	n.d.	n.d.		
n.d.	Obtaining land.				
n.d.	Obtaining credit.	n.d.	n.d.	They meet in the community hall of Jesús María.	The leader has leftist tendencies.
n.d.	Obtaining credit.	n.d.	n.d.	They meet in the community hall of Jesús María.	
n.d.	Organization for credit, housing, basic services.			They meet in the community hall of Labrador.	
n.d.	Organization for production and marketing.	n.d.	n.d.	They meet in the Pozo Azul farm on Wednesdays.	
n.d.	Purchase and distribution of the Hacienda San Marcos.	n.d.	n.d.	Owner interested in selling.	Some interest on the part of involved government institutions.
n.d.	Development of two production projects: shrimp cultivation and purchase-distribution of Finca El Cimarrón de la Bajura.	n.d.	n.d.	Few possibilities because of poor organization and lack of interest.	Democratic group composed of small agriculturalists, peons on cattle ranches, and some fishermen.
	Create more sources of jobs and stop in-migration to area.	n.d.	n.d.	They present problems of irrigation, roads and transport.	

Name	Location	Area of influence	Leaders	Number of members	Objectives	Political position
San Luis en marcha	Puntarenas	San Luis de Monteverde	Gilbert Lobo Navarro, Zallo Brenes (secondary)	n.d.	Development of the zone.	Democratic

Paquera

Name	Location	Area of influence	Leaders	Number of members	Objectives	Political position
Asociación de Agricultores Proyecto Río Grande	Puntarenas	Asentamiento Río Grande	Eduardo Cubero V.	n.d.	Development of agricultural projects.	Social Democratic
COOPEPAQUERA R.L.	Puntarenas	The peninsular zone	Hernán Guido Cruz	n.d.	Improve income levels.	Social Democratic
COOTRAPAQUERA	Puntarenas	From Punta Leona de Paquera to Cabuya de Cóbano	Víctor Manuel Barboza	n.d.	Improve income levels.	Social Democratic
Asociación de Fruticultores de Paquera (ASOFRUTA)	Puntarenas	Nicoya Peninsula	Albín Jiménez Jiménez	n.d.	Export of fruit.	Social Democratic
Unión de Campesinos Orotinenses (UCAMPO)	Puntarenas	Orotina	Elpidio Avila	n.d.	Solve members' problems.	n.d.
Asociación de Productores del Pacífico Central	Puntarenas	Esparza	Juan Araya, Ing. Olman Quesada (secondary)	n.d.	Looking for better marketing alternatives.	n.d.

Montes de Oro

Name	Location	Area of influence	Leaders	Number of members	Objectives	Political position
Coopelagos R.L.	Puntarenas	Montes de Oro	Leonel Sibaja, Gerardo Solano	14	Agricultural production.	n.d.
UTACA	Puntarenas	Cedral, Arancibia	Efrain Ramírez, Porfirio Azofeifa	37	Purchase of land.	n.d.
Asociación de Productores de Zapotal de Puntarenas	Puntarenas	Asentamiento Zapotal IDA	Juan José Mesén, Rafael Calderón	22	Agricultural production.	n.d.
UTAN	Puntarenas	Miramar	Efraín Ramírez	35	Purchase of land.	n.d.

Affiliation	Reason for which it arises	Economic activities in which it participates	Surface area [of its lands]	Observations	*Observations*
n.d.	Achieve better social relations.	n.d.	n.d.	They need land purchases, roads and electrification.	
n.d.	Resolve problems of irrigation, potable water, roads, and credit.	n.d.	n.d.	The group is composed of small agriculturalists.	
n.d.	Develop the cooperative movement.	Fruit, cattle	n.d.	They present problems of lack of working capital.	The group is composed of small agriculturalists.
n.d.	Provide fishermen with better services and better prices.	Fish	n.d.	They propose the elimination of intermediaries.	
n.d.	Eliminate intermediaries.	Mangos	n.d.	They plan to export directly.	Small- and medium-size producers.
n.d.	Solve members' problems.	n.d.	n.d.	The participation of the MAG is of vital importance in solving their problems.	Because they are a homogeneous group, they have no secondary leader.
n.d.	Technical assistance and planning of planting areas.	Mangos	n.d.	The MAG should appoint a full-time specialist for them.	
n.d.	Self-managed cooperative [coooperativa autogestionaria].	Coffee, cardamon, macadamia, vegetables	96 hectares	Composed of small agriculturalists.	
n.d.	Purchase of a farm.	Fruit trees, coffee	n.d.	Small producers with little or no land.	The size of the farm they need is not known.
n.d.	Exploitation of farm by parcel holders [parceleros].	Forestry, dairy, fruit trees	1,200 hectares	Financed by the European Economic Community.	
n.d.	Purchase a farm to divide in parcels.	Bamboo, fruit trees, coffee		Small producers.	

Name	Location	Area of influence	Leaders	Number of members	Objectives	Political position
Asociación de Productores de Marañón	Puntarenas	Esparza, Miramar	Ing. Gerardo Rudín	n.d.	Encourage cashew cultivation.	n.d.
Coopemontes de Oro	Puntarenas	Montes de Oro, Arancibia	Agronomist Víctor Arce	n.d.	Marketing of coffee.	n.d.

Jicaral

Name	Location	Area of influence	Leaders	Number of members	Objectives	Political position
Comité Pro-Asentamiento Campesino Agrario	C. Blanco	Jicaral	Franklin Obando R.	n.d.	Obtain lands.	n.d.
Comité Cívico	Jicaral	Lepanto District	Benito Villegas L., Francisco Hernández L. (secondary)	n.d.	Struggle to solve the community's problems.	n.d.
Cámara de Ganaderos	Jicaral	Lepanto District	Digno Chavarría S.	n.d.	n.d.	n.d.
Asociación de Agricultores	Jicaral	Jicaral and surrounding areas	Fernando Escalante A.	n.d.	Obtain lands for small producers.	n.d.
Comité de Desarrollo de Camaronal	Camaronal (Jicaral)	Camaronal	Lisímaco Morales, Antonio Calvo (secondary)	n.d.	n.d.	n.d.
Comité Pro-Cultivo de Mango	Jicaral	Lepanto District	Carlos L. Solórzano, Evelio Hernández (secondary)	n.d.	Marketing of fruit.	n.d.
Organización de Trabajadores Agrícolas Independientes del Cantón de Puntarenas	Jicaral	La Fresca	Martín Quirós M.	n.d.	Obtain lands for small producers.	n.d.
Comité Auxiliar CAC de Jicaral Puntarenas	Jicaral	Lepanto District	Alejandro Rodríguez Q., Miguel Durán J. (secondary)	n.d.	Improve the socioeconomic condition of the members.	n.d.

Affiliation	Reason for which it arises	Economic activities in which it participates	Surface area [of its lands]	Observations	*Observations*
n.d.	Marketing and technology.	Cashews	350 hectares	Medium and large producers.	
n.d.	Marketing of coffee.	Coffee	500 hectares		
n.d.	Obtain lands.	n.d.	n.d.	They are presently negotiating with Evelio Benavides an option to purchase a farm.	
n.d.	Form a Municipal District Council.	n.d.	n.d.		
n.d.	n.d.	Livestock	n.d.	Medium-size and large producers.	
n.d.	Obtain lands for small producers.	n.d.	n.d.	They are presently negotiating the purchase of a farm from Luis Ugalde.	
n.d.		n.d.	n.d.	They meet every two weeks in the community hall.	
n.d.	Consolidate a group and struggle for a secure market with PINDECO.	Mangos	n.d.		
n.d.	Obtain lands.	n.d.	n.d.	They are presently negotiating options to purchase Palo Arco farm and Y Griega farm in Nandayure.	
n.d.	They meet the first and third Thursdays of each month in the local MAG.				

Name	Location	Area of influence	Leaders	Number of members	Objectives	Political position
Cobano						
Cooperativa de Suministros Agrícolas	Cóbano	Cóbano District	Ing. Miguel Escalante A., Norma Quirós (secondary)	n.d.	Supply agricultural inputs at reasonable prices.	n.d.
Cooperativa de Pescadores Malpaís (COOPEMALPAIS)	Cóbano	Malpaís, Santa Teresa, San Martín, Manzanillo, B. Horizonte	Elías Núñez G., Róger Rodríguez (secondary)	n.d.	Marketing of fish.	n.d.
Grupo de Agricultores de Cabuya	Cabuya [Cóbano]	Cabuya	Eladio Vega Arguedas, Javier Méndez (secondary)	n.d.	Promote agriculture and livestock projects.	n.d.
Comité de Parceleros Proyecto COS-2761	Cóbano	Asentamiento de Cabuya, Santa Teresa, San Martín, B. Horizonte	Eladio Vega Arguedas, Javier Méndez C. (secondary)	n.d.	Coordinate with the MAG.	n.d.

REGIONAL DIRECTORATE OF THE EASTERN CENTRAL VALLEY

Name	Location	Area of influence	Leaders	Number of members	Objectives	Political position
Cartago						
Seccional UPANACIONAL	Cartago	Cartago	Olman Montero Aguilar, Norman Asenjo (secondary), Luis Federico Vásquez (secondary)	40 representatives	n.d.	
Unión de Pequeños Agricultores de Los Santos (UPAS)	?	Los Santos	Jorge Manuel Monge S.	n.d.	n.d.	n.d.

Affiliation	Reason for which it arises	Economic activities in which it participates	Surface area [of its lands]	Observations	*Observations*
n.d.	Improvement of the rural population of the district.	n.d.	n.d.	A high percentage (95%) believe in the cooperative's objectives.	
n.d.	Creation of a storage facility to secure a market for their products.	n.d.		Interest in strengthening the organization with aid from state institutions.	
n.d.	Coordinate with agricultural sector state institutions.	n.d.	n.d.	They receive donations from various international foundations.	
n.d.	Coordinate with the MAG.	n.d.	n.d.	The committe has become more efficient in different aspects of this project. It has coordinated other projects.	
UPANACIONAL		n.d.	n.d.	They remain very united in demanding debt forgiveness payments.	Care should be taken with Sr. Asenjo since his participation has been that of an agitator. Sr. Vásquez supports the violent reactions of Sr. Asenjo.
n.d.		n.d.	n.d.		The leader is president of the National Confederation of Cantonal Agricultural Centers and president of the CAC de Tarrazú. He is demanding with the MAG but is tolerable. They participated in blocking the southern highway. Lately they have been calm. He speaks a lot but says little.

Name	Location	Area of influence	Leaders	Number of members	Objectives	Political position
Unión Campesina Agraria de Cartago (UCAC)	Turrialba	?	Sara Arguedas, Luis Sánchez A.	n.d.	n.d.	n.d.
Unión de Trabajadores Industriales de Cartago	Turrialba	?	Guillermo Barrantes	n.d.	n.d.	n.d.
Asociación de Agricultores del Guarco	Guarco	?	Ramón González Vaglio	n.d.	n.d.	n.d.

REGIONAL DIRECTORATE OF THE WESTERN CENTRAL VALLEY

Alajuela

Name	Location	Area of influence	Leaders	Number of members	Objectives	Political position
Coopemontecillos	Montecillos (Alajuela)	National		2,121	Get better prices in the national and international markets.	n.d.
Coopealajuela R.L.	Alajuela	Alajuela		800	Greater profits for its members.	n.d.
Centro Agrícola Cantonal de Alajuela	Alajuela	Canton of Alajuela		91	Assist and orient the producers of the canton.	n.d.

Atenas

Name	Location	Area of influence	Leaders	Number of members	Objectives	Political position
Coopeatenas R.L.	Atenas	Atenas	Lic. Leonidas López G., Rigoberto Morera (secondary), José Campos (secondary)	1,100	Organize agriculturalists to defend their interests.	n.d.

Affiliation	Reason for which it arises	Economic activities in which it participates	Surface area [of its lands]	Observations	*Observations*
n.d.		n.d.	n.d.	n.d.	Both leaders are catalogued as true mass agitators. They are dangerous because their interventions lead to land invasions (Tayutic Forest Reserve). They have support from employees of other state institutions, such as the CCSS.
n.d.	n.d.		n.d.	n.d.	Their demands are similar to those of UPANACIONAL, although in recent months they have lost enthusiasm and are largely inactive.
n.d.	n.d.		n.d.	n.d.	A passive group. Their leader may become violent, but in the end he is tolerable.
n.d.	Establish more hygienic and modern slaughterhouses.	Cattle, horses, pigs			
n.d.		Coffee	n.d.	Their principal activity is coffee processing.	
n.d.		n.d.	n.d.	The services they offer are: credit, renting of land, sale of inputs, and administration of a farmers' market.	
n.d.	Seek to avoid intermediaries in the marketing of their products.	n.d.	n.d.	Seek to educate the community about the principles of cooperative organization.	

Name	Location	Area of influence	Leaders	Number of members	Objectives	Political position
Centro Agrícola Cantonal de Atenas	Atenas	Atenas	Ing. Mario Campos (MAG), Jorge Arredondo (secondary)	125	Aid and orient the producers of the canton.	n.d.
Asociación de Desarrollo Específico de Fruticultura de Atenas (ADEFA)	Atenas	Atenas	Ing. Mario Campos (MAG), Jorge Arredondo (secondary)	80	Increase the area in production, apply technology to new plants to obtain better quality and size.	n.d.
Seccional UPANACIONAL	Atenas	Atenas, San Mateo, La Garita		1,308	Organize agriculturalists in defense of their interests.	n.d.

Grecia

Name	Location	Area of influence	Leaders	Number of members	Objectives	Political position
Cooperativa Victoria R.L.	Grecia	Grecia, Esparza, San Ramón, Palmares, Naranjo, Atenas, Alajuela, Poás	Marcos T. Solís R.	2,500	Offer to purchase and process the partners' harvest and to market it, obtaining the best prices.	n.d.
Seccional UPANACIONAL	Grecia	Grecia	Dagoberto Murillo E.	820	Organize agriculturalists in defense of their interests.	Democratic and pacific.
Centro Agrícola Cantonal de Grecia	Grecia	Grecia	Horacio Rodríguez P.	280	Seek agricultural, social and economic alternatives.	n.d.
Cámara de Productores de Caña	Grecia	Grecia, Guanacaste, Puntarenas, Parrita, San Ramón, Atenas, Naranjo, Sarchí, Poás, Alajuela	Miguel Alfaro Bolaños	4,600	Better benefits for its members.	n.d.

Affiliation	Reason for which it arises	Economic activities in which it participates	Surface area [of its lands]	Observations	*Observations*
n.d.	An organization that represents them in the search for benefits.	n.d.	n.d.	They have problems related to finance.	
n.d.	Export the fruit directly to obtain greater income for the members.	n.d.		They have problems of lack of credit for infrastructure. Lack of support from the National Banking System.	
UPANACIONAL	Higher prices for their products and lower prices for agricultural inputs.	n.d.	n.d.		
n.d.	For better organization of the agriculturalists.	Coffee and sugarcane	n.d.	They are now acquiring 51% of the stock of CATSA, so their influence will extend to Guanacaste.	
UPANACIONAL	Part of a union organization without any political party affiliation.	n.d.	n.d.	Through a committee, they coordinate with the local MAG office the development of the highland avocado project.	
n.d.	n.d.	n.d.	n.d.	They have two auxiliary committees, one in Río Cuarto and another in Tacares.	
n.d.	Offer coffee producers agricultural chemicals at lower prices.	n.d.		They have four storage facilities for inputs in Grecia, Poás, San Ramón and La Garita.	The Cámara does not constitute a problematic organization. It does not react with violence, but with dialogue.

Name	Location	Area of influence	Leaders	Number of members	Objectives	Political position
Heredia						
Coopepirro	?	Barva, San Lorenzo, Santo Domingo, Heredia, etc.	Francisco Salazar Vargas	153	Offer to purchase and process the partners' harvest and to market it, obtaining the best prices.	n.d.
Coope-Santa Rosa R.L.	?	Northern sector of Heredia, Alajuela, San José	Ing. Jorge Maroto Casorla	785	Improve the socio-economic conditions of its members.	n.d.
Coope-Libertad R.L.	?	?	Lic. Juan B. Moya, Ing. Rolando González (secondary)	1,550	Improve the socio-economic conditions of its members.	n.d.
Coope-Fresa	Heredia	Heredia, San José, Alajuela	Ing. Jorge Manuel González E.	43	Market strawberries in international markets.	n.d.
Centro Agrícola Cantonal Santo Domingo	San Luis	Santo Domingo	Audencio Zamora	40	Improve the socio-economic conditions of its members.	n.d.
Naranjo						
Coopenaranjo R.L.	Naranjo	Naranjo	Edwin Acuña, López, Olman Ramírez C. (secondary)	2,050	Improve the socio-economic level of the small- and medium-size agriculturalists.	n.d.
Coopesanjuanillo R.L.	Naranjo	Naranjo, Grecia, Valverde Vega, Poás	Luis Gonzaga Rojas, Manuel Núñez Ramírez (secondary)	2,500	Obtain a better living standard for the members through higher coffee prices.	n.d.

Affiliation	Reason for which it arises	Economic activities in which it participates	Surface area [of its lands]	Observations	*Observations*
n.d.	Resolve problems specific to the period (1970) in the cultivation, processing and sale of the beans.	Coffee	n.d.		
n.d.	Established in a split off from Coopelibertad.	Coffee	n.d.		
n.d.	Organize small coffee producers so that they are not exploited by private enterprise.	Coffee	n.d.	They manage capital worth one billion colones and benefit 105,000 families.	
n.d.	Market strawberries in international markets.	n.d.	n.d.		
n.d.	Improve the socio-economic conditions of its members.	n.d.			
n.d.	Improve the conditions of the small- and medium-size coffee producer.	Coffee	n.d.	They provide loans for irrigation projects, housing, advances on harvests, renovation of coffee fields, etc. They provide services, including an input warehouse, super-market, store, savings plan, and others.	
n.d.	Improve members' socioeconomic level.	Coffee	n.d.		

Name	Location	Area of influence	Leaders	Number of members	Objectives	Political position
Coopenaranjo R.L.	Naranjo	Naranjo, Palmares, San Ramón, Alajuela, Heredia, San Carlos, Guatuso	Olga Chinchilla, Rodrigo Mora	7,559	Achieve a better living standard for the members through savings.	n.d.
Coopeagrona	Rosario (Naranjo)	Rosario	Manuel Vásquez, Leonel Jiménez (secondary)	12 families	Achieve a better living standard for the members.	n.d.
Asociación de Agricultores	Los Robles, San Jerónimo (Naranjo)	Los Robles, San Jerónimo	Alfonso Salazar	15	Generate sources of employment appropriate to members' socioeconomic level.	n.d.
Seccional UPANACIONAL	Naranjo	Naranjo	Gilberto Vargas R., Antonio Vargas H. (secondary)	952	Defend the interests of the small- and medium-size agriculturalists.	n.d.
Centro Agrícola Cantonal Naranjo	Naranjo	Naranjo	n.d.	200	Develop the organization in order to improve the living standard of the members.	n.d.

Palmares

Name	Location	Area of influence	Leaders	Number of members	Objectives	Political position
Cooperativa de Caficultores de Palmares R.L.	Palmares	Palmares		1,400	Improve members' socioeconomic level.	n.d.
Coopeindia R.L.	Palmares	The entire country		1,315	Improve members' socioeconomic level.	n.d.
Seccional UPANACIONAL	Palmares	Palmares	Víctor J. Alvarado, Juan B. Pacheco (seondary)	334	Work for just treatment for the producers and for a more just treatment from the government.	n.d.

Affiliation	Reason for which it arises	Economic activities in which it participates	Surface area [of its lands]	Observations	*Observations*
n.d.	Need for a savings and credit organization.	n.d.	n.d.	They provide credit to groups [*créditos dirigidos*] for agriculture, housing, small-scale industry. They offer supply and retail services.	
n.d.	Need for an organization that backs them in obtaining land.	Coffee, ornamental plants [*caña india*]	n.d.	This organization is in the process of developing, but has great economic problems.	
n.d.		n.d.	17–25 hectares	Organization in process of developing.	
n.d.		n.d.	n.d.		
n.d.		n.d.	n.d.	Its activities center on Naranjo, but its fruit and forestry nursery project also works in surrounding cantons.	
n.d.	Process and market coffee.	Coffee	n.d.	Their services include a supermarket, store, medical center, supply warehouse, etc.	
n.d.	Process ornamental plants [*caña india* and *itabo*] and develop their cultivation.	Ornamental plants [*caña india* and *itabo*]	n.d.	They have members and process materials from the entire country.	
n.d.	To have an UPA chapter that groups together the producers.	n.d.	n.d.	They sell inputs and agricultural tools to the members, who can also purchase social security insurance through the UPANACIONAL–CCSS agreement.	

Name	Location	Area of influence	Leaders	Number of members	Objectives	Political position
Centro Agrícola Cantonal Palmares	Palmares	Palmares		120	Improve members' socioeconomic level.	n.d.

Poás

Name	Location	Area of influence	Leaders	Number of members	Objectives	Political position
Coopemerca	San Pedro	Poás	Ing. Rodolfo Blanco	56	Improve members' socioeconomic level.	n.d.
Coopecorrales R.L.	San Pedro	Poás	Ismael Flores P.	5,900	Improve members' socioeconomic level.	n.d.
Seccional UPANACIONAL	San Pedro	Poás	Julio Antonio Ugalde	226	Socioeconomic demands of the agriculturalists.	n.d.
Cámara de Productores de [Caña?] del Pacífico	San Pedro	Poás	Luis Fernando Alfaro	1,000	Improve members' socioeconomic level.	n.d.

San Isidro de Heredia

Name	Location	Area of influence	Leaders	Number of members	Objectives	Political position
Cooperativa Isidreña R.L.	San Isidro de Heredia	San Isidro de Heredia		4,335	Improve members' socioeconomic level.	n.d.
Centro Agrícola Cantonal de San Isidro de Heredia	San Isidro de Heredia	San Isidro de Heredia		110	Work for the interests and improve the socioeconomic level of the zone's agriculturalists.	

San Ramón

Name	Location	Area of influence	Leaders	Number of members	Objectives	Political position
Coope San Ramón R.L.	San Ramón	San Ramón	Célimo Montero	1,500	Improve members' socioeconomic level.	n.d.
Coopecafira R.L.	San Ramón	San Ramón	Alvaro Ramírez	3,500	Improve members' socioeconomic level.	n.d.

Affiliation	Reason for which it arises	Economic activities in which it participates	Surface area [of its lands]	Observations	*Observations*
n.d.		n.d.	n.d.	They collaborate with the MAG on a model farm and related research projects.	
n.d.	Develop rabbit production and the processing and sale of meat.	Small species.	n.d.		
n.d.	Promote savings among citizens in general and agriculturalists in particular.	n.d.	n.d.		
UPANACIONAL	Defend the interests of the agriculturalists.	n.d.	n.d.		
n.d.	Supply the producers with favorably priced inputs.				
n.d.		n.d.	n.d.	This is a consolidated cooperative made up primarily of agriculturalists.	
n.d.	Develop savings and train the members.	n.d.	n.d.	An agroindustrial cooperative.	
n.d.	Market the coffee of the zone's producers, provide training, develop a savings program.	Coffee	n.d.	Provides artificial insemination services and trains producers.	

Name	Location	Area of influence	Leaders	Number of members	Objectives	Political position
Coopeleche R.L.	San Ramón	San Ramón Guanacaste, San Carlos	Miguel Arias	150	Improve members' socioeconomic level.	n.d.
Coopesira R.L.	San Ramón	San Ramón		200	Improve members' socioeconomic level.	n.d.
Coopecañera R.L.	San Ramón		Alvaro Rojas	450	Improve members' socioeconomic level.	n.d.
Agrivolio	Volio (San Ramón)	San Ramón	José R. Campos	15	They seek to unite forces to resolve the socioeconomic problems of the families.	n.d.
RAGASO	San Ramón	San Ramón		55	Breeding, growth, and fattening of cattle.	n.d.
Seccional UPANACIONAL	San Ramón	San Ramón	Olger Sancho	2,300	Work for the interests and to improve the socio-economic level of the agriculturalists.	n.d.
Asociación de Mujeres Ramonenses Activas	San Ramón	San Ramón	Margarita Castro	5	Improve members' socioeconomic level.	n.d.
Centro Agrícola Cantonal San Ramón	San Ramón	San Ramón	Olger Sancho	17	Promotes the participation of the local population in the planning and execution of regional agricultural development programs.	n.d.

Santa Bárbara de Heredia

Name	Location	Area of influence	Leaders	Number of members	Objectives	Political position
Coopebotánica R.L.	San Pedro [Santa Bárbara]	San Pedro	Minor Dibella, Herson Dibella (secondary)	12	Improve members' socioeconomic level.	n.d.

Affiliation	Reason for which it arises	Economic activities in which it participates	Surface area [of its lands]	Observations	*Observations*
n.d.	Market the milk of the zone's producers.	Milk			
n.d.	Market the *caña india* of the zone's producers and train them in its production.	Ornamental plant [*caña india*]	n.d.		
n.d.	Market the sugarcane of the zone's producers and train them in its production.	n.d.			
n.d.	Market members' harvests.	n.d.	n.d.	It is a purely agricultural cooperative.	
n.d.	Market their products.	Meat	n.d.	This group benefits the entire community.	
UPANACIONAL		n.d.	n.d.	Provides equipment to members.	
n.d.	Unite efforts to market their products.	n.d.	n.d.	This is an industrial association which makes sauces.	
n.d.		n.d.	n.d.		
UNACOOP, COOPEPLAN, COOPEINDIA	Impossibility of involving individual producers in projects.	n.d.	n.d.		

Name	Location	Area of influence	Leaders	Number of members	Objectives	Political position
Seccional UPANACIONAL	Santa Bárbara	Santa Bárbara	Ricardo Herrera A.	200	Organize and participate in the solution of problems that negatively affect producers.	n.d.

Valverde Vega

Coopevalverdevega	Valverde Vega	Valverde Vega, Naranjo, part of Grecia	Ing. Luis Castro	1,130	Provide orientation to the producers.	n.d.
Coopetrojas	Trojas de Valverde Vega	Valverde Vega	Enrique Zamora, José Manuel Arias	13	Improve members' socioeconomic level.	n.d.
Centro Agrícola Cantonal Valverde Vega	Valverde Vega	Valverde Vega		315	Organize the canton's producers for greater socioeconomic well-being.	n.d.

REGIONAL ATLANTIC DIRECTORATE

Frente Agropecuario Zona Atlántica (FAZA)	Limón	Limón	Guido Velásquez, Emilio Torres, Sergio Velásquez (secondary)	n.d.	Obtain indemnification [for crop losses].	Leftist group
Coordinadora Campesina Limonense	Limón	Batáan, southern Limón, Río Banano	Rafael Murillo, Guido Velásquez, Sergio Velásquez	300	Pressure for lands.	Mixed. The leadership is leftist.
Sindicato de Pequeños Agricultores Limonenses (SPAL)	Talamanca	Talamanca, Sixaola, Paraíso, Savala	Ricardo Araya, Freddy Meléndez, Daylin Luna (secondary)	300	Pressure for lands and indemnification for crop losses.	Leftist group of the PVP [Communist Party]

Affiliation	Reason for which it arises	Economic activities in which it participates	Surface area [of its lands]	Observations	*Observations*
UPANACIONAL	A more just treatment by the government and better incomes for the producers.	n.d.	n.d.	This chapter has little support from the local population.	
n.d.	Because of a felt need for organization among the agriculturalists.	Coffee	n.d.	This is a consolidated cooperative, but it presently has serious economic problems. It has a warehouse for inputs and a coffee processing and exporting facility.	
n.d.		n.d.	n.d.	In certain periods, the cooperative sells its products on the national market.	
n.d.		n.d.	n.d.	It has a supply warehouse and a veterinary pharmacy.	
n.d.	Because of the founding of UNSA.	n.d.	n.d.		The Velásquez brothers are direct relatives of a well-known leader of the National Liberation Party [PLN]. As a group they are weak.
n.d.	Farms belonging to foreigners in southern Limón Province.	n.d.	n.d.	[Legislative] Deputy Cruickshank offered support for their cacao project. They are advised by groups from the National University [UNA].	
FENAC	Pressure for lands.	n.d.	n.d.	The leaders do not live in the region. They are weak.	They have disputes with other unions in the region, such as USATA and UNSA.

Name	Location	Area of influence	Leaders	Number of members	Objectives	Political position
SPAL Siquirres	Siquirres	Southeast of Siquirres [banks of Río Reventazón]	Alberto Espinoza	100	Establish a beachhead for the PVP [Communist Party].	PVP
Asociación Arroceros [?]	Batáan	Batáan	Walter Céspedes, Fidel Luna (secondary)	300	Debt forgiveness.	n.d.
UPAGRA	Guácimo (south)	Guácimo (south)	Carlos Campos. Secondary leaders: Juan J. Herrera, Emilio Torres, Ricardo Araya P.	1,000	Indemnification for crop losses.	n.d.
Asociación de Productores de Pococí	Pococí	High zone of Guápiles, Guácimo	Ulises Blanco	100	Legalize their holdings in the watershed and forest reserve.	n.d.
SPAL (El Indio)	Northeast of Guápiles	Northeast of Guápiles	Angel Gómez	200	Negotiate price of [occupied] lands.	n.d.

Affiliation	Reason for which it arises	Economic activities in which it participates	Surface area [of its lands]	Observations	*Observations*
n.d.	Pressure for lands and indemnification for crop losses.	n.d.	n.d.		The leader is a peón of Ricardo Araya of the FENAC.
n.d.	Better rice prices, debt forgiveness.	Rice	n.d.	Leader Céspedes is indebted for many millions to banks (12 million colones). They seek permission from IDA for a large housing loan from BAHNVI [public-sector bank].	The leader is a partisan of the PUSC [Social Christian Unity Party]. He dances with whoever plays him the best tune.
n.d.	1978 land invasion at NEGUEV.	Maize, cassava	n.d.	They have international economic and logistical aid. With the payment of maize losses in 1985, they received 10 million colones.	A radical leftist (Trotskyist) group. MRP.
n.d.	Land invasion in the Guápiles watershed area.	n.d.	n.d.		This is an unconditional support arm for UPAGRA. They have kidnapped a functionary of the Forestry Directorate.
n.d.	The price of parcels in El Indio agrarian reform settlement.	n.d.	n.d.	Group became stronger with the seizing and kidnapping of an IDA functionary.	This is the strongest arm of FENAC.

INTRODUCTION

1. Biersteker (1983b) provides an excellent analysis of the events preceding the 1982 Mexican debt crisis, though his list of worrisome financial symptoms does not include Costa Rica's default one year earlier. He terms the August 13 – 15 negotiations the "Washington weekend," since the negotiations took place in the U.S. capital.

2. Obviously, Costa Rica was not the first Latin American country *ever* to default on its debts—simply the first during the 1980s debt crisis.

3. It is perhaps necessary to remind U.S. readers that "liberalism" and related terms, as employed here, bear no relation to their colloquial use in U.S. political discourse. Indeed, what is "liberal" in the rest of the world is generally "conservative" in the United States. As David Korten (1995, 72) remarks, the political implications of this semiotic inversion are profound: "In its various guises, this ideology is known by different names—neoclassical, neoliberal, or libertarian economics; neoliberalism, market capitalism, or market liberalism. . . . Latin Americans commonly use the term *neoliberalism*. However, in most countries—including the United States—it goes without a generally recognized name. Unnamed, it goes undebated, its underlying assumptions unexamined."

4. The literacy figure is from the 1984 population census.

5. This hyperbole was not limited to self-interested Costa Rican politicians. A 1993 Inter-American Development Bank analysis declared that Costa Rica was "back in the winners' circle" (Richter 1993, 4–5). Recognition that the Costa Rican case has more general relevance is widespread among Latin America specialists. Tardanico (1993), for example, remarks that "insofar as Costa Rica is the benchmark for gauging the regional prospects of Central America, debate over its development options carries extra-national weight." A multi-country study of nontraditional export promotion notes that "despite its small size, Costa Rica presents a crucial case for evaluating NTAX strategies," since it is the only Latin American country where a long history of democratic government, concern for social equality, and a relatively successful record of NTAX promotion all intersect (Barham et al. 1992, 67). Another study of structural

adjustment programs points out that "Costa Rica's relatively long experience with SAPs deserves special scrutiny, because it provides an example of what the rest of the region can expect in the future" (Development GAP 1993, 4; see also Rodríguez 1990). Even scholars who have at times been prone to radical left positions concede that economic structural adjustment in Costa Rica has been largely "successful" (Irvin 1991, 94; Vilas 1996, 25).

6. The latter sentiment derives in no small measure from the often muddled prose of key postmodern theorists. Nederveen Pieterse (1992, 27) links this to a "tendency to 'theorrea.'" Sangren (1988, 408) points out that this characteristic style constitutes a "rhetoric of power" which "communicates the message that what most readers find difficult the writer finds pleasurable." In a similar vein, Murphy (1990, 332) notes, not entirely accurately, that "the chief practitioners of what I choose to call 'thick writing' are men, who seem to be engaged in a curiously competitive game in which obscure literary allusions and baroque rhetorical forms are weapons, a kind of egghead rap-talk."

7. In contrast to dependency theory, a paradigm developed primarily in the Third World and then "consumed" (Cardoso 1977) in the First, postmodernism arose in the First and is now consumed—or as Colás (1994, ix) suggests rather tongue-in-cheek, "dump[ed] . . . like so much First-World toxic waste"—in the Third.

8. Like many postmodernist tenets, the claim that ethnographies (or "development") are fictions has an intellectual lineage that its proponents rarely acknowledge. The idea was, of course, important in Geertz's interpretive anthropology (1973) and was employed even earlier, albeit somewhat differently, by Leach (1964, ix–xii).

9. In an early essay (1984, 389) Escobar acknowledges that the "fictitious construct" is based on "a certain materiality . . . certain conditions of life . . . " and that "there is a situation of economic exploitation that must be recognized and dealt with." These concessions largely disappear in his later work. DuBois (1991, 25) echoes Escobar: "Certainly one cannot deny the existence of certain political, economic, and social conditions of existence that threaten life itself, but 'underdevelopment,' one interpretation of these conditions, is a construction."

10. Clifford (1986, 6) maintains that "'fiction' . . . as commonly used in recent textual theory has lost its connotation of falsehood, as something opposed to truth. It suggests the partiality of cultural and historical truths." If this meaning were as conventional or as widely accepted as Clifford suggests, the word would lose its shock value—which derives from its standard rather than its postmodernist sense—and would likely cease to be employed in his and others' writings. Even when postmodernists concede the "partiality" of truths, they rarely give any methodological expression to the obvious question: just how partial are they? The categories "partial truth" and "fiction" both presuppose some broader criterion of "truth" from which they diverge.

Assertions of the "fictional" character of ethnographic thought and practice have become so *de rigueur* in postmodernist writing that they appear as an almost automatic and un-thought-out reflex, even among authors with explicit and deeply felt political commitments. Lancaster (1992, 299), for example, ends a powerful and unabashedly engaged report of the hardships of life in late-1980s Sandinista Nicaragua with the disappointing conclusion that "one truth is as good as any other." This trite afterthought undermines an otherwise compelling account, the entire thrust of which suggests that while all truths may be partial, some are nonetheless more valid than others.

11. Portes and Kincaid (1989, 486) accurately note that such positions resemble "earlier dependency arguments in locating a new external explanation of the region's problems." The argument of self-proclaimed Foucauldians, such as Escobar and Ferguson, about the inexorable expansion of state power is all the more curious since Foucault himself broke early on with the notion that power is ultimately located within the state (Foucault 1980, 159, in Harvey 1989, 45). Slater (1992, 298) appropriately suggests that it is important to distinguish "types of power within the state." For example, the state's technical capacity to carry out surveillance of its citizens may increase, even as its power over the economy diminishes in the face of global market forces.

12. Ferguson (1990), who locates himself within the Foucauldian camp but who nonetheless links "development" discourse to other kinds of political-economic change, is more sensitive than Escobar to the danger of such false syllogisms. Noting that "development" is conventionally understood as either growth of the forces of production or improvement in quality of life, he charges that "it seems to be a theoretical necessity in 'development' discourse . . . for the two notions of 'development' to be co-present and even conflated" (55).

13. Esteva's mention of the initial Spanish connotation of "development" echoes Raymond Williams's (1983, 204) comment on the original English meaning: "the unfolding, the unrolling, indeed the evolution, of an inherent process." W. Sachs and Escobar also cite Truman's inauguration speech as the charter for the new "development" era (see Sachs [1992, 2], Escobar [1995, 3] and Esteva [1992, 6], all of whom place the speech on January 20, ten days later than Esteva [1988]). Kearney (1996, 34) uncritically appropriates this view of Truman as deus ex machina in his stimulating, though frequently problematical, intellectual history of peasant studies in anthropology.

14. Nor do critics of "development" discourse generally recognize the extent to which many of their critiques were anticipated, often with greater attention to empirically based argument, in the "anti-aid" literature of the 1970s and 1980s (George 1977; Hayter 1971; Hill 1986; Payer 1982; Tendler 1975).

15. The closest the postmodernist critics of "development" come to acknowledging this is in a 1993 essay by Esteva, which is a much-revised expanded version of the 1988 *Comercio Exterior* article cited above; while Esteva

notes the reinvention of various biological evolutionary theories as ideologies of economic development, he paints Truman as an all-powerful deus ex machina of post–World War II history and fails to mention either the Latin American Liberalism or the populist-Marxist polemics that were so central to discussions of development in the Americas. Escobar, on the other hand, in his earlier work, leaves the antecedents of "development" to a sketchy footnote: "Even if the roots of development are to be found in colonialism, 19th-century ideas of progress, and, more generally, Western European modernity, something drastic happened in the early post–World War II period when an *entirely new* discourse, "development," emerged. . . . There was no 'development,' 'underdevelopment,' or 'Third World' before 1945. *Inventions of the postwar period,* these notions have resulted in the deployment of a very efficient apparatus through which the 'Third World' was and is largely produced" (1991, 679 n.18, emphasis added). Somewhat later, he introduces a few nuances into the argument, but still leaves key elements, such as Latin American liberalism, largely unexamined (Escobar 1995, 26–30; Alvarez, Dagnino, and Escobar 1998, 9–10). Cowen and Shenton provide a detailed historical analysis of the nineteenth-century roots of "development," including a brief critique of the Foucauldians' view of Truman (1996, 7–9).

16. "Ministerio de Fomento" is best glossed as "Development Ministry," just as the verb *fomentar,* when used in the same sense, is one equivalent of "to develop." The term retains some of the volitional flavor of its cognate, "to foment." It thus differs from the broader meaning of "development," or "*desarrollo.*" This, as Esteva points out "is used equally to allude to the awakening of a child's mind, the middle part of a chess match, the explosive growth of a fifteen-year-old girl's breasts, or a group of houses" (1988, 665).

In an important case study of the Guatemalan Ministerio de Fomento, McCreery stresses that "the driving force behind the new Liberal regime was the quest for 'development,' by which they meant the acquisition as rapidly as possible of the readily apparent characteristics of modern, that is, North Atlantic, society" (1983, 13). This was equally true elsewhere in Latin America.

17. This use of "development" by United Fruit Company officials was typical of the period (cf. Dosal 1993, 38).

18. "Before the American era," William Smith Bryan wrote in *Our Islands and their People* (1899), "there was no such thing as underground drainage in Santiago [de Cuba], and all such work was a revelation to the inhabitants. They came in crowds every day to witness the progress of the work, and were enthusiastic in their praise of American methods" (quoted in Black 1988, 14). Frederick Ober, in *Our West Indian Neighbors,* declared:

When the Americans came [to Havana] they found a horrible condition of affairs in matters of sanitation, and it is to their credit that they almost performed the impossible task of cleansing the city. . . . Even the Spaniards and Cubans admit that the Americanos have improved their city vastly. . . . It "riled" them awfully to be told, in effect, that they had been heedless of the simplest laws of sanitation, and they bitterly resented the inspection and consequent disinfection of their houses. But the great and good work went on, nevertheless, and to-day it is continued by the Cubans, along the lines laid out by their teachers. (1907, 56–57)

19. Mariátegui's calls for skipping the capitalist "stage" and the importance he attributed to the indigenous peasantry were at odds with Stalin's theories of development and "nationality" policies. These positions earned Mariátegui condemnation as a "populist" and "Trotskyite" at the First Congress of Latin American Communist Parties in 1929. The Comintern called for creating independent Quechua and Aymara "republics" in the Peruvian Andes—and some delegates even favored the creation of separate Italian, Polish, and Jewish "nations" for immigrants in Argentina (Caballero 1987, 58; Munck 1984, 11; Vanden 1986, 66–69, 125; Basadre 1971, xxvii–xxviii). Ironically, Mariátegui's view that indigenous community institutions might permit leaping over the capitalist stage directly to socialism paralleled the later Marx's ideas about the Russian peasant commune (see Edelman 1984; Esteva 1983, 203; Shanin 1983).

20. Haya de la Torre founded the APRA (Alianza Popular Revolucionaria Americana) in Peru in 1924. Initially, APRA was an international party influenced by the Mexican and Russian Revolutions, but it never attained significant support outside Peru and eventually became more conservative. José Batlle y Ordóñez, president of Uruguay from 1903 to 1907 and again from 1911 to 1915, was a crusader for labor legislation and state intervention in the economy. Getulio Vargas ran Brazil from 1930 to 1945. While he at times flirted with domestic and foreign fascism, he was immensely popular among the poor and contributed significantly to industrialization. Juan Domingo Perón, during his first term as president of Argentina from 1946 to 1955, promoted industrialization, an expanded role for the public sector in the economy, and an improved standard of living for industrial workers. Rómulo Betancourt, founder of Acción Democrática (AD) in Venezuela, came to power in 1946 with the support of a faction of the military. In the three years before he was toppled, his government intervened actively in the economy to advance industrialization and founded workers and peasant confederations. "Development" was among the most salient themes in AD's programs.

21. Some have argued that in the United States, though not elsewhere, the military draft gave the upheavals a rarely acknowledged "rational" character and led to the decline of the anti–Vietnam War movement after 1973, when the draft was discontinued. While this "rational" impulse may have figured in some young people's calculations, it is also true, as Gitlin (1987, 411–12) points

out, that the anti-war movement arose at a time when student deferments were safe, that many protesters took the highly risky step of destroying or turning in their Selective Service cards, and that draft-exempt women also took many risks.

22. The central role of Argentine-born theorist Ernesto Laclau in the European debate doubtless contributed to diffusion of NSMs theories first in Buenos Aires and then elsewhere in Latin America (Gledhill 1988, 257; Wood 1986, 48).

23. Whereas in Europe the sixties upheavals gave rise to the "identity-oriented," "constructivist," or "NSMs" paradigm, in the United States the main framework became "resource mobilization theory." The latter, "strategy-oriented" approach, like NSMs theory, is the subject of a vast literature with competing variants. Its roots are in rational-choice theory, but rather than focusing primarily on individual strategizing, it emphasizes the rational pursuit of interests by groups and the resources, social networks, and social pressures that explain why strategizing individuals might take part in collective activities that might otherwise pose unacceptable personal risks (Tilly 1985; Zald 1992). Several authors (Cohen 1985; Eyerman and Jamison 1991) have noted how similar historical events produced disparate theoretical responses in post-sixties European and North American students of social movements, but few have probed the political antecedents or contexts that might underlie this split. Foweraker suggests that the "social democratic consensus," institutionalized labor movement, and strong welfare state institutions of Western Europe made new social movements look genuinely "new"; in the United States, in contrast, "social movements were explained not by big societal changes but by the continuing ability of outsider groups to mobilize resources and gain representation within the system" (1995, 2).

24. Touraine has insisted that "the notion of social movement is inseparable from that of class" (1988, 68). But he defines classes not in relation to their position in the process of production and appropriation of an economic surplus or even in relation to their consumption possibilities, but as groups that are opposed to each other in a central conflict for the appropriation of "historicity"— "the set of cultural, cognitive, economic, and ethical models by means of which a collectivity sets up relations with its environment" (40). New social movements thus become the bearers of "historical projects," much like "classes-for-themselves" in the "old" days.

25. This is part of the broader "urban gaze" of postmodernism and cultural studies, which gives little or no attention to rural peoples and places. As Ching and Creed (1997, 7–12) point out, urban intellectuals who examine rural issues within "development" frameworks, frequently end up doing so in part to validate their own culture or place.

26. Proponents of the model, such as Melucci, sometimes concede that the

NSMs category lacks coherence (Escobar and Alvarez 1992, 15), but they typically give this acknowledgment little methodological expression in their work.

27. A poignant example of this phenomenon occurred during my fieldwork in Carrillo cantón, Guanacaste province, Costa Rica, during 1991. The leader of a cooperative of landless peasants that as yet had no land but that hoped, with government help, to acquire 830 hectares of a nearby foreign-owned *latifundio*, told me why co-op members had set their hearts on obtaining that piece of land as opposed to some other. "You have to understand," he said, "that half of this land is in primary growth forest [*montaña virgen*], it's the only *montaña virgen* in the entire cantón of Carrillo. When the people outside find out about this, there won't be anybody who won't want to come see it and we will have a first-class ecotourism project in Carrillo."

Carrillo cantón was his world, and while he understood that outsiders might pay good money to visit a virgin tropical forest, it did not seem to occur to him that they might just as soon do this somewhere in the Amazon, or even elsewhere in Costa Rica.

28. Similarly amnesiac is the assertion that "conventional social science has not systematically explored the connections between culture and politics" (Alvarez, Dagnino, and Escobar 1998, 2). Vincent's (1990) history of anthropology's relation to politics—academic and extra-academic—constitutes a detailed and forceful argument to the contrary.

29. Of course, not all social movements are naturally progressive or radical either, as is sometimes assumed in the social movements literature. Critics of this premise include Tilly (1984) and Foweraker (1995).

30. Similarly problematical is the current insistence that rural Latin America is becoming a "postdevelopment" society (Escobar 1995, chap. 6; Kearney 1996, 116). Those residents or observers of the Latin American countryside who commit the error of taking this too literally might be inclined to think that they somehow missed what was supposed to come before the present period. Here, as in many writings about NSMs, the occasional caveats about the ultimate importance of material forces (Escobar 1992a, 412; Slater 1985, 10) have rarely led to systematic consideration of political-economic issues within the NSMs–postmodernist framework.

31. I did, however, write a few brief articles that attempted to bring to a larger audience some background about the situation (Edelman 1983, 1985; Edelman and Hutchcroft 1984).

32. Cartago, just south of San José, was Costa Rica's colonial capital. In peripheral areas of the country, people from the central valley region are often called "Cartagos," whether or not they are from Cartago province. In Guanacaste, where regionalist feelings have long been pronounced, the term sometimes has a pejorative ring to it, connoting dishonesty, greed, individualism, or unreliability (Edelman 1992, 127–33).

33. This was eventually published (Edelman 1990, and [in Spanish] 1991a).

34. In an overview of twenty years of "peasant studies," Warman (1988, 657) suggests this kind of occurrence has become more common: "Studies of peasant movements express with greater clarity and less rhetoric the commitment that links researchers and historical subjects. . . . [Researchers'] works are immediately 'consumed,' analyzed and incorporated by the actors of the social movements, who draw conclusions and lessons from them."

35. Nash (1992, 276) recently described a similar relationship that evolved in a study of an anti-IMF movement in Bolivia: "Balancing a latent mistrust of Yankee intruders against the hope of getting their message to the American people, the protesters chose to put me in the role of interlocutor."

36. I early on concluded that Spivak's (1988) question—"Can the Subaltern Speak?"—could be answered resoundingly and in the affirmative. Not only could subalterns speak, but they often did so with great eloquence and understanding. This is not to deny, however, either that some subalterns cannot speak, or that even sophisticated subalterns may seek out social scientists as a kind of "cognitive resource" able to connect them to broader fields of knowledge and power (Melucci 1992, 51; cf. Huizer 1979).

37. Stern (1987) provides a concise and compelling theoretical statement about the importance of analyzing peasant movements over long periods.

38. Both regions had highly skewed distributions of income and wealth, with populations consisting largely of impoverished rural laborers and small agricultural producers. The pro-Cuban MRP may have chosen the Santa Cruz area as a strategic focus because of its proximity to Nicaragua and the organization's efforts to aid the Sandinistas' war against Somoza. The MRP may also have been drawn to the zone's large sugar plantation proletariat and the small, but rugged peaks of the Nicoya Peninsula, where some members reportedly practiced "mountain tactics" during the late 1970s. As in Tucumán, Argentina, where guerrillas established a column in roughly the same period, it is possible that "to many, the rugged, densely forested mountains and the flat sugarcane growing plain that sprawled from it evoked eastern Cuba" (Andersen 1993, 127). Years later, MRP founder Sergio Erick Ardón recognized that "in the beginning we responded to many idealistic visions without root in Costa Rican reality, which for some years made us act more in relation to regional and Latin American situations than national ones" (*La Nación Internacional*, Nov. 24–30, 1983, p. 15).

39. The presence of anthropologists in the MRP, and my acquaintance with them, very likely contributed to easing whatever doubts former MRP peasant militants might have had about dealing with me.

40. I briefly analyzed this issue in a later article (Edelman 1991b).

41. At this time, the CEPAS agrarian research team also proposed that I write up and publish my research through their organization, offering me re-

sponsibility for "covering Guanacaste," a region in which they had little experience. When they broached this idea, I couldn't help but be reminded of Ramírez's warning that the NGOs were always trying to "appropriate" others' ideas and work. But after the controversial CEPAS roundtable on my research (see below), I never heard anything more about the CEPAS team's proposal.

42. For a critique of the "urban bias" of Costa Rican social scientific research practice, see Edelman 1998b.

43. Jakobson wrote of "the two cardinal and complementary traits of verbal behavior": that "inner speech is in essence a dialogue," and that "any reported speech is *appropriated* and remolded by the quoter, whether it is a quotation from an *alter* or from an earlier phase of the *ego* (*said I*)" (Jakobson 1981, 11, italics in original). "Montage," however, the polyvocal style to which many postmodernist writers aspire, is forthrightly described by one of its early advocates as "the art of quoting without quotation marks" (Benjamin 1983, 3).

CHAPTER 1   RISE AND DEMISE OF A TROPICAL WELFARE STATE

1. On the "white legend," see Heath (1970) and Creedman (1977). The critical literature is now quite large. Among the best synthetic treatments are Gudmundson (1986) and Acuña and Molina (1991). See also Fonseca (1983), Molina Jiménez (1991), and Samper (1990).

2. The advent of coffee, as Gudmundson demonstrated beyond any doubt, initially brought *greater* occupational homogeneity and a process of *ruralization*, as people moved out of nucleated village settlements and into the coffee-producing countryside (1986).

3. Analyses that downplay or deny the relevance of political culture and historical experience in explaining Costa Rica's stability typically take reformism and traditions of compromise as givens. In an otherwise outstanding analysis, Lehoucq (1992b), for example, makes the following telling assertions: "By de-emphasizing the role of the executive branch in political life, *reform-oriented politicians* increased the benefits associated with complying with democratic institutions for those who failed to win presidential elections" (12, emphasis added); "*Compromise* offered an attractive solution of regulating access to key public offices" (13); "Democratic stability was *a product of a decision* by incumbents and their opponents *to share* and not to monopolize state power" (14, emphasis added). One might ask what historical experiences—collective and individual—produced these reform-oriented politicians, with their inclination to compromise and to share power.

4. I am not including here the small number of cases in which chief executives have assumed office for brief periods as legal designates or through extraconstitutional compromises between parties reached in the aftermath of inconclusive elections (for details, see Lehoucq 1992a).

5. In contrast, the assertion of Jonas (1984, 14) and Salazar (1981, 27, 195)

that the ideology and practices of the National Liberation Party (Partido de Liberación Nacional, or *PLN*) were fundamentally Liberal (or neo-Liberal) is most curious, given the PLN's commitment, at least until ca. 1980, to statist rather than laissez-faire solutions to economic and social problems.

6. The 1936 Colombian agrarian law, often viewed as a socially progressive measure, actually provided large proprietors with a basis for legally claiming lands usurped from the public domain (LeGrand 1986, 143–53).

7. See Edelman and Kenen (1989, chap. 2) for further discussions of Liberalism and early reformism. Palmer (1992, 1996) provides a very suggestive analysis of how early-twentieth-century Liberal regimes promoted various "social hygiene" and public-health measures as means of controlling the lives of poor families in the urban areas.

8. He failed to serve the remaining two years of his term after he led a quixotic armed uprising and was then briefly committed to a European mental hospital (Volio 1972, 240–49).

9. On the "shortage of hands" in one region of Costa Rica, see Edelman (1992, chap. 3).

10. Rodolfo Cerdas, son of a founder of the Costa Rican Communist Party and a political scientist who has become increasingly conservative since the 1970s, argues that the Costa Rican CP in this period was relatively successful because it remained adaptable and independent from Moscow. This relative autonomy resulted from the Comintern's abandonment of Central America following its unsuccessful attempt to co-opt Nicaraguan nationalist Augusto Sandino and its posthumous condemnation of Salvadoran Communist leader Agustín Farabundo Martí as a traitor in the aftermath of the failed 1932 peasant uprising and the subsequent army massacre (1991, 279–80).

11. The system was financed by contributions from the government, employers, and the insured. In 1971 social security became obligatory for all salaried workers.

Throughout this book, dollar equivalents for colones are from Albarracín and Pérez (1977, 26) for the period up to 1946, and from BCCR (1986, 211–13) for the period 1950–85.

12. The alliances and allegiances of these years did not always have profound ideological roots. Picado, for example, originally sympathetic to the fascism of Francisco Franco (Rojas 1979, 82–83), had been a leading figure in Cortés's party until December 1942, when Cortés defeated his bid to become the party's presidential nominee for the 1944 elections. He then went over to Calderón's PRN and, despite his recent conversion, was able to make a successful run for the presidency and beat Cortés as the PRN candidate (Brenes 1990, 22). Picado and members of his family and administration also had close business ties to Nicaraguan dictator Anastasio Somoza García, who intervened in

Costa Rica during the 1948 civil war to try to prevent Picado's overthrow (Edelman 1992, 236–40). After Picado fell, he went into exile in Nicaragua, where he became a frequent contributor to the Somoza family's newspaper, *Novedades* (Estrada 1967, 203, 252).

13. That this was less a matter of principal than of expedience is suggested by the fact that the Congress let stand the same day's legislative elections in which the *calderonista*–Communist block maintained its majority (Aguilar 1969, 291–92). The Communists had elected 12 of the 45 members of Congress and had been reluctant to press for annulling the vote, unlike their *calderonista* allies, who had lost the executive branch (Cerdas 1991, 290).

14. The *figueristas* could hardly have been happy about Ulate's long anti-reformist trajectory. As far back as 1917, he had organized street celebrations to celebrate the overthrow of reformist president González Flores. The editorials in his newspaper, *El Diario de Costa Rica*, were consistently ultraconservative. But his administration was "stigmatized" by his secondary role in the 1948 civil war and by the long delay separating his election and inauguration. He thus led a weak government that posed no threat to the radical social transformation begun by Figueres's Junta (Brenes 1990, 96).

15. ICE's rates were not only the lowest in Central America, but they remained unchanged between 1959 and 1973 at 0.13 colones (about $0.02) per kilowatt-hour (Sojo 1984, 46).

16. The nationalization was also a punishment for the private bankers, who had backed the *calderonistas*, and a reward for bank employees, who played a key role in a 1947 opposition strike against the Picado government (Bulmer-Thomas 1987, 124).

17. In 1956 the CNP became an autonomous public-sector institution.

18. This ceased to be the case, however, after July 1989, when the collapse of the International Coffee Organization's export quota system brought unprecedentedly low prices and led many producers to abandon coffee production.

19. On a smaller scale, a similar process of private-sector penetration of the public-sector occurred with ALCORSA (Algodones de Costa Rica, S.A.), CODESA's cotton-ginning subsidiary (Edelman 1992, 319–20).

20. In July 1990 an agriculturalist from Guácimo reflected bitterly on his experience with Agriculture Ministry and other public-sector cacao extension workers, unintentionally echoing neoliberals' cynical view of the state:

> If the MAG disappears, they are the only ones who will notice, not the agriculturalists. The MAG can disappear, we don't need it for anything, because it has never helped us at all. The only thing it has done is involve us in foolish risks [*embarcarnos*] instead of helping us. In a JAPDEVA seminar on cacao, I asked the man, "How is it possible that four technicians have come to see my cacao and each said something different? To which do I pay atten-

tion? To the one or two from the Ministry? To the ones from the bank? To the one from CINDE? A heap of experts with different, contradictory versions!"

21. Costa Rica was, nonetheless, the first country in the 1980s to negotiate a multiyear repayment schedule with the private banks (Vargas Peralta 1987, 205–6).

22. After 1985, Congress prohibited formal linkage of USAID programs to IMF or World Bank conditionality, but informal coordination has continued (Kahler 1992, 112; Sojo 1991, 40).

23. In 1985, for example, a minor technicality meant that Costa Rica was temporarily not in compliance with IMF guidelines. Banks refused to disburse loans without a letter from the IMF. But the letter could only be obtained from the IMF's board, which was not scheduled to meet for more than a month. This then required complex new negotiations to restructure much of the country's commercial bank debt. Another, more extreme, case occurred in 1983–87, when the Costa Rican Central Bank had to pay interest on undisbursed USAID funds deposited there. By 1986, interest payments to USAID amounted to nearly one-third of the Central Bank's deficit and had come to constitute a stumbling block in negotiations for a new IMF accord.

24. In an otherwise salutory effort to explain neoliberal transitions as, in part, the outcome of domestic political processes rather than solely international financial institutions' conditionality, Bruce Wilson makes the curious assertion that "though USAID and [the] IMF did tie their assistance to the fulfillment of certain conditions concerning reforms of the financial system, they did not demand the denationalization of Costa Rica's banking sector. . . . When the banking reforms were held up in the legislative assembly, it was a coalition of Costa Rican neoliberals that forced the measures through, and they acted in their own interest instead of being mere puppets of international lending agencies" (1994, 155–56).

It is doubtful that these claims could be considered accurate even in the most restricted, literal sense. USAID, in particular, aggressively pushed denationalization since the early 1980s. In addition to withholding promised disbursements when the Costa Rican assembly balked at passing currency reforms, it also allocated funds to private financial institutions and, together with the U.S. Embassy and the Reagan White House, applied intense political pressure on both the legislative and executive branches of the Costa Rican government. In 1984 the IMF also conditioned renewal of its standby credit agreement on passage of the currency reform measure and the dismissal of 3,300 government employees (Honey 1994, chap. 4).

25. Privatization, however, often meant giveaways to the already well-off. When publicly-owned cotton gins and sugar mills were put on the auction

block, they were sold for only a tiny fraction of their assessed value (Edelman 1992, 299, 321–22).

26. For the text of the plan, see Céspedes, Di Mare, and Jiménez (1985, 199–225).

27. The only exceptions were monies for the new Export Promotion Fund (FOPEX) and Industrial Development Fund (FODEIN).

28. For the text of SAL II, see "Programa de ajuste estructural," *La Nación,* May 5, 1987.

29. In late 1990, the IMF and World Bank, which had long been dissatisfied with CATs, pressured Costa Rica to reform the system so that tax credits would be based on a percentage of the local value-added rather than the total value of the exports.

30. Large unregistered inflows of dollars, primarily from the flourishing drug trade, almost certainly contributed to strengthening the newly liberalized financial institutions, lessening the impact of negative trade balances, and maintaining relatively stable exchange rates.

31. Investors also liked the fact that the labor force appeared relatively docile; social democracy in Costa Rica had been associated with controls on organized labor, a particularity that arose from the repression of the Communists after the 1948 civil war.

32. Bananas, ironically, are increasingly cultivated on the edges of the few remaining wilderness zones in the north, with devastating environmental effects.

33. See "Carta de intenciones entre el Gobierno y el FMI," *La Nación,* Oct. 18, 1995.

CHAPTER 2   PEASANTS CONFRONT THE FREE MARKET

1. FESIAN was the most important of these party-linked groups. Founded in 1972, it had extremely close ties to the social democratic PLN until 1982 and slightly more autonomy thereafter (Mora Alfaro 1987; Román 1993, 140–44, 162–63). FENAC, the Communist peasant federation, also led many land invasions in the 1970s and early 1980s, particularly in the Atlantic region and in the southern Pacific banana plantation zones abandoned by the United Brands Company in the early 1980s (Menjívar, Portuguez, and Moy 1985; Portuguez and Moy 1984). When the Communist Party (PVP) divided in 1983–84, a breakaway faction founded UNAC, linked to the short-lived Costa Rican People's Party (PPC). Both the PVP and the PPC had largely disappeared by 1990 and with them their respective peasant federations.

An idea of the growing extent of peasant ferment is provided by data on the rising number of new *campesino* unions and associations registered with the Ministry of Labor and Social Security. In the years 1970–78, only 4 new organizations were founded; in 1979–82, another 10 were established; but in 1983–

90, an impressive 126 registered with the Ministry (Mora Alfaro 1990b, 49). Many more never obtained legal status. Sometimes this was because of lack of resources and bureaucratic obstacles, but at least occasionally government agencies blocked applications for "legal personality" from organizations they perceived as "subversive."

2. The importance of inflation as a stimulus to political mobilization has at times been exaggerated in the literature on anti-austerity protest (e.g., Walton 1989).

3. "Scissors crisis" refers to a rapid shift in the terms of trade between industry and agriculture in a direction unfavorable to the latter. In Russia in the early 1920s, where the phrase was first widely used, it suggested a sudden opening of a shears' blades ("price scissors") that threatened political stability. Closing scissors implied converging relative prices (Nove 1972, 93–96).

4. Jorge Luis Hernández Cascante, taped interview by author, Tibás de San José, July 25, 1990; José Miguel Gómez Víquez, taped interview by author, Tierra Blanca de Cartago, Nov. 22, 1990.

5. In this, as in other peasant road blockades discussed below, protesters, the media, and government functionaries all labeled the action a "strike" (*huelga*) or a "work stoppage" (*paro*). I use quotation marks only to indicate that the term's meaning here differs from the employee actions against employers to which it usually refers.

6. UPANACIONAL supporters (and some social scientists) assert that this was the first highway blockade protest in Costa Rican history (Cartín and Castro 1986, 23; Menjívar, Moy, and Portuguez 1985, 464; also, author's field interviews, 1990). In fact, peasant organizations used similar tactics at least as early as the 1970s (Cartín 1990, 37).

7. Gómez Víquez, interview.

8. Ibid.

9. According to an official UPANACIONAL publication, the union "is nonpartisan [*apartidista*], that is, it does not obey any political party and much less those of the left" (UPANACIONAL n.d., 3). While UPANACIONAL members for the most part looked favorably on Costa Rica's social democratic development model, this did not necessarily translate into support for the PLN. Several UPANACIONAL leaders I interviewed in Tierra Blanca displayed banners from the Social Christian Unity Party (PUSC) on their homes.

10. Gómez Víquez, interview. Hernández (1990, 5, 11) is among those who mention Gómez's key role in founding the union.

11. These were carried out by the National Production Council (Consejo Nacional de Producción, or CNP), the state commodities board.

12. Even those small producers organizations that originally had links to the leftist groups MRP, FENAC, or UNAC have tended to shun the term "*sin-*

dicato," in part because the many *campesinos* from lowland areas who had worked on banana plantations became disillusioned and bitter about the organized Left and the labor organizations that in the early 1980s hurled them into poorly prepared, easily defeated strikes.

13. Local-level endogamy is widely recognized as extremely high in this region. One elderly resident cited in a recent monograph remarked about the mid–twentieth century: "In those times already our parents had changed a little their way of thinking about marriages. Because it was already known that it was bad for first cousins to marry and they said then that we should bring outside blood to the family so that there would be healthier children and to renew the stock [*cepa*]. . . . We're all one family because of marriages among ourselves" (in Aguilar et al. n.d., 28).

14. The funds came from export taxes on the difference between the free-market and official exchange rates that were intended to prevent exporters from obtaining windfall profits as a result of the huge currency devaluation of 1981–82.

15. Part of UPANACIONAL's strength in the late 1980s derived from its successful negotiation of social security health and pension coverage for independent producers who would not otherwise have enjoyed these protections (*La Nación,* May 23, 1989). Even union officials acknowledged that many peasants joined only in order to obtain benefits (Olger Sánchez, taped interview by author, San Ramón de Alajuela, July 27, 1990).

16. Foweraker (1995, 52) points out that political generations are a key component of identity that is rarely mentioned in the social movements literature. Sociologist Philip Abrams (1982, 240) provides a succinct analysis: "The problem of generations is a problem of the mutual phasing of two different calendars: the calendar of the life-cycle of the individual and the calendar of historical experience. . . . New life-histories are constantly being lived in relation to new world-histories."

The biographies of peasant activists outlined below suggest that it may be useful to view the rise of militant agriculturalists organizations in part as an outgrowth of the worldwide rise of a New Left in the late 1960s and early 1970s. On the anti-ALCOA movement and its importance for this generation of Costa Rican radicals, see González (1985, 281–83) and Ugalde (1985).

17. On the history and ideology of the MRP, see Salom (1987, chap. 3) and Solís (1985). Various leaders of organizations allied with UPAGRA have openly discussed their former MRP ties with the author. A few published sources explicitly address this connection (G. Molina 1985, 54–55; Rivera 1991, 39; Román 1993, 150, 218).

18. Wilson Campos Cerdas, taped interview by author, Aug. 1, 1990. Antonio Mendoza was murdered in San José de Upala on July 17, 1983, almost cer-

tainly by Nicaraguan *contras* (*Libertad,* July 22–28, 1983). *Contras* murdered a half dozen other Costa Rican peasants in Upala around this time, but Mendoza's death received the most attention, probably because he was a prominent local leader of the Communist Partido Vanguardia Popular and its peasant organization, FENAC.

19. In 1991 he became coordinator of a Central America-wide coalition of peasant organizations (Edelman 1996).

20. Campos is a common last name in Costa Rica. Wilson Campos and Carlos Campos are not related.

21. Anderson (1990b, 83; 1994, 95) presents El Hogar as "quite typical" of Costa Rican peasant villages, at least in Limón, ignoring its status as a center of UPAGRA strength.

22. In late 1983, Communist leader Manuel Mora, who had headed the Partido Vanguardia Popular for almost fifty years, was forced out of the PVP and founded a short-lived Partido del Pueblo Costarricense. The following year, the MRP changed its name to Movimiento Nueva República and moved closer to the ruling PLN. The small Partido Socialista also suffered a series of splits that left it completely debilitated. By the end of the decade, all of these groups had ceased to function, although some of their former militants continued to work in other kinds of organizations.

23. Anderson (1990a, 102) mistakenly suggests that UPAGRA was initially backed by the Communist Party. Somewhat contradictorily (and again erroneously), she claims that this union was always free of official connections to political parties. In a later work she revises her initial assessment, reporting UPAGRA was founded by "a local schoolteacher from Guácimo" (1994, 101–2). Carlos Campos, the key figure in the founding of UPAGRA, was an engineering student from San José.

24. The Oscar Arias administration announced its program for "the agriculture of change" in November 1986. The most detailed exposition of what the term meant is in Alvarez Desanti (1988).

25. This local currency also supported U.S. geopolitical objectives and the broader effort to supplant public-sector Costa Rican institutions with well-funded "parallel state" entities that carried out the same or similar functions (see Chapter 1). Garst (1990, 30) provides a detailed breakdown of the programs that received local currency under PL-480 in the years 1984–89. Many of the largest expenditures were for land titling or road building in the strategic northern zone along the Nicaraguan border. After 1990, when the Sandinistas lost the Nicaraguan presidential election, the use of PL-480 funds in Costa Rican road projects extended to the rest of the country. In the 1992 PL-480 agreement, the largest local currency grants, aside from road building, were for irrigation and controlling plant pests and pathogens, both key ele-

ments of the new, export-oriented agriculture (Asamblea Legislativa 1992, 22–37).

26. In May, a major hurricane devastated maize-producing areas in the Atlantic region and fed the growing sense of distress among small producers. Following the storm, UPAGRA began to bring pressure to bear on the government to obtain emergency payments for crop losses from the National Agricultural Contingencies Fund (Fondo Nacional de Contingencias Agrícolas, or FNCA).

27. Traditionally, Costa Rican farmers had produced both white maize, used primarily for human consumption, and yellow maize, used for poultry and animal feed.

28. The Director General of the International Center for Tropical Agriculture, writing in a house organ of the Inter-American Development Bank, shares this assessment:

> The magnitude of the problem [of agricultural subsidies] is clear from the size of the transfers to the agricultural producers in the developed countries—that is, the subsidies paid by the national treasuries and the higher costs paid by consumers as a result of protectionism, equal to some $300 billion a year. This compares with the $301.4 billion represented by all world trade in agricultural products in 1989. The lowering of trade barriers as part of Latin America's economic reform will make its agricultural producers subject to aggressive foreign competition, in many cases subsidized. As IDB President Enrique V. Iglesias has said, the region's farmers are capable of competing with foreign farmers, but not with the treasuries of the developed countries. (Nores 1993, 3)

29. Dollar amounts are based on average exchange rates of 10.52 for 1980 and 50.77 for 1985 (BCCR 1986,211–13).

30. This has been a recurrent theme in interviews and group discussions during the author's fieldwork. For an insightful study from another context of folk conceptions of the rural household as a metaphor for larger social units, see Gudeman and Rivera (1990).

31. This unspoken acknowledgment of the accessibility of senior government figures to members and leaders of radical grassroots organizations was a recurrent theme in my fieldwork and surely accounts in some measure for Costa Rica's much-vaunted political stability. I was frequently startled to find, as I mention in Chapter 4, that *campesinos* from remote communities, who were not organization leaders, had participated in face-to-face meetings with cabinet ministers or even presidents of the republic.

32. Other organizations that participated included: UPAP, UCADEGUA, FEDEAGRO, FENAC, UNAC, Cooperincón, and committees of small producers from the South Pacific, Coto Sur, Osa Peninsula, and Upala regions.

33. In interviews, several march participants attributed the civil guards' brutality to a desire to "try out" the training they had recently received from U.S. Army Special Forces at Murciélago, in northern Costa Rica.

34. The origins of the Maize Plan actually date to 1984, when various peasant organizations began to discuss basic grains policies together. In 1986, after hashing out the final details during the Cathedral occupation, they proposed that the government institute a national plan for raising yields and area planted, providing adequate low-cost credit, and assuring national food self-sufficiency. Negotiations over the Maize Plan's proposals continued intermittently until 1987, with few successes for the peasant organizations (Román 1993, 242–49).

35. Arias's third Agriculture Minister, José María Figueres Olsen, son of PLN founder and former President José Figueres Ferrer, took over in mid-1988, following events described in the next chapter. He was elected president in 1994.

36. Costa Rica's second SAL with the World Bank took two years to negotiate, surely an indication of the extent of controversy it provoked.

37. Several agreements with international agencies had already been published. See, for example, "Programa de ajuste estructural," *La Nación*, May 5, 1987, pp. 16A–17A. Costa Rica's letters of intent to the IMF had been published in *La Nación*, the country's major daily, since 1982. Curiously, the IMF and World Bank appear unaware of this practice. Country officers of both institutions, interviewed by telephone in Washington in April 1991, expressed surprise that I had obtained these documents; they claimed that the agreements were confidential and declined to release English versions.

38. The conservative newspaper *La Nación* editorialized that the occupations of government offices constituted a "kidnapping of public-sector functionaries" and lamented that the "taking" of the Cathedral and similar measures "went completely beyond the traditional style and behavior of our *campesinos*" (Sept. 26, 2987, p. 14A).

39. For a case study of how the cattle lobby employed this power, see Edelman (1992, chap. 10).

40. Under the 1987 Agricultural Development Law (Ley de Fomento de Desarrollo Agropecuario, or FODEA), the government committed itself to issuing bonds that in effect rescheduled producers' debts (Asamblea Legislativa 1989). But the application of the law was uneven and it became another point of friction between the agriculturalists organizations and the government.

CHAPTER 3   ORGANIZING IN "THE CRADLE OF MAIZE"

1. The Committee had a fairly affluent constituency. It set monthly dues at 50 colones (US$5.80) for the "better-off" members and at 25 colones (US$2.90) for "small agriculturalists" (CAG Actas, Jan. 14, 1980, 10).

2. By the mid-1980s, the MRP had moderated its political stance and changed its name to the New Republic Movement (Movimiento Nueva República, or MNR), moving ever closer to the mainstream social democratic PLN (a few years later the MNR, too, was defunct). The Filadelfia holdup team was almost certainly independent of the MNR, even though participants were former members and the police and media tried to blame the operation on the organization. The robbers apparently employed a jeep belonging to the National Museum, allegedly obtained from one of the anthropologists who worked there (information from interviews).

3. Years later, reflecting back on this period, Ramírez told me, "Here in Guanacaste I didn't know anybody, especially anybody I could trust, to whom I could say 'Look, take charge of this, let's make this happen.' So I said to myself, 'Well, how is it possible that these [MRP] people, with that level of consciousness are here loose, unconnected? Why not link them to what we were doing?'"

4. *Concuño* (or *concuñado*) is a term (derived from *cuñado*, or brother-in-law) with no precise equivalent in English. It refers to the relation between two men who are married to a pair of sisters.

5. Between 1950 and 1989, the only instance of more than one drought year in a row is 1975–77; although data for 1975–76 are not complete, this drought may have been more severe than that of 1985–87.

6. Cooperincón, despite having a membership of only sixteen, was one of eight organizations, mainly much larger unions and federations, that signed an open letter to the President of the Republic following the march (UNAC et al. 1987). The twelve Cooperincón representatives went to San José for a week around the time of the march; in addition, the cooperative "authorized three *compañeros* to stay [in San José] for one month, incorporated in the dynamic of the march" (CENAP 1988, 40). These were almost certainly the cadres of urban origin—Ramírez, Hernández, and Sánchez—who had formed the co-op in the first place.

7. Negotiations concerned a range of issues: credit conditions and availability; technical assistance; the agrarian reform agency's budget; continued financing for the CNP; and access to agreements with foreign creditors that were thought to affect negatively producers of food crops for the domestic market (cf. CENAP et al. 1988, 9–15; Rivera and Román 1988). On events in Guanacaste in this period, see *El Amanezquero* (1988, 6–7).

8. Radio Chorotega, the most popular station in rural Santa Cruz, was also for a time an important forum for discussion of the agriculturalists' problems. In late 1988, the Church dismissed staff members who had promoted this activist role for the station.

9. In Guanacaste, protesters blocked highway bridges in Santa Cruz, Guar-

dia de Liberia, and Cañas. Other blockades occurred in Guácimo, in Limón province, and in Parrita, Puntarenas province.

CHAPTER 4   "IN JAIL, WE'LL EAT CEMENT"

1. Several of those named in warrants had not participated in the building occupation. Some had blocked the highway bridge, but had not entered the *"muni."* Others had no involvement at all, as in the case of one man who had been hospitalized for surgery on the day he was accused of being in the municipality.

2. "Paisa" is short for *"paisano,"* or "compatriot." Nicaraguans outside of Nicaragua often greet each other as "Paisa." In Guanacaste the term is sometimes simply synonymous with "Nicaraguan."

3. The Contingencies Fund and the MAG argued that this per-hectare amount represented one-half of average production costs. The agriculturalists maintained that it was closer to one-fifth, and less in the case of those who had to rent land to cultivate.

4. The AAA's Principles of Professional Responsibility were adopted in 1971 and amended various times until 1990. In the mid-1990s, an AAA Commission drafted a new Code of Ethics, which better reflected both the real complexity of most anthropological research and the divergent points of view within the profession.

5. At one point, for example, Pizarro declared that Ramírez was the "intellectual author" of the action, while at another he testified that he had heard one of the peasants who took over the municipal building say that they ought to call Rodolfo Brenes and report that the operation had been a success. This suggested that Brenes, a son of a local elite landowning family who was known to be sympathetic to the agriculturalists' movement, might be "the intellectual author." Brenes had participated in some of the agriculturalists' demonstrations just before the occupation of the Santa Cruz municipality, but he did not participate in the latter operation.

6. My first accounts of these events (Edelman 1990, 1991a), written well before Ramírez's trial, reflected this ingenuous and premature interpretation, which was an outgrowth both of my fieldwork data up to that time and of a somewhat overprotective attitude, early in the research, toward my peasant movement interlocutors (a limitation of much other social movements scholarship as well—see Hellman 1992, 55).

7. ASPPAS leader Ezequiel Gómez was a veteran of the 1948 civil war, who fought on the losing side in a banana workers militia unit commanded by Communist author Carlos Luis Fallas. He later told me that his "military experience" consisted of firing a few shots from an antiquated and defective rifle during a night battle in which it was impossible to see anything.

CHAPTER 5   MOVEMENTS EVOLVE, ORGANIZATIONS ARE BORN AND DIE

1. Indeed, around this time, the shift "from protest to proposal" became a common part of activist and NGO networks' philosophy and practice throughout Latin America and elsewhere as well (Fals Borda 1992, 305). Its use here is indicative of the Costa Rican peasant movement's increasing awareness of this broader, global civil society and of the kinds of discourse that *campesino* leaders thought would "play" well with European funding organizations.

2. Alvarez conceded as much, complaining that "it is frustrating to see how each day the MAG has fewer of the political, agricultural and economic instruments needed to provide solutions to the crisis" (*La República*, July 24, 1988, p. 3).

3. Somewhat later, the Minister charged that UPAGRA had employed state subsidies to build its modern, two-story headquarters in Guácimo de Limón (*La Nación*, May 30, 1989, p. 8A). UPAGRA leaders said in interviews that the building was financed with voluntary contributions of a small percentage of the emergency payments for crop losses which the organization won for its members from the government's National Agricultural Contingencies Fund (*Fondo Nacional de Contingencias Agrícolas*).

4. Similarly, the report noted that two leaders of a small, "weak" organization called the Frente Agropecuario de la Zona Atlántica, "the brothers [Guido and Sergio] Velásquez[,] are close relatives of a well-known leader of [the] National Liberation [Party]."

5. This comment may have had another connotation as well, at least for those familiar with Latin American music. The "*son*" is a typical musical form from Cuba. As in some of its other entries, the report may thus have sought to create an association, however indirect, between this individual and Cuban "subversion."

6. The actual utterance ("*¿Quién te mandó a vos aquí?*") implies both "Who sent you here?" and "Who ordered you here?" In polite Costa Rica, the Minister's use of the informal, second-person form of address was likely deliberately discourteous as well.

7. Carlos Campos, taped interview by author, San José, Nov. 20, 1990. The reported threat may have had a certain credibility because of circumstantial evidence linking Figueres to the extrajudicial killing of a minor marijuana trafficker during his Civil Guard years (see Romero and Romero 1991).

8. This was part of a vastly increased European attention to the region after the mid-1980s (Cáceres and Irvin 1990, 191–229). In particular, the European Economic Community's strong support for CADESCA (*Comité de Acción de Apoyo al Desarrollo Económico y Social de Centroamérica*), which held frequent regional seminars for peasant leaders, had a major impact on how agriculturalists' organizations viewed questions of food security (Edelman 1998a).

On the activities of foreign NGOs in Central America, see Concertación Centroamericana de Organismos de Desarrollo (1990), Visser and Wattel (1991), and Biekart (1994).

9. On the concept of "commodity chains," see Conroy, Murray, and Rosset (1996, 92–95).

10. Campos, interview.

11. This section is based on interviews with those on both sides. The first published document to discuss these disputes was Hernández Cascante, Hernández, and Monge (1991).

12. One colleague who sat through several such meetings asked me with a snicker, "Hey, have they laid that rap on you about how 'We don't want to be objects of study any more?' (*Maje, ¿a vos te han echado esa hablada de que 'No queremos ser más objetos de estudio'?*)."

13. Carlos Campos, Ramírez, and Hernández were of urban origin. Alvarez and Blanco were unambiguously of peasant origin and had long histories of involvement in agrarian struggles. Wilson Campos was from a peasant family in central Costa Rica, but managed to attend (though not to graduate from) the University of Costa Rica.

14. Technically, Nuestra Tierra was a limited-responsibility partnership (see RPSM, fiche 102,569). It was closely associated with two other enterprises: "Productico," a peasant-controlled exporting company; and Communication Initiatives for Development (Iniciativas de Comunicación Para el Desarrollo, or ICODE), a publishing arm. During the early 1990s, ICODE published *Evidencia*, an attractively designed magazine that frequently published short articles by *campesino* leaders, particularly those in the "group of six" (e.g., Blanco 1991), as well as exclusive interviews with well-known Central Americans, such as Nobel Peace Prize winner Rigoberta Menchú and writer and former Vice-President of Nicaragua Sergio Ramírez. The *campesino* movement's capacity for forming alliances with other sectors is apparent in the composition of *Evidencia*'s editorial board, which included many of Costa Rica's leading progressive journalists, educators, and artists.

15. Another former ASPPAS activist, interested in shifting his coffee producers' cooperative to organic production, told me in 1990 that a San José–based leader of the Justice and Development Council had appeared one day in Santa Cruz and unexpectedly invited him to Mexico, where there was going to be an international conference on organic coffee:

> One day before these people tell me, "You can go tomorrow to Mexico."
> "Tomorrow? Why tomorrow?" [I asked]. "Because tomorrow is the activity in Mexico and we need to send someone and you can go. . . ." "No, you people are charlatans," I told him. "You can all go to hell!" Maybe I was too cruel, too hard, my way of saying things. But to tell me one day before was

a lack of respect. I don't ever want to see those bastards again on the face of this earth!

16. A year later, ASPPAS's Cola de Gallo committee head ruefully reflected, "My people are vice-ridden, as addicted to being in debt as they are to alcohol."

17. Edwin Cabalceta, Sub-Regional Director of the agrarian reform institute (IDA) in Santa Cruz recalled, "They [the security personnel] asked me if I had seen him and I said, sure, I'd given him lifts many times in the jeep, that he had been working for a long time with a machete alongside the *campesinos*. And they told me that he had encouraged some big land invasions in the Atlantic zone and that he was a sociologist. But even he couldn't get anyone around here to occupy a finca." Taped interview by author, Santa Cruz, Dec. 4, 1990.

18. Even the confidential Security Ministry report cited above describes the organization in this region as having 1,500 members in 1988 (MAG 1988; see also Appendix).

19. Calderón, the son and namesake of a popular Social Christian reformist who was president from 1940 to 1944, won the 1990 election in part because voters identified him with his father's progressive policies. He nonetheless advocated a more extreme version of economic structural adjustment than even the orthodox members of Arias's party, who were traditionally social democratic.

20. Even the touchingly naive article by sociologist Cecilia Arguedas (1994), which cites an October 1992 interview with Ramírez, identifies him as the Justice and Development Council's coordinator for the Northwest "Región Chorotega," not as an official of ASPPAS.

21. In 1988, when ASPPAS was at its height, Higinio Rodríguez, who was elected president of the association at its founding convention, hinted at this problem in a conversation that included a few of his neighbors, Ramírez, and me. Sitting on his small porch in the beautiful mountaintop village of Vistalmar, he teased Ramírez: "Marcos, when I first saw you, I thought to myself, 'This guy isn't an agriculturalist. He doesn't have an agriculturalist's features. Nor does he speak like us.'"

22. In 1984, for example, a "Cartago" con artist calling himself Marcos Morales appeared in the village of Río Seco and rented a room from a family of evangelical Protestants. He claimed that he had access to a tripartite fund sponsored by the Banco Popular, Asignaciones Familiares, and INFOCOOP that would provide a matching grant for the creation of a cooperative. Seventeen peasants, some influenced by the evangelicals' reputation for probity, provided him substantial sums as their stake in the cooperative. Morales then vanished with the money and the evangelical family's teenage daughter (field interviews, 1990).

23. Campos, interview. Campos's understanding of the international lending institutions' stance derived in part from his attendance at a joint IMF–World Bank governors' meeting in Washington in September 1990. This trip, facilitated by U.S. and European NGOs, was preceded by a detailed letter to the Chair of the House Committee on Foreign Affairs, Representative Dante Fascell, whose office assisted the peasant organizations in gaining an invitation to the IMF–World Bank event.

24. This section is based on interviews with several members of the "group of six" (including one who defended Carlos Campos and left the group with him), as well as with personnel of German and other international "cooperation" institutions who were privy to the discussions.

25. I once pointed out to Campos in 1990 that the founder of UPANACIONAL, whom I interviewed in his home in Tierra Blanca de Cartago, flew the red-and-blue flag of the Social Christian Unity Party from his roof, not that of the PLN. He disregarded my intervention and continued to lambaste UPANACIONAL for its supposed alliance with the PLN.

26. Significantly, Wilson Campos (no relation to Carlos), who became one of Carlos Campos's main adversaries in the "group of six," had helped to form an UPANACIONAL Chapter in his home community. Later, in the northern zone region of Guatuso, he fostered collaboration between UPANACIONAL and his own organization, UCADEGUA (see Chapter 2). In 1994 he told me that he had never liked it when Carlos attacked UPANACIONAL and that it had always made him feel uncomfortable, because he knew much of what Carlos said was exaggerated or untrue.

27. In 1991, UPANACIONAL, the Justice and Development Council, and COOPEAGRI, a highly successful cooperative in the southern canton of Pérez Zeledón, formed a coordinating body (Coordinadora Agraria Nacional) to carry out joint negotiations with the government. Two years later, this coordinating body renamed itself the Mesa Nacional Campesina (National Peasant Roundtable, or MNC).

28. In the mid-1990s, Campos re-emerged in the political arena, this time as a prominent figure in the Costa Rican Pork Producers Chamber (Cámara Costarricense de Porcicultores). He also participated in the internal (primary) elections of the Social Christian Unity Party (PUSC), seeking unsuccessfully to be a candidate for legislative deputy from Limón province.

29. A detailed outline of the MNC's proposal for "the reconversion of production" is in Román (1997b, 109–11).

30. The Consorcio Frijolero was formally called the Consorcio de Comercialización Cooperativa R.L. It received additional financial backing from the cooperative sector and banking system.

31. Between 1987 and 1996 the proportion of the economically active rural

population working in agriculture fell from 47 percent to 37 percent (Román 1987a, 7).

CONCLUSION

1. A similar reticence exists regarding movements that falter or die. Indeed, success is sometimes a criterion for framing the object of study. The author of a first-rate study of women's organizing in the Americas concedes that "the movements chosen were . . . included because of their relative success in achieving some of their self-defined goals. While it is equally important to study movements that fail and why, relatively little is written about successful women's organizing" (Stephen 1997, 4).

2. The de-historicization and exoticization of a timeless peasant have been constant themes in anthropological peasant studies since their inception. Robert Redfield, for example, famed for his 1930 portrait of the idyllic, solidary social order in Tepotzlán, never reported in his published work that he had been forced to evacuate his family from the town after a shootout between local "Bolsheviks" and pro-clerical "Cristeros" (Godoy 1978, 66–70)

3. Somewhat contradictorily, Kearney maintains elsewhere that "the peasant" was a discursive construct "peculiar to the aftermath [sic] of the Cold War [when] the containment of communism became in large part the containment of masses of rural peoples" (1996, 35). Curiously, this assertion that "the peasant" is a [post-?] cold war "invention" occurs nearly in the same breath as the claim that anthropology (in particular, Redfield, whose key works predate the onset of the cold war by fifteen years or more) "invented the peasant." These incompatible affirmations are not accompanied by any treatment of the theorization of "peasants" as revolutionary subjects by writers as diverse as Mao Tse-tung and Gerrit Huizer (1973).

4. The intellectual genealogy of these ideas is substantially older than Kearney indicates (as often seems to be true with studies of the history of thought influenced by postmodernism's penchant for seeing novelty at every turn). Kearney's argument, for example, echoes a number of ideas articulated by, among others, Lambros Comitas in the 1960s (1973 [1964]) and Arturo Warman (1976) and Anthony Leeds (1977) in the 1970s. It is simply incorrect to say that there was a "late recognition in anthropology of the extent and import of informal economic activities in 'peasant' and 'proletarian' communities" (Kearney 1996, 62).

5. Kearney's insistence on this point appears to grow out of his research in and on Oaxaca, Mexico, with people who had high levels of migration to the United States and for whom an indigenous (and not just a *campesino*) identity is still salient. However, to map the experience of this region onto the rest of rural Latin America, much less Asia or Africa, presents significant difficulties.

6. In other words, "peasant" is thus often an "identity" rather than simply a "role," a distinction which was lost or blurred in much of the early peasant studies literature. "In simple terms," as Manuel Castells (1997, 7) puts it, "identities organize the meaning while roles organize the functions."

7. My argument here derives in part from observing the decline of UPA-GRA after it purged Carlos Campos and the similar decline in UCADEGUA after Wilson Campos, its founder and most prominent leader, left for several years to direct a Central America-wide network of *campesino* organizations (Edelman 1998a).

8. It is necessary also to recognize that the "peasant-ness" claim, in this case and in others, frequently conceals an unstated premise: that women are excluded from the designation or included in subordinate ways (see Chapter 4 and Appendix). Both those who are the subjects of claims and counterclaims, and those who engage in the debate, tend to be largely or exclusively men.

9. Excellent summaries of this debate, from opposing positions, are in Feder (1977, 1978) and Hewitt de Alcántara (1984, chap. 5); the former was a self-identified *descampesinista*, while the latter is sympathetic to the *campesinistas*.

10. Theorists of diverse stripes frequently overestimate the attraction of agriculture for capital (J. Berger 1992; Edelman 1992). This becomes increasingly relevant in the globalized economy of the 1990s with the growing separation of capital from production (Castells 1996).

11. Warman's (1980, 173–74) objections to the uncritical use of census data in analyzing the Mexican context are almost certainly relevant for Costa Rica as well. Few alternatives exist, however, for the type of global study attempted by Rodríguez Solera for Costa Rica or by Feder for Mexico. Since, as Warman points out, agricultural censuses tend to underestimate the extent of rural people's de facto access to land, it is all the more striking that Rodríguez Solera finds that the *descampesinización* process reversed in Costa Rica in the 1980s. Nevertheless, it is certainly the case that too few social scientists have paused to consider the epistemological issues underlying the use of this sort of data (see Edelman and Seligson 1994).

12. Rodríguez estimates that "between 1950 and 1984 the proportion of peasants in the economically active population dropped 7 percent, approximately 0.2 percent per year. At this pace, it would take 220 years for the peasantry to completely disappear" (1992, 211). Even this estimate, though, does not take into account the increase in the absolute size of the peasantry in the period for which census data are available.

13. De Janvry et al. do not, however, always draw entirely accurate conclusions from their descriptions of these two groups. Writing of the commercially oriented peasantry, they say that "the motor of economic well-being for these peasants is . . . the effective demand for wage goods in the economy; *their level of well-being is thus a reflection of that of the urban population* (de Janvry

et al. 1989, 106, emphasis added). Curiously, this assertion ignores the unceasing struggle over terms of trade between rural and urban, or agricultural and nonagricultural, sectors. As UPANACIONAL leader Guido Vargas summed up this eternal problem,

> We have seen discrimination around import substitution, where we endured huge subsidies for industry, and in the fixed-price "basic market basket," which caused and, even now, causes us enormous harm. And now that they speak of market openings and globalization, the paradigm hasn't truly changed and they continue speaking to us of fixed prices for our products and of free importation, but with restrictions on exports in order not to cause shortages. (Vargas Artavia 1997, 15–16)

14. Another factor contributing to the *recampesinización* process is the massive influx into Costa Rica of impoverished Nicaraguans. These immigrants, frequently undocumented, have played a direct part in the *recampesinización* process and have also nearly monopolized key parts of urban informal-sector employment, thus forcing an undetermined number of the poorest Costa Ricans to seek survival in the countryside.

15. Here, I paraphrase Nicaraguan *campesino* activist Sinforiano Cáceres, interviewed in 1994 (Edelman 1994b, 33).

For a complete list of the abbreviations used in these references, see pp. xv–xxii.

ARCHIVES

JISC   Juzgado de Instrucción, Santa Cruz, Guanacaste, 1988–89
CAG   Comité de Agricultores Guanacastecos, Actas, 1979–80
RPSM   Registro Público, Sección Mercantil, San José

NEWSPAPERS AND PERIODICALS

El Amanezquero (Santa Cruz, Guanacaste)
Central America Report (Guatemala)
Esta Semana (San José)
La Gaceta Diario Oficial (San José)
Inforpress Centroamericana (Guatemala)
Journal of Commerce (New York)
Latin America Regional Report: Mexico and Central America (London)
LDC Debt Report / Latin American Markets (Syracuse, N.Y.)
Libertad (San José)
La Nación (San José)
La Nación Internacional (San José)
New York Times
La Prensa Libre (San José)
La República (San José)
Rumbo en Costa Rica (San José)
Tico Times (San José)

BOOKS, ARTICLES, AND UNPUBLISHED DOCUMENTS

Abarca Vázquez, Carlos. 1992. *Los movimientos sociales en el desarrollo reciente de Costa Rica*. San José: Editorial de la Universidad Estatal a Distancia.
Abrams, Philip. 1982. *Historical Sociology*. Ithaca, N.Y.: Cornell University Press.

Achío Tacsan, Mayra, and Ana Cecilia Escalante Herrera. 1985. *Azúcar y política en Costa Rica*. San José: Editorial Costa Rica.

Acuña Ortega, Víctor Hugo. 1986. *Los orígenes de la clase obrera en Costa Rica: Las huelgas de 1920 por la jornada de ocho horas*. San José: CENAP–CEPAS.

———. 1987. La ideología de los pequeños y medianos productores cafetaleros costarricenses (1900–1961). *Revista de Historia* 16 (July–Dec.): 137–59.

Acuña Ortega, Víctor Hugo, and Iván Molina Jiménez. 1991. *Historia económica y social de Costa Rica (1750–1950)*. San José: Editorial Porvenir.

Adam, Barry D. 1993. Post-Marxism and the New Social Movements. *Canadian Review of Sociology and Anthropology* 30, no. 3:316–36.

Agricultores del Distrito. 1987. Agricultores del Distrito de Cartagena y Santa Cruz [Actas, 20 de diciembre]. Manuscript, 3 pp.

Aguilar, Jesús, José Soto, Miguel Garita, and Enrique March. n.d. *Monografía histórica de Tierra Blanca*. San José: Servicios Litográficos Comárfil, S.A.

Aguilar Bulgarelli, Oscar. 1969. *Costa Rica y sus hechos políticos de 1948*. San José: Editorial Costa Rica.

Albarracín, Priscilla, and Héctor Pérez Brignoli. 1977. *Estadísticas del comercio exterior de Costa Rica (1907–1946)*. San José: Universidad de Costa Rica, Proyecto de Historia Social y Económica de Costa Rica, Avance de Investigación N° 5.

Alfaro Rodríguez, Dionisio. 1990. Transformaciones de la politica económica de ajuste estructural en el subsistema espacial de granos básicos. In *Los campesinos frente a la nueva década: Ajuste estructural y pequeña producción agropecuaria en Costa Rica*, ed. William Reuben Soto. San José: Editorial Porvenir.

Alforja [Centro de Estudios y Publicaciones Alforja]. 1988. *Esta lucha había que darla. Hay que darla y ganarla también. Asientamiento campesino el Indio 1979–1988*. San José: Alforja.

Altenburg, Tilman, Wolfgang Hein, and Jürgen Weller. 1990. *El desafío económico de Costa Rica: Desarrollo agroindustrial autocentrado como alternativa*. San José: Departamento Ecuménico de Investigaciones.

Alvarez, Sonia E. 1998. Latin American Feminisms 'Go Global': Trends of the 1990s and Challenges for the New Millennium. In *Cultures of Politics / Politics of Cultures: Re-Visioning Latin American Social Movements*, ed. Sonia E. Alvarez, Evelina Dagnino, and Arturo Escobar. Boulder, Colo.: Westview.

Alvarez, Sonia E., Evelina Dagnino, and Arturo Escobar. 1998. Introduction: The Cultural and the Political in Latin American Social Movements. In *Cultures of Politics / Politics of Cultures: Re-visioning Latin American Social Movements*. Boulder, Colo.: Westview.

Alvarez Desanti, Antonio. 1988. *Agricultura de cambio*. San José: Imprenta Nacional.

Andersen, Martin Edwin. 1993. *Dossier Secreto: Argentina's Desaparecidos and the Myth of the Dirty War*. Boulder, Colo.: Westview.

Anderson, Leslie E. 1990a. Alternative Action in Costa Rica: Peasants as Active Participants. *Journal of Latin American Studies* 22 (Feb.): 89–113.

———. 1990b. Post-Materialism from a Peasant Perspective: Political Motivation in Costa Rica and Nicaragua. *Comparative Political Studies* 23, no. 1:80–113.

———. 1991. Mixed Blessings: Disruption and Organization among Peasant Unions in Costa Rica. *Latin American Research Review* 26, no. 1:111–43.

———. 1994. *The Political Ecology of the Modern Peasant: Calculation and Community*. Baltimore: Johns Hopkins University Press.

Apfell Marglin, Frédérique, and Stephen Marglin, eds. 1990. *Dominating Knowledge: Development, Culture, and Resistance*. Oxford: Clarendon Press.

Appendini, Kirsten. 1992. La 'modernización' en el campo y el futuro del campesinado: Iniciamos el debate de 'los noventa.' *Estudios Sociológicos* 10, no. 29:251–62.

Apter, David E. 1992. Democracy and Emancipatory Movements: Notes for a Theory of Inversionary Discourse. *Development and Change* 23, no. 3:139–73.

Arguedas Marín, Cecilia. 1994. Los campesinos quieren decir. . . . *Revista de Ciencias Sociales* 63 (March): 11–23.

Arias Peñate, Salvador. 1989. *Seguridad o inseguridad alimentaria: Un reto para la región centroamericana. Perspectivas al año 2000*. San Salvador: UCA Editores.

Aronowitz, Stanley. 1988. Foreword. In Alain Touraine, *The Return of the Actor: Social Theory in Postindustrial Society*. Minneapolis: University of Minnesota Press.

Asad, Talal, ed. 1973. *Anthropology and the Colonial Encounter*. London: Ithaca Press.

Asamblea Legislativa. 1989. *Ley de fomento a la producción agropecuaria y sus reglamentos anotados y concordados*. San José: Editorial Universidad Estatal a Distancia.

———. 1992. Aprobación del convenio entre el gobierno de los Estados Unidos de América y el gobierno de Costa Rica para la venta de productos agrícolas, firmado en San José, Costa Rica, el 27 de febrero de 1992. Expediente No. 11467. Manuscript.

Barham, Bradford, Mary Clark, Elizabeth Katz, and Rachel Schurman. 1992. Nontraditional Agricultural Exports in Latin America. *Latin American Research Review* 27, no. 2:43–82.

Bartra, Armando. 1985. *Los herederos de Zapata: Movimientos campesinos posrevolucionarios en México*. Mexico: Ediciones Era.

Bartra, Roger. 1975. Las vías de disolución del campesinado en México: Notas sobre la coyuntura actual. In *Los problemas de la organización campesina*, ed. Iván Restrepo Fernández. Mexico: Editorial Campesina.

BCCR. 1986. *Estadísticas 1950–1985*. San José: BCCR.

———. 1988. *Anuario estadístico cuentas monetarias 1984–1988*. San José: BCCR.

———. 1990a. *Anuario estadístico fascículo de índices 1985–1989*. San José: BCCR.

———. 1990b. *Anuario estadístico finanzas públicas 1985–1989*. San José: BCCR.

BCCR et al.1989a. *Renegociación de la deuda pública externa de Costa Rica 1981–1989 (recopilación de documentos)*. Parte 3: *Renegociación de la deuda pública externa bilateral de Costa Rica*. San José: BCCR, Comentarios sobre asuntos económicos N° 82.

———. 1989b. *Renegociación de la deuda pública externa de Costa Rica 1981–1989 (recopilación de documentos)*. Parte 4: *Algunos comentarios publicados sobre la deuda externa de Costa Rica*. San José: BCCR, Comentarios sobre asuntos económicos N° 82.

Bebbington, Anthony. 1996. Movements, Modernizations, and Markets: Indigenous Organizations and Agrarian Strategies in Ecuador. In *Liberation Ecologies: Environment, Development, Social Movements*, ed. Richard Peet and Michael Watts. London: Routledge.

Behar, Ruth. 1993. *Translated Woman: Crossing the Border with Esperanza's Story*. Boston: Beacon Press.

Benjamin, Walter. 1983. Theoretics of Knowledge; Theory of Progress. *Philosophical Forum* 15, nos. 1–2:1–40.

Bergad, Laird W. 1983. *Coffee and the Growth of Agrarian Capitalism in Nineteenth-Century Puerto Rico*. Princeton: Princeton University Press.

Berger, John. 1992 [1979]. *Pig Earth*. New York: Vintage.

Berger, Mark T. 1993. Civilising the South: The U.S. Rise to Hegemony in the Americas and the Roots of 'Latin American Studies,' 1898–1945. *Bulletin of Latin American Research* 12, no. 1:1–48.

Berger, Peter, and Thomas Luckmann. 1966. *The Social Construction of Reality: A Treatise in the Sociology of Knowledge*. Garden City, N.Y.: Doubleday.

Biekhart, Kees. 1994. *La cooperación no-gubernamental europea hacia Centroamérica: La experiencia de los ochenta y las tendencias en los noventa*. San Salvador: PRISMA.

Biersteker, Thomas J. 1993a. International Financial Negotiations and Adjustment Bargaining: An Overview. In *Dealing with Debt: International Financial Negotiations and Adjustment Bargaining*, ed. Thomas J. Biersteker. Boulder, Colo.: Westview.

———. 1993b. Mexico, 1982: Paving the Way with Exceptions. In *Dealing with Debt: International Financial Negotiations and Adjustment Bargaining*, ed. Thomas J. Biersteker. Boulder, Colo.: Westview.

Black, George. 1988. *The Good Neighbor: How the United States Wrote the History of Central America and the Caribbean*. New York: Pantheon.

Blanco, Gustavo, and Orlando Navarro. 1984. *El movimiento solidarista costarricense*. San José: Editorial Costa Rica.

Blanco, Ulises. 1991. Lamento . . . o encuentro. *Evidencia* 1, no. 2:10–11.

Blanco M., Ulises, and Carlos Campos R. 1988. Declaración de organizaciones campesinas de Costa Rica, ante la XVII Asamblea General de la Unión Internacional para la Conservación de la Naturaleza y los Recursos Naturales (UICN). In *La situación ambiental en Centroamérica y el Caribe*, ed. Ingemar Hedström. San José: Departamento Ecuménico de Investigaciones.

BNCR et al. 1988. Reunión celebrada el día 7 de julio de 1988. Manuscript, 4 pp.

Botey Sobrado, Ana María. 1990. El movimiento popular costarricense en el contexto de la crisis actual. In *Historia de Costa Rica en el siglo XX*, ed. Jaime Murillo Víquez. San José: Editorial Porvenir.

Boudreau, Vincent. 1996. Northern Theory, Southern Protest: Opportunity Structure Analysis in Cross-National Perspective. *Mobilization: An International Journal* 1, no. 2:175–89.

Bourdieu, Pierre, and Loïc J. D. Wacquant. 1992. *An Invitation to a Reflexive Sociology*. Chicago: University of Chicago Press.

Bourgois, Philippe I. 1989. *Ethnicity at Work: Divided Labor on a Central American Banana Plantation*. Baltimore: Johns Hopkins University Press.

———. 1990. Confronting Anthropological Ethics: Ethnographic Lessons from Central America. *Journal of Peace Research* 27, no. 1:43–54.

Bozon, Michel, and Anne-Marie Thiesse. 1986. The Collapse of Memory: The Case of Farm Workers (French Vexin, pays de France). *History and Anthropology* 2: 237–59.

Brass, Tom. 1991. Moral Economists, Subalterns, New Social Movements, and the (Re-)Emergence of a (Post-)Modernised (Middle) Peasant. *Journal of Peasant Studies* 18, no. 2:173–205.

Brenes, Esteban R., and Noel Ramírez. 1989. Costa Rica: El ajuste estructural y el sector agrícola. In *Procesos de ajuste en países en desarrollo*, ed. Mark Lindenberg and Noel Ramírez. San José: Libro Libre.

Brenes, Lidiette. 1990. *La nacionalización bancaria en Costa Rica: Un juicio histórico*. San José: Facultad Latinoamericana de Ciencias Sociales.

Brenes Castillo, Carlos. 1988. ¿Desarrollo forestal campesino? In *La situación ambiental en Centroamérica y el Caribe*, ed. Ingemar Hedström. San José: Departamento Ecuménico de Investigaciones.

Brockett, Charles D. 1988. *Land, Power, and Poverty: Agrarian Transformation and Political Conflict in Central America*. Boston: Unwin Hyman.

———. 1991. The Structure of Political Opportunities and Peasant Mobilization in Central America. *Comparative Politics* 23 (Apr.): 253–74.

Bryan, William Smith. 1899. *Our Islands and Their People*. New York: N. D. Thompson Publishing Company.

Brysk, Alison. 1996. Turning Weakness into Strength: The Internationalization of Indian Rights. *Latin American Perspectives* 23 (spring): 38–57.

Bulmer-Thomas, Victor. 1987. *The Political Economy of Central America Since 1920*. Cambridge: Cambridge University Press.

Burbach, Roger, Orlando Núñez, and Boris Kagarlitsky. 1997. *Globalization and Its Discontents: The Rise of Postmodern Socialisms*. London: Pluto Press.

Burdick, John. 1992. Rethinking the Study of Social Movements: The Case of Christian Base Communities in Urban Brazil. In *The Making of Social Movements in Latin America: Identity, Strategy, and Democracy*, ed. Arturo Escobar and Sonia E. Alvarez. Boulder, Colo.: Westview.

———. 1995. Uniting Theory and Practice in the Ethnography of Social Movements: Notes Toward a Hopeful Realism. *Dialectical Anthropology* 20: 361–85.

Bustelo, Eduardo S., Andrea Cornia, Richard Jolly, and Frances Stewart. 1987. Hacia un enfoque más amplio en la política de ajuste: Ajuste con crecimiento y una dimensión humana. In *Políticas de ajuste y grupos más vulnerables en América Latina: Hacia un enfoque alternativa*, ed. Eduardo S. Bustelo. Bogotá: Fondo de las Naciones Unidas para la Infancia–Fondo de Cultura Económica.

Caballero, Manuel. 1987. *Latin America and the Comintern, 1919–1943*. Cambridge: Cambridge University Press.

Cáceres, Luis René, and George Irvin. 1990. La reconstrucción del MCCA y la cooperación europea. In *Centroamérica: El futuro de la integración económica*, ed. George Irvin and Stuart Holland. San José: Departamento Ecuménico de Investigaciones.

Calderón, Fernando, Alejandro Piscitelli, and José Luis Reyna. 1992. Social Movements: Actors, Theories, Expectations. In *New Social Movements in Latin America: Identity, Strategy, and Democracy*, ed. Arturo Escobar and Sonia E. Alvarez. Boulder, Colo.: Westview.

Calhoun, Craig. 1993. New Social Movements of the Early Nineteenth Century. *Social Science History* 17, no. 3: 385–427.

Campos, Carlos. 1987. ¿Cuál puede ser la alternativa? In *Costa Rica: Crisis y desafíos*, ed. Edelberto Torres-Rivas. San José: Departamento Ecuménico de Investigaciones.

———. 1988. En busca de alternativas. In *La situación ambiental en Centroamérica y el Caribe*, ed. Ingemar Hedström. San José: Departamento Ecuménico de Investigaciones.

Cardoso, Ciro F. S. 1975. Historia económica del café en Centroamérica (siglo

XIX): Estudio comparativo. *Estudios Sociales Centroamericanos* 10 (Jan.–
Apr.): 9–55.

Cardoso, Fernando Henrique. 1977. The Consumption of Dependency in the
United States. *Latin American Research Review* 12, no. 3:7–12.

Cartín Herrera, Sandra. 1990. *Lucha social en el agro costarricense: La experiencia de la UPIAV*. San José: CEPAS.

Cartín Herrera, Sandra, and Carlos Castro V. 1986. *Lucha social en el agro costarricense: La experiencia de UPANACIONAL*. San José: CEPAS.

Castells, Manuel. 1996. *The Rise of the Network Society*. Oxford: Blackwell.

———. 1997. *The Power of Identity*. Oxford: Blackwell.

Castro Valverde, Carlos. 1995. Sector público y ajuste estructural en Costa Rica
(1983–1992). In *La transformación neoliberal del sector público: Ajuste estructural y sector público en Centroamérica y el Caribe*, ed. Trevor Evans.
Managua: CRIES.

CENAP. 1988. Evaluación de la marcha campesina de setiembre de 1987. San
José: CENAP (mimeo).

———. 1989. *La situación agraria, hechos y palabras*. San José: CENAP.

CEPAL. 1988. *Agricultura, comercio exterior y cooperación internacional*. Santiago: Naciones Unidas, Estudios e Informes de la CEPAL N° 73.

CEPAS. 1987. La readecuación de deudas a los productores agropecuarios. *Panorama Campesino* 2 (Dec.): 1–15.

———. 1988a. Readecuación de deudas por medio de la ley FODEA y la situación actual y futura de la cartera crediticia agropecuaria de los pequeños y
medianos productores (memoria del taller 19–3–88). Mimeo.

———. 1988b. Taller: UNSA y los pequeños productores enfrentando la crisis
nacional. Memoria. Mimeo.

———. 1992. *Costa Rica en el umbral de los años noventa: Deterioro y auge
de lo social en el marco del ajuste*. San José: CEPAS.

Cerdas, Rodolfo. 1991. Costa Rica since 1930. In *Central America since Independence*, ed. Leslie Bethell. Cambridge: Cambridge University Press.

Céspedes, Víctor Hugo, Alberto Di Mare, and Ronulfo Jiménez. 1985. *Costa
Rica: Recuperación sin reactivación*. San José: Academia de Centroamérica.

Ching, Barbara, and Gerald W. Creed. 1997. Recognizing Rusticity: Identity
and the Power of Place. In *Knowing Your Place: Rural Identity and Cultural
Hierarchy*, ed. B. Ching and G. W. Creed. London: Routledge.

Clifford, James. 1986. Introduction: Partial Truths. In *Writing Culture: The
Poetics and Politics of Ethnography*, ed. James Clifford. Berkeley: University
of California Press.

———. 1988. *The Predicament of Culture: Twentieth-Century Ethnography,
Literature, and Art*. Cambridge, Mass.: Harvard University Press.

Cohen, Jean. 1985. Strategy or Identity: New Theoretical Paradigms and Contemporary Social Movements. *Social Research* 52, no. 4:663–716.

Cohen, Myron L. 1993. Cultural and Political Inventions in Modern China: The Case of the Chinese 'Peasant.' *Daedalus* 122, no. 2:151–70.

Colás, Santiago. 1994. *Postmodernity in Latin America: The Argentine Paradigm.* Durham, N.C.: Duke University Press.

Comaroff, Jean, and John Comaroff. 1991. *Of Revelation and Revolution: Christianity, Colonialism, and Consciousness in South Africa, vol. 1.* Chicago: University of Chicago Press.

Comisión Campesina (UPAGRA, FEDEAGRO, UCTAN, UNAC, UCADEGUA, CCA, FECOPA). 1987. 15 días sin respuesta. Leaflet, files of author.

———. 1990. Letter to the Honorable Dante Fascell, files of author.

Comisión Centroamericana de Pequeños y Medianos Productores Agropecuarios. 1991. Posición ante el programa de ajuste estructural, las relaciones con las ONGs locales y la cooperación internacional solidaria. Mimeographed, in files of author.

Comitas, Lambros. 1973 [1964]. Occupational Multiplicity in Rural Jamaica. In *Work and Family Life: West Indian Perspectives,* ed. Lambros Comitas and David Lowenthal. Garden City, N.Y.: Anchor Doubleday.

Concertación Centroamericana de Organismos de Desarrollo [Central American Concordat of Development Organizations]. 1990. *Cooperación externa y desarrollo en Centroamérica.* San José: CECADE.

Conroy, Michael E., Douglas L. Murray, and Peter M. Rosset. 1996. *A Cautionary Tale: Failed U.S. Development Policy in Central America.* Boulder, Colo.: Lynne Rienner Publishers.

Consejo Nacional de Pequeños y Medianos Productores Justicia y Desarrollo. 1991. Síntesis de la carta a los presidentes centroamericanos: La urgencia del desarrollo exige concertar. Mimeographed, in files of author.

Corrales, Jorge. 1981. *De la pobreza a la abundancia en Costa Rica.* San José: Editorial Studium–Universidad Autónoma de Centro América.

Cowen, M. P., and R. W. Shenton. 1996. *Doctrines of Development.* London: Routledge.

Creedman, Theodore S. 1977. *Historical Dictionary of Costa Rica.* Metuchen, N.J.: Scarecrow Press.

Dagnino, Evelina. 1998. The Cultural Politics of Citizenship, Democracy, and the State. In *Cultures of Politics/Politics of Cultures: Re-Visioning Latin American Social Movements,* ed. Sonia E. Alvarez, Evelina Dagnino, and Arturo Escobar. Boulder, Colo.: Westview.

Deere, Carmen Diana. 1979. Rural Women's Subsistence Production in the Capitalist Periphery. In *Peasants and Proletarians: The Struggles of Third World Workers,* ed. Robin Cohen, Peter C. W. Gutkind, and Phyllis Brazier. New York: Monthly Review Press.

de Janvry, Alain, Robin Marsh, David Runsten, Elisabeth Sadoulet, and Carol Zabin. 1989. Impacto de la crisis en la economía campesina de América

Latina y el Caribe. In *La economía campesina: Crisis, reactivación y desarrollo*, ed. Fausto Jordan. San José: Instituto Interamericano de Cooperación para la Agricultura.

De La Cruz, Vladimir. 1986. Notas para la historia del movimiento campesino en Costa Rica. In *Las instituciones costarricenses del siglo XX*, Carmen Lila Gómez et al. San José: Editorial Costa Rica.

de Soto, Hernando. 1989 [1986]. *The Other Path: The Invisible Revolution in the Third World*. New York: Harper & Row.

Development GAP [Development Group for Alternative Policies]. 1993. *Structural Adjustment in Central America: The Case of Costa Rica*. Washington: Development GAP.

Dosal, Paul J. 1993. *Doing Business with the Dictators: A Political History of United Fruit in Guatemala, 1899–1944*. Washington: Scholarly Resources Inc.

DuBois, Marc. 1991. The Governance of the Third World: A Foucauldian Perspective of Power Relations in Development. *Alternatives* 16, no. 1:1–30.

Dunkerley, James. 1988. *Power in the Isthmus: A Political History of Modern Central America*. London: Verso.

Eckstein, Susan. 1989. Power and Popular Protest in Latin America. In *Power and Popular Protest: Latin American Social Movements*, ed. S. Eckstein. Berkeley: University of California Press.

ECLA. 1984. *Statistical Abstract of Latin America*. Santiago: ECLA.

Edelman, Marc. 1981. *Apuntes sobre la consolidación de las haciendas en Guanacaste*. San José: Instituto de Investigaciones Sociales, Universidad de Costa Rica, Avances de Investigación 44.

———. 1983. Recent Literature on Costa Rica's Economic Crisis. *Latin American Research Review* 18, no. 2:166–80.

———. 1984. A Particular Road. *Monthly Review* 36, no. 7:55–59.

———. 1985. Back from the Brink: How Washington Bailed Out Costa Rica. *NACLA Report on the Americas* 19, no. 6:37–48.

———. 1987. El distrito de riego de Guanacaste (Costa Rica) y la política del agua. *Anuario de Estudios Centroamericanos* 13, no. 1:95–111.

———. 1989. Illegal Renting of Agrarian Reform Plots: A Costa Rican Case Study. *Human Organization* 48, no. 2:172–80.

———. 1990. When They Took the 'Muni': Political Culture and Anti-Austerity Protest in Rural Northwestern Costa Rica. *American Ethnologist* 17, no. 4:736–57.

———. 1991a. La cultura política de una protesta campesina contra el ajuste estructural económico, 1988. *Revista de Historia* 23 (Jan.–June): 145–90.

———. 1991b. Shifting Legitimacies and Economic Change: The State and Contemporary Costa Rican Peasant Movements. *Peasant Studies* 18, no. 4: 221–49.

————. 1992. *The Logic of the Latifundio: The Large Estates of Northwestern Costa Rica since the Late Nineteenth Century.* Stanford, Calif.: Stanford University Press.

————. 1994a. Landlords and the Devil: Class, Ethnic, and Gender Dimensions of Central American Peasant Narratives. *Cultural Anthropology* 9, no. 1: 58–93.

————. 1994b. Three Campesino Activists [interviews with Leoncia Solórzano, Honduras; Wilson Campos, Costa Rica; Sinforiano Cáceres, Nicaragua]. *NACLA Report on the Americas* 28, no. 3:30–33.

————. 1995. Rethinking the Hamburger Thesis: Deforestation and the Crisis of Central America's Beef Exports. In *The Social Causes of Environmental Destruction in Latin America,* ed. Michael Painter and William Durham. Ann Arbor: University of Michigan Press.

————. 1996. Reconceptualizing and Reconstituting Peasant Struggles: A New Social Movement in Central America. *Radical History Review* 65 (spring): 26–47.

————. 1998a. Transnational Peasant Politics in Central America. *Latin American Research Review* 33, no. 3:49–86.

————. 1998b. De la fría Nueva York al cálido Guanacaste. In *Ciencia social en Costa Rica: Experiencias de vida e investigación,* by Marc Edelman, Fabrice Lehoucq, Iván Molina, and Steven Palmer. San José: Editorial de la Universidad de Costa Rica & Editorial de la Universidad Nacional.

————. n.d. The Society and Its Environment. In *Costa Rica: A Country Study,* ed. Rexford Hudson. Washington: Library of Congress (forthcoming).

Edelman, Marc, and Jayne Hutchcroft. 1984. Costa Rica: Resisting Austerity. *NACLA Report on the Americas* 18, no. 1:37–40.

Edelman, Marc, and Rodolfo Monge Oviedo. 1993. Costa Rica: The Non-Market Roots of Market Success. *NACLA Report on the Americas* 26, no. 4: 22–29, 43–44.

Edelman, Marc, and Mitchell A. Seligson. 1994. Land Inequality: A Comparison of Census Data and Property Records in Twentieth-Century Southern Costa Rica. *Hispanic American Historical Review* 74, no. 3:445–91

Escobar, Arturo. 1984. Discourse and Power in Development: Michel Foucault and the Relevance of His Work to the Third World. *Alternatives* 10 (winter): 377–400.

————. 1988. Power and Visibility: Development and the Invention and Management of the Third World. *Cultural Anthropology* 3, no. 4:428–43.

————. 1991. Anthropology and the Development Encounter: The Making and Marketing of Development Anthropology. *American Ethnologist* 18, no. 4:658–82.

————. 1992a. Culture, Practice and Politics: Anthropology and the Study of Social Movements. *Critique of Anthropology* 12, no. 4:395–432.

———. 1992b. Culture, Economics, and Politics in Latin American Social Movements Theory and Research. In *The Making of Social Movements in Latin America: Identity, Strategy, and Democracy*, ed. Arturo Escobar and Sonia E. Alvarez. Boulder, Colo.: Westview.

———. 1995. *Encountering Development: The Making and Unmaking of the Third World.* Princeton: Princeton University Press.

Escobar, Arturo, and Sonia E. Alvarez. 1992. Introduction: Theory and Protest in Latin America Today. In Arturo Escobar and Sonia E. Alvarez, eds., *The Making of Social Movements in Latin America: Identity, Strategy, and Democracy.* Boulder, Colo.: Westview.

Esteva, Gustavo. 1983. *The Struggle for Rural Mexico.* South Hadley, Mass.: Bergin & Garvey.

———. 1988. El desastre agrícola: Adiós al México imaginario. *Comercio Exterior* [Mexico] 38, no. 8:662–72.

———. 1992. Development. In *The Development Dictionary: A Guide to Knowledge as Power*, ed. Wolfgang Sachs. London: Zed Books.

Estrada Molina, Ligia. 1967. *Teodoro Picado Michalski: Su aporte a la historiografía.* San José: Imprenta Nacional.

Evers, Tilman. 1985. Identity: The Hidden Side of New Social Movements in Latin America. In *New Social Movements and the State in Latin America*, ed. David Slater. Amsterdam: CEDLA.

Eyerman, Ron, and Andrew Jamison. 1991. *Social Movements: A Cognitive Approach.* London: Polity Press.

Fallas, Helio. 1990. El programa de ajuste estructural y la agricultura en Costa Rica. In *Los campesinos frente a la nueva década: Ajuste estructural y pequeña producción agropecuaria en Costa Rica*, ed. William Reuben Soto. San José: Editorial Porvenir.

Fals Borda, Orlando. 1992. Social Movements and Political Power in Latin America. In *The Making of Social Movements in Latin America: Identity, Strategy, and Democracy*, ed. Arturo Escobar and Sonia E. Alvarez. Boulder, Colo.: Westview.

Feder, Ernest. 1977. Campesinistas y descampesinistas: Tres enfoques divergentes (no incompatibles) sobre la destrucción del campesinado. Primera parte. *Comercio Exterior* [Mexico] 27, no. 12:1439–46.

———. 1978. Campesinistas y descampesinistas: Tres enfoques divergentes (no incompatibles) sobre la destrucción del campesinado. Segunda parte. *Comercio Exterior* [Mexico] 28, no. 1:42–51.

Fonseca Corrales, Elizabeth. 1983. *Costa Rica colonial: La tierra y el hombre.* San José: Editorial Universitaria Centroamericana.

Foucault, Michel. 1972. *The Archeology of Knowledge and the Discourse on Language.* New York: Pantheon Books.

Fowerwaker, Joe. 1995. *Theorizing Social Movements.* London: Pluto Press.

Fox, Jonathan. 1990. Editor's Introduction. *Journal of Development Studies* 26, no. 4:1–18.

Franco, Eliana, and Carlos Sojo. 1992. *Gobierno, empresarios y políticas de ajuste.* San José: Facultad Latinoamericana de Ciencias Sociales.

Frieden, Jeffry. 1989. Winners and Losers in the Latin American Debt Crisis. In *Debt and Democracy in Latin America,* ed. Barbara Stallings and Robert Kaufman. Boulder, Colo.: Westview.

Fürst, Edgar. 1989. Costa Rica 1982–1987: ¿Una aplicación heterodoxa "sui generis" de políticas de ajuste estructural? In *Crisis económica en Centroamérica y el Caribe,* ed. Mats Lundhal and Wim Pelupessy. San José: Departamento Ecuménico de Investigaciones.

Gaete Astica, Marcelo, Ana Ligia Garro Martínez, and Aida Rivera Montero. 1989. El movimiento social campesino de la segunda mitad de los años ochenta (El caso de las marchas campesinas de 1986 y 1987). Licenciatura thesis, University of Costa Rica, San José.

Gallardo, María Eugenia, and José Roberto López. 1986. *Centroamérica: La crisis en cifras.* San José: Instituto Interamericano de Cooperación para la Agricultura—Facultad Latinoamericana de Ciencias Sociales.

Gamson, William A. 1992. The Social Psychology of Collective Action. In *Frontiers in Social Movement Theory,* ed. Aldon D. Morris and Carol McClurg Mueller. New Haven: Yale University Press.

Garita, Luis. 1981. El proceso de burocratización del Estado costarricense. *Ciencias Económicas* 1, no. 1:105–18.

Garnier, Leonardo. 1991. *Gasto público y desarrollo social en Costa Rica.* Heredia, Costa Rica: Maestría en Política Económica, Universidad Nacional, Cuadernos de Política Económica 2.

———. 1994. Ajuste extructural e inserción externa: La experiencia en economías pequeñas. In *Apertura externa y competitividad,* ed. Leiner Vargas. Heredia, Costa Rica: Editorial Fundación UNA.

Garst, Rachel. 1990. *Ayuda alimentaria de Estados Unidos a Costa Rica.* San José: Centro de Estudios para la Acción Social, Documento de Análisis Nº 13.

Garst, Rachel, and Tom Barry. 1990. *Feeding the Crisis: U.S. Food Aid and Farm Policy in Central America.* Lincoln: University of Nebraska Press.

Geertz, Clifford. 1973. *The Interpretation of Cultures.* New York: Basic Books.

———. 1988. *Works and Lives: The Anthropologist as Author.* Stanford, Calif.: Stanford University Press.

George, Susan. 1977. *How the Other Half Dies: The Real Reasons for World Hunger.* Montclair, N.J.: Allanheld, Osmun.

Gitlin, Todd. 1987. *The Sixties: Years of Hope, Days of Rage.* New York: Bantam Books.

Gledhill, John. 1988. Agrarian Social Movements and Forms of Consciousness. *Bulletin of Latin American Research* 7, no. 2:257–76.

Godio, Julio. 1983. *Historia del movimiento obrero latinoamericano*, vol. 2: *Nacionalismo y Comunismo, 1918–1930*. Mexico City: Nueva Sociedad— Editorial Nueva Imagen.

Godoy, Ricardo. 1978. The Background and Context of Redfield's Tepoztlán. *Journal of the Steward Anthropological Society* 10, no. 1:47–79.

Gómez, Carmen Lila. 1985. *La pena de muerte en Costa Rica durante el siglo XIX*. San José: Editorial Costa Rica.

González, Paulino. 1985. Las luchas estudiantiles en Centroamérica 1970– 1983. In *Movimientos populares en Centroamérica*, ed. Daniel Camacho and Rafael Menjívar. San José: EDUCA.

González Vega, Gonzalo. 1984. Fear of Adjusting: The Social Costs of Economic Policies in Costa Rica in the 1970s. In *Revolution and Counterrevolution in Central America*, ed. Donald E. Schultz and Doughlas H. Graham. Boulder, Colo.: Westview.

Gordillo, Gustavo. 1988. *Campesinos al asalto del cielo: De la expropiación estatal a la apropiación campesina*. Mexico City: Siglo XXI.

Gould, Jeffrey L. 1990. *To Lead as Equals: Rural Protest and Political Consciousness in Chinandega, Nicaragua, 1912–1979*. Chapel Hill: University of North Carolina Press.

Grupo Esquel. 1989. Las políticas de desarrollo rural en América Latina: Balance y perspectivas. In *La economía campesina: Crisis, reactivación y desarrollo*, ed. Fausto Jordan. San José: Instituto Interamericano de Cooperación para la Agricultura.

Guardia, Tomás. 1989. Law on Individual Rights, 1877. In *The Costa Rica Reader*, ed. Marc Edelman and Joanne Kenen. New York: Grove Weidenfeld.

Gudeman, Stephen, and Alberto Rivera. 1990. *Conversations in Colombia: The Domestic Economy in Life and Text*. Cambridge: Cambridge University Press.

Gudmundson, Lowell. 1983. The Expropriation of Pious and Corporate Properties in Costa Rica, 1805–1860: Patterns in the Consolidation of a National Elite. *The Americas* 39, no. 3:281–302.

———. 1986. *Costa Rica Before Coffee: Society and Economy on the Eve of the Export Boom*. Baton Rouge: Lousiana State University Press.

Güendell G., Ludwig, and Roy Rivera A. 1993. *Los fondos sociales en Centroamérica*. San José: Facultad Latinoamericana de Ciencias Sociales, Cuadernos de Ciencias Sociales 64.

Gutiérrez Haces, María Teresa. 1993. Centroamérica en la visión del libre comercio de los Estados Unidos. In *Democracia emergente en Centroamérica*, ed. Carlos M. Vilas. Mexico City: Universidad Nacional Autónoma de México.

Haggard, Stephan, and Robert R. Kaufman, eds. 1992. *The Politics of Economic Adjustment*. Princeton: Princeton University Press.

Hale, Charles A. 1989. Political and Social Ideas. In *Latin America: Economy and Society, 1870–1930,* ed. Leslie Bethell. Cambridge: Cambridge University Press.

Hale, Charles R. 1997. Cultural Politics of Identity in Latin America. *Annual Review of Anthropology* 26: 567–90.

Hall, Stuart. 1991. Brave New World. *Socialist Review* 21, no. 1:57–64.

Handelman, Howard, and Werner Baer. 1989. Introduction: The Economic and Political Costs of Austerity. In *Paying the Costs of Austerity in Latin America,* ed. Howard Handelman and Werner Baer. Boulder, Colo.: Westview.

Harvey, David. 1989. *The Condition of Postmodernity: An Enquiry into the Origins of Cultural Change.* Cambridge, Mass.: Blackwell.

———. 1993. Class Relations, Social Justice, and the Politics of Difference. In *Principled Positions: Postmodernism and the Rediscovery of Value,* ed. Judith Squires. London: Lawrence and Wishart.

Hayter, Teresa. 1971. *Aid as Imperialism.* Baltimore: Penguin.

Heath, Dwight B. 1970. Costa Rica and Her Neighbors. *Current History* 58, no. 342:95–101, 113.

Hellman, Judith Adler. 1992. The Study of New Social Movements in Latin America and the Question of Autonomy. In *The Making of Social Movements in Latin America: Identity, Strategy, and Democracy,* ed. Arturo Escobar and Sonia E. Alvarez. Boulder, Colo.: Westview.

———. 1995. The Riddle of New Social Movements: Who They Are and What They Do. In *Capital, Power, and Inequality in Latin America,* ed. Sandor Halebsky and Richard L. Harris. Boulder, Colo.: Westview.

———. 1997. Social Movements: Revolution, Reform, and Reaction. *NACLA Report on the Americas* 30, no. 6:13–18.

Hernández, Hermógenes. 1985. *Costa Rica: Evolución territorial y principales censos de población.* San José: Editorial de la Universidad Estatal a Distancia.

Hernández Cascante, Jorge Luis. 1990a. Las propuestas de la organización campesina frente al ajuste: El caso de UPANACIONAL. In *Los campesinos frente a la nueva década: Ajuste estructural y pequeña producción agropecuaria en Costa Rica,* ed. William Reuben Soto. San José: Editorial Porvenir.

———. 1990b. *Política agraria para los 90's: UPANACIONAL toma la palabra.* San José: Centro de Capacitación para el Desarrollo.

Hernández Cascante, Jorge, Carlos Hernández, and Oscar Monge. 1991. *El campesino ve el ajuste estructural así.* San José: Centro de Estudios y Publicaciones Alforja.

Herrera Balharry, Eugenio. 1988. *Los alemanes y el Estado cafetalero.* San José: Editorial de la Universidad Estatal a Distancia.

Hess Araya, Erick, and Sui Moy Li Kam. 1994. Perfil de la nueva estrategia de desarrollo de Costa Rica. *Revista de Ciencias Sociales* 66 (Dec.): 69–82.

Hewitt de Alcántara, Cynthia. 1984. *Anthropological Perspectives on Rural Mexico*. London: Routledge and Kegan Paul.

Hidalgo, Jorge. 1997. Las propuestas campesinas de los años noventas. In *Organización campesina y modelos de gestión productiva en Costa Rica*, ed. Isabel Román. Heredia, Costa Rica: Editorial Fundación UNA.

Hill, Polly. 1986. *Development Economics on Trial: The Anthropological Case for a Prosecution*. Cambridge: Cambridge University Press.

Hirschman, Albert O. 1988. The Principle of Conservation and Mutation of Social Energy. In *Direct to the Poor: Grassroots Development in Latin America*, ed. Sheldon Annis and Peter Hakim. Boulder: Lynne Rienner Publishers.

Honey, Martha. 1994. *Hostile Acts: U.S. Policy in Costa Rica in the 1980s*. Gainesville: University Press of Florida.

Huizer, Gerrit. 1973. *El potencial revolucionario del campesino en América Latina*. Mexico City: Siglo XXI.

———. 1979. Anthropology and Politics: From Naiveté Toward Liberation? In *The Politics of Anthropology: From Colonialism and Sexism Toward a View from Below*, ed. Gerrit Huizer and Bruce Mannheim. The Hague: Mouton.

IDB. 1985. *Economic and Social Progress in Latin America: 1985 Report*. Washington: IDB.

———. 1989. *Economic and Social Progress in Latin America: 1989 Report*. Washington: IDB.

———. 1991. *Economic and Social Progress in Latin America: 1991 Report*. Washington: Johns Hopkins University Press.

Iglesias, Enrique V. 1989. Poverty: A Social Policy without Paternalism. *The IDB* 16 (March): 10.

Irvin, George. 1991. New Perspectives for Modernization in Central America. *Development and Change* 22, no. 1:93–115.

Jackson, Michael. 1989. *Paths Toward a Clearing: Radical Empiricism and Ethnographic Inquiry*. Bloomington: Indiana University Press.

Jakobson, Roman. 1981 [1964]. "Language in Operation." In *Selected Writings*, vol. 3: *Poetry of Grammar and Grammar of Poetry*, ed. Stephen Rudy. The Hague: Mouton Publishers.

Jameson, Fredric. 1984. Foreword. In *The Postmodern Condition: A Report on Knowledge*, ed. Jean-François Lyotard. Minneapolis: University of Minnesota Press.

———. 1989. Marxism and Postmodernism. *New Left Review* 176 (July-Aug.): 31–45.

Jelin, Elizabeth, ed. 1989. *Los nuevos movimientos sociales: Mujeres, rock nacional, derechos humanos, obreros, barrios*. Buenos Aires: Centro Editor de América Latina.

————. 1990. Citizenship and Identity: Final Reflections. In *Women and Social Change in Latin America*, ed. Elizabeth Jelin. London: Zed.

Jonas Bodenheimer, Susanne. 1984. *La ideología social demócrata en Costa Rica*. San José: Editorial Universitaria Centroamericana.

Jordan, Fausto, Carlos De Miranda, William Reuben, and Sergio Sepúlveda. 1989. La economía campesina en la reactivación y el desarrollo agropecuario. In *La economía campesina: Crisis, reactivación y desarrollo*, ed. Fausto Jordan. San José: Instituto Interamericano de Cooperación para la Agricultura.

Kahler, Miles. 1992. External Influence, Conditionality, and the Politics of Adjustment. In *The Politics of Economic Adjustment*, ed. Stephan Haggard and Robert K. Kaufman. Princeton: Princeton University Press.

Katz, Friedrich. 1991. The Liberal Republic and the Porfiriato, 1867–1910. In *Mexico since Independence*, ed. Leslie Bethell. Cambridge: Cambridge University Press.

Kay, Cristóbal. 1991. Reflections on the Latin American Contribution to Development Theory. *Development and Change* 22, no. 1:31–68.

Kearney, Michael. 1996. *Reconceptualizing the Peasantry: Anthropology in Global Perspective*. Boulder, Colo.: Westview.

Kit, Wade. 1993. The Unionist Experiment in Guatemala, 1920–1921: Conciliation, Disintegration, and the Liberal Junta. *The Americas* 50 (July): 31–64.

Knight, Alan. 1994. Weapons and Arches in the Mexican Revolutionary Landscape. In *Everyday Forms of State Formation*, ed. Gilbert Joseph and Daniel Nugent. Durham, N.C.: Duke University Press.

Laclau, Ernesto. 1985. New Social Movements and the Plurality of the Social. In *New Social Movements and the State in Latin America*, ed. David Slater. Amsterdam: CEDLA.

————. 1992. Beyond Emancipation. *Development and Change* 23, no. 3:121–37.

Laclau, Ernesto, and Chantal Mouffe. 1985. *Hegemony and Socialist Strategy: Towards a Radical Democratic Politics*. London: Verso.

Lal, Deepak. 1983. *The Poverty of 'Development Economics'*. Cambridge, Mass.: Harvard University Press.

Lancaster, Roger N. 1992. *Life is Hard: Machismo, Danger, and the Intimacy of Power in Nicaragua*. Berkeley: University of California Press.

Landsberger, Henry A., and Cynthia N. Hewitt. 1970. Ten Sources of Weakness and Cleavage in Latin American Peasant Movements. In *Agrarian Problems and Peasant Movements in Latin America*, ed. Rodolfo Stavenhagen. Garden City, N.Y.: Anchor-Doubleday.

Lara, Silvia, Tom Barry, and Peter Simonson. 1995. *Inside Costa Rica: The Essential Guide to its Politics, Economy, Society, and Environment*. Albuquerque, N.M.: Interhemispheric Resource Center.

Launay, Robert. 1992. Representations and Misrepresentations: Is There Life After Positivism? *Reviews in Anthropology* 21, no. 3:181–92.

Leach, Edmund. 1964 [1954]. *Political Systems of Highland Burma*. Boston: Beacon Press.

Leeds, Anthony. 1977. Mythos and Pathos: Some Unpleasantries on Peasantries. In *Peasant Livelihood: Studies in Economic Anthropology and Cultural Ecology*, ed. Rhoda Halperin and James Dow. New York: St. Martin's Press.

LeGrand, Catherine. 1986. *Frontier Expansion and Peasant Protest in Colombia, 1830–1936*. Albuquerque: University of New Mexico Press.

Lehoucq, Fabrice Edouard. 1990. Explicando los orígenes de los regímenes democráticos: Costa Rica bajo una perspectiva teórica. *Anuario de Estudios Centroamericanos* 16, no. 1:7–29.

———. 1991. Class Conflict, Political Crisis, and the Breakdown of Democratic Practices in Costa Rica: Reassessing the Origins of the 1948 Civil War. *Journal of Latin American Studies* 23, no. 1:37–60.

———. 1992a. The Origins of Democracy in Costa Rica in Comparative Perspective. Ph.D. diss., Duke University, Durham, N.C.

———. 1992b. Presidentialism, Electoral Laws, and the Development of Democratic Stability in Costa Rica, 1882–1990. Paper presented at the Seventeenth Congress of the Latin American Studies Association, Los Angeles, Sept. 24–27.

———. 1993. Política, democracia y guerra civil en Costa Rica (1882–1948). *Suplemento de La Gaceta* 25 (June 23): 2–3.

León, Rosario. 1990. Bartolina Sisa: The Peasant Women's Organization in Bolivia. In *Women and Social Change in Latin America*, ed. Elizabeth Jelin. London: Zed.

Lewis, Oscar. 1951. *Life in a Mexican Village: Tepoztlán Restudied*. Urbana: University of Illinois Press.

Lizano Fait, Eduardo. 1988a. *Programa de ajuste estructural*. San José: Banco Central de Costa Rica, Serie "Comentarios sobre asuntos económicos," no. 76.

———. 1988b. Los principales problemas de la política de ajuste estructural. *Actualidad Económica* 5, no. 3:41–49.

———. 1991. *Economic Policy Making: Lessons from Costa Rica*. San Francisco: International Center for Economic Growth, Occasional Papers no. 21.

Lomnitz, Larissa, and Ana Melnick. 1991. *Chile's Middle Class: A Struggle for Survival in the Face of Neoliberalism*. Boulder: Lynne Rienner Publishers.

Lomnitz-Adler, Claudio. 1992. Rural Cultures in Morelos: Transformations of Peasant Class Culture. In *Exits from the Labyrinth: Culture and Ideology in the Mexican National Space*. Berkeley: University of California Press.

López, José Roberto. 1989. *El ajuste estructural de Centroamérica: Un enfoque comparativo.* San José: Facultad Latinoamericana de Ciencias Sociales, Cuadernos de Ciencias Sociales 26.

Lubasz, Heinz. 1992. Adam Smith and the Invisible Hand—of the Market? In *Contesting Markets: Analyses of Ideology, Discourse and Practice,* ed. Roy Dilley. Edinburgh: Edinburgh University Press.

Lundhal, Mats, and Wim Pelupessy, eds. 1989. *Crisis económica en Centroamérica y el Caribe.* San José: Departamento Ecuménico de Investigaciones.

Luria, Keith, and Romulo Gandolfo. 1986. Carlo Ginzburg: An Interview. *Radical History Review* 35 (April): 89–111.

Lynd, Robert S. 1939. *Knowledge for What? The Place of Social Science in American Culture.* Princeton: Princeton University Press.

Macdonald, Laura. 1994. Globalising Civil Society: Interpreting International NGOs in Central America. *Millennium: Journal of International Studies* 23, no. 2:267–85.

MAG. 1986. *Un diálogo permanente. Políticas y programas para el sector agropecuario.* San José: mimeo.

———. 1988. Información básica para el despacho del ministro. Información confidencial. Document in files of author.

Magagna, Victor V. 1991. *Communities of Grain: Rural Rebellion in Comparative Perspective.* Ithaca, N.Y.: Cornell University Press.

Mamdani, Mahmood. 1973. *The Myth of Population Control: Family, Caste, and Class in an Indian Village.* New York: Monthly Review Press.

Mariátegui, José Carlos. 1979 [1928]. *Siete ensayos de interpretación de la realidad peruana.* Mexico City: Serie Popular Era.

Martínez, Alberto. 1990. *Costa Rica: Política y regulación de precios en granos básicos.* Panama: Comité de Acción de Apoyo al Desarrollo Económico y Social de Centroamérica CADESCA, Comisión de la Comunidades Europeas & Gobierno de Francia.

McAdam, Doug. 1994. Culture and Social Movements. In *New Social Movements: From Ideology to Identity,* ed. Enrique Laraña, Hank Johnston, and Joseph R. Gusfield. Philadelphia: Temple University Press.

McCreery, David. 1983. *Development and the State in Reforma Guatemala, 1871–1885.* Athens: Ohio University Center for International Studies, Latin America Series no. 10.

Melucci, Alberto. 1989. *Nomads of the Present: Social Movements and Individual Needs in Contemporary Society.* Philadelphia: Temple University Press.

———. 1992. Liberation or Meaning? Social Movements, Culture and Democracy. *Development and Change* 23, no. 3:43–77.

Mendiola, Haydée. 1988. Expansión de la educación superior costarricense en los 1970's: Impacto en la estratificación social y en el mercado de trabajo. *Revista de Ciencias Sociales* 42 (Oct.–Dec.): 81–98.

Menjívar, Rafael, Sui Moy Li Kam, and Virginia Portuguez. 1985. El movimiento campesino en Costa Rica. In *Movimientos populares en Centroamérica*, ed. Daniel Camacho and Rafael Menjívar. San José: Editorial Universitaria Centroamericana.

MIDEPLAN. 1990. *Costa Rica: Indicadores sociodemográficos. Período 1975 – 1989*. San José: MIDEPLAN.

Miller, Eugene D. 1993. Labour and the War-Time Alliance in Costa Rica, 1943 – 1948. *Journal of Latin American Studies* 23, no. 3:515 – 41.

Miller, George A. 1919. *Prowling About Panama*. New York: Abingdon Press.

Mills, C. Wright. 1959. *The Sociological Imagination*. New York: Oxford University Press.

Mintz, Sidney W. 1989. The Sensation of Moving, While Standing Still. *American Ethnologist* 16, no. 4:786 – 96.

Mitchell, Tim. 1991. America's Egypt: Discourse of the Development Industry. *Middle East Report* 21, no. 2:18 – 36.

Moguel, Julio, Carlota Botey, and Luis Hernández, eds. 1992. *Autonomía y nuevos sujetos sociales en el desarrollo rural*. Mexico City: Siglo XXI.

Molina, Guiselle. 1985. El nuevo problema agrario en Costa Rica y las organizaciones campesinas. *Revista Mensual COPAN* 2 (Sept.–Oct.): 48 – 56.

Molina, Jonathan. 1988. Ministro Figueres: No existe crisis en el agro nacional. *Semanario Universidad*, November 25: 16 – 17.

Molina Jiménez, Iván. 1991. *Costa Rica (1800 – 1850): El legado colonial y la génesis del capitalismo*. San José: Editorial de la Universidad de Costa Rica.

Monge Alfaro, Carlos. 1962. *Historia de Costa Rica*. San José: Trejos Hermanos.

Mora, Jorge Cayetano. 1989. *La organización comunal y DINADECO 1964 – 1987*. San José: Instituto Costarricense de Estudios Sociales.

Mora Alfaro, Jorge A. 1987. Crisis y movimientos campesinos en Costa Rica, 1978 – 1986. *Revista Abra* 5 – 6 (Jan.–June): 137 – 86.

———. 1989. Costa Rica: Agricultura de cambio y producción campesina. *Revista de Ciencias Sociales* 43 (March): 7 – 25.

———. 1990a. Los campesinos y la exportación de productos agropecuarios. In *Los campesinos frente a la nueva década: Ajuste estructural y pequeña producción agropecuaria en Costa Rica*, ed. William Reuben Soto. San José: Editorial Porvenir.

———. 1990b. Estructura agraria y movimientos campesinos en Costa Rica, 1950 – 1990. Heredia, Costa Rica: Universidad Nacional, mimeo.

Morris, David. 1979. *Measuring the Condition of the World's Poor: The Physical Quality of Life Index*. New York: Pergamon Press – Overseas Development Council.

Murillo Jiménez, Hugo. 1981. *Tinoco y los Estados Unidos: Génesis y caída de un régimen*. San José: Editorial Universidad Estatal a Distancia.

Murillo V., Jaime E. 1986. Desarrollo histórico y proceso de descentralización de la administración pública en Costa Rica: El caso de las instituciones autónomas. In *Las instituciones costarricenses del siglo XX*, ed. Carmen Lila Gómez. San José: Editorial Costa Rica.

Murphy, Robert F. 1971. *The Dialectics of Social Life*. New York: Basic Books.

———. 1990. The Dialectics of Deeds and Words: Or Anti-the-Antis (and the Anti-Antis). *Cultural Anthropology* 5, no. 3:331–37.

———. 1991. Anthropology at Columbia: A Reminiscence. *Dialectical Anthropology* 16:65–81.

Myrdal, Gunnar. 1969. *Objectivity in Social Research*. New York: Pantheon.

Nash, June. 1992. Interpreting Social Movements: Bolivian Resistance to Economic Conditions Imposed by the International Monetary Fund. *American Ethnologist* 19, no. 2:275–93.

———. 1997. When Isms Become Wasms: Structural Functionalism, Marxism, Feminism, and Postmodernism. *Critique of Anthropology* 17, no. 1: 11–32.

Nederveen, Pieterse. Jan. 1992. Emancipations, Modern and Postmodern. *Development and Change* 23, no. 3:5–41.

Nelson, Diane M. 1996. Maya Hackers and the Cyberspatialized Nation-State: Modernity, Ethnostalgia, and a Lizard Queen in Guatemala. *Cultural Anthropology* 11, no. 3:287–308.

Nelson, Joan M. 1989. Crisis Management, Economic Reform and Costa Rican Democracy. In *Debt and Democracy in Latin America*, ed. Barbara Stallings and Robert Kaufman. Boulder, Colo.: Westview.

———. 1990. The Politics of Adjustment in Small Democracies: Costa Rica, the Dominican Republic, and Jamaica. In *Economic Crisis and Policy Choice: The Politics of Adjustment in the Third World*, ed. Joan M. Nelson. Princeton: Princeton University Press.

Nietzsche, Friedrich Wilhelm. 1977 [1968]. *The Portable Nietzsche*, ed. Walter Kaufmann. New York: Penguin Books.

Nores, Gustavo A. 1993. Agriculture's Brave New World. *The IDB* 20, no. 7:3.

Nove, Alec. 1972. *An Economic History of the U.S.S.R.* London: Penguin-Pelican.

Novick, Peter. 1988. *That Noble Dream: The "Objectivity Question" and the American Historical Profession*. Cambridge: Cambridge University Press.

Nuestra Tierra [Fondo Nacional de Desarrollo Agropecuario Nuestra Tierra]. n.d. Nuestra Tierra. Leaflet, 1 p.

Núñez Vega, Benjamín. 1994. Las propuestas de UPANACIONAL: Alternativa o inserción en el ajuste estructural. *Revista de Ciencias Sociales* 63 (March): 89–100.

Ober, Frederick A. 1907. *Our West Indian Neighbors*. New York: James Pott & Company.

Obregón Loría, Rafael. 1981. *Hechos militares y políticos.* Alajuela, Costa Rica: Museo Histórico Cultural Juan Santamaría.

OFIPLAN. 1982. *Evolución socioeconómica de Costa Rica, 1950–1980.* San José: Editorial Universidad Estatal a Distancia.

Olofsson, Gunnar. 1988. After the Working Class Movement? An Essay on What's "New" and What's "Social" in the New Social Movements. *Acta Sociologica* 31, no. 1:15–34.

Olson, Mancur. 1965. *The Logic of Collective Action.* Cambridge, Mass.: Harvard University Press.

Ortega, Emiliano. 1992. Evolution of the Rural Dimension in Latin America and the Caribbean. *CEPAL Review* 47 (August): 115–36.

Palma, Diego. 1980. El Estado y la desmovilización social en Costa Rica. *Estudios Sociales Centroamericanos* 27 (Sept.–Dec.): 183–206.

Palmer, Bryan D. 1990. *Descent into Discourse: The Reification of Language and the Writing of Social History.* Philadelphia: Temple University Press.

Palmer, Steven. 1992. El consumo de heroina entre los artesanos de San José y el pánico moral de 1929. *Revista de Historia* 25 (Jan.–June): 29–63.

———. 1993. Getting to Know the Unknown Soldier: Official Nationalism in Liberal Costa Rica, 1880–1900. *Journal of Latin American Studies* 25 (Feb.): 45–72.

———. 1996. Confinement, Policing, and the Emergence of Social Policy in Costa Rica, 1880–1935. In *The Birth of the Penitentiary in Latin America: Essays on Criminology, Prison Reform, and Social Control, 1830–1940,* ed. Ricardo D. Salvatore and Carlos Aguirre. Austin: University of Texas Press.

Payer, Cheryl. 1982. *The World Bank: A Critical Analysis.* New York: Monthly Review Press.

Pelupessy, Wim. 1989. El papel de la agroexportación en la reactivación económica de América Central. In *Crisis económica en Centroamérica y el Caribe,* ed. Mats Lundhal and Wim Pelupessy. San José: Departamento Ecuménico de Investigaciones.

Pérez Brignoli, Héctor. 1985. *Breve historia de Centroamérica.* Madrid: Alianza Editorial.

Phillips, Lynne, ed. 1997. *The Third Wave of Modernization in Latin America: Cultural Perspectives on Neoliberalism.* Wilmington, Del.: Scholarly Resources.

Pira, Lars. 1989. La producción campesina de alimentos y el desarrollo económico del istmo centroamericano: Su promoción ante las políticas macroeconómicas y sectoriales. In *Crisis económica en Centroamérica y el Caribe,* ed. Mats Lundhal and Wim Pelupessy. San José: Departamento Ecuménico de Investigaciones.

———. 1990. Acciones diferenciales e integración económica dentro del ajuste:

Hacia una mayor eficiencia productiva del agro centroamericano. In *Los campesinos frente a la nueva década: Ajuste estructural y pequeña producción agropecuaria en Costa Rica,* ed. William Reuben Soto. San José: Editorial Porvenir.

Piven, Frances Fox, and Richard A. Cloward. 1977. *Poor People's Movements: Why They Succeed, How They Fail.* New York: Pantheon.

Polanyi, Karl. 1957 [1944]. *The Great Transformation.* Boston: Beacon Press.

Popkin, Samuel L. 1979. *The Rational Peasant: The Political Economy of Rural Society in Vietnam.* Berkeley: University of California Press.

Portelli, Alessandro. 1991. *The Death of Luigi Trastulli and Other Stories: Form and Meaning in Oral History.* Albany: State University of New York Press.

Portes, Alejandro, and A. Douglas Kincaid. 1989. Sociology and Development in the 1990s: Critical Challenges and Empirical Trends. *Sociological Forum* 4, no. 4:479–503.

Portuguez, Virginia, and Sui Moy Li Kam. 1984. El movimiento campesino en Costa Rica (1970–1983). Entrevista al Sr. José Meléndez Ibarra, Dirigente de FENAC. *Documento de Estudio Serie Movimientos Populares Nº 1* (Facultad Latinoamericana de Ciencias Sociales, San José): 1–29.

Prakash, Gyan. 1990. Writing Post-Orientalist Histories of the Third World: Perspectives from Indian Historiography. *Comparative Studies in Society and History* 32 (Apr.): 383–408.

Price, Richard. 1983. *First-Time: The Historical Vision of an Afro-American People.* Baltimore: Johns Hopkins University Press.

Primer Encuentro Campesino. 1987. "Primer Encuentro Campesino Guanacaste Oct. 87." Mimeographed, in files of author.

Ramírez, Marcos. 1990. Carta al Ing. Juan Rafael Lizano, Ministro de Agriculture y Ganadería, 11 de julio. Photocopy.

Raventós Vorst, Ciska. 1989. *El agro costarricense y el programa de ajuste estructural.* San José: Instituto de Investigaciones Sociales, Universidad de Costa Rica, Contribuciones Nº 2.

———. 1995. The Production of an Order: Structural Adjustment in Costa Rica. Ph.D. diss., New School for Social Research, New York.

Redfield, Robert. 1930. *Tepotzlán: A Mexican Village.* Chicago: University of Chicago Press.

Reuben Soto, William. 1990. El potencial de la economía campesina en la reactivación económica y el desarrollo de Costa Rica. In *Los campesinos frente a la nueva década: Ajuste estructural y pequeña producción agropecuaria en Costa Rica,* ed. William Reuben Soto. San José: Editorial Porvenir.

Richter, Charles. 1993. Costa Rica: Back in the Winners' Circle. *The IDB* 20, no. 7:4–5.

Rivera Sánchez, Rolando. 1991. *Lucha social en el agro costarricense: Las or-*

ganizaciones campesinas de la Región Atlántica. San José: Centro de Estudios Para la Acción Social, Documento de Análisis N° 15.

Rivera Sánchez, Rolando, and Isabel Román. 1990. Ajuste estructural y alternativas productivas para los pequeños productores. In *Los campesinos frente a la nueva década: Ajuste estructural y pequeña producción agropecuaria en Costa Rica,* ed. William Reuben Soto. San José: Editorial Porvenir.

Rivera Urrutia, Eugenio. 1982. *El Fondo Monetario Internacional y Costa Rica, 1976–1982.* San José: Departamento Ecuménico de Investigaciones.

———. 1986. Macroeconomía y geopolítica de deuda externa centroamericana. *Revista Centroamericana de Economía* 7, no. 21:55–68.

Robles Macaya, Carlos Hernán. 1990. Aspectos jurídicos de la renegociación de la deuda externa. *Banca, Bolsa & Seguros,* no. 4 (Nov.–Dec.): 13–20.

Rodríguez Céspedes, Ennio. 1988. Costa Rica: En busca de la supervivencia. In *Deuda externa, renegociación y ajuste en la América Latina,* ed. Stephany Griffith-Jones. Mexico City: Fondo de Cultura Económica.

Rodríguez Céspedes, Ennio, and Mario Alberto Carrillo Cháves, eds. 1987. *Deuda externa: El caso de los países pequeños latinoamericanos.* San José: Banco Centroamericano de Integración Económica.

Rodríguez Solera, Carlos Rafael. 1992. Las grandes transformaciones del agro y su impacto sobre la reproducción de los campesinos en el período 1950–1984. Master's thesis, University of Costa Rica, San José.

Rodríguez V., Adrián. 1990. La deuda pública externa de Costa Rica: Crecimiento, moratoria y renegociación. In *Deuda externa y políticas de estabilización y ajuste estructural en Centroamérica y Panamá,* ed. José Roberto López and Eugenio Rivera. San José: CSUCA.

Rojas, María de los Angeles, and Blanca Arce. 1989. Cooperativas agrícolas de la región chorotega: Extensión, tenencia, uso y situación jurídica de la tierra. *Revista de Ciencias Sociales* 43 (Mar.): 43–51.

Rojas Bolaños, Manuel. 1979. *Lucha social y guerra social en Costa Rica, 1940–1948.* San José: Editorial Porvenir.

———. 1990. *Ajuste estructural y desajuste social.* San José: Centro de Estudios Para la Acción Social, Documentos de Análisis N° 11.

Rojas Bolaños, Manuel, and Isabel Román. 1993. *Agricultura de exportación y pequeños productores en Costa Rica.* San José: Facultad Latinoamericana de Ciencias Sociales, Cuadernos de Ciencias Sociales 61.

Rojas Víquez, Marielos. 1990. *Anuario del cooperativismo en Costa Rica.* San José: Instituto de Investigaciones Sociales, Editorial de la Universidad de Costa Rica.

Román Vega, Isabel. 1989. Los planteamientos de UPANACIONAL frente a la agricultura de cambio. *Panorama Campesino* 3 (May): 1–17.

———. 1992. Efectos del ajuste estructural en el agro costarricense. *Polémica* 16 (Jan.– April): 13–25.

———. 1993. Estilos de negociación política de las organizaciones campesinas en Costa Rica durante la década de los ochenta. Master's thesis, University of Costa Rica, San José.

———. 1997. Mundo rural en transición. San José: Proyecto Estado de la Nación (manuscript).

ed. 1997. *Organización campesina y modelos de gestión productiva en Costa Rica.* Heredia, Costa Rica: Editorial Fundación UNA.

Román Vega, Isabel, Sandra Cartín, and Rolando Rivera. 1988. *UNSA: Por el derecho a producir.* San José: Centro de Estudios para la Acción Social, Cuaderno de Estudio Nº 8.

Román Vega, Isabel, and Roy Rivera Araya. 1990. *Tierra con fronteras (Treinta años de política de distribución de tierras en Costa Rica).* San José: Centro de Estudios para la Acción Social, Documento de Análisis Nº 13.

Romero Mora, David E., and José Manuel Romero Mora. 1991. *El caso Chemise.* San José: Editorial D. Mora.

Rosaldo, Renato. 1989. *Culture and Truth: The Remaking of Social Analysis.* Boston: Beacon Press.

Roseberry, William. 1993. Beyond the Agrarian Question in Latin America. In *Confronting Historical Paradigms: Peasants, Labor, and the Capitalist World System in Africa and Latin America,* by Frederick Cooper, Allen F. Isaacman, William Roseberry, and Florencia E. Mallon. Madison: University of Wisconsin Press.

Rosenberg, Mark. 1980. *Las luchas por el seguro social en Costa Rica.* San José: Editorial Costa Rica.

Rovira Mas, Jorge. 1982. *Estado y política económica en Costa Rica: 1948–1970.* San José: Editorial Porvenir.

———. 1987. *Costa Rica en los años '80.* San José: Editorial Porvenir.

———. 1992. El nuevo estilo nacional de desarrollo. In *El nuevo rostro de Costa Rica,* ed. Juan Manuel Villasuso. San José: Centro de Estudios Democráticos de América Latina.

Rubin, Jeffrey W. 1998. Ambiguity and Contradiction in a Radical Popular Movement. In *Cultures of Politics / Politics of Cultures: Re-Visioning Latin American Social Movements,* ed. Sonia E. Alvarez, Evelina Dagnino, and Arturo Escobar. Boulder, Colo.: Westview.

Rudé, George. 1980. *Ideology and Popular Protest.* New York: Pantheon.

Sachs, Ignacy. 1976. *The Discovery of the Third World.* Cambridge, Mass.: MIT Press.

Sachs, Wolfgang. 1992. Introduction. In *The Development Dictionary: A Guide to Knowledge as Power,* ed. Wolfgang Sachs. London: Zed Books.

Salas U., Walter, Jorge León S., Justo Aguilar, and Carlos Barboza V. 1983. *El sector agropecuario costarricense: Un análisis dinámico, 1950–1980.* San José: Universidad de Costa Rica, Escuela de Economía Agrícola.

Salazar, Jorge Mario. 1981. *Política y reforma en Costa Rica, 1914–1958*. San José: Editorial Porvenir.

———. 1987. Luchas sociales e intervencionismo estatal en Costa Rica (1920–1940). *Revista de Ciencias Sociales* 37–38 (Sept.–Dec.): 61–69.

———. 1990. El sistema político-electoral costarricense del período 1914–1948. In *Historia de Costa Rica en el siglo XX*, ed. Jaime Murillo Víquez. San José: Editorial Porvenir.

Salom, Roberto. 1987. *La crisis de la izquierda en Costa Rica*. San José: Editorial Porvenir.

Salvatore, Ricardo D. 1993. Market-Oriented Reforms and the Language of Popular Protest: Latin America from Charles III to the IMF. *Social Science History* 17, no. 4:485–523.

Samper, Mario. 1990. *Generations of Settlers: Rural Households and Markets on the Costa Rican Frontier, 1850–1935*. Boulder, Colo.: Westview.

Sandoval García, Carlos. 1997. *Sueños y sudores de la vida cotidiana: Trabajadores y trabajadoras de la maquila y la construcción en Costa Rica*. San José: Editorial de la Universidad de Costa Rica.

Sangren, P. Steven. 1988. Rhetoric and the Authority of Ethnography: "Postmodernism" and the Social Reproduction of Texts. *Current Anthropology* 29, no. 3:405–35.

Santos, Eduardo A. 1988. La seguridad alimentaria mundial y el proteccionismo agrícola. *Comercio Exterior* [Mexico] 38, no. 7:635–44.

Sartre, Jean-Paul. 1963. *The Problem of Method*. London: Methuen.

Scheper-Hughes, Nancy. 1992. *Death Without Weeping: The Violence of Everyday Life in Brazil*. Berkeley: University of California Press.

Schmais, Michael. 1991. Explaining Contemporary Rural Protest: Land Occupations in Costa Rica, 1950–1990. Paper presented at the annual meeting of the American Political Science Association, Washington, D.C., Aug. 29–Sept. 1.

Scholte, Bob. 1972. Toward a Reflexive and Critical Anthropology. In *Reinventing Anthropology*, ed. Dell Hymes. New York: Vintage Books.

Scudder, Thayer. 1988. The Institute for Development Anthropology: The Case for Anthropological Participation in the Development Process. In *Production and Autonomy: Anthropological Studies and Critiques of Development*, ed. John Bennet and John Bowen. Lanham, Md.: University Press of America and Society for Economic Anthropology.

Segura Bonilla, Olman. 1991. *Costa Rica y el GATT*. San José: Editorial Porvenir.

Seligmann, Linda. 1995. *Between Reform and Revolution: Political Struggles in the Peruvian Andes, 1969–1991*. Stanford, Calif.: Stanford University Press.

Seligson, Mitchell A. 1980. *Peasants of Costa Rica and the Development of Agrarian Capitalism*. Madison: University of Wisconsin Press.

Sen, Amartya. 1987. *The Standard of Living.* Cambridge: Cambridge University Press.

SEPSA. 1982. *Información básica del sector agropecuario 2.* San José: SEPSA.

———. 1985. *Información básica del sector agropecuario 3.* San José: SEPSA.

———. 1989. *Información básica del sector agropecuario 4.* San José: SEPSA.

Shallat, Lezak. 1988. Costa Rica: Los agricultores se enfrentan al gobierno. *Pensamiento Propio* 6, no. 3:27–29.

———. 1989. "AID and the Secret Parallel State. In *The Costa Rica Reader,* ed. Marc Edelman and Joanne Kenen. New York: Grove Weidenfeld.

Shanin, Teodor. 1982. Defining Peasants: Conceptualisations and De-Conceptualisations: Old and New in a Marxist Debate. *Sociological Review* 30, no. 3:407–32.

———, ed. 1983. *Late Marx and the Russian Road: Marx and the "Peripheries of Capitalism."* New York: Monthly Review Press.

Sikkink, Kathryn. 1988. The Influence of Raúl Prebisch on Economic Policy-Making in Argentina, 1950–1962. *Latin American Research Review* 23, no. 2:91–114.

Singelmann, Peter. 1974. Campesino Movements and Class Conflict in Latin America: The Functions of Exchange and Power. *Journal of Interamerican Studies and World Affairs* 16, no. 1:39–72.

Slater, David. 1985. Social Movements and a Recasting of the Political. In *New Social Movements and the State in Latin America,* ed. David Slater. Amsterdam: CEDLA.

———. 1992. Theories of Development and Politics of the Post-modern— Exploring a Border Zone. *Development and Change* 23, no. 3:283–319.

Smelser, Neil J. 1962. *The Theory of Collective Behavior.* New York: Free Press.

Smith, Adam. 1976 [1776]. *An Inquiry into the Nature and Causes of the Wealth of Nations.* Chicago: University of Chicago Press.

Smith, David, and Rolando Rivera. 1987. Organización, movilización popular y desarrollo regional en el Atlántico costarricense. *Revista de Ciencias Sociales* 37–38 (Sept.–Dec.): 43–59.

Smith, Gavin. 1989. *Livelihood and Resistance: Peasants and the Politics of Land in Peru.* Berkeley: University of California Press.

Sojo, Ana. 1984. *Estado empresario y lucha política en Costa Rica.* San José: Editorial Universitaria Centroamericana.

Sojo, Carlos. 1991. *La utopía del Estado mínimo: Influencia de AID en Costa Rica en los años ochenta.* Managua: CRIES.

———. 1992. *La mano visible del mercado: La asistencia de Estados Unidos al sector privado costarricense en la década de los ochenta.* Managua: Ediciones CRIES.

Solís, Manuel Antonio. 1985. *La crisis de la izquierda costarricense: Conside-*

raciones para una discusión. San José: Centro de Estudios Para la Acción Social, Serie Tiempo Presente N° 1.

———. 1992. *Costa Rica: ¿Reformismo socialdemócrata o liberal?* San José: Facultad Latinoamericana de Ciencias Sociales.

Spivak, Gayatri Chakravorty. 1988. Can the Subaltern Speak? In *Marxism and the Interpretation of Culture,* ed. Cary Nelson and Lawrence Grossberg. Urbana: University of Illinois Press.

Starn, Orin. 1992. "I Dreamed of Foxes and Hawks": Reflections on Peasant Protest, New Social Movements, and the *Rondas Campesinas* of Northern Peru. In *The Making of Social Movements in Latin America: Identity, Strategy, and Democracy,* ed. Arturo Escobar and Sonia E. Alvarez. Boulder, Colo.: Westview.

Stephen, Lynn. 1997. *Women and Social Movements in Latin America: Power from Below.* Austin: University of Texas Press.

Stern, Steve J. 1987. New Approaches to the Study of Peasant Rebellion and Consciousness: Implications of the Andean Experience. In *Resistance, Rebellion, and Consciousness in the Andean Peasant World, 18th to 20th Centuries,* ed. Steve J. Stern. Madison: University of Wisconsin Press.

Stone, Samuel. 1975. *La dinastía de los conquistadores: La crisis del poder en la Costa Rica contemporánea.* San José: Editorial Universitaria Centroamericana.

Summers, Robert, and Alan Heston. 1988. A New Set of International Comparisons of Real Product and Price Levels Estimates for 130 Countries, 1950–1985. *Review of Income and Wealth* 34, no. 1:1–25

Tarrow, Sidney. 1994. *Power in Movement: Social Movements, Collective Action, and Mass Politics in the Modern State.* Cambridge: Cambridge University Press.

Tendler, Judith. 1975. *Inside Foreign Aid.* Baltimore: Johns Hopkins University Press.

Thorner, Daniel. 1986 [1966]. Chayanov's Concept of Peasant Economy. Introduction to *The Theory of Peasant Economy,* by A. V. Chayanov. Madison: University of Wisconsin Press.

Tilly, Charles. 1984. Social Movements and National Politics. In *Statemaking and Social Movements: Essays in History and Theory,* ed. Charles Bright and Susan Harding. Ann Arbor: University of Michigan Press.

———. 1985. Models and Realities of Popular Collective Action. *Social Research* 52, no. 4:717–47.

Tolchin, Susan J., and Martin Tolchin. 1983. *Dismantling America: The Rush to Deregulate.* Boston: Houghton Mifflin.

Torres, Oscar, and Hernán Alvarado. 1990. *Política macroeconómica y sus efectos en la agricultura y la seguridad alimentaria. Caso: Costa Rica.* Panama:

Comité de Acción de Apoyo al Desarrollo Económico y Social de Centro-américa CADESCA & Comisión de las Comunidades Europeas.

Touraine, Alain. 1974. Las clases sociales. In *Las clases sociales en América Latina*, ed. Raúl Benítez Zenteno. Mexico City: Siglo XXI.

———. 1981. *The Voice and the Eye: An Analysis of Social Movements*. Cambridge: Cambridge University Press.

———. 1985. An Introduction to the Study of Social Movements. *Social Research* 52, no. 4:749–87.

———. 1988. *Return of the Actor: Social Theory in Postindustrial Society*. Minneapolis: University of Minnesota Press.

Trejos S., Rafael A. 1992. Desarrollo del sector servicios en Costa Rica. In *El nuevo rostro de Costa Rica*, ed. Juan Manuel Villasuso. San José: Centro de Estudios Democráticos de América Latina.

Ugalde Quirós, Rafael Angel. 1985. Al tío Caimán le majaron la colita. *Semanario Universitario* 19 (April): 16–18.

Ulate Q., Anabelle. 1992. Aumento de las exportaciones: Obsesión del ajuste estructural. In *El nuevo rostro de Costa Rica*, ed. Juan Manuel Villasuso. San José: Centro de Estudios Democráticos de América Latina.

UNAC, UPAGRA, UCADEGUA, FECOPA, Coordinadora Campesina del Atlántico, UCTAN, y Cooperativa del Rincón de San Vicente. 1987. Carta abierta al Presidente de la República, San José, 21 de setiembre de 1987. Letter, in files of author.

UNDP. 1995. *Human Development Report*. New York: Oxford University Press.

UPAGRA. 1985. Nuestras tareas en la crisis. Ponencia al Foro Los Movimientos Sociales ante la Crisis, Universidad Nacional, Heredia, Costa Rica.

UPANACIONAL. n.d. *UPANACIONAL . . . en pocas palabras*. San José: UPANACIONAL.

U.S. Embassy. 1985. "Costa Rica: Key Economic Indicators." U.S. Embassy, San José, Costa Rica. Photocopy.

Valverde, José Manuel. 1993. *Proceso de privatización en Costa Rica . . . ¿Y la respuesta sindical?* San José: ASEPROLA.

Valverde, José Manuel, Elisa Donato, and Rolando Rivera. 1989. Costa Rica: Movimientos sociales populares y democracia. In *Costa Rica: La democracia inconclusa*, ed. Manuel Rojas Bolaños. San José: Departamento Ecuménico de Investigaciones.

Vanden, Harry E. 1986. *National Marxism in Latin America: José Carlos Mariátegui's Thought and Politics*. Boulder: Lynne Rienner Publishers.

Vargas Artavia, Guido. 1997. Nuestra lucha contra la discriminación. In *Organización campesina y modelos de gestión productiva en Costa Rica*, ed. Isabel Román. Heredia, Costa Rica: Fundación UNA.

Vargas Peralta, Federico. 1987. Experiencias de negociación de la deuda externa: Caso de Costa Rica, 1982/1983. In *Deuda externa: El caso de los países pequeños latinoamericanos,* ed. Ennio Rodríguez Céspedes and Mario Alberto Carrillo Ch. San José: Banco Centroamericano de Integración Económica.

Vargas R., Jorge E. 1992. El cooperativismo en los años ochenta: Balance de una década. In *El nuevo rostro de Costa Rica,* ed. Juan Manuel Villasuso. San José: Centro de Estudios Democráticos de América Latina.

Vega, Mylena. 1982. *El Estado costarricense de 1974 a 1978: CODESA y la fracción industrial.* San José: Editorial Hoy.

Vega Carballo, José Luis. 1981a. *Orden y progreso: La formación del Estado nacional en Costa Rica.* San José: Instituto Centroamericano de Administración Pública.

———. 1981b. Costa Rica: Coyunturas, clases sociales y Estado en su desarrollo reciente, 1930–1975. In *América Latina: Historia de medio siglo,* vol. 2: *Centroamérica, México y el Caribe,* ed. Pablo González Casanova. Mexico City: Siglo XXI.

———. 1982. Decadencia política y crisis económica en Costa Rica. *Cuadernos Centroamericanos de Ciencias Sociales,* no. 8:38–54.

Vermeer, René. 1990a. La política agraria de la administración Arias en el marco del ajuste estructural. In *Los campesinos frente a la nueva década: Ajuste estructural y pequeña producción agropecuaria en Costa Rica,* ed. William Reuben Soto. San José: Editorial Porvenir.

———. 1990b. *El cambio en la agricultura: El caso de los granos básicos durante la administración Arias.* San José: Centro Nacional de Acción Pastoral and Escuela de Economía, Universidad Nacional.

Vilas, Carlos M. 1993. The Hour of Civil Society. *NACLA Report on the Americas* 27, no. 2:38–42, 44.

———. 1996. Neoliberal Social Policy: Managing Poverty (Somehow). *NACLA Report on the Americas* 29, no. 6:16–25.

Villasuso, Juan Manuel. 1992. La reforma democrática del Estado costarricense. In *El nuevo rostro de Costa Rica,* ed. Juan Manuel Villasuso. San José: Centro de Estudios Democráticos de América Latina.

Villasuso, Juan Manuel, Rafael Celis, Rafael A. Trejos, Rosario Domingo, Marvin Taylor, Enrique Vásquez, Julio Kierzerson, Adrián Vargas, and Alejandro Desarraga. 1984. *Costa Rica: El sector productivo crisis y perspectivas.* San José: Editorial Porvenir.

Vincent, Joan. 1990. *Anthropology and Politics: Visions, Traditions, and Trends.* Tucson: University of Arizona Press.

Volio, Marina. 1972. *Jorge Volio y el Partido Reformista.* San José: Editorial Costa Rica.

Wagley, Charles. 1964. The Peasant. In *Continuity and Change in Latin America,* ed. John J. Johnson. Stanford, Calif.: Stanford University Press.

Walton, John. 1989. Debt, Protest, and the State in Latin America. In *Power and Popular Protest: Latin American Social Movements,* ed. Susan Eckstein. Berkeley: University of California Press.

Warman, Arturo. 1972. *Los campesinos: Hijos predilectos del régimen.* Mexico City: Nuestro Tiempo.

——. 1976. *. . . Y venimos a contradecir: Los campesinos de Morelos y el estado nacional.* Mexico City: Ediciones de la Casa Chata.

——. 1980. *Ensayos sobre el campesinado en México.* Mexico City: Editorial Nueva Imagen.

——. 1988. Los estudios campesinos: Veinte años después. *Comercio Exterior* [Mexico] 38, no. 7:653–58.

Warren, Kay B. 1998. Indigenous Movements as a Challenge to the Unified Social Movement Paradigm for Guatemala. In *Cultures of Politics / Politics of Cultures: Re-Visioning Latin American Social Movements,* ed. Sonia E. Alvarez, Evelina Dagnino, and Arturo Escobar. Boulder, Colo.: Westview.

Wertheim, Wim F. 1992. The State and the Dialectics of Emancipation. *Development and Change* 23, no. 3:257–81.

White, Stephen K. 1991. *Political Theory and Postmodernism.* Cambridge: Cambridge University Press.

Williams, Raymond. 1983. *Towards 2000.* London: Chatto & Windus–The Hogarth Press.

Williams, Robert G. 1994. *States and Social Evolution: Coffee and the Rise of National Governments in Central America.* Chapel Hill: University of North Carolina Press.

Wilson, Bruce M. 1994. When Social Democrats Choose Neoliberal Economic Policies: The Case of Costa Rica. *Comparative Politics* 26 (Jan.): 149–68.

Wolf, Eric R. 1966. *Peasants.* Englewood Cliffs, N.J.: Prentice-Hall.

——. 1969. *Peasant Wars of the Twentieth Century.* New York: Harper & Row.

Wood, Ellen Meiksins. 1986. *The Retreat from Class.* London: Verso.

Yashar, Deborah J. 1997. *Demanding Democracy: Reform and Reaction in Costa Rica and Guatemala, 1870s–1950s.* Stanford, Calif.: Stanford University Press.

Zald, Mayer N. 1992. Looking Backward to Look Forward: Reflections on the Past and Future of the Resource Mobilization Research Program. In *Frontiers in Social Movement Theory,* ed. Aldon D. Morris and Carol McClurg Mueller. New Haven: Yale University Press.

Zamosc, León. 1986. *The Agrarian Question and the Peasant Movement in Colombia: Struggles of the National Peasant Association, 1967–1981.* Cambridge: Cambridge University Press.

——. 1989. Peasant Struggles of the 1970s in Colombia. In *Power and Popular Protest: Latin American Social Movements,* ed. Susan Eckstein. Berkeley: University of California Press.

INDEX

In this index an "f" after a number indicates a separate reference on the next page, and an "ff" indicates separate references on the next two pages. A continuous discussion over two or more pages is indicated by a span of page numbers, e.g., "57–59." *Passim* is used for a cluster of references in close but not consecutive sequence.

Abrams, Philip, 257
Acción Demócrata, 54
Adam, Barry, 19
Agency for International Development, *see* USAID
Agrarian reform, 22f, 33, 49, 59f, 68f, 94, 99, 109, 140, 174, 180, 183, 205. *See also* IDA (Instituto de Desarrollo Agrario)
Agricultural price supports, 25, 80, 91, 96, 99, 102–5 *passim*, 116f, 131, 139, 158f, 163f, 176, 180, 259
"Agriculture of change," 26, 80–83 *passim*, 89f, 100–103 *passim*, 109, 158, 160, 164
ALCOA (Aluminum Company of America), 97, 257
Alliance for Progress, 59
Alvarez, Pedro, 162, 264
Alvarez Desanti, Antonio, 106–10, 141, 158, 263
American Anthropological Association, 150f, 262
Anderson, Leslie E., 258
Anthropologists and anthropology, 4, 6, 30–33, 37, 42f, 119f, 150f, 185, 189–92, 210, 249f, 261
Anti-Communism, 54, 57, 96, 119, 164
Antioquia, 46f
Aportes, 145f
Araujo, Arturo, 51
Arce, Heidi, 140f
Archaeological sites, 144, 153
Ardón, Sergio Erick, 250
Argentina, 2, 12, 15f, 181, 247, 250
Arias Sánchez, Oscar, 3, 86, 100–11 *passim*, 130f, 139, 143f, 152, 157f, 169, 265. *See also* Penón de Arias, Margarita
Aronowitz, Stanley, 5

Asignaciones Familiares, 29f, 61, 87, 89
Asociación Cívico-Agropecuaria y de Desarrollo Integral de Guanacaste, 175f
ASPPAS (Asociación de Pequeños Productores del Pacífico Seco), 26–35, 130–33, 135–55, 164–67, 215f; disintegration of, 34–36, 152, 168–75, 188, 197f
Autonomous public-sector institutions, 56–68 *passim*, 199

Bananas and banana industry, 13, 44, 51, 57, 82ff, 89, 95, 99, 112–15 *passim*, 120, 123, 172, 183, 200, 206, 209, 255
Banco Anglo-Costarricense, 127
Banco Central de Costa Rica, 25, 41, 78–81 *passim*, 91, 103ff, 131, 211, 254
Banco Nacional de Costa Rica, 100f, 120, 127, 131, 140
Banco Popular y de Desarrollo Comunal, 60
Banks and banking, 25, 38, 41, 55–60 *passim*, 68, 74, 79, 105, 116, 125–27, 167, 253
Bartra, Armando, 204
Bartra, Roger, 203, 209
Basic grains and basic grains producers, 25, 58–63, 80, 96, 101f, 109, 123–27, 166–74, 180–83, 205. *See also individual crops by name*
Batlle y Ordóñez, José, 15, 247
Bean Consortium, 181f, 199, 266
Beans and bean producers, 101f, 125–26, 139f, 148f, 164f, 181f
Bebbington, Anthony, 192
Belgium, 52
Benjamin, Walter, 251
Berger, John, 210
Berger, Mark, 13
Betancourt, Rómulo, 15, 247

301

Library of Congress Cataloging-in-Publication Data

Edelman, Marc.
　　Peasants against globalization : rural social movements in Costa
Rica / Marc Edelman.
　　　　p.　　cm.
　　Includes bibliographical references and index.
　　ISBN 0-8047-3401-1 (cloth : alk. paper). — ISBN 0-8047-3693-6
(pbk. : alk. paper)
　　　　1. Peasantry—Costa Rica—Political activity.　2. Social
movements—Costa Rica.　3. Costa Rica—Economic policy.　I. Title.
　　HD1339.C8E33　2000
　　322.4'4'097286—dc21　　　　　　　　　　　　　　　　　99-31301

⊗　This book is printed on acid-free, recycled paper.

Original printing 1999
Last figure below indicates year of this printing:
08　07　06　05　04　03　02　01　00　99